REFLECTIONS

Life After the White House

Barbara Bush

A LISA DREW BOOK

Scribner

New York   London   Toronto   Sydney

A LISA DREW BOOK / SCRIBNER
1230 Avenue of the Americas
New York, NY 10020

First Lisa Drew/Scribner trade paperback edition 2004
SCRIBNER and design are trademarks of
Macmillan Library Reference USA, Inc., used under license
by Simon & Schuster, the publisher of this work.

A Lisa Drew Book is a trademark of Simon & Schuster, Inc.

For information about special discounts for bulk purchases,
please contact Simon & Schuster Special Sales:
1-800-456-6798 or business@simonandschuster.com

Text set in Garamond 3

Manufactured in the United States of America

1   3   5   7   9   10   8   6   4   2

Library of Congress Control Number: 2003054365

ISBN 0-7432-2359-4
0-7432-5582-8 (Pbk)

This book is dedicated to six beloved, marvelous children and the world's best man . . . President George Bush #41.

Author's Note

Let me say up front this is a very slanted book—slanted in favor of my family and friends. It is how I see the world.

I have so many people to thank—all of whom will be glad to see this project finished:

Lisa Drew, our editor and publisher at Scribner, who has encouraged me through three other books. Lisa has overlooked my tardiness and has not pushed me to say things that I might be sorry about later.

Jean Becker, the busiest person I know, edited *Memoirs* and now *Reflections*. She has held my hand throughout the two years it has taken me. Jean also tells me that I owe the folks at Google many thanks for saving her hours of fact-checking.

Two people at The George Bush Presidential Library: Laura Spencer, who spent hours looking up and verifying facts; and Mary Finch, who helped us find all those elusive pictures.

Nancy Lisenby, who works in George's Houston office, put together an index for me. (I don't want my precious brother complaining that the dog got more mention than he did, again.)

All our friends who put up with me.

Our family who continue to be so interesting, so loving, and often so very funny.

I make no apologies for the fact that I still live a life of ease. There is a difference between ease and leisure. I live the former and not the latter. I complain a little about being too active at seventy-eight years old and not being allowed to be in one place long enough to unpack, exercise, and be with friends. But the truth is, I LOVE MY LIFE. I love George Bush, our children, their children, our family, and friends. I have great faith in God; although His will is not always done, I always trust His wisdom.

       For clarity, I must explain some of the family names used in this book. Because he is known this way to readers, I refer to our son, President George Walker Bush, as George W. Never did his father, brothers, sister, or I EVER call him George W. Then he got into politics. People referred to him as Junior. He is not and never was a "junior." Over the years we have called him "Gugliami." For some strange reason he reminded us of a well-known bald sports announcer whose name was not even similar, but that's what we affectionately called our bald baby fifty-some years ago. For many years I called him "Georgie" to differentiate between all those Georges in our family.* After he was elected to office, he said, "Mom, I bet George Washington's mother didn't call him 'Georgie.'" (I bet she did in an affectionate moment.) There was a period when he was called "Geo" because that was the way he signed his name—although only a mother could read his writing! And he grew to be just George.

Thanks to Congressman John Dingell, we now call him "43" if we are trying to distinguish one George from the other. At the 2002 Alfalfa Club dinner, Congressman Dingell said that he had gone to numbers when referring to the 41st president and 43rd president. But what did you call them when they are in the same room? Do you say "President Bushes?" or "Presidents Bush?" He said he had settled on "84."

So George H. W. is now "41" and George W. is "43." And our grandson is "George P." or "P."

We are a family of "nicknamers," but not as bad as 43. He calls

*And there are many. Three George Walkers and one George Holden come to mind immediately, all named after George Herbert Walker, maternal grandfather of "my George." I'll let the others solve their own problems.

everyone by a nickname. I remember reading that the press was shocked that GWB called Texas lieutenant governor Bob Bullock "Bully."

No. 41 was called Poppy for the first eighteen years of his life. That was because his namesake, George Herbert Walker, was called "Pop" by his children (at least behind his back). So when George was born, his uncles immediately started calling him "Little Pop," or "Poppy."

When I first met 41's family, his older brother Pres (Prescott Sheldon Bush, Jr.) was occasionally called "Penguin"; his sister Nancy was and still is "Nan"; his brother Jonathan James Bush, "Johnny Jim"; and his brother William Henry Trotter Bush, "Bucky." So it was natural that I was called "Bar," after Barsil, the horse that pulled a wagon at Walker's Point during World War II. "Penguin" called me "Babar" and does to this day occasionally. (Would you prefer to be named after a horse or an elephant? I don't care—nicknames are a sign of affection.) George and our children call me "The Silver Fox," for obvious reasons.

Our daughter Pauline Robinson Bush was named after my mother, who died in a car accident in 1949, the year our baby was born. We nicknamed our little girl "Robin," and I suspect that even her brothers and sister don't remember her real name. I do.*

Our son John Ellis Bush, "Jeb," the great Governor of Florida, was named after 41's brother Jon and Nan's husband, "Sandy" Ellis—Alexander Ellis, Jr.—whom we both admired and loved.

Our son Neil Mallon Bush was named after the man who took us to Texas in 1948, 41's first boss, Henry Neil Mallon, who was the most heavenly man. To this day we call Neil "Whitney," often shortened to "Whit." (He started out as "Whitey" because of his blond hair and somewhere along the way it became "Whitney.") Paula Rendon, who has lived with us for forty-four years, called him "Hüerito," which we think was because Neil was a blue-eyed blond and truly sweet.

Our son Marvin Pierce Bush was named after the most wonderful father anyone ever was lucky enough to have—Marvin Pierce, my dad—whose nickname, of course, all through college was "Monk." You might well wonder why we waited through four sons to name a

*Robin died of leukemia in 1953, right before her fourth birthday.

child after this fine, funny, smart, generous-of-spirit, beloved man? Each time we had a baby we would tell Daddy that if we had a son, we were going to name him Marvin. And he would say, "Please don't." He said it was a difficult name and he always hated it. His mother was Mabel Marvin Pierce, so he was given her maiden surname, as that was popular in those days and is again today. As a footnote to this, when "Marty" was born and we called Daddy to tell him that we had named the baby Marvin, he seemed hesitant and asked what we were going to call him. We said: "Marvin." I'll never forget it. He was quiet for a while and when he spoke, he was choked up. So all the time he really wanted a namesake. He would be proud—very proud—of all our sons, but I suspect fine, funny, loyal, smart, generous-of-spirit Marvin would be a favorite.

Our sixth child, Dorothy Walker Bush, was named after 41's precious mother. I read some place later that "Dorothy" means "a gift from God." Certainly both Dorothys were just that. George's father called his wife "Doe-ie" sometimes, and I notice that Bobby Koch, our son-in-law, calls our child "Doe." From birth we nicknamed the baby "Doro," and Doro she remains to the world.

⟿ This book was to start and end on January 20, 2001. But the world did not stop on that day and so the book lingers on, I hope not too long.

REFLECTIONS

PROLOGUE

January 20, 2001

Being kissed by the President of the United States, January 20, 2001.
ASSOCIATED PRESS PHOTO BY AMY SANCETTA

There is a myth in the United States—you've heard it many times. It says that all American mothers hope that their child will grow up to be President of the United States. In my case that certainly is a myth. I never dreamed that any of ours would; there were days when I hoped that they'd just grow up!

I did hope for our children to be happy. I also hoped they would be decent, responsible, independent, and caring. Besides that, I hoped they would believe in a greater being, God. All our children have achieved those dreams.

But on January 20, 2001, even without having wished that one of our children would grow up to be president, there we were sitting on the west side of the United States Capitol, waiting for our son, George W., be sworn in as the forty-third president of the United States of America. Can anyone understand how we felt? I'm not sure we did. Afterward, I wrote down my thoughts during the Inauguration:

In a few moments our son will walk down the steps, take a seat and at noon will be sworn in surrounded by family, friends, the [Supreme] Court, the incoming Cabinet, the Congress, the outgoing president and Vice President, and many others. We are thrilled to see former President Jimmy Carter and his wife Rosalynn Carter sitting on the platform. Rosalynn had written me such a nice card:

Dear Barbara,
   Congratulations! How proud you must be.
   As a mother, I can feel the exhilaration you are experiencing having a son become president of the United States. Jimmy and I will be thinking of you and George and be in prayer, too, for George W. as he assumes this most powerful position.
   We are happy for you and know our country is in good hands.
   Merry Christmas to all your family,
                                        Sincerely,
                                        Rosalynn Carter

We received hundreds of cards and letters after that very painful election finally ended. These messages came from Democrats and Republicans alike. I believe that this card meant more to me than all the others we received about the election and the final results. I thought that was most generous of her and meant a lot coming from someone who knew exactly what the job entailed . . .

I know I should be thinking marvelous deep and lofty thoughts, but I find myself thinking of Al Gore and what he must be feeling. He walked down the steps with a broad smile on his face and I saw him shaking hands with Coretta Scott King and other friends. His step faltered a little when he came to Jim Baker. He shook his hand and moved on. Jim Baker, a longtime Bush family friend and distinguished former Secretary of State, was George W.'s lead lawyer in Florida. Jim certainly acted as a statesman throughout the whole hideous vote recount debacle. He is credited by many of us, along with 50-plus lawyers, with seeing that the recounts were honest. The V.P. walked down the steps and took his seat one over from the Supreme Court. I'm sure that Al Gore has no love for them after their vote to stop the recount. And, if one can believe many of the speculative stories about why Al Gore lost the election, he is sitting next to the man who he believes lost the election for him, Bill Clinton. I'm sure he thinks he won the race, and although I don't, I do feel sorry for him. He is gracious, and a minute ago came over to shake our hands and to meet Jenna and Barbara, George and Laura's twin daughters. We've lost and losing is not easy.

This all took me back eight years ago to January 20, 1993, when many of the same cast of characters were on the same Capitol steps— the difference being that my George and Dan Quayle were sitting in the seats where Bill Clinton and Al Gore were sitting that day, and where George W. Bush and Dick Cheney would sit in a few moments. What an incredible eight years it had been . . .

Visiting with Croatian refugees while on a mission for
AmeriCares, December 1993.
PHOTO COURTESY OF THE GEORGE BUSH LIBRARY

January 20, 1993, was a tough day for us. But we had two and a half months to get used to the idea, and my mind had already gone home to Houston. We spent the last few weeks saying some very emotional good-byes to the Republican members of the Senate; George's cabinet; the military at Camp David; all the armed services at Fort Myer; the White House staff; and our many dear friends who lived in Washington.

The hardest good-byes were to our children who lived there, Doro and Bobby Koch, Marvin and Margaret, and all their children. How we had loved it when they dropped in. They all left town the week of

Bill Clinton's Inauguration with the exception of Bobby who stayed in Washington and came for dinner our last night in town along with our dear friends, Ann and Alan Simpson, senator from Wyoming, and Cathy and Lud Ashley, whom we had known since George's Yale days.

Another memory from those final days was a phone call George received from Billy Graham. Because of our close friendship, he was worried about what we would think if he accepted Bill Clinton's invitation to give the inaugural invocation. George assured him that nothing would please him more, and he meant it.

By this time I was sort of out of tears, emotionally wiped out. I wrote in my diary:

> Well, this is the day. Both of us are ready. The news and TV programs are full of end-of-term stories about George, his successes and his failures, and "the new beginnings" by Clinton. All this was expected, but we need to get out of here. The *Los Angeles Times* has George leaving office with a 68% popular vote. We have felt no ill will.

We came home to Houston to a totally unpacked house, and flowers in the house and garden, all done by our new neighbors and friends. Longtime friends and next-door neighbors Jack and Bobbie Fitch were the ringleaders in this thoughtful, life-saving deed.

Our days were spent getting used to being back on our own, living in a rented house with two dogs after four years in that glorious house with ninety-three staff. George set up his office, and we both had thousands of letters that needed answering.

We realized fairly quickly how much life had changed. George W. came for dinner a few days after our return home. He wanted pasta, as he was running the Houston Marathon the next morning. (He was nervous about the race as he wasn't sure he could make it. He finished in the middle of the pack.) I had not cooked in twelve years, so it is not surprising that my pasta was NOT too good. In fact, it was dreadful. George W. was polite, but his dad said, "I like my pasta rare." By that time, I had cooked about five meals, and I figured I was two for five. George told me the good news was that he had lost two pounds without even trying.

I also hadn't driven in twelve years and was panicked about driving for the first time. It seemed easy, but I confess that I did not stray too far away from our neighborhood for a long time. George told everyone in speeches that if anyone saw a blue Sable station wagon on the road—get out of the way!

One weekend we went to Galveston—just a short hour's drive from Houston on the Gulf of Mexico—and stayed in our friend Hugh Liedtke's house on the water. When George went in to get a fishing license, the woman said to him, "You look familiar. Have we met before?"

Something very similar happened to me, although a while later. My good friend and neighbor, Mildred Kerr, and I went to Luby's cafeteria for lunch. A perfectly strange, attractive woman came over, put her face in mine, and said, "Aren't you somebody? I know I know you." She never took a breath and continued, "Are you a teacher? Have you waited on me in a store? Didn't you help me at Sears?" I never had a chance to say a word, but just kept nodding. She left as quickly as she arrived, muttering as she went: "I thought she was somebody."

〜 Here are some of my diary notes from those first few weeks after we left Washington:

February 14—Pop and I have had a lot of fun since we've been back playing house, after 12 years of being waited on hand and foot. We have all modern equipment, and our needs are not great. My cooking leaves a lot to be desired, that's for sure.

February 19—I, of course, have deep tinges of regret, but mostly for George. I have been so proud of him. He is not bitter, but just cannot seem to focus in on anything yet, but it has only been one month since the Inauguration. The office in Houston is going strong with a small paid group and a large group of volunteers. I guess there are tons of mail . . . I am working away on my book.* It is so much fun looking back.

*I'm talking about *Barbara Bush: A Memoir*, which was published in 1994 and covered the first sixty-eight years of my life.

Before we had left the White House, our lawyer Terri Lacy came to see me and asked me how I planned to pay my staff. I couldn't believe my ears. What did she mean? Why would I need a staff? She explained that former first ladies received lots of mail, including invitations and other requests, all of which would have to be answered. I would need someone to answer the mail and to schedule me. She had checked with Betty Ford's office and although they had been out of office some 16 years, Betty still spent $100 a month on postage alone. I felt like crying. Everyone knew that I had never earned any money as I had never seriously worked in the 48 years we had been married. So besides losing the election, now at 68 years old I was going to have to make some money. I honestly thought Terri was slightly crazy. Fortunately, several book publishers and a speaking bureau came to my rescue shortly after that, and I could afford all the above. I am a diary-keeper and I had so much information [for a book] that I was like Yogi Berra—I "had insurmountable opportunities" or too much information.

And as for public speaking, I found I was being paid for something that I had done for free for twelve years. I met many people from past administrations on the speaking tour, including former Presidents Jerry Ford and Jimmy Carter; former Senators Howard Baker and Bob Dole along with Elizabeth Dole; Generals Colin Powell and Norman Schwarzkopf; VIPs from overseas including former Prime Ministers Shimon Peres of Israel and John Major of Great Britain; many athletes and coaches; and finally the political "odd couple," Mary Matalin and James Carville. Many of us agreed that speaking qualified as "white collar crime." For most of them, after working for years for the government, it seemed like stealing to be paid half a year's salary for one speech.

I admit I took a great deal of pleasure when a dear friend of mine, Margie Jenkins, called from Santa Rosa, California, to give me a heads-up that I was going to be invited to speak to a group in which she was involved. Several days later she called back to tell me that when the speakers bureau had told them my fee, they realized they could not afford me and so they had gotten David Gergen instead! I loved that. I was particularly amused because he had been so self-serving with everyone. He was with us in the 1980 campaign when things looked good and then the day George lost in New Hampshire, he went off our radar screen. No "good-bye"—he just took off!

Then, during the 1992 election, Gergen was the Conservative spokesman, opposite Mark Shields for the Liberals, on one of those cable "point counterpoint" talk shows. I would think his job was to defend the president in the face of Mark's penetrating attacks. He seldom did that. After the election was over, he announced he was an independent and that he had voted for Bill Clinton. He ended up working in the White House as an adviser to the new president, but left after 18 months when things got tough.

So, Margie's call amused me. If she had called me directly, I would, if my schedule had permitted, have come for free as she is a very dear friend. George and I have tried hard to balance our talks between "for pay" and "for good causes."

⁓ Back during the 1988 election, I had told George that if he didn't become president, not to worry, there were ten things I really wanted to do and couldn't do if he were president. One was for our springer spaniel, Millie, to have puppies. "Easy," he said, and Millie did have six pups while we were in the White House.* Another was to go on a cruise. So in February 1993, a month after he left office, George surprised me by booking us on the *Regal Princess*, one of the "Love Boat" ships.

We boarded the ship early to avoid the crowd and were met by both the captain of the *Regal Princess* and the Hollywood "Love Boat" captain, Gavin MacLeod. Gavin, a charming man, was going to be on a sister ship where 450 couples planned to renew their vows on Valentine's Day. I remember that George was not pleased with me as that struck me as very funny and I said so. Imagine renewing your vows with 449 couples you didn't know and away from family and friends! I was rude and I apologized. But it still seems very funny to me. I just should not have said it.

---

*One of Millie's puppies, Spot, is now back at the White House with her family, George W. and Laura. This could be a historical first, a dog living in the White House in two different administrations.

I realized I must be careful not to be like Alice Roosevelt Longworth. I think she was in her nineties when we moved to Washington in 1967. President Theodore Roosevelt's daughter—the Alice of the song "Alice Blue Gown"—was the darling of old Washington. We were invited to a dinner one night where she was also present. Everyone was in awe of her and hung on her every word. It suddenly came to me that Alice felt that she could say anything that she wanted because she was old. She ripped many people apart and spoke, I felt, for shock effect; it didn't matter who she hurt. Old age is no excuse for being rude and hurtful, and I was that day on the ship.

It reminds me of a favorite story that I like to use in my talks. Unfortunately, more often than not, I do feel a lot like the woman who was determined to become a better person. She said this prayer every single day:

Dear Lord,
    So far today, I am doing all right. I have not gossiped, lost my temper, been greedy, grumpy, nasty, selfish, or been self-indulgent. I have not whined, cursed, or entertained evil thoughts. However, I am going to get out of bed in a few minutes, and I will need a lot more help after that. Amen.

Just before we set sail, George went across the bay to visit a new American submarine at the invitation of its captain. When he returned, we went up on our captain's bridge to see our cruise ship leave harbor. It was really thrilling, and when we went past the submarine, the crew were lined up on the deck. We exchanged blasts of our horns, and the officers saluted George until we were out of sight. It was one of those magic moments. He saluted back, but it was hard for him to control his feelings. I didn't bother trying. How I love my good man.

There were 1,600 other passengers and 900 staff—at best half voted for George (on second thought, that is very optimistic), but they all acted as though he was their favorite man in the world. Every time we stepped foot out of our room, he was swamped by requests for autographs and pictures. The captain took pity on us and invited us to eat every meal with him and the officers. It was about the best food I have ever eaten. We went early every morning to a spa where we exercised, had massages, etc., before the crowd arrived. One morning George was coming out of the shower toweling off when a man approached him with a camera saying, "Do you mind if I take your picture?" George, dripping wet and stark naked, suggested that the time was not quite right.

We read a lot, slept, and I worked on my book. I know I have said this before, but I loved writing my memoir, and I am loving writing this book. I am reminded once again of just how lucky I am and what a great life we are living. I would urge everyone to keep a diary. The memory fails as one adds years. You forget what you thought and felt.

We jumped ship, as planned, in St. Martin's and caught a plane to Miami to be with our son Jeb and his wife Colu and family—the second commercial flight for George in twelve and a half years. We had dinner together at Joe's Stone Crab and went to bed at Jeb and Colu's house.

The next morning, George and Jeb played golf with Arnie Palmer and Joe DiMaggio. Even for a former president who's a first-class name-dropper, that was pretty tall cotton. The treat for me was that Winnie Palmer came and rode the golf cart with me. Winnie was a truly precious friend and both George and I have missed her since she died in 1999. She was a great clipper of articles about books or movies that she thought we would enjoy. One time she had highly recommended a movie. We saw it and it was poor at best. When I was talking to her on the phone next, I mentioned that we thought the movie she had recommended was really awful. Her answer was: "Oh, well, now I won't go see it." I loved that. I know more people who think Winnie was one of their best friends and no one who didn't love and admire her.

That night I flew to Jacksonville, Florida, to attend my first Mayo Clinic Board meeting. Fairly soon after the election, I was visited at the White House by Dr. Robert Waller, head of the Mayo Foundation at that time; Ed Spencer, chairman of the board; and former Senator Howard Baker, a member of the board. (Actually I'm not sure if Howard came to the meeting or just called in.) All three urged me to come on the Mayo Clinic Foundation Board. The Mayo Clinic had been called in by the White House doctor, Burt Lee, when George and

I had been separately diagnosed with Graves' disease and the staff had treated us with the great care they are known for. I didn't kid myself that I was invited to join because of my medical knowledge or even my brilliance. I was invited because I married well. So many great things have happened to me because I married well! This was not totally an altruistic act on my part because going on the board guaranteed that both George and I would receive the best medical care there is. I think of this as a gift to our children.

The board is made up of fourteen inside trustees: doctors and administrators from the three clinics, located in Rochester, Minnesota; Scottsdale, Arizona; and Jacksonville; and sixteen public trustees. The latter are academics, CEOs of major U.S. companies, political types, and so on. I may be missing a category or two, but I truly was the only person on the board who was there because of my husband's position. My other claim to fame was that I was the oldest member when my age forced me off the board.

Howard Baker followed Ed Spencer as chair of the foundation board, and after Howard's resignation, Frances Fergusson, president of Vassar College, became the first female chair. Since the board is heavy on the male side, I thought it spoke so well for those gentlemen that they No. 1, recognized Fran's ability; and No. 2, were secure enough to ask a woman to lead them. She was a really great choice.

I made some very nice friends, had some marvelous experiences while there, and tried hard to do what was asked. I flew home from Spain one year and missed dinner with King Juan Carlos and Queen Sophia, and another year I flew from the Far East to attend board meetings.

Having just said how great I was, I should explain that this clinic has been fantastic to us. I promise I only will mention this once, but in the last seven years, between the two of us, we have had ten operations. For people who feel like a million dollars, that is hard to explain. I have had two hip replacements and George has had one. I have had five feet operations (now wait a minute—I didn't say I have five feet, just five operations) and two back operations. Six of these were done at the Mayo Clinic.

I swore George into secrecy about one operation on my foot. He obviously didn't listen because lying in the hospital bed I turned on

C-SPAN and there was George in Chicago speaking. To my horror I heard him saying that I was sorry not to be with them, but I was in the hospital after a foot operation. He went on to say that I had made him promise not to tell, so all he would say was that now "I was a perfect NINE." I'm sure people were still confused. The truth is, I had a toe removed, and had a second one removed a few years later. Anyone who has ever had problems with their feet will understand how great it feels to get rid of the pain, even if it means amputation. I'm in heaven now.

The other day I walked into the beauty parlor and a woman said, "You look great. How do you feel?" I answered her, "I feel great, but let me give you a little advice. When you see a friend who is over seventy-five, stop at 'You look great.' Otherwise you can be sure that nine times out of ten they'll tell you, at great length, just how they feel." It is horrible to get older and have to listen to others' ailments when yours are so much more interesting!

I stayed on the Mayo board from February 1993 to February 2001 and was very proud when year after year *U.S. News & World Report* put them at the top of the medical care list in most categories. Patient care is their top priority. Although I am off the board as I write, I will never lose my interest in this great institution.

March—Pop is coming along slowly, but surely. I will be glad when he starts on his book.* It will give him something to focus on. He still reads the papers from cover to cover and listens to the commentators laud Bill Clinton and dump on him.

April 6—What a year this has been. Today we are sick at heart. Our gallant, funny, awkward Ranger Boy† died. He had to be put down. He was riddled with cancer. . . . George didn't need this now. Everyone loved our Ranger Boy. I immediately thought of all our White House friends who loved Ranger. Poor little Millie, all alone. George said at lunch today, "Ranger had no enemies."

---

*George was getting ready to write a book with his national security adviser and great friend, Brent Scowcroft. *A World Transformed* was published by Knopf in 1998.
†One of Millie's puppies, her only son.

I felt so sorry for George. He loved Ranger and got such pleasure walking, playing, and laughing with and at him. He and Don Rhodes, our dear friend who has been in our lives for almost forty years and without whom we really could not exist, truly mourned Ranger's death. George had been so brave about losing the election and then the death of his wonderful mother, who died shortly afterward. But he couldn't hide his feelings about Ranger. I believe Ranger's death allowed him to vent his accumulated grief over the three losses. I am not in any way comparing Ranger's death to that of George's mother, but just saying that this was the straw that broke the camel's back.

A greater sadness for me that spring was the illness and eventual death of my brother Jim. He had diabetes and cancer, suffered a heart attack and blood clots. It was a vicious circle in that he had to stop the chemotherapy when he had the heart attack and go off blood thinner. That caused clots and they had to amputate his leg. He was like Job, with the very most courageous heart you can imagine. His wife Margie also was so caring and brave. My darling, funny brother Jim died on June 22 at home with hospice and a loving wife at his side.

On April 15 we flew to Kuwait with a planeload of family and friends at the invitation of the Kuwaiti government. George had not been there since it was liberated from Iraq during Desert Storm two years earlier. I wrote in my diary:

> We were met at the airport by the Emir and Crown Prince, members of the cabinet, and our ambassador and his wife, Skip and Peggy Gnehm. We did all the usual things, men in one room and ladies in the other. We drove to Bayan Palace and all along the way were people cheering and waving George Bush posters and American flags and Kuwaiti flags. And the women make a unique high keening sound with their tongues at the top of their mouths. All were screaming and smiling. They blew kisses, etc.
>
> We later heard after we left the country that all were not so very pleased to see us. A group of Iraqis (under the direction of

Saddam Hussein's minions) had planned to bomb our car, but were discovered before they could accomplish the nasty deed. President Clinton bombed some strategic military sites to let Saddam know that he would not tolerate such action.

It was a very moving trip for us all. We were hosted at the most beautiful dinner parties during our visit. Shaikha Awatif had a beautiful dinner for me attended by 400 ladies, and the Emir had 600 men for George and gave him Kuwait's highest decoration. It only has been given four other times and was a very warm and moving ceremony, I heard.

We did so many things, all interesting, but the highlights for me were a meeting with the Emir and Crown Prince in a huge tent; and a visit to Parliament where George gave a short from-the-heart talk. A poem was read and George was highly lauded. George got teased by Fitchy [our neighbor Jack Fitch] as he was referred to as "a stallion."

. . . The occupation [of Kuwait had] started in August of 1990 and ended February of 1991. Just before liberation, the Iraqi invaders burned, broke, and bombed that which they had not already stolen. They took around 800 hostages those last few days, many tortured, many still detained, and many dead. So there is a big POW-MIA group. Every building we went into has been rebuilt in the last two years. The Parliament was rebuilt by the U.S. Army Corps of Engineers. It is beautiful. We saw before and after pictures and they are hard to believe.

. . . We went from the Parliament to a museum. It is a large shambles now. The Iraqis visited the museum in July of 1990 as guests of the Kuwaitis, spotted all the treasures they wanted, and then when they invaded a month later, they knew what they wanted and where it was. The same people went immediately to the museum and took as many of their treasures as they could. They burned and bombed the building the last week of the war, including the films and all records.

April 14—We went out to the oil fields and saw oil lakes and burned twisted equipment, etc. It looked like a bad nightmare. Amazingly enough, the blackened desert is showing a touch of color. It turns out that the oil slick kept the moisture in and now the desert is greening just a little. Nature is tough and wonderful.

Later we went to visit a home and a hospital for sick and deformed children. They had been thrown into the streets, [their] incubators were taken and sent to Baghdad during the invasion. These invaders were animals.

We returned to Kuwait in 2001 to celebrate the tenth anniversary of the liberation, along with General Norman Schwarzkopf, Margaret Thatcher, John Major, and many others involved in the coalition. The city has been rebuilt, but the prisoners of war are still unaccounted for* and the museum is still in shambles. The memories of the atrocities are still there, and the affection for the coalition members is stronger than ever. It was a poignant return.

April 27—We had Margaret Thatcher for breakfast. She is on a speaking tour. She had just come from the Reagan Library's celebration of Ron's birthday. She said it was a great evening, but very long. When Ron got up to speak he had his cards, and when he looked up from the cards and then looked down again, he read the same card again. She said that it was very embarrassing and that people were marvelous and all clapped and laughed in the same places. It never made the papers. Amazing.

I did read about this incident after President Reagan wrote that incredible letter and told us all he had Alzheimer's. What a glorious man and what a tragedy for both him and Nancy.

In early May, we moved our household to Kennebunkport. To give you a flavor of our first summer out of office, I'd like to share just a few of my diary notes:

The town had the warmest welcome home for us on the Town Green in front of The Captain Lord Mansion. It was so sweet.

*They were still unaccounted for in June 2003 and feared dead.

. . . G. went to visit Nick and Kitty Brady* in the Bahamas, played golf and went fishing. He said the bone fishing was spectacular.

On Monday May 17th I left Maine and flew to NYC . . . We went right to McMillan's (better learn how to spell it, now they are my publisher!)† There we met with Benita Somerfield‡ and talked about The Barbara Bush Foundation for Family Literacy. Things seem to be going well there. We are going on with our grant giving—$100 thousand to MRS. BUSH'S STORY HOUR for starters. We have around $8 million in the bank and $2 million more promised. Not bad.

After a literacy event in NYC, I flew to Houston to do two fund-raisers for Kay Bailey Hutchison. Kay is running for the United States Senate. She's a good candidate and can win this race IF we get the vote out.§

From Houston to Boise, Idaho, where I had lunch with my dear friend, Louise McClure, U.S. Senator Jim McClure's wife. After lunch we went to call on their Literacy Lab at the public library, a good adult program and dear children. I read a book to the children. In the evening there were two receptions and my speech. This was sort of a typical speaking day—visit a local program, read to kids, and speak. This way one can call attention to the local program and the need for volunteers and money.

(While I was on my trip George was on a trip to Argentina and Brazil giving speeches and visiting with our friend President Carlos Menem. In early June he was in Cannes, France, and Geneva and Lugarno, Switzerland, with our son Marvin's wife Margaret. Before the year was out he traveled to Puerto Rico, Hong Kong, Taiwan, England, Mexico, Canada, and Sweden. He was working too hard and still does today, at age seventy-nine.)

---

*Nick Brady was George's secretary of the Treasury and they both are old, wonderful friends
†The correct spelling is Macmillan.
‡Executive director of the Barbara Bush Foundation for Family Literacy.
§Kay won, and then won again in 2000.

May 21—I am in Rochester at a Mayo Clinic Board meeting. It has been a very exciting week for us all. First of all DORO AND BOBBY HAD A BIG BABY BOY yesterday at 2:15. Robert Daniel Koch weighing in at 10 lbs. 6 oz., our 13th grandchild. I cannot believe it. Thank God that my baby and hers are well and strong. Bobby says that both are doing very well and that the little one has a full head of black hair. 10 lbs. 6 oz.—a whale!!! I also thank God that he has been so good to all Bushes. We have our health and each other.

We had some interesting houseguests, some invited and some not. Larry and Janis Gatlin and their daughter and son came for a brief stay. They were such fun. George loved playing golf with Larry. Larry was starring in WILL ROGERS on the stage in New York. They arrived on Sunday afternoon and flew back to NYC with us on Tuesday in time for the evening show. THE GATLINS were invited.

Monday at lunch we were sitting on the deck overlooking the Atlantic Ocean when Larry started wiping at his head and shifting his chair. Some birds had nested in the eaves over his head and were using Larry as a repository for their droppings. I'm afraid we all got laughing so hard and were not very sympathetic. Larry was a very good sport. THE BIRDS were the uninvited guests.

June 12—We had a wonderful weekend over Pop's birthday. For months he had been planning a visit for the military nurses who were so nice to him at the White House. They had given him neck treatments to loosen up those knots [in his neck]. During these White House treatments, they would play tapes. One of the tapes they listened to was Roger Whittaker's.* Kim Siniscalchi became the president of "The Roger Whittaker Fan Club" and George, the recording secretary. They had a lot of fun with all of this.

George found Roger's agent in Florida and got his United States tour schedule and his telephone number in England. I

---

*A popular British ballad singer.

think that Natalie Whittaker did not believe it when George said that he was the President of the USA,* explained about the nurses and that he wanted to invite them for a weekend in June to Kennebunkport. I believe she called the White House switch board to verify the call and only then accepted his invitation. Only Kim knew he was coming. Natalie and Roger drove up in the early afternoon and we immediately liked them. We threw a sandwich down them and rushed out to play golf. We got home in time to greet the nurses, all 6 of them, who had driven up in a van. They were so cute, 5 ladies and 1 man, Kim, Ellen Tolton, Paula Trivette, Debbie Beatty, Mary Jackson, and Art Wallace. They are all married and all officers. They all had on T-shirts with Roger's picture on one side and their own on the other. They also had their motto on the shirt, "More Roger in Our Lives." They said when they stopped for a bite on the way up they raised a lot of eyebrows and could see that people were wondering just who they were.

. . . When they got to our gate a guard looked at them and said, "Who is this Roger Whittaker anyway? He's up at the house right now." So our surprise was out seconds before they arrived. The girls threw themselves out of the car and into George's and Roger's arms. That started a great weekend of singing, golf, bike riding and walking.

Unfortunately, there was no walking for me, as I can't walk into town to this day because I get stopped by people asking for autographs and pictures. George says if I would just dye my hair, I could go anywhere I wanted.

The Whittakers have become good friends and Natalie and I exchange e-mails often. Hers are so funny and delightful. I understand the nurses go to every concert they can when Roger is in the U.S.A.

⁓ We entertained a lot that summer, with houseguests galore. All our children came at different times and also together. They

---

*George had made the phone call after we lost the election but before leaving the White House.

all had guests. This prompted George to say: "Don't houseguests know they don't have houseguests?" The answer is that our children don't know that, thank heavens. The Point sang with the noises of horse-shoes, tennis, water polo, and bike riders. It was not unusual to look in the tiny playroom off the kitchen and dining room and to see eight grandchildren of all ages curled like puppies on the sectional couch watching television.

Our wonderful housekeeper, Paula Rendon, who has been with us since Doro was born, fed armies with some high school and college youth to help with beds, dishes, and cleaning. Sometimes Paula's patience would wear a little thin—especially with the sweet young girl who worked for us—and I would hear Paula muttering in Spanish under her breath, *"stupido, stupido."* I was so worried she had offended the girl that I asked her one day if she had hurt feelings. "Oh, don't worry," she said sweetly. "I don't speak Spanish."

We did lots of buffets. A favorite menu was lemon chicken; a rice ring filled with baby peas, fresh if possible; and sliced tomatoes on the side. (Fresh Maine corn and fresh Maine vine-ripened tomatoes are the best in the world.) This was followed by Paula's blueberry or pecan pie with ice cream.

LEMON CHICKEN, BY PAULA RENDON
(Marvin Bush's favorite dish)
SERVES 6

3 breasts of chicken (halved and halved again)
½ cup flour
1 stick butter
2 tablespoons dry vermouth
2 tablespoons lemon juice
¼ teaspoon grated lemon rind
Salt and pepper to taste
1 cup heavy cream (variable to thicken into gravy consistency)

Lightly flour and salt and pepper chicken; fry the chicken golden brown in butter for 14 minutes, then set aside. Discard butter, but 1 tablespoon. Scrape flour sediment and soften with vermouth, lemon juice, and lemon rind. In moderate heat, add heavy cream (I lighten with half-and-half to make a little more gravy) and stir. Arrange chicken in layers in casserole and pour gravy over. The more gravy the better. Sprinkle with parmesan cheese.

Bake for 30 minutes in 350-degree oven.

This recipe reminds me of a letter I received in the White House from a doctor suggesting that I was trying to kill George Bush with such unhealthy meals. I think he saw one of my recipes printed in a magazine or something. Unhealthy maybe, but oh, so good!

In early July President F. W. de Klerk of South Africa came for lunch. He arrived in style as president of a large country, in a government plane and with many staff. (Strange for me to say, I guess, when the American president seems to travel with an army of security, staff, and a gigantic press corps.) Several years later he visited us in Houston as South Africa's vice president. Quite a difference. He flew commercially and only had two others in their party. One of them told me that de Klerk had only stayed on in hopes of helping Nelson Mandela with a peaceful transition, which they managed quite successfully. I'm sure that it wasn't easy to go from president to vice president, but he loved his country that much.

I might add here a note about Nelson Mandela: He and George also have stayed friends and occasionally talk on the phone. We had a nice conversation with him in 2001 during a visit to South Africa. At age eighty-two, he walked straight as an arrow and told us he was happily married to his second wife. He is dedicating the rest of his life to peace, concentrating at this moment on Africa and the Middle East.

On July 14, we hosted the first meeting of the board of trustees for the George Bush Presidential Library Foundation. This was a group of our closest friends who were coming together to help raise money for George's Library, to be built on the campus of Texas A&M University in College Station, Texas. Most of the board stayed downtown, but we invited Lee and Walter Annenberg* to stay in the renovated Bungalow, Mrs. Bush's summer cottage that George bought from her estate. Unlike many summer cottages that are enormous, this is truly a cottage. We have often stayed with Lee and Walter at their beautiful home in Palm Springs, California, and everything is perfect. Everything was and is not perfect in the Bungalow. It's nice and clean. The master bedroom is about the size of Lee's closet at home, but the ocean view is grand and the air is heavenly. Both Lee and Walter were so dear about their tiny little quarters; Lee raved over everything and everyone.

We were so thrilled by the people who came, especially ninety-year-old Don Luis Ferre, the former governor of Puerto Rico, and his wife Tiody. I wrote in my diary:

> They came in trolleys from the Colony Hotel for cocktails, then back by trolley to the River Club for a catered lobster bake. After dinner we went across the street to the Casino.† Dick Cheney, Tip O'Neil, and Dick Jackman‡ spoke and dear Jane Weintraub§ sang. It was a great evening.
>
> The next day we all met at the Colony Hotel for a library meeting, and it was amazing that so many people were so surprised about Texas A&M. They showed a superb film and no one realized that it is the third or fourth largest university in the country, fifth in National Merit scholars, and eighth in research funding. I remember Walter Annenberg said that when he goes back to college he thinks he'll go to A&M.

⟆ In August George and I, along with Noelle, our beautiful eldest granddaughter and Jeb's daughter, flew to Madrid with our

---

*Great friends and great philanthropists. Walter, among other things, founded *TV Guide*. He also was a very popular ambassador to Great Britain for President Nixon and Lee was chief of protocol for Ronald Reagan.

†Another building that is part of the River Club in Kennebunkport. There is *no* gambling there.

‡Dick, retired from Sun Oil (now Sunoco), is a well-known, very funny after-dinner speaker.

§Jane, now married to movie producer Jerry Weintraub, was Jane Morgan, the fabulous singer. She grew up in Kennebunkport and is possibly one of the nicest people I know. One of her many hits was "Fascination."

much younger cousins, Debbie and Craig Stapleton,* and their daughter Wendy for a wonderful trip. The girls were around fifteen or sixteen at the time, and we had a fabulous time with all of them. Back to my diary notes:

> George gave his speech at Euroforum to Universidad Conplutense—*cursos de verano.*† Meanwhile the girls and I went to visit the unbelievable monastery. I don't know if they call it the EL ESCORIAL or if that is the name of the town.‡ We were greeted by the director and a marvelous guide and shown all over this famous cathedral. King Felipe built this lovely edifice in the 15th century in 22 years. It is filled with El Greco's and many famous Spanish, Italian, and Dutch paintings. It is enormous and has one of the most ornate and large altar areas that I have ever seen. The church part is square, in the style of a Greek cross. There are many Turkish influences, the most obvious being the blue and white tiles. Room after room is filled with paintings of the Spanish royalty starting with Charles. Every single Spanish king and many wives have been buried in the most ornate, domed room in the bowels of the building. The caskets are layered (one on top of the other) and are made of marble. The walls are fine pink and gray marble. There is an enormous chandelier in the middle.

(We then went from Madrid to Rabat for George and Craig to play golf with the king of Morocco, King Hassan II, a respected and close friend.)

> Craig said that they had the biggest crowd of ball markers, advisors, etc. There were three teams and so they played a sixsome. It took hours. George later told me that he thought there were about 100 people and that his majesty had 50 clubs in the biggest golf bag he had ever seen.

---

*Craig is now the U.S. ambassador to the Czech Republic.
†I'm assuming this means summer courses.
‡El Escorial is actually a palace, monastery, and mausoleum and also is the name of the town where it is located. It was built to combine all functions of church and state.

. . . The ladies were taken to Bouznika to see the King's Arabian horses. [The King's wife]* greeted us with the young princess who had met us at the plane wearing a black Chanel suit with a blue and black blouse and very clunky funky platform shoes. Noelle and Wendy died over her clothes, they loved them so. It was very hot. I had on a blue denim dress that I had worn for years with navy blue pumps. I asked Her Highness if I should wear my sneakers (I did not, thank heavens) to the horse farm and she said, "yes," and that she was going to change her shoes and I would be surprised. When we got to the farm she had on high top tennis shoes made of the same material as her blouse and, the girls noticed, as the lining of her Chanel skirt. The girls seemed to know that these shoes cost $700. They were drooling.

I thought that I had seen some pretty great farms, but this is like nothing I had ever seen before. First of all this farm is in the middle of a very big desert. From the moment we arrived at the gate the desert turned into a flower garden. The stables were of ornate plaster carving with glorious tiles and domed roofs. (Somewhat like the brick Mexican domes.) The horses were led out and were like ballet dancers. And incidentally they were much better dressed than I was.

. . . We went to the same summer palace (Skhirat) that George and I had been to before. Beautiful, on the beach, and we sat with the wife of the King, a charming woman, their three daughters and two sons on a large terrace overlooking a small harbor that held the King's boats. Two of the daughters were married and the third is engaged. The third, who is 25, will be married when it rains. "It would not be appropriate to have a celebration when the country is suffering from a drought." The princess did not seem to be praying for rain.

. . . Then His Majesty and George arrived. Shortly after that three of the dearest children arrived, two boys in linen suits and one little girl. They raced up to hug His Majesty. All the middle generation seemed to watch the King all the time. They bowed over his hand as did all the servants. An amazing country.

---

*And in 2003 the mother of the current king.

(In spite of all the grandeur, King Hassan and his family made the Bushes and Stapletons feel very much at home. As I edit this in 2002, I am pretty sure the present king, King Muhammad VI, was there that night.)

We flew that night to Tangier and boarded Trammell Crow's lovely yacht THE MICHAELA ROSE and cruised to Gibraltar. We toured after a breakfast with the Governor Sir John and Lady Isabel Chapple. It's a fascinating "Rock" with extraordinary history and is now British territory and a thorn in the Spanish side. There are 32 miles of tunneling in the rock, more underground miles than there are on the surface. There is a population of 30,000 and hundreds of thousands of tourists. It is a tremendous maintenance and refueling port. Our 6th Fleet was here during Desert Storm, I believe.

We drove up to several sites and fed the "apes." I would call them monkeys. If a monkey could be called spoiled, these monkeys were really spoiled rotten. They grabbed bananas from our hands and made rude noises.

We continued cruising along the coast of Spain. I jumped ship in Palma to fly back to attend the August Mayo Clinic meeting, so our daughter-in-law Margaret Bush joined the party. Trammell and Margaret Crow, our great friends in Dallas, were so generous to lend their boat to us.

~ I felt that summer we all began to settle into our new life and our new routine. I wrote this letter to Julie Cooke, my No. 2 at the White House, on August 30:

We have had all our gang up here at one time or another . . . Jeb and George are both running for governor of their respective states. WOW! I am flabbergasted that they want to run, but they do. Jeb has sold out of all his business and has a tough primary campaign ahead for a year. George will have less trouble in the primary, but a really ugly general

election. Meanwhile we are all watching the Texas Rangers*
from afar and each morning awaken to race for the papers to
see if they won or lost the night before.

That precious and wonderful George Bush hasn't
changed one bit. He is still inviting the world over and
regrets those he left out. We have the oddest groups staying
here that you have ever heard of. Brent Scowcroft; [his
secretary] Flo Gantt; Ginny and Rob Mulberger (Brent's
right hand assistant who worked at the NSC with him, and
her husband); Condi Rice (now provost at Stanford!!); and
Arnie Kanter.† This group is known as "The Book Group."
They are working with George and Brent on their book.

Also staying with us are Barbara Patton and Jack Steel,
two close friends from Houston who are big volunteers in
our office.

AND . . . get this . . . THE OAK RIDGE BOYS are
here . . . all four of them with wives. Why Paula doesn't
collapse, I don't know. We have so many beds now and, as I
said, George wants them all filled.

I heard him on the phone yesterday inviting Cardinal
Law (Boston), Cardinal O'Connor (New York), Cardinal
Baum (St. Louis), and Father Murphy [from Boston] all for
lunch tomorrow. They will be here with "The Book Group";
and Chrissie Evert, Andy Mill, and their baby will be
arriving later today. Some combination, huh?

George discovered during the visit just before lunch
that the Cardinals knew Bishop Jack Allin, our minister at
St. Ann's by the Sea,‡ so he called Jack and asked him to join
us. During this lunch our cousin John Walker, his wife
Katharine and daughter dropped by with their friend and
houseguest, Kimba Wood, a very attractive judge who was

---

*George W. was then managing partner of the Texas Rangers baseball team.

†Arnie Kanter served as under secretary of state from 1991 to 1993. Ginny Lampley
was senior director of legislative affairs on the National Security staff from 1989 to 1993. He
and Ginny both were founding partners of Brent Scowcroft's "The Scowcroft Group," an
international advisory group based in Washington.

‡Bishop Allin at one time was presiding bishop of the Episcopal Church. At this time
he was retired, spending part of the summer in Kennebunkport. He died in 1998.

nominated by Bill Clinton for Attorney General and was caught up in a "nanny gate" situation. What fun and what a nutty household we are running!

My reading of the summer has not been of the highest type so have no recommendations. I tried *Colony* after loving *Outer Banks*,* but just couldn't concentrate.

Love to you Julie,
BPB

That letter painted a good picture of the summer of 1993. Hectic, but fun.

Thinking back on it, I was really surprised that George and Jeb wanted to have anything to do with politics after 1992. Both of them had worked hard in the campaign, and both of them had seen the tough, dirty side of politics—the lies and negative campaigning. Both of them saw and felt how much losing hurt. It does. As I recall, George W. asked us what we thought, and I told him that he should NOT run against the very popular Governor Ann Richards. I did not think he could win. His father was much wiser and offered no advice. To this day George W. teases me about that advice. You notice he didn't take it either.

September 6—We are beginning to wind down. Yesterday was the last Sunday at St. Ann's by the Sea. At church yesterday we sang a hymn, and George leaned over and said, "That's the way Mom went." The theme was about being "prepared to go home." Then a little later he said, looking at a stained glass window of Jesus holding out his arms to a child, "That makes me think of Robin."

That seemed so strange to me for when the second lesson (Romans 12:9–21) was read I thought about George and his great generosity. He forgives. He works on the theory that it is better to make a friend than an enemy. When I told George that I thought of him when I heard the lesson, he said that wasn't true, but that is what I see. He is a good man.†

*Books by Anne Rivers Siddons.

†The entire passage reminds me of George, but especially the part that says: "Be joyful in hope, patient in affliction, faithful in prayer. Share with God's people who are in need. Practice hospitality."

September 13—Prime Minister Rabin of Israel and Yassir Arafat of Palestine were signing a peace accord on the White House lawn. George and I were invited to go and stay at the White House. It was right and proper that he be there. I am just not ready to go back yet. George was going anyway on Tuesday to push for the NAFTA Treaty* to be passed by Congress, an initiative that he was such a part of. He is more generous than I am. During the campaign Clinton did not take a side on NAFTA, but now that he needs help he calls on George, Jerry Ford, and Jimmy Carter.

I am very happy George is there, as this signing would never have taken place without him, ever. And R.R. [Ronald Reagan] must get a lot of credit for rebuilding our defenses and keeping us strong. AND if G. hadn't fought the pressure from the Jewish lobby to make immense loan guarantees without Israel's word that they wouldn't build in the occupied territories, the Arabs would NOT have come to the table. If G. had not gathered the free world together and freed Kuwait and secured the safety of Israel, the Arabs and the Jews would NOT have come to the table. The whole world knows this. Brian Mulroney† and Colin Powell called George to tell him that they knew that and to congratulate him.

G. met with Arafat and said he was charming. Amazing. Whoever thought that we'd recognize him—a sworn terrorist? . . . One man's terrorist is another man's hero.

. . . The next morning they had the NAFTA push in the East Room. We all saw it on the TV. Bill gave an impassioned speech. All the others spoke. George said after hearing B.C. speak he understood why Bill was living in the White House and he wasn't. He got a nice laugh. J. Carter made news speaking up about the dangers of Ross Perot, "a demagogue, who because he has money, feels he can buy his way through life." . . . Ross has intimidated members of Congress by telling them that if they vote for NAFTA his "army" will work to defeat them. . . .

---

*The trade agreement among the United States, Canada, and Mexico.
†Then the prime minister of Canada.

September 17—I spoke in Richmond, Virginia, for a New Women's Center and Peggy Swift met Nancy Huang* there and helped her. Peg slipped out during dinner and did not say goodbye. How I will miss her and wish her all the best. She has been the greatest help and done the best job. She is like a member of our family. I think that Nancy will be wonderful, also.

∽ In October we headed back to Houston, where our new house had been under construction all summer. The house was—and is—a dream. Finally, it was moving day.

October 18—Laura [Bush] and [her friend] Lynn Munn came from Midland and Dallas and worked for two full days opening barrels and boxes and putting things away. Those girls lined all our drawers with white poster paper that they cut to fit the drawers. They were fabulous. Mark Hampton's† assistant Nancy came from New York and put my beautiful new couches in place and helped place our old furniture. Nancy Huang, my new personal aide, and Jean Becker [who came to Houston to do research for my book and help me with speeches] unpacked my office and literally after two days everything was almost unpacked and put away. Ed Eubanks, our architect, was in there pitching in all day long. Paula gave orders and worked hard. The beautiful curtains went up in the house . . . We were all sitting on the floor eating when George walked in. There were workmen all over the place finishing up and he joined us for a bite and returned to the office. They teased him badly, but it was just right that he dropped in and then left. I heard that he stopped and had his picture taken with all those talented workmen who worked day and sometimes late in the evening to get us in our house. Nice. He had

---

*Peggy had come to Houston with me when we left the White House. She was my aide there and became almost my "everything" in Houston. My aide travels with me, makes my schedule, does some errands, and stays in touch with our family. Peggy was leaving and Nancy was my new "everything."

†Mark Hampton helped me decorate at the vice president's house, Camp David, the White House, and Walker's Point. He was a wonderful friend who sadly died in 1998.

already moved his clothes in over the weekend and set up his closet.

That afternoon I washed my hair and went with George to the Houston Convention Center* where they named a large room THE GEORGE BUSH GRAND BALLROOM. There was a big crowd and it was so touching. That night we could barely move, we were so tired.

The next day Mark Hampton arrived and what a touch he has. Laura, Lynn, and Ed spent the day handing him things. He placed every book and hung every picture without hesitation. Every single thing we own never looked better than they do in this house. It is truly a golden house and everywhere I look I am reminded of some wonderful beautiful happy part of our life. What a life it has been.

I love our new house!!! It is twice as pretty as I thought it would be!!!

≈ It was a very full fall. In November, we went to Washington where first we saw Doro and her new, very huggable, squishy baby Robert. Then we went to Colin Powell's retirement ceremony from the military. It was a beautiful "good-bye" to a great man and friend. We would never have gone back to Washington if it hadn't been for our love and respect for Colin. I sat next to Michael Powell, Alma and Colin's very attractive lawyer son. We had a good cry together. Colin was the "first" in many things: the first African-American to come up through the ranks of the ROTC, the first to become chairman of the Joint Chiefs of Staff; and now of course the first African-American Secretary of State.

Here are some diary notes from some of our other activities that fall:

I read two books that Caroline Seitz† had given me. Loved them both. *Devices and Desires* by P.D. James and *The Light Years*

---

*Its official name is the George R. Brown Convention Center.
†Wife of our ambassador to Great Britain, Raymond Seitz.

Attending Colin Powell's retirement ceremony, November 1993.
FAMILY SCRAPBOOK

by Elizabeth Jane Howard. Ms. Howard writes in the most pleasant fashion and seems to notice things that happen to all of us, so you find yourself saying, "How funny. That is just exactly the way it is."

November 13—I flew with Lod* and Carole Cook to Beijing. We will meet up with George in Hong Kong later in the week. Lod was there on business and Carole and I shopped and went sightseeing.

After our bags arrived we, Chinese security, U.S. security and a lady from the Chinese protocol went for a walk down the street, looking like a small army, towards the Friendship Store. What a change [from when we lived there]. Many neon lights. Many street vendors. Many beggars. I saw a mother with a baby in her arms holding her hands out and one with the boy's hands cupped in the same position. That killed me. That did not happen in the "bad old days."

*Lod was then CEO of ARCO.

. . . The number of new buildings is unending. I was told with pride that "this is a joint venture building with Canada" or "this building is owned by China's richest man, a many times millionaire . . ." China's richest man! China never had a "richest man" when we lived there. If they did, they never let us know about it.

Looking from my hotel window I can see that the pollution is worse than ever. Rather amazingly I am looking at an overpass that certainly was not here the last time I was here. I am told that the new toll road from the airport was built in eleven months. It is a very different entrance into Beijing now. The old allowed you to get into the "China mood." Maybe that is what the new one does also. Somewhere along the line someone suggested that Chairman Mao was like a dam; now the dam is broken, and free enterprise is flooding the country.

. . . The stores and restaurants are filled with Chinese, the streets are filled with cars and small yellow van taxis. It is amazing.

. . . All Americans think that China is "on hold" because of Tiananmen Square. While we are talking about human rights being connected to MFN* status, many many companies are doing big business in China. I was amused to see that McDonald, Kentucky Fried Chicken, Shakey's, and Pizza Hut are all firmly ensconced in Beijing and are filled and have waiting lines.

. . . CNN is big in Beijing. How we would have loved that when we lived here! All the news is bad or ugly about the USA—rapes, murders, lying, and cheating. That's what people see about our country. Now maybe nationals from other countries feel their countries are being badly depicted, too. In any case COMMUNICATION is the biggest change in a world of big changes.

. . . Just before lunch the NAFTA vote was announced, and the President won his vote. He got 100 Democrat and 125 Republican votes . . . some place in there I lost ten votes as the

---

*MFN stands for Most Favored Nation; the term refers to special trading partnerships.

final vote was 235 pro. George worked hard on this and called many congressmen for the president.

     ∽ We went on to Taiwan, Sweden, and England; home for Thanksgiving, and then back to England for a speech George was giving and a very special lunch with Queen Elizabeth.

     November 30—At exactly 12:55 p.m. we arrived at the side entrance of Buckingham Palace. We were led upstairs to the private rooms where Her Majesty and Prince Philip were standing looking out a window at geese that were walking on their enormous lawn or park. We had a little sherry and small talk and Her Majesty said: "Well, I guess we better get on with what we are here for" and gave George with no fanfare the Knight Grand Cross of the Most Honourable Order of the Bath. Six generals in WW II and President Reagan are the only Americans to be so honored. Had he been British, George would be called "Sir" and been down on one knee and touched on the shoulder with a sword. The order came in two velvet boxes. One held a sunburst and the other a long collar—gold covered with enamel and very handsome. We were amused when we got back to the hotel to be asked to sign papers saying that IF George resigned from the order or on his death, the collar is to be returned to Great Britain. He may keep the sunburst. We were told that the collar was worth 25,000 pounds.* Rather amazing. That made me wonder if they put it in a museum or do they loan it to someone else? As we were sipping sherry the door opened and six little Welsh Corgis came in. They were all ages and absolutely adorable. Her Majesty and the Prince were dear to them. They did not take over or yap. Very important!

     We went into a sunny small dining room and had a very relaxed pleasant lunch. Her Majesty and Prince Philip are very

*The equivalent of $37,075.

versed on the world and also seemed to know all about our sons running for office. We will certainly never forget that day!

⮑ I can't forget it for it became a joke in George's speeches. He says that when we got home he asked me how it felt to be married to a real live knight. My answer was, "Get the coffee, SIR George!" Sir George and I both still get the coffee and walk the dog.

One night in December we went to the Houston Museum of Fine Arts for a dinner sponsored by the Texas Heart Institute. George was to receive the Denton Cooley* Leadership Award. George gave an off-the-cuff acceptance talk, saying he really didn't deserve the great honor except that briefly last year he had "an achy breaky heart."† I loved that and thought it was so funny.

December 15—Saturday night Lauren and Pierce [two of Neil and Sharon's children] came for the night. They came after dinner (I guess their mother and father didn't trust my cooking) and were so good. We played a little PEGGITY and a game of CLUE. I had made beds on the third floor and they looked comfortable. (They didn't want to sleep in our guest room; they wanted to sleep up on the third floor.) The only thing is that they have to use the elevator to go to the bathroom. First they wanted a drink. They were thirsty. Then they needed to go to the bathroom. Of course they didn't close the door and so the elevator wouldn't move. We finally solved all those problems and they settled down to sleep like babies. They are so nice, easy good children.

While we were gone the next summer we had one closet made into a half bath on the third floor!

---

*Dr. Cooley, a good friend, is a renowned heart surgeon. He performed the first heart transplant in the United States in 1968.
†Title of a country-western music song by Billy Ray Cyrus.

〜 Earlier that year George's remarkable classmate from Andover, Bob Macauley, had called and asked if he could come to lunch in Kennebunkport. At that lunch, Bob asked me to become the ambassador-at-large for AmeriCares. Bob founded this incredible relief organization in 1982 because he saw a need to get aid to people without government red tape. AmeriCares supports treatment for immediate and long-term health problems, primarily with medical supplies, but they also try to tackle other problems that follow disasters. A lot of their supplies—95 percent—are in-kind gifts, meaning that pharmaceutical companies donate the supplies or large corporations lend their planes for transportation. An astonishing 98.62 percent of the money raised goes to care of the victims—victims of floods, tornadoes, landslides, hurricanes, etc., both in this country or anywhere in the world. The staff is mostly unpaid or underpaid. In 1993, AmeriCares was the biggest nongovernmental group in Yugoslavia, having already sent thirty airlifts.

In December, Bob asked me if I would accompany a planeload of supplies to Split, Croatia. He said I could bring a friend, and I immediately thought of our new family doctor, feeling that he would be of the most help if a doctor was needed. We only had several days notice, and Dr. Ben Orman rearranged his life in no time and came. So, accompanied by my aide Nancy Huang, Ben and I flew off to New York City to start our adventure. Here are some of my diary notes from the trip:

We had a press conference and then dramatically climbed on a DC-8 packed with hospital supplies and medicine in the front, and seats for about 20 in the back. Nancy and I got the two front seats—the best. They waived the "no smoking" rule, several of them smoked the whole way there. We stopped in Ostend, Belgium, at 2 a.m. and went to a darling hotel called Royal Astor Hotel, the plainest little inn, but clean and great plumbing. I got my wake-up call at 4:45 and we left for the airport at 5:30 a.m. The plane didn't take off until 6:45 a.m. Oh boy, were we ever spoiled at the White House. We did not "hurry up and wait."

All during the trip Bob talked about going to Sarajevo. Out of courtesy George called the State Department and CIA to let them know I was going; for advice, he called Larry Eagleburger, a friend and former ambassador to Yugoslavia [and former Secretary of State]. All three said absolutely "no" to Sarajevo. It was too dangerous as a civil war was raging there at that very moment and that if I went the USA could be blamed for any accidents. So I was to wave Bob off . . . Bob was hell bent to take medicine and hospital supplies to Sarajevo and had a small plane loaded when they got the word that the airport was under siege and on red alert. The pilots would not fly.

Meanwhile we went to visit refugee camps, mostly Moslem . . . It was so sad. Everyone wanted to return home. Families are divided. They share bedrooms with other families and have community baths. No hot water, etc. We were told that the toughest thing that the people had to fight was depression. We brought medicine for depression. I think one reason they are so depressed is that they have nothing to do. The women knit socks with the design of their villages as patterns. One woman told me that when she finishes a sock she pulls it out and starts all over. We should have taken yarn for them.*

They want to go home. They want to be with family and friends. They are worried. They've lost everything. The last camp we went to was the worst with housing for 100 people all sharing 4 toilets and sinks and no showers. At the camp we were to eat with the families, but hepatitis had broken out (20 cases) and our Secret Service man said we couldn't eat with them so we brought food to eat with several chosen families, not the whole camp. We shouldn't have eaten at all if everyone couldn't eat. I sat across from a young couple. The man had grenade shrapnel in his leg. They had a three-month-old baby. They want to come to America. We are taking ten thousand people and they are not on the list. I could cry.

We had some press on the trip, all nice, caring people. ABC's Anne Compton and a crew of four came along, as did syndicated

---

*I suggested this to Bob, and this miracle man sent all sorts of sewing and knitting equipment to them on the next cargo plane.

columnist Georgie Ann Geyer; Massimo Calabrisi from *Time*; and that very famous *Time* photographer Carl Mydans. Carl was eighty-six at the time, a tiny little man. We all adored him. On the plane he told us, with some probing, that he and his wife Shelley were Japanese prisoners of war for three years in the Philippines during World War II. He had more energy at eighty-six than most of the rest of us.

On the way home we refueled at Rein Military base in Frankfurt, where I saw some of the military people we had met over the years at bases all over the world. After a 10-hour, 55-minute trip back to Houston, there was George with Millie waiting for me at the foot of the plane steps. We had a press conference at Ellington Air Force Base and then went home.

ᕲᕫᕫ Christmas was more meaningful in 1993 than most, and we really counted our blessings.

With Betsy Heminway at Kennebunkport, August 1994.
FAMILY SCRAPBOOK

All throughout 1993 I worked on my memoirs. I carried my little Think Pad computer and pulled it out on boats, trains, planes, and in every foreign country we visited. I had more fun, and each happy memory brought forth yet another one. Lisa Drew, my editor at Scribner, insisted that I have a local editor and work from an outline. Enter Jean Becker, who really helped me. I wrote from copious diaries and letters, and then Jean edited. She read each chapter as I finished it and made tactful suggestions like "maybe you have said this or that before," or "this might be better in another chapter." She corrected my spelling, which is the worst, and checked on my facts, names, and stories to be sure I was truthful. Jean was a joy to work with, and I felt free to share my diaries with her. They are so personal that I can't think of anyone else I would share them with. She knows way too much about me. After we finished the book, Jean became and still is George's chief of staff.

After a chapter had been corrected, we sent it to Lisa, who has a very active red pencil and is not half as tactful as Jean. She's probably sharpening it right now. Lisa hates exclamation points. She is not crazy about the words "dearest," as in "dearest friends"; "greatest," as in "greatest children" or grandchildren; "best," as in "best friend." Lisa actually has become a great friend and if she behaves, she will be in danger of becoming a great dearest best friend.

The day after Christmas, Jean and I went to the Golden Door, a fabulous spa in Southern California, and spent two weeks working on the body in the morning and the book in the afternoon. To be honest, more got done on the book than the body. "The Door" is a lovely place and we had wonderful weather. Every morning we awakened at 5 a.m. and walked over to a small lounge, got coffee, and carried it back to our beds. At 6 a.m. a group took off for a 1½-mile walk straight up a hill for the view. It was stunning to see the sun rising, with the Pacific way off on the horizon, and to watch the valleys with farms and ranches below us come to life.

Then it was back to my room and a bath, and at 7 a.m., breakfast and the newspaper were brought in. After breakfast we started in on bike riding, aerobics, stretching, toning, and for me, swimming. We ate a lot of vegetables and fruit and very little fat. By lunch, we were starved. The afternoon was massage and facial time, but from 4 to 6 p.m. every day I read the book to Jean, the whole book. We deleted and moved and laughed and even shed a tear or two.

In the evening I missed the scheduled programs and worked on the last few chapters. One night I went to bed, having finished a difficult chapter, and the next morning, when I turned the computer on, it looked like there had been a war and either Egyptian hieroglyphics or Chinese calligraphy had won. Enough words were left in English to show that my chapter was in there—but where? Jean and I worked on it and could not retrieve it. Finally we decided to call Chris Emery, the White House usher and a computer expert who had set up my computer when we were still at the White House. He had saved me over and over again. Jean talked to him, and eventually we got most of that chapter back although we had to do a little reconstructing.

The book was finally turned in the day before the March 1 due date.

Lisa returned it to us with seventy-five pages cut. We agreed with most of the cuts, but not with the names of books that I had read and enjoyed. They went back in because we wanted people to know that reading was and is an important part of my life.

Sad to say, in March of 1994 we read in the papers that Chris had been fired from his usher's job at the White House. The reason given was that Chris had been in touch with me. There is no question that we had called Chris and the other ushers for information for the book—verification, etc. Our calls, and they were not that many, were returned. They rarely talked to me, but spoke to Jean or Peggy Swift. Chris was a professional public servant who loved working at the White House. I felt very badly that Chris lost his job. The good news is that he has gone on to other jobs and seems happy.

Then in March a reporter from *The New York Times* called George to ask him if he had talked to John Magaw in the past year. John was then the director of the United States Secret Service, and had been head of the president's detail for part of the time we were at the White House. George checked with Rose Zamaria, his chief of staff, and she reminded him that he had called when John's mother died. George told the reporter that, and he said: "That is what we heard." He also told George that the next day, John got a call from White House adviser Vince Foster asking him what he was doing talking to the former president. Shortly after that, John was moved to another job. This, too, broke our hearts. To think that we may have hurt these two fine men really upset us.

Life after the White House did allow us to do many things that we couldn't do in government. George was invited to play in the AT&T Golf Tournament in Pebble Beach, California. (For years it was called the Bing Crosby Golf Tournament.) It is so much fun and exciting for golf lovers and name-droppers. Movie stars, CEOs from many major companies, and an army of famous golfers take part in this tournament. George was teamed up with pro golfer Hale Irwin, the nicest, most laid-back young man. He and his darling wife Sally are close to perfect people. To make it even better, they played all three days with Arnie Palmer and his partner, Russ Meyer. Following them was a joy. Seeing Arnie stride up to the green to loud applause was unforgettable. The tournament is played on three great courses: Pebble Beach, Spyglass, and Poppy Hills. The views on those courses of the Pacific Ocean are spectacular, with otters floating on their backs eating abalone or some shellfish, waves crashing against rocks, birds flying overhead, and boats of all kinds at sea.

The only better view is from Cypress Point Golf Club, where our dear friend Daphne Gawthrop has treated me to a couple of rounds over the years. It is an impossible game, but gives such pleasure. Although George did not play as well as he would have liked, he helped Hale on thirteen holes in the three days. George is so funny; he reported that "Bryant Gumbel hit a sea gull and made the news on all the major networks. I hit four spectators and got no coverage at all."

Thanks to Winnie and Arnie Palmer we went to dinner at the home of Rolande and Hank Ketcham, who is the creator of "Dennis the Menace." They have a dream house filled with lovely paintings, some of them done by Hank. He sent Millie a marvelous drawing, which I have hung in my little Houston office. It is a cozy house and Rolande is a great cook. She served a dish she called "Corn Spoon Bread"—more of a deep-dish grits dish than bread. It was delicious, and she generously gave me the recipe.

CORN SPOON BREAD, BY ROLANDE KETCHAM
SERVES 6

1 can creamed corn
1 cup yellow corn meal
3/4 cup milk
1/3 cup oil
3 eggs
1 teaspoon salt
4 ounces chopped green chili (fresh)
1 cup grated sharp cheese

*Mix all together and bake in a round deep-dish Pyrex bowl in a
375-degree oven for 25 to 30 minutes. (If you double the recipe,
cook for 35 to 45 minutes.)*

Rolande seems to leave the kind of oil, milk, and cheese up to the
cook. One can experiment. It has been a winner in our house.

I can hear it now: Does she not know any healthy dishes? We all
know how to steam vegetables, but do we all know the easiest and best
dish for a buffet? It can be prepared before your guests arrive and spices
up any meal.

~~~ We had our annual physicals at the Mayo Clinic Scottsdale.
While I was having mine, I kept thinking that George was lucky that
he did not have female parts. He told me that he was thinking the
same thing about male parts. We both did very well with one exception: "Lose weight, Barbara!"

About this time I finished Michael Crichton's *Disclosure*, and
enjoyed it. George told me I would. I also had just read *Remains of the
Day*, by Kazuo Ishiguro. My neighbor Mildred Kerr had suggested it,
and I loved it.

During all this both our Texas and Florida sons were working hard
on their campaigns. George and I helped them when we were asked,
mostly at fund-raisers. I wrote in my diary:

> We attended a huge fund-raising dinner for George W. in
> Dallas and both of us got teary when the emcee announced:
> "Ladies and Gentlemen, the next governor of Texas and Mrs.
> Laura Bush." The crowd roared and I was afraid that I might
> really cry. I didn't, but Pop told me that he felt the same surge
> of pride that I did.
>
> We went to Naples for Jeb. He was so good, like George W.,
> and yet so different. Jeb's lovely, patient manner is there. He
> speaks without notes. He is clear and firm . . .

At sometime during the campaign Jeb was asked why he was running. He answered that he had three reasons: George P., Noelle, and

Jebby. Shortly thereafter when George was asked the same question, he answered that he had two reasons: Jenna and Barbara. The press quickly caught him on that and said that his brother had answered the same way the week before and accused George W. of stealing his brother's line. Quick as a wink, George answered: "I did. And if my brother has any other great answers, I'm going to steal them, too."

So now I'd like to turn Jeb in for stealing from his older brother. George W. loves telling people he gets lots of unsolicited advice from his mother. So imagine my surprise when, during his second inauguration as Florida's governor in 2003, I heard Jeb say the following:

"Now my mother, she doesn't usually wait for my call. She calls me. And what she lacks in coddling, she more than makes up for in smaller phone bills by keeping her comments short, to the point, and right on target."

The truth is, no one has shorter conversations in our family than Jeb, who is infamous for getting to what HE thinks is the end of a conversation and just hanging up!

∽ We did a great deal of campaigning for candidates other than our two sons in 1994. For instance, we flew one afternoon to Memphis to attend a dinner for Don Sundquist, an old friend who was running for governor of Tennessee. It was typical of many such campaign trips:

> We were delivered about an hour and a half early and promptly put in a hotel suite. As I was dressed for the evening, and stupidly did not have a comb or brush, I just sat and watched TV. George went right into the bedroom and slept. I hate it when we could have spent an hour more at home, and to be tucked into a suite without a book is really a criminal offense! Finally we went to a room where "other" head table guests were gathering and found old friends Lamar Alexander, Howard Baker, Congressman Jimmy Quillen from East Tennessee, the dinner committee, and Don and Martha Sundquist. Then we were all herded through to another room. From here to a reception for 300 people, all of whom came through a receiving line.

Considering the crowd it was fairly fast. We were then led into a very crowded room and asked to walk down a long rope line on one side and back out on the other side. I was convinced that they would rip us apart, but, no, we lived. Then we were led through an overflow crowd of 300 and on into the main dining room with some 800 people. This is a big year for Tennessee. This is due to the vacancy left by Al Gore when he became Vice President and so there are two Senate seats up this year along with the Governor's seat. Howard told me that he thought we could win all these races.* Darling Jimmy Quillen told a story he is famous for during dinner, but I certainly hadn't heard it:

"Two boys decided to stay out of school, walk up the hill, and fool the wise old man at the top. As they set off up the hill they had no idea what they were going to do when they saw a lit-tle red bird walk across their path. One boy quickly caught it in his hand and said: 'I know what we can do. We'll knock on the wise man's door and ask him if the bird is dead or alive. If he says dead, I'll let him go and if he says alive, I'll squeeze the life out of him before I open my hand.' They proceeded up the hill and did knock on the wise man's door. The wise man opened the door and the boy asked the question. The wise man answered: 'You have that bird's life in your hands.'"

Jimmy went on to say that everyone in this room had the future in their hands, etc.

Jimmy dragged that story out by describing the old man: "Deep penetrating blue eyes, hair to his shoulders, and a beard that came below his belt buckle." There was not a sound in the room as his voice got lower and lower. He was marvelous.

To sum the evening up: It was a roaring success, the largest fund-raiser ever in the state, and they worked us to death!

❧ For Easter we went to Hillary Farish's wedding to Stan Stratton in Boca Grande, Florida. We stayed at Gasparilla Inn, and it

---

*Howard was right. Tennessee sent Fred Thompson and Dr. Bill Frist to the Senate, and Don Sundquist won as well.

was perfect. Marvin, Margaret, and Marshall were there on vacation, and our great friends Will and Sarah Farish, the bride's mother and father, included them in on everything. They had golf tournaments, tennis, and beautiful weather. We went to a really nice family and close-friends rehearsal dinner. The groom's mother and father both attended with second spouses. They all seemed very comfortable with each other with much laughter and teasing. At one time the stepfather gave a toast to the father and thanked him for not getting along with the mother, so he could marry her! If there has to be a parting, this is certainly the way to do it.

The night we arrived, George found a box with an Easter necktie from a very nice guest, a Mrs. Holmes, who was staying in the inn. The next day, George decided to wear his new necktie to the wedding with his navy jacket and light pants. When we got to the wedding we were greeted by the ushers who pinned a large yellow boutonniere on George's lapel, and we were led to sit with Mary and Bayard Sharp, the bride's grandparents. When the wedding party came down the aisle it was clear why George had gotten a boutonniere—the groom had given similar ties to all the groomsmen and ushers! It was also a coincidence that they all wore blue jackets and light pants. They thought that George was in the wedding party. How Marvin teased his dad.

That was about the prettiest wedding I have ever seen. There have never been so many beautiful flowers, and the bridesmaids were adorable and lovely in Easter colors. George would tell you that I say this at every wedding. I think when the sweet groom looked at Hillary with tears of happiness in his eyes, that did it for me. As I write this, I immediately think of our nephew Jon Bush's wedding where he and his best man, brother Bill, both had tears of love streaming down their faces; or our niece Louisa Bush's wedding that was perfection itself; or Gian-Carlo Peressutti's wedding (he was one of George's aides) where he walked down the aisle with his mother and father on either side. That was pretty touching. I might add the bride did the same sweet thing, but I didn't know her family. As you can see, weddings are a favorite of mine. I can't remember one where I didn't shed a tear.

In April, we finally got around to having a party for all the talented people who had worked on our house. I found it interesting that several of the carpenters' wives home-schooled their children. They must be saints. I would never have had the patience. They were worried about what their children were learning and not learning. Their children all were active in league sports, so they were interacting with children their own age. Statistics show that in most cases home-schooled children do as well if not better than children who attend a traditional school, public or private. That absolutely amazes me. I guess I am surprised that there are so many mothers who have the knowledge and dispositions to teach their own children. Now I am not urging home schooling on any or all mothers. I am thinking that we are all different and there are "many ways to skin a cat" as my father used to say.

       We went on many foreign trips in 1994, and certainly one of the most interesting was to Singapore where George spoke as part of a business leadership series.

      We arrived in Singapore at a difficult time as a young American boy, along with a gang of other 17 and 18 year olds, had apparently gone on a 10-day rampage, spray-painting cars and generally breaking things. The American boy was sentenced to caning, a harsh punishment unique to this part of the world. The pressure from the American press is on George to speak to the government of Singapore and ask them to lift the caning part of the punishment. This is very hard as a Singapore citizen would be caned and the government does not feel they can make an exception in this boy's case. As I understand it, interference from the U.S. Government, plus the boy's father, has made it impossible to do anything other than cane the boy to save face.

      We met with our chargé, a fine career Foreign Service officer. No ambassador has been appointed as yet, so he has to cope with this problem by himself and has done his level best. I was amazed when he mentioned that he had asked the White House to tell him just what the President had said in his letter to the prime minister of Singapore, only to be told by the NSC [National Security Council] that the contents of the letter were personal, privileged information. He is supposed to speak for the administration and yet cannot know what the President thinks or is saying on the subject!

We had a lunch with Deputy Prime Minister Lee, our dear friend Lee Kuan Yew's* son, and George tried to explain that we were not asking for leniency for the boy. He certainly understood the need to punish the boy. But the relationship between our two countries was so much more important than this one case. He went on to explain that although the polls showed at this moment that the American public say they are for caning, they could easily change. George feels the polls would change overnight if the boy was badly scarred. I mentioned that I was sure the boy would go public and bare his backside if his body was cut and scarred. This seemed to surprise the deputy prime minister. George suggested a compromise. Why not "gently" cane him, which would not leave scars and cuts, and then deport him. Which I think they did on their own. The boy later got into trouble at home in the United States.

At an embassy reception a young girl asked George what he thought about her classmate. George asked, "Classmate?" She then gave George the name of the boy. George asked her what she thought and she said, "He's a jerk and a troublemaker."

Because this is my memoir, I feel free to speak for myself. Every foreigner who goes to Singapore is clearly and firmly warned about breaking the law and told just how harsh the punishment will be. Anyone involved in this spree deserved to be punished, severely in my opinion. They have very strict rules in Singapore, such as no chewing gum, litter, etc. It is the world's cleanest, safest city, and they have a right to make their own laws.

After Singapore, we flew to Korea. One thing that was unusual was the fact that the masseuses were blind. Two beautiful girls were led to our door and gave us wonderful massages. After they left,

*The longtime prime minister, then a "senior" minister, and an old friend.

George said, "Are you sure they were blind?" I said, "I HOPE they were." He gave me a scare when he said: "Then why did my lady walk in the room and say, 'I've never seen such a beautiful body!'" George, of course, was teasing me.

The other very unusual happening on this trip was that we played golf on the Sung Nam U.S. Military Golf Course. George played with four-star General Luck, Lieutenant General Crouch, and Major General Abrams. I played with their wives. The golf was dreadful, but lots of fun. The course was lovely. Seoul was way off in the background, and we were surrounded by hills covered with forsythia and other spring blooms. The pollution was pretty bad so we saw things through a haze. I kept wanting to pinch myself—I was playing golf in South Korea! I could hardly believe it. The new course is right next to a Korean military compound, and we could hear those strident unfamiliar voices coming over the hillside magnified by bullhorns and loudspeakers.

∽ I was a great fan of Pat Nixon's, so I agreed to speak at the Nixon Library that April. Pat had died the previous June. She was such a gentle lady and got little or no credit for all she accomplished for the White House and for the country. I was told by two curators at the White House and by the White House staff that Pat Nixon collected more antiques for the house than any other first lady. She also encouraged volunteerism. Much of this was overshadowed by Watergate. I remember seeing President Nixon's face crumble at her funeral and realized how little we really knew about this very complicated man. I felt like I was looking into a window and seeing someone we didn't even know lived in the house. He was not a man given to sharing his feelings, but his love for Pat certainly showed that day. She was a great wife, mother, and first lady.

The day before I was to speak at the Nixon Library, the former president went into a coma from a stroke he had suffered a few days earlier. I decided that I would go anyway and, if he died, I would convert the speech and luncheon into a celebration of his and Pat's lives. He died that night after my talk.

Bill Safire wrote a lovely column about his old boss. He had several Nixon quotes that I liked: "A man's not finished when he's defeated;

he's finished when he quits." He wrote that to Teddy Kennedy after Chappaquiddick. That certainly was Dick Nixon. He never quit. Another Nixon quote that I liked was: "Those who hate you don't win, unless you hate them and then you destroy yourself."

Dick's funeral at the Nixon Library in Yorba Linda, California, was attended by all the presidents and their wives. It was freezing, but thank heavens Carole Cook brought a shawl for me to wear over my long-sleeved silk dress. Henry Kissinger, Bob Dole, Pete Wilson, and Bill Clinton gave eulogies. Bill Clinton really set the tone for this funeral by suggesting that we look at the "whole man and not just one small flaw." There was a lot of Watergate (the flaw) in the news. I wrote in my diary at the time that maybe President Clinton was thinking of his own legacy as he was then dealing with the Paula Jones controversy. Billy Graham was superb, and must have really comforted the girls, Julie Eisenhower and Tricia Cox. Among other things, Billy pointed out that we will all die and must be ready.

I smiled at that, for although Billy was not thinking about one's actual funeral service, every president and spouse was. Certainly George and I had talked about our services. Actually, this funeral persuaded me that George and I should be buried at his Presidential Library at Texas A&M University. We had planned on being buried in Kennebunkport in our much-loved First Congregational Church graveyard, thinking that it would be convenient for our children "to visit," among other things. Well, of course our children will visit George's Library, and the thought of schoolchildren and tourists plowing through that sweet cemetery in Maine was suddenly wrong. It would disrupt the cemetery for others. And besides that, it would be under snow for two or three months a year. So we will be tucked in at College Station in the loveliest resting spot I have ever seen. We moved Robin to our burial spot in the year 2000.

Nixon's funeral was very impressive, with the former president's childhood home in the background, that tiny little Sears, Roebuck house that his dad had ordered from a catalogue and put together himself. It had not been that long ago—1990, when his Library opened—that Dick Nixon showed us through the home with great pride. I remember wondering that day just what his grandchildren were feeling when they saw it. One of these children grew up on Park

Avenue in New York City and the others in the stylish suburbs of Philadelphia.

Pat and Dick Nixon did many commendable things, but the greatest of these was raising two marvelous daughters under very difficult circumstances.

∽ In May, I flew to Washington to join the other former first ladies and President and Mrs. Clinton at a fund-raiser for the National Botanical Gardens. It was a great black-tie affair, and our dear persuasive friend Lod Cook talked me into going. I was very glad that I did, but it reminds me that former first ladies are invited to many fundraisers for worthy causes. Most of them have causes of their own and work very hard raising money and attend many dinners.

One year, when we kept track, I gave forty luncheon or dinner speeches for charities, and the same year gave thirty-nine speeches for which I was paid. At every talk I tried to urge people to support their local literacy programs, libraries, hospitals, schools, etc. Believe me, that is a lot of travel, a lot of talking, a lot of meals (woe is me), a lot of handshakes, and a lot of standing.

When the call comes about a big first lady event, and you are told that "all the other first ladies are attending and you must come," we have learned to call each other and ask if, in truth, they are attending. Many times they are not.

For instance, I got a call from my aide one time asking me if I would attend a dinner in New York City one Saturday night for the Charles A. Dana Foundation. "All the other first ladies will be there." I was tired and said that I just do not leave George Bush on a weekend, and I wasn't even sure that all the others were attending anyway. My aide asked me if it would make a difference to me that they were giving all the ladies $100,000 each to donate to their favorite charities? It will come as no surprise that I was not as tired as I thought and that I do leave George Bush on a weekend. Lady Bird Johnson gave her money to The Lady Bird Johnson Wildflower Center. I can't remember to which causes Betty Ford, Nancy Reagan, and Rosalynn Carter gave their money. At the last moment Nancy could not attend because of Ronald Reagan's health. The Dana Foundation allowed me to give

$25,000 to four groups that I care strongly about: The Barbara Bush Foundation for Family Literacy, The Maine State Family Literacy program, the Mayo Clinic, and The Barbara Bush Children's Hospital in Portland, Maine.

I have been on panels with Betty Ford and Rosalynn Carter on both coasts—once in Washington, D.C., and another time in Bakersfield, California. They were easy and fun. I feel very close to both these ladies and have enormous respect for them. Betty is very active at the Betty Ford Clinic, which she founded along with Leonard Firestone. With fifty thousand alumni worldwide, this clinic now has an international reputation for helping people break drug and alcohol addictions. In January 2003, two presidents—George Bush and Jerry Ford; five former first ladies—Betty Ford, Rosalynn Carter, Nancy Reagan, Hillary Clinton, and yours truly; and a roomful of celebrities and friends got together to celebrate the twentieth anniversary of this remarkable place. Betty also raises money for the Arthritis Foundation and cancer research.

Rosalynn Carter has many interests. She is perhaps best known for Habitat for Humanity and her work with mental illnesses. She is active in programs at her husband's Library, and she travels with him on his many foreign trips.

Nancy Reagan has a full-time job taking care of her precious husband, but still does what she can for drug abuse programs and Alzheimer's. Lady Bird Johnson, although frail, works on her beloved wildflower and highway beautification projects.

⚬

꙳ We shifted our whole household and a small staff to Kennebunkport from May 11 until October 11. This has become our pattern over the years, give or take a few days on either end.

In June, Jean Becker and I flew to California to attend the American Booksellers Association Convention. This is attended by some twenty thousand people. My publisher, Simon & Schuster (which owns Scribner) invited fifty booksellers and buyers to have dinner with me. This group represented 460,000 books that already had been ordered. Imagine ordering that many copies when not one person had read it, buying sight unseen. Eventually 750,000 books were printed, I believe. (There was another printing of 5,000 books in the year 2001.)

The next day, we went to look for the Simon & Schuster booth on the convention floor. There was a ghastly moment when we rounded the corner and there was my face blown up, bigger than life-size. It was huge and very embarrassing. It was around there that I saw our dear friend Mary Matalin and her husband James Carville, the "odd couple," whose jointly written book was also just going on the block. They were cruising the book displays. I remember being so jealous, wishing that I could look at every book there, but then I would have wanted to buy them all.

Back at the hotel I met author Mary Higgins Clark for tea. She had another book coming out, *Remember Me.* We had the most interesting talk. I told her that I had loved writing my book and that I hated finishing it and was missing writing. (Maybe I was missing the memories?) She said that I must write and that I should try my luck at writing a novel. She said that it was really easy. She picks a plot, knows the ending, and works back. Mary told me that when her characters talk to her and won't let her write something, then she knows she is on the right track. It's as if they tell her, "I wouldn't do or say this or that." It sounded easy.

As the grandchildren would say: "NOT."

I made up a rather interesting plot, started at the end, and worked my way back. My characters never said a word to me—good or bad. The book was lousy and as for writing conversations, mine were stiff and unnatural. I gave up.

My plot centered on two female roommates, a flight attendant, and a Secret Service agent, who worked too hard and therefore had no love lives. So they went to a very discreet dating service. All the men who dated the Secret Service agent ended up dead. Guess who the jealous murderer was?

One of the books I was reading around this time was Terry Kay's *Shadow Song.* I loved it. I also read and loved Judith Rossner's *Olivia.*

In May, our son Marvin organized a fund-raiser for the Crohn's & Colitis Foundation of America. He and three others, including Rolf Benirschke, a former field goal kicker for the San Diego Chargers, got sponsors and played 100 holes of golf on a course in

North Carolina in one day. (Marvin shot 485 on the first 100 holes.) As there was still light enough to see, they went on and played 17 more holes. They were thrilled as they raised $125,000. I remember they were all so stiff the next day that they could hardly move. Rolf and Marvin certainly proved that people with a colostomy can do anything they want to do. And as I write this, seven years later, I am so proud of these fine young men. Marvin has two near-perfect children, a great wife, a successful business—the Winston Partners Group—and plays superb tennis. He is a dear, thoughtful man and has more friends than anyone I know. We hear from friends that he is a fine businessman. George's mother would love the fact that he never "brags."

∽ Paula went to Mexico for a month in July, and I was really worried about the household. All those meals! What was I going to do? As in the movies, my hero arrived—not on a white horse, but via the U.S. Navy. Ariel DeGuzman had been a Navy chief petty officer assigned to the vice president's house and later moved to the White House with George as a personal attendant. That July he took a month's vacation from the Navy and joined us in Maine. His first big dinner was for Vaclav Havel, the president of the Czech Republic, on the Fourth of July. We invited our dear friends Spike and Betsy Heminway and Dan and Bunny Burke to join Vaclav and his entourage for a delicious dinner. It was a great evening, and after dinner we invited the group to come up to our little widow's walk and watch the fireworks. Across the Atlantic Ocean we can see all the way to York, Ogunquit, Wells, and Kennebunkport. The fireworks were spectacular from all the little towns on the coast. Poor Vaclav was flying home that night after dinner and needed to get on his way. For the very first time in my memory the fireworks went on forever. We finally let the exhausted man go to his plane in Portland before the grand finale.

So far that year Carlos Menem of Argentina, F. W. de Klerk of South Africa, and now Vaclav Havel had stopped by to see George. He really enjoys seeing old friends and loves catching up on current events.

George was briefed several times that summer and continues to this day to be briefed by the CIA. It is a courtesy paid all former presidents.

George is still vitally interested in both domestic and foreign affairs. He is very careful not to disagree with the president. He told Bill Clinton that he would not interfere, criticize, or cause trouble. He didn't and has continued this policy with the current president—our son.

✑ That summer we hosted a big event for Brent Scowcroft's Forum for International Policy, a nonprofit foreign policy foundation. Here are my diary notes from that event:

> Larry and Janis Gatlin and their daughter Kristin arrived with Kristin's fiancé on Friday [July] 8th for the Scowcroft Forum. Saturday morning we went to the Colony Hotel at 9 a.m. and listened to a discussion led by Brent and George. It was a prestigious group of businessmen and a group of advisors to the Forum. Some wives attended also. The discussions were on " U.S. Opportunities in Asia: Problems and Opportunities." Kim Il Sun* died on the previous Friday night and so that made Korea the hot item on the plate. It seems that all of Asia's future depends on Korea and nuclear weapons. It seems as though we are the only ones who can or who have the will to step in and stop them.† The next three or four months are important. Bob Gallucci‡ (who stopped on his way to Bonn to brief George) is in Bonn right now trying to negotiate. (We heard this morning that the talks will continue after a decent period of mourning.)
>
> We had a nice lunch and then the group took off for golf, tennis, and swimming. That night we had a reception at our house and a dinner in a tent on the Bungalow§ drive. This would have been brilliant, BUT for the fact that for the first time this summer we had a little rain and a lot of fog. You would never guess that you were only 20 feet from the Atlantic Ocean, it was

*The president of North Korea.

†I find it eerie how true this still is in 2003 as the current president deals with a serious crisis involving North Korea's nuclear capabilities.

‡A career State Department diplomat.

§That was the name of the house where George's mother lived, and which we now use as a guest cottage.

such a deadly night. Larry Gatlin and our dear friend Dick Jackman entertained and all went well until the uninvited guests appeared. Mosquitoes the size of seagulls arrived and broke the party up pretty quickly! I believe that we could get 160 people in that tent at 16 round tables.

I hope George doesn't read this as it surely will give him ideas.

⌒ Early in the summer I had the "Ladies of the Club" come for a few days. This was a group of women whose husbands were all elected to Congress—the House and Senate—in 1966. This was a large class, but eleven of us became great friends and have remained friends for thirty-three years. As George was out of town, they were invited without their husbands. Life has not always been easy for these ladies, but they are exceptional women. Congressmen Bill Steiger, Jim Collins, and Jerry Pettis died at very young ages. Janet Steiger became the first female chairman of the Postal Commission as a Reagan appointee and later the first female chairman of the Federal Trade Commission for George. Dee Collins went back to Texas and took over Jim's estate, which included running ranch and complicated business affairs. Shirley Pettis took her husband's seat in Congress.

Louise McClure's husband Jim left the House for the Senate, where he joined Antoinette Hatfield's husband, Senator Mark Hatfield. Olga Esch has fought awful health with a great spirit and faith with her Marvin by her side back in Michigan. Mary Jane Dellenback returned to Oregon when her husband left the Congress. Both she and John have worked hard for Christian causes all their lives and this allowed them to devote full time to helping others. We were not amazed to hear that Mary Jane wanted to give John a kidney which he needed badly to keep active in his World Vision mission work, but many of their friends thought it was too dangerous at their ages. She did, and both of them were in good health for years until John died very unexpectedly in 2002.

Joan Winn's dear son, the father of her grandchildren, died and she and Larry left the House of Representatives to help their wonderful daughter-in-law and be near their grandchildren. Carol and Guy Vander Jagt also have left Congress. She campaigned hard for George and George W.

Loret Ruppe was the director of the Peace Corps during the Reagan administration and then became the ambassador to Norway in the Bush administration. She returned to private life and was very happy as she adored her husband and five daughters. She arrived in Maine later than the others as one of her daughters was getting married the very next Saturday. She admitted to us that her back was hurting and that she was going to the doctor on the Monday following the wedding.

Loret did go to the doctor and soon found that her body was riddled with cancer. She had radical surgery immediately, and chemotherapy was started while she was still on the operating table. I don't believe that any two people showed such courage as Loret and Phil Ruppe did for the next months. Loret's faith was very strong, and she took great comfort in prayer groups, family, and friends. There were good times when she was well enough to play tennis at their new winter home in Florida, and there were those other not such good times.

In the summer of 1995, Loret was in the hospital, and we heard that she was really very ill. Jim Baker, George, and I were having coffee in Maine one summer morning and decided to call her. Both men spoke to her and then passed the phone to me. Loret told me that she was comfortable and at peace. She then told me that the most marvelous thing happened. She was to have a very tough procedure done where something had to be inserted into her liver. She had been really frightened about the pain. Her sister told her that there was a new book out dealing with pain and that she would send it to her. Loret told her sister that she didn't have time to read a book—please just give her a shortened version over the phone. Well, her sister told her the essence of the book was to say a prayer—a mantra—over and over again, which she did. She told me that she fell asleep and during the sleep had a dream. She saw the most beautiful beach that one could imagine. Loret was almost poetic about the glory of this beach. Way down the beach she saw a couple walking hand-in-hand. The dream—as could only happen in a dream—sort of zoomed in, and she saw that she was part of the couple and holding her hand was Jesus. She went on to tell me, in a joyful voice, that at that moment she knew that she would not have to face what lay ahead alone. Jesus would be with her.

She said that nothing like that had ever happened to her before. She also said that she wondered if those doing the procedure had wondered just what that happy look on her face meant.

After I hung up, I told George and Jimmy about our conversation and we all felt that was a very special phone call. Loret's husband, Phil, her five beautiful daughters, so many friends, and hospice helped Loret through this awful time with such love and tenderness. Loret died on August 7, 1995. There is no doubt in my mind who she is with. She certainly taught us all so much about faith, courage, generosity, and love.

 Summer 1994 was the summer of the big baseball strike. This was a stunning blow to many of our friends and family, especially George W. as the managing partner of the Texas Rangers. The Houston Astros had just changed hands, so it also hurt the new owner and our new friend, Drayton McLane from Temple, Texas. The fields closed down and so many were put out of work. The owners were hurt, but so were the hot dog vendors, the ticket sellers, ground crew, umpires, etc. Most of all, baseball fans were hurt and hurt badly. The price of a ticket went up so much that one thought twice about running out to the ball game with the neighborhood kids at the last moment. America's pastime became a real luxury item. We are baseball fans and for several years awakened every morning checking first on the Texas Rangers and the Houston Astros before the world news. I would know from George's first words—a "Darn" or a "Great"—whether we had won or lost. Half our family were Astros fans, led by Neil's son Pierce, and half were Ranger fans because of Uncle George. I love baseball and have ever since George played at Yale University. My dream was that the Astros and the Rangers would be in a World Series, and then I couldn't lose. Don Rhodes was so upset about the strike that he swore he would not go to a ball game for ten years. I honestly cannot remember whether he was on the owners' or the players' side, but I know that "greed" came into it. For nine years Don has stuck to this vow even though he has been invited by the owners to see both my teams and on the opening days of their new stadiums. Don is a man of true principle and discipline.

That fall I lost another aide but gained a new one. Nancy Huang left to get her master's degree from Harvard Business School, and Quincy

Hicks, the receptionist in the Houston office, took her place. Nancy was a brilliant girl with an adorable laugh, and I missed her very much. She graduated from school, had several fascinating jobs, then got married and went to the west coast. Quincy became a member of our family.

∽ One morning in September I turned on the television and suddenly realized that, with the exception of Arafat, I knew every single person personally that I had seen on the tube during that hour. That's the life that George Bush has given me. Amazing life. Lucky, lucky me. The very sad thing was that Jessica Tandy, that glorious actress, had died during the night. So sad for her darling husband Hume Cronyn. I first met them in Canada with Mila and Brian Mulroney at a cystic fibrosis dinner. He later came to the White House, and when George introduced Hume he said: "Barbara Bush told me that she fell in love with Hume Cronyn. Now I get to meet him and honor him and his wonderful wife." George wasn't teasing. I had told him that. I fell in love with them both.

∽ Betsy Heminway and I took to the book-promoting trail in the early fall as *Barbara Bush: A Memoir* hit the bookstores. We started unofficially in Kennebunkport at the Community House at the South Congregational Church. The Kennebunkport Book Port sponsored the event and some of the proceeds from the sales went to the local Graves Public Library. As we drove through the town for the next month or so after the event there was a large poster of me in the Book Port window.

We then went to New York City for the official kick-off, then on to Stamford, Connecticut.; Washington, D.C.; Boston; Chicago; San Francisco; Los Angeles; Denver; Dallas; Houston; Tampa; and Miami. We laughed our way across the country and stood in at least one bookstore and usually two a day. We did lunches and even one or two brunches. I had signed thirty thousand book plates in the six months before the tour; so I did not sign books, but just shook hands and often had a picture taken. This was much easier and more satisfactory for me. It saved my arthritic hands and allowed me to look someone in the eye and chat. That way you can see twice as many people. In almost every city a local literacy program or library benefited from our visit, so I didn't feel quite so self-serving. We did radio, television, and newspaper interviews in every city, plus many of the national media. It was exhausting, profitable, and fun. I even did the *Tonight Show* with Jay Leno and the *Late Show with David Letterman*, where they talked me into going out onto the streets of New York and trying to get a hot dog for free, just to show up a bear. (You really would have to be there to understand this but I think it was very funny.)

Besides selling the book, the tour brought the problems of illiteracy to the forefront. Along the way we helped Literacy Volunteers of Stamford; Literacy Chicago; Marin Education Fund near San Francisco; The Read to Me campaign in Denver; The Friends of the Dallas Public Library; The Selby Library Foundation in Florida; and The Miami Book Fair.

I believe every mother in America got my book for Christmas that year, and I think I signed every single one. I am still signing the book almost every day in 2002, which is nice.

One more book story: One day I needed to buy a few of my books to take as presents on a trip. I ran into Sam's Club and couldn't find any, so I asked the girl if they had any in the back where I had found some before. To my horror, the girl got on the loudspeaker and through the store rang out, "Mrs. Bush is here and wants to buy her own book. Do we have any left?" I was stampeded by customers and raced out. From then on I let the office go out for books.

∿ I read Maeve Binchy's *The Glass Lake.* I love everything she writes.

∿ That fall, besides the book tour, George and I joined a group with AmeriCares and took medicine and other supplies to Guatemala. This was a long down and back one-day trip. George and I put on old clothes expecting to work, only to be greeted by high officials dressed to the teeth, I guess because they were meeting the former president. We toured several shantytowns and one enormous garbage pit. As far as the eye could see there were women, children, and dogs scouring the pit for anything that could be recycled and sold. Close by, a new school had been built and The Ronald McDonald Charities had put in a large, safe children's playground with the most marvelous equipment.

Speaking of Ronald McDonald Charities, on October 15 I flew to Chicago for their annual fund-raising dinner. This was another invitation that I literally could not turn down. The crowd was made up of two thousand McDonald franchise owners, plus suppliers like Coca-Cola. They honored three people that night with big checks for their favorite charities. The one I remember most was a marvelous African-American, LeRoy Walker, from Jackson, Mississippi, who is close to a saint. He owns six McDonald's restaurants, but he is doing a lot more than cooking hamburgers. First, he mandated that all his student employees had to maintain a C average in school. To make sure this happens, he started his own tutoring program. He has taken a number of troubled boys under his own wing and shown them that if LeRoy Walker can do it, anyone can do it. All of this has blossomed into a program called 100 Black Men of Jackson, where LeRoy recruited one hundred mentors—also successful black businessmen—to be a part of this now nationwide program.

They also honored a fabulous doctor, Dr. Audrey Evans, who saw a need and started the first Ronald McDonald House. She specializes in children's oncology at The Children's Hospital in Philadelphia.

I wondered how they could afford to give us so much money at that one dinner. It turned out to be quite easy as they raised $8 million that night from that crowd of grateful Americans. We were all asked to speak for two minutes and then were entertained by Gladys Knight and dancers. I gave $25,000 to both the Ronald McDonald Houses in Washington, D.C., and Houston, and $50,000 to The Barbara Bush Foundation for Family Literacy.

❧ Here are some random diary notes from that fall:

In October George was honored at West Point.* He said that it was a marvelous ceremony. He was very moved. Among

*He received the Thayer Award.

other things they thanked him for keeping politics out of the military and letting them carry out their missions. I was really sorry that I couldn't be there as it meant so much to him.

. . . Fax from Lisa [Drew]: Book is in 6th printing and now totals 750,000. It has been on the *NY Times* bestseller list for 6 weeks. We will have had a 4-week run as #1. Not bad.

. . . George W. had his debate with [Governor] Ann Richards. I just can't watch. I did not have to watch as I was on an airplane. The reports are that it was "even-Stephen." I hate debates. I feel just like George W. did in 1988. During a debate between his dad and Mike Dukakis, our sons, George and Marvin, went to the movies. Marvin later told me that George was so nervous that he sent him out every 15 minutes to call some friends who were watching the debate for a report on how it was going.

. . . Jeb had his debate last Thursday night and was superb. So both boys are good.

It is easier to debate a man than a woman unless you are another woman. If a man is tough or rude to a woman he is "condescending" or "demeaning." She can be all those things and just be a good debater.

We spent a lot of time on the campaign trail that fall—not always for our boys, although we were there when they asked. I campaigned several times for George W., sometimes with Laura, and sometimes we would meet up with George W. at the end of the day.

The biggest treat of all was a day spent campaigning with baseball great Nolan Ryan. We went to a school and talked to the kids about gangs, drugs, and sex. I could not tell you what I said, but I did my best. Hard to do because when sex was mentioned, a titter ran through the crowd. Needless to say, when Nolan appeared they really went wild. What a very nice man, married to a very beautiful nice lady, Ruth Ryan. We heard later that the teachers' union was furious that I had been allowed to speak, but the principal stuck to his guns and told them that I had spoken only about drugs, staying in school, etc., and that it was not a political speech. It wasn't.

On October 27, I met George W. and Laura in Houston at a "We Are the World" rally, sponsored by Texans' War on Drugs. I wrote in my diary:

Laura introduced me and was so articulate. My respect for Laura has soared, and although I always thought she was the best, now I think she is even better than the best. She is so peaceful, calm and natural, even-tempered, and so sweet. Lucky George. George is confident that he is going to win. I don't think so.

That night George and I went to a big dinner for M. D. Anderson, Houston's world-class cancer hospital. The most amazing thing happened. Among other things they honored a few folks who joined the "Anderson Assembly," which is made up of $1 million–plus donors. We were told that George Foreman, the heavyweight boxing champion, was a new member. He had given $1,000,007. When asked why he had given that strange amount, he said, "Everyone gives $1 million." Would that they did, as this great research hospital serves so many and always needs money for patients who can't pay and for research. The same week we attended a big cancer dinner in Washington, for the Cancer Research Foundation of America, in which our daughter-in-law and cancer survivor Margaret Bush is involved

✑ Betsy Heminway called me one day to check in. She knew just how miserable I would be so close to the election. She told me the dearest story about our Doro. Doro was in Greenwich and had taken a walk by George's mother's house, which made her sad. The next day in New York City she had a few moments to spare and popped into St. Patrick's Cathedral to light a candle for her Ganny. There she saw a small wedding going on, and so she went to the wedding. There were more tourists than wedding guests. She said she stood next to a shabby, smelly, homeless man and wept at the wedding of people she didn't even know. Doro is the captain of the Bush "bawl team" and the most sensitive, kind, caring soul. We are so proud that she currently is attending Wesley Theological Seminary in Washington, D.C.

November 6—This is a very nervous time for all Bushes. I am in agony over my boys' elections. Both boys have worked so hard and are so very close. This morning's polls show GWB as doing very well and Jeb going down. It kills me for Jeb. He has worked hard and stuck to his vow not to knock the [Florida] governor. I might add that Lawton Chiles has not felt that need. He blasted Jeb every chance he got and questioned his honesty and anything else he could think of.

I had not realized how much worse it seems when your children run than when your husband runs. And that's pretty stressful. Three days before the end of the campaign we both felt almost sick worrying about our sons.

The weekend before the election, 750,000 Florida senior citizens received phone calls, allegedly from the AARP, saying that voters should beware: Jeb would cut Social Security. It was later proved that the phone calls were not from AARP but organized by some of Lawton Chiles' followers. Governor Chiles later apologized, but the election was over.

Jeb lost by 65,000 votes, and George W. had a big victory. So, although we celebrated for George W. and Laura, we wept over Jeb and Colu's loss. Both ran great races, and Jeb lost by such a tiny amount. I was sure he would run again. Thirty years ago, at about the same age, my George had lost his first race.

Thank heavens for humor. The day after the election I went to the beauty parlor to have my hair done before George and I left for Europe. Eddie, my regular hairdresser, said: "I can't believe it. I just can't believe I'm doing the hair of the mother of the Governor-elect of Texas." I laughed and said, "Come on, Eddie. How about doing the hair of the wife of the former President of the United States?" Eddie replied quick as a wink: "Oh, that, too." Boy, when you're out, you're really out!

∽ On that trip we went to Lisbon, Rome, Tirana in Albania, and back to Italy to attend a conference of many world leaders in Rimini. Mikhail and Raisa Gorbachev were there. It was wonderful to see them again. Raisa never seemed exactly the same after the coup attempt in 1991. She was quieter and frailer. I felt sorry for her as they had not arranged for an interpreter for her, and we sat for hours listening to speeches in English.

George kept us jumping that fall, and on November 19 we were on our way to Australia for a speaking tour. During one Q&A session, one big burly Aussie got up and asked a question that I had heard before, but not quite so graphically: "How come you didn't go for Saddam Hussein when you had him by the short and curlys?"

George called him an "articulate devil" and then went on to answer the question. He reminded the man that this was a thirty-country coalition whose U.N.-sanctioned mission was to kick Saddam Hussein out of Kuwait, period. Once they freed Kuwait, the mission was complete. Had they gone on into Baghdad, the Arab world and many of our other allies would not have stayed with us and the coalition would have fallen apart. Had we gone into Iraq, many civilians would have been killed, and we probably would not have found Saddam, who has the best security in the world and is rumored to change his sleeping place every night. We would have lost many young men and women. And whose son and daughter should he have sent? He finished with, "To kill for the sake of killing is just not our way." One of George's great strengths was bringing people together, which he certainly did in this case.*

From Australia we went on to Jakarta, Indonesia, and then on to Hong Kong for an Eisenhower Exchange Fellowships dinner. George was then chairman of the board of trustees for this wonderful program, which invites to the United States mid-level career men and women from all over the world who have promise of rising in their own fields. They stay for around three months, visiting several cities to learn about our country and see how Americans in the same field operate. We certainly learn from each other. It is privately funded and, of course, is named for President Eisenhower. Many of these fellows go on to serve in cabinet positions in their governments or hold down top-level jobs.

On December 1, George went with our two older sons to the swearing in of Mexico's new president, and on December 4 he took Doro on an exhausting trip to Taiwan and Japan, where he was speak-

---

*Unfortunately, eight years then went by where the world let Saddam build up weapons and brutalize his own people.

ing. He loves taking the children on trips. It almost makes me feel guilty to go, but not enough to stay home!

We had a marvelous Christmas with Neil and his family; he has such beautiful, fascinating children.

⤸ What a year! What a man! George was supposedly retired. Just listen to these numbers: in 1994, he gave 111 speeches; campaigned for 48 political candidates; traveled to 22 foreign countries—two of them twice—and to more than half the states. We won't even count the people he invited to our house for breakfast, lunch, dinner, and cocktails. We broke ground for his Presidential Library; took our entire family to Greece and Euro Disney; played golf from California to Florida to Maine and, yes, Korea. He even baby-sat for a few grandchildren.

I managed to finish my memoir, go on a nationwide book tour, sign thousands of bookplates, play dreadful golf, and was lucky enough to share with George many of his trips and activities. It was such a fun year, but a little exhausting. I wrote in my diary, as a joke:

> I sometimes find retirement so exhausting that I think I'll get a job.

Cutting our fiftieth wedding anniversary cake.
DAVID VALDEZ

The year started with a bang, our fiftieth wedding anniversary in early January. I remember thinking, when I'd see those pictures of people in the newspapers celebrating their fiftieth: "They are SO old. How can they be having fun?" And here we were, those "old people," and we were having lots of fun.

I also distinctly remember that we had decided NOT to do anything for our fiftieth wedding anniversary. Early in December, I was reading the newspaper and noticed a small item in a newsmaker column saying that we were going to celebrate our fiftieth anniversary at the Grand Ole Opry in Nashville. I laughed and called it to George's attention. He looked puzzled and said, "You knew that. I'm sure I told you." Well, he hadn't. Donna Sterban, the fabulous wife of the Oak Ridge Boys' Richard Sterban, had read the wedding date in my memoir and planned this amazing party for us with the cooperation of George's office.

We also do not give each other presents, supposedly. This is one year that George cheated—really cheated. Under the Christmas tree I found a big box. George had ordered china from the People's Republic of China that has the dates 1945 on one side and 1995 on the other, our names on the top and the bottom, and the symbol for double happiness in the middle—all in beautiful Chinese characters. He gave each of our children a set and three sets for us: one for Maine, one for Houston and one, eventually, for George's Library at College Station. (If all else fails we could open a Chinese family restaurant.) He also sent a small plate to many of our family and friends.

The most amazing thing of all was that I also found under the tree a note saying that on the actual day of our fiftieth, we were going to The Cloister at Sea Island, Georgia, where we had spent our honeymoon. And the note added that I would be playing golf with my friend Louise Suggs. Louise really was a pioneer female golfer—she is a great teacher and a golf legend. She has taught golf for many years in Florida and at Sea Island, switching with the seasons. When we left there after our honeymoon, George and I swore we would go back often, but we had returned only one time. It is the most beautiful place, with golf, tennis, swimming, beaches, and great food, and one is surrounded by flowers, moss-covered trees, and soft-spoken, charming people.

When we arrived at The Cloister, to add to the surprise, an unbelievable gold bracelet inscribed with our wedding and anniversary dates and initials was in our room. I wear it all the time, and often feel it and think just how lucky I am.

We played golf on our fiftieth anniversary in the morning with Louise and Bill Jones, boys against girls. Bill is the owner of The Cloister; his grandparents, Bill and Kit Jones, were there when we went in 1945.

My golf was never in that league, but it was great fun and Louise gave the men a run for their money. The men won as Bill had a 76. We four had lunch with Griffin Bell—a good friend who was Jimmy Carter's Attorney General and one of George's attorneys during the Iran-Contra controversy—and his wife, Mary; local residents Fran Green and Caroline Carter; and Rees Jones, who is following the footsteps of his father, Robert Trent Jones, the famous golf course architect.

After lunch the men went out on the course and the ladies followed. Once again my golf was horrid, but such fun for me. That night we went to Bill and Sally Jones' house for an oyster and shrimp roast and a delicious buffet dinner. Not bad for two old people to play thirty-six holes of golf on their fiftieth wedding anniversary and to go to a wonderful party that night.

The next day the ladies decided to watch the men play on a beautiful course, the Ocean Forest Club. This course was not even opened officially; Bill Jones and Rees Jones (not related) had played it at least one other time but that maybe was it. Those playing were Rees, Bill, golf great Davis Love, Griffin, and George. There were many water holes. I kept thinking what a thrill Rees must be feeling, playing on a course that he designed and built. It was cut out of 350 virgin acres of jungle and marshlands. I heard that they really went out of their way to be environmentally correct. I can vouch for the fact that they were— I was eaten alive by mosquitoes!

We flew to Nashville the next morning, and drove forty-five minutes from our hotel out to The Golf Club of Tennessee, a beautiful course designed by Tom Fazio, where twelve of us played golf: our cousin Craig Stapleton; sons George, Jeb, and Marvin; the country/Gospel singers Vince Gill and Amy Grant; and two or three pros and a friend of Jeb's. The course was especially opened for us as it had closed for the winter. It was damp, but beautiful and a joy. Vince Gill is a really fine golfer. Many entertainers take up golf because they have all day in strange towns to wait around for their evening performances.

The evening event was perfect. All children and grandchildren came and that huge hotel was rocking. We were so touched by the friends and stars who were there. The Oak Ridge Boys, of course, who sang "Amazing Grace" and "My Baby Is American Made." Michael W. Smith, Vince Gill, Lorrie Morgan, Ricky Skaggs, Amy Grant, and Eddie Rabbitt all performed. Lee Greenwood sang "The Wind Beneath My Wings" and "God Bless the USA." Roger Whittaker and Natalie came all the way from England. Our dear friend Loretta Lynn sang "Coal Miner's Daughter." Lamar Alexander played the piano. In betwixt and between all this great music, Marilyn Quayle, Mary Matalin, Delta Burke and her husband Gerald McRaney ("Major Dad"), Tommy Lasorda, Phyllis Diller, and Chuck Norris all spoke. Yakov Smirnoff of "What a Country!" fame spoke. We were very touched when George's great friend from Congress, Sonny Montgomery, a Democrat from Mississippi, said: "I have served under five presidents and you, Mr. President, were the best, the very best." It almost killed me. True, but so dear. It was an evening of tears, much laughter, and great music.

Three charities benefited from the proceeds: The Barbara Bush Foundation for Family Literacy received $45,000; the George Bush Presidential Library Foundation received $49,000; and MusiCares Foundation—which is a charity for people in the music industry—received about $20,000. I can't tell you how happy that evening was. We were surrounded by family and friends, and helped others, too.

∽ On January 16, George and I flew to Austin, Texas, for George W.'s inauguration. It was fun to see all George and Laura's friends who came for his big day—college, business, West Texas, baseball, and golfing friends. And all the family turned out full force. Jeb and Colu came and were so dear. Everyone who saw George W. with Jeb or Marvin (who apparently looks very much like Jeb) said: "Great work, George. You'll make it next time, Jeb." Marvin got tired of explaining and after a while just said, "Thanks." He said that he got very bored with it, and I can't imagine how Jeb felt, but neither he nor Colu showed anything but happiness for their brother. How I love them.

We started the day with a church service and then went on to the state Capitol for the ceremony. We had visits with many former governors and their wives or widows while waiting for the exact moment. When we walked out, there must have been 25,000 spectators. Lieutenant. Governor Bob Bullock was sworn in and spoke first, followed by George. Both men said they were going to work together, although they were from different parties. I suspect that all politicians say this at the beginning. The difference was, in this case, they did and became great personal friends. Bob Bullock, by reputation, was a tough man and very partisan. He was also very powerful. I don't think Bob expected George to be fair, and I'm sure George did not expect Bob to work with him. Both men were Texans and put Texas and its people first. Bob supported George for re-election in 1998, and when Bob was very ill in 1999, he asked George if he would give his eulogy. That was very hard for George because in that very short span of time they had become very close. Bob's widow, Jan Bullock, has become a friend of our whole family and is now very active on the advisory board for The George Bush School of Government and Public Service at Texas A&M University.

George, Marvin, Margaret, and I flew home after a family luncheon in that stunning Governor's Mansion, having decided we would not stay for the ball that night. On the short commercial flight from Austin to Houston, we discussed our dinner plans. We were all exhausted and wanted to have a light supper and go right to bed.

We walked into a dark house, which was unusual. I called "hoo hoo" and suddenly the kitchen lights came on and there were three beautifully dressed Chinese men. We were startled, and although they looked familiar and were so welcoming, we weren't quite sure exactly who they were. One either kissed me or kissed my hand. I thought they were diplomats, and before George could really see, he thought it was some friends that we were expecting the next week and that one of us had gotten mixed up on the date. George and I were stammering when Marvin came to our rescue: "Surprise, Peking Gourmet. Happy Anniversary!"

This was so sweet. Our favorite restaurant in the Washington area is The Peking Gourmet. The owners wanted to do something for our anniversary, so Marvin arranged this surprise. George Tsui, his son, and one of his staff flew down for the evening, sending all sorts of ovens ahead that were stored in the Fitches' garage. Our own had been emptied, plastic put on the floor, and they had cooked a great Peking duck dinner right there. They would not use our lovely kitchen or the Fitches' because they didn't want to "smell up" our houses! Some of our great, longtime Houston friends—Mildred and Baine Kerr, Bobbie and Jack Fitch, and Sally and Charles Neblett—joined Marvin and Margaret and us for a feast beyond belief. These darling people gave us such a wonderful evening. It was a perfect end to a memorable day.

Our boy was governor of Texas!

After dinner, the three gentlemen brought in a really lovely big, framed, scroll painting of peonies in all colors that I love. The next day, Jack Fitch came over and we hung the painting in our dining room. A week or so later our expected Chinese friends did come, and I could see them looking at the scroll. I told them the story and they said that explained the mention of The Peking Gourmet characters on the side! So we are, to this very day, still advertising for the restaurant and glad to do it. They really touched us with this great gift—the dinner and the scroll.

༄ Now one might think that this would be the last of our fiftieth wedding anniversary, but it was not to be. What a surprise we had! In April, on our way to Bucharest, Romania, we stopped in Deauville, France, to stay with our friends Issam and Hala Fares. They have a glorious horse farm and had been urging us to come to Normandy, which we were eager to do. First of all, we like them very much, and we also wanted to see the place where so many Americans fought and died on D-Day.

We visited Omaha Beach, where the troops landed and jumped off their landing craft into enemy gunfire. It must have taken unimaginable courage. Eighty percent of the first wave was killed immediately. It was so touching to walk through the American Cemetery. Among other graves we saw those of the two sons of Theodore Roosevelt: one killed in World War I, and the other a general who died in World War II.

That night we dressed for dinner in our beautiful guesthouse and walked over to the chateau or farmhouse. Enormous bouquets of flowers, created by an artist who had been brought down from Paris and worked until 4 a.m. the night before, filled the house. He used those big variegated leaves that we see in Houston and sprayed them gold. They looked like ribbons. It turned out there was a reason for all that gold! The Fareses had about thirty friends in to meet us, and when it came time for dessert, Issam made a little speech and in came a five-foot wedding cake with a Statue of Liberty on the top. Hala chose the Statue of Liberty because it represents the United States and because it was made in France. She also chose it because it represents freedom, and freedom is so important to the Lebanese. Issam and Hala are from Lebanon, that lovely little country that has been torn asunder by wars for many years. Issam is now the deputy prime minister.

This, I promise, is the end of our fiftieth wedding anniversary.

᭡ Several days after George W. was sworn in, I went to Austin to a Distinguished Speakers Event at the LBJ Library for Lady Bird Johnson. I respect and love her and certainly would do anything I could for her. It was truly a very happy evening for me as the great governor of Texas* introduced me. I was very touched that he and Laura came on Day Three of his administration.

The next day we received a letter from our Governor that really moved us. This letter was written by hand on the official paper of the governor's office and dated 1–18–95:

> Dear Mom and Dad,
>   This is my first letter written on my first day as your governor.
>   What a day!
>   Your letter moved me so much that I knew I could not look at either of you after I was confirmed. I would have wept with love and pride to be your son.
>   I am where I am because of you. You should always know this.
>
> With Love,
George

This seems a little self-serving, but I put this letter in because it shows a little about the forty-third President of the United States that people might not know. Family matters enormously to him and to us. We hurt when our children hurt and we are happy when they are happy. We've been known to shed a tear on either occasion.

---

*I will tell you now that whenever I refer to our governor sons, I will always put "great" in front of governor.

∝ Our friend Mildred Hilson—a delightful and elegant lady—had died before Christmas. We met Mildred when George was the U.S. Ambassador to the United Nations, and we both lived in the Waldorf-Astoria Towers. I was invited by her granddaughter, Wendy Levy, to be one of her eulogists. The service was held at the glorious Temple Emmanuel at One East 65th Street in New York. Wendy, knowing her grandmother would have loved it, invited an all-star cast to be eulogists: Walter Cronkite, Hollywood producer David Brown, David Eisenhower, two grandchildren, and one great-grandchild. The head of the Hospital of Special Surgery, which was Mildred's great passion, also spoke.

At different times in George's career Mildred had urged one or both of us to attend a dinner for the hospital, which specializes in orthopedics and rheumatology. And since Mildred did not know the meaning of "no," we attended. When George was president, Mildred put the hard press on me once again and because I loved her, I finally said yes. When I got to the dinner, they had two main speakers, a CEO of a large pharmaceutical company and me. (She had hedged her bet in case one of us had the nerve to back out or get sick.) The three-tiered dais was filled with folks like the mayors of New York—former and present—TV stars, and New York celebrities. The dinner was honoring Mildred, who at age ninety-some looked like a fairy godmother in her Paris gown. Several spoke, and then my co-speaker, a truly lovely man and a friend of ours, got up to speak briefly. It was clear from the beginning that he did NOT know Mildred as this is the story he told:

"A man went into a senior citizen home to see a friend. As he was walking through the lobby, another friend he knew came up to him to say hello. Surprised, the man asked what HE was doing there. Before his friend could answer, a voice from the back called out: 'We're all here because we aren't all there!'" My fellow speaker then went on to say: "We all know why we are here tonight. We're all here to honor MARION Hilson. The Mayor is here tonight to honor MARION Hilson. Barbara Bush is here to honor MARION Hilson," etc. He named quite a few folks. Mildred leaned over and asked me what he was saying. A titter ran through the crowd, but he never knew until his wife and brother told him his mistake. I confess that it made a rather long evening more fun for me.

⤳ When George and I got home from another trip to the AT&T Golf Tournament, Paula told us that Millie had done "dookies" in the living room. That reminded me of the time George and I returned from a trip to be told that one of our boys had been sick with a high fever and they called the doctor. The doctor, longtime friend Lillo Crain, couldn't understand Paula's mixed Spanish/English very well, and so he asked to speak to the child. Among other things, Dr. Crain asked when the child had last had a bowel movement? No answer. So he tried again, "Done number two?" A third time: "When did you last eliminate?" Again, no response. "Ca-ca?" Quiet on the end of the phone. Desperate, the doctor asked him when "you had last taken a s—t?" This the child understood. Later, I saw Lillo and he asked me just what word the Bush family used. I told him that our word was "dookies." He suggested that we teach our children what "bowel movement" meant! We did. Our dear friend died in January 2003, and George and I both attended the funeral.

⤳ We continued to travel all over the country. We went to Hernando, Florida, for the ground-breaking of the Ted Williams Museum and Hitters Hall of Fame. Ted had gathered many baseball greats, among them Willie Mays, Willie McCovey, Bob Feller, Mickey Mantle, Stan "the Man" Musial, and on and on. My George was in heaven. At a lunch following the ceremony George sat next to comic Henny Youngman, who spoke in sound bites: "Take my wife— PLEASE." "I've been on a great trip—I took my mother-in-law to the airport," etc. We read the little corny book he gave George going to the airport and died laughing. We must have been tired, but the late Henny Youngman was funny.

As I write this in July 2002, Ted Williams has just died and his children are fighting over his remains. He was not only a great hero to so many, but he was George's friend and loyal supporter. They stayed in touch, and George had talked to him as recently as the May before he died.

⤳ We read one great book that late winter: Doris Kearns Goodwin's *No Ordinary Time,* a warm, revealing book about Franklin and Eleanor Roosevelt. I felt very differently about both Roosevelts when I finished the book. Their personal life was sad, I thought.

I was amazed to read that, like Bill Clinton, Franklin let public opinion polls influence him a great deal. Polls are important, but are only part of the equation as public opinion can be misjudged by the phrasing of the pollsters' questions, strong lobbyists, and so on. The president must be able to weigh the facts his advisers have gathered, his own strong convictions, and the polls before he makes a decision.

I was amused to read that my George and Franklin both hated broccoli, the difference being that I did not serve broccoli in the White House and do not serve it now as George really detests the smell. When Eleanor spoke to the White House cook about broccoli, she responded, "It's good for him. Tell him to eat it!"

I also read a shockingly bad book about the personal lives of the presidents from Roosevelt through Clinton. Things we read about George are just not true, and some of the author's stories about the others are even worse. Therefore I came to the conclusion that they are not true either. How can someone write a book without talking to the person about whom they are writing, or checking with people who were there? It used to be, in the old-fashioned days, you had to check with two or three sources to verify information—and you couldn't get away with a "Deep Throat" either.

This brings up another point: inaccuracies on the Internet, where a lot of people get their information. History is being written by gossip, untruths, half-truths, and mistakes passed along by unreliable websites. Anyone can start their own website and many have. I have more people tell me something they've heard, and I'll say, "How interesting. That's not true." Then they'll tell me they saw it on the Internet.

Instead of complaining, I think I'll start my own web page.

It is all about being accountable. Sadly, many writers are not.

I read and enjoyed a lot Alison Scott Skelton's *Family Story: A Novel.* I thought about the book and family quite a bit. It was a great read—poignant, real, warm, and loving. It also was shocking and sad.

〜 At the end of February we flew to Managua, Nicaragua, to celebrate the fifth anniversary of Violetta Chamorro's election. All was not smooth sailing, to say the least. For starters, there were twenty-seven different political parties. How could they get anything done? This speaks to the benefit of a two-party system. One should choose the party nearest to one's beliefs and work within the party to change the policies rather than weakening the country by forming many little parties.

I went to a ladies luncheon where I sat across from two sisters. One had worked for Sandinista leader Daniel Ortega, and the other was the spokesperson for the Contras. As with the Chamorros, they stayed close to their families, but were on different sides of the civil war. Amazing.

It was very hot, but not unbearable. We went to open "La Casita," a recovery program for children who were addicted to sniffing glue. It was run by the Mother Teresa order of sisters, three of whom greeted us with a handful of children who danced to music played by a small group of musicians. The darling sisters smelled like billy goats. I guess bathing was not easy. "La Casita" was in a restored building that was paid for by our friends, George and Annette Strake from Houston. A plaque was unveiled, the ribbon cut, a blessing, the president spoke, George Strake said a very few nice words, and we took a tour.

We then went on with Violetta to the opening of a day care center, CDI Columbia. It was a similar ribbon-cutting with the exception that the blessing went on longer than the speeches while a crowd stood out in the blazing sun.

We all met up with George—who had been meeting with the leadership in the legislature—at the Park of Peace, where they unveiled a rock with a plaque honoring George. They had the most fascinating ceremony where truckloads of confiscated or freely given guns were backed up to a ditch and dumped and burned. They were collected by people favoring both sides of the war. It was very symbolic and very hot. By now we probably all smelled like billy goats!

After each event we plunged out into the crowds and were enveloped in hugs and kisses. I'm sure it was a security nightmare, but what loving, warm, nice people.

Although we did many interesting things on that brief trip, the dinner at Violetta's house was memorable. Her house is a rabbit warren of rooms that open onto junglelike gardens. The rooms are filled with memorabilia, gifts from foreign countries, and so on. There is a cabinet containing the clothes her husband, a newspaper publisher and an opposition leader, was wearing when he was shot. Outside is the car he was sitting in at the time of his death. She says the constant reminder makes her strong.

The house was filled with family, including three of her children. Her son Carlos was there. Carlos is a Sandinista and opposes his mother. Now that is unusual!

We left feeling once again that we are the luckiest people in the world to live in the United States of America.

✐ Here are some of my random diary notes from early 1995:

Eddie my hairdresser told me the funniest story the other day. He said that a customer of his who had two golden retrievers lived next door to a family that had several young children and a large white family rabbit. One day when the family had gone on a day's outing to Galveston, the dogs got out and returned home with a dirty bloody rabbit dangling out of one of the dog's mouths. The poor lady panicked, didn't know what to do, and finally decided to take it upstairs, shampoo it, fluff it up, and return it to the rabbit cage next door. She hoped the neighbors might think the rabbit had died peacefully in its cage. So she did just that. The family returned home and a little while later she heard such screaming and yelling that she went over to inquire what happened. She was told that several days earlier their rabbit had died and they buried it in their backyard and now it appeared back in its cage! Eddie swears this really happened.

All during this period Republicans are announcing for President, to run against Bill Clinton in 1996. So far Lamar Alexander and Phil Gramm have announced and as of March 21, Pat Buchanan. In the wings we have Bob Dole, Pete Wilson, with Colin Powell as a big question mark. Am I glad we are out of this.

We both did a lot of speaking in 1995. At least George appeared at gatherings where he knew something about the companies or business. I often spoke to groups where I hardly understood their profession. Sometimes I wondered what I possibly could tell them that they already didn't know. I was reminded of Winston Churchill, who once said something like: "Never try to walk up a wall that is leaning towards you. Never try to kiss somebody who is leaning away from you and NEVER EVER try to speak to a group that knows more about a subject than you do."

For instance, what do I know about animal science? And yet one year I spoke at the annual veterinarians' conference in Florida. George sent me off to that group suggesting that I tell them about a veterinarian he knew who merged with a taxidermist. Their motto was "Either way you get your dog back."

I gave so many talks in Houston that our friend and publisher of the *Houston Chronicle*, Dick Johnson, introduced me once by claiming he said to someone: "I guess you've heard a thousand speeches by Barbara Bush." "No," came the answer, "I've heard Barbara Bush give the same speech a thousand times!" True.

Once when George W. introduced me, he said, "My mother taught me so much. One of the things she said was to keep my feet on the ground, my nose to the grindstone, my shoulder to the wheel, and get to work. I ask you—How can anyone work in that position?"

In March, neighbor Jack Fitch had yet again another body part replaced, a knee this time. He told me that while he was in the hospital three Methodists came into his room. He said he was an Episcopalian, but they asked if they could pray with him. The next thing he knew he was holding hands with three strange men and they were praying over him. He was sputtering. He just doesn't hold hands with strange men. Although these people were trying to be kind, I do not think that strangers should be allowed in a sickroom. I am sure that the patient should be asked if he wants visitors. Then, one of the many ministers from our huge church also came by, and, according to Bobbie Fitch, apparently started talking about the dreadful things that the Republicans were doing. Now Jack is a dyed-in-the-wool Republican and he once again got sputtering. Another editorial note: Don't go to the hospital and talk politics, especially if you don't know the politics of the patient.

We watched the Masters Tournament at Augusta, Georgia, and were thrilled to have so many friends in the final group: Hale Irwin, Greg Norman, Davis Love, and Ben Crenshaw. "Gentle Ben" won against those giants, which was truly amazing as he had skipped the practice day and flown home to be a pallbearer for his mentor, well-known golf instructor Harvey Penick. I teased George and told him that these men all had something in common: They had played golf with George Bush and survived.

> *April 13*—Bob Dornan announced for President and so now the field is Dole, Gramm, [Richard] Lugar, Buchanan, Alexander, [Arlen] Specter, and Dornan. Yikes!
>
> The O. J. Simpson trial is still the top of the news.*
>
> The baseball strike finally ended. The season started two weeks late!

꙳ On April 19, we awakened to a normal day to find that the Alfred P. Murrah Federal Office Building in Oklahoma City had been blown up. Among the 168 dead was a lovely young man, Al Whicher, who had served on George's Secret Service detail. He was a devoted husband and father.

As fate would have it, the next day George and I were due to go to Tulsa, Oklahoma. I was to speak at a Junior League event at noon and that night join George at The Salvation Army annual dinner. We debated about going because of their great loss, but then decided that both groups help people in need and, of course, we must go. What a dreadful tragedy.

I wrote in my diary at the time:

> The press is reporting that they suspect Middle Eastern terrorists, but they really do not know. How quick we are to judge before the facts are in.

---

*Simpson was on trial for the murder of his wife, Nicole, and Ronald Goldman, on June 12, 1994. He eventually was found "not guilty."

April 26—I rode my bike this morning, looked at catalogs, and decided that the most insulting, worst thing is for a large woman to see a dress she loves and it will say: "Extra Large—size 14." Now that is heart rending. Not only do they not carry my size, but they insult me along the way!

∽ One of the highlights of the spring was that the May issue of *Outlaw Biker* magazine named me "Biker Babe of the Century" and said that I was a "classy broad." As this magazine usually features topless and tattooed women, and bikers in black leather, I really was honored. Referring to Desert Storm, they also had a line in there about "Babs' ol' man who kicked a little butt in the White House." Definitely a very fine honor!

∽ April and May are always busy times with graduations, charity events, and a lot of spring conferences. It is almost as though people are trying to get it all in before summer vacation. A couple of trips stand out in my mind, including the Air Force Academy, where George addressed the corps and received the T. D. White Award. The military are very special to George, and to this day he is moved by their patriotism, loyalty, and dedication to serving others.

I went to Columbus, Ohio, to speak for The Speech and Hearing Center. The luncheon was held at the convention center and attended by 1,600 people. I was introduced by a dear friend, Janet Voinovich, wife of then Governor, now Senator George Voinovich. She is a darling young woman, and she and her George are two of the most decent people I know. She told me that she was loving George W. and Laura since George W. had become governor of Texas. Apparently, governors and their wives had wondered what George and Laura would be like, and they were pleasantly surprised. That there would be doubts never occurred to me. But George W. was the son of a former president and had defeated a very popular governor. I could see that they might think he was going to be a "big shot," but she said they loved them both, which was nice for this mother to hear!

On Long Island I visited a family literacy program, Center for

Family Resources, that my foundation had helped, and I attended a luncheon of seven hundred ladies. They raised $40,000, which was terrific. A group of thirty mothers and one father greeted me, all either Hispanic or African-American, who had their hair done by a sister of one of the students—very elaborate and very wild. Two of the women were chosen to say what the program meant to them. One was painfully shy, but the other stood up and described her life before and after coming to the center. She said that she yelled and screamed at her children; that she hated her life and awakened each day to "another day of hell." Now she wants her GED and wants to go to computer school. She had trouble not weeping when she told us that she no longer ties her children to the kitchen table and screams at them. She had us all weeping when she told us that her children now say for the first time, "I love you, Mummy." One African-American said that these thirty mothers and one father "were all family and helped each other." God bless the man. But, of course, that is a large part of the problem. The fathers must be responsible also.

One night in late May I attended a black-tie dinner for the Hadley School for the Blind in Chicago. This is not a bricks and mortar building, but mail-order courses that are sent around the world. Approximately twelve thousand people are learning Braille now through this parent-taught program. Only 15 to 20 percent of the blind learn Braille. That means the other 80 percent are illiterate. I learned a great deal that night about an almost totally neglected population.

⌒ In the middle of May, the National Rifle Association sent out the most offensive fund-raising letter. Their timing was really bad—just after the Oklahoma bombing—but at any time it would have been appalling. Among the wording they used: "The semi-auto ban gives jack-booted government thugs more power to take away our constitutional rights, break in our doors, seize our guns, destroy our property, and even injure or kill us." The whole three-page letter was paranoiac—"the government against us," etc. George resigned from the organization and released his letter to the media. It certainly caused a lot of excitement. It is so sad to think that there are a lot of people out there arming and feeling that the U.S. government is out to get them. Incidentally, George's resignation did not mean that he was for more gun control or against the right to bear arms. It meant that he was against rabble-rousing and irresponsible rhetoric.

All our children visited that summer with their children, friends of ours, and friends of theirs. I try to remember our children's favorite dishes when they come, such as baked peaches for Jeb. I really like this dish, and of course, it is bad for you. It is so easy to make; the ingredients are usually in the house; it's hard to burn or overcook; most important, everyone likes it.

BAKED PEACHES

1 or 2 cans Del Monte peach halves in heavy syrup (how many depends on the number of guests; as they cook down, I usually allow for three halves per guest)

Lay peach halves, cavity side up, in a low casserole or pie dish
Cover with half the peach syrup from can
Put a dab of butter and a touch of brown sugar in each peach half
Sprinkle with cinnamon
Squeeze the juice of a lemon over all

Bake in a 350-degree oven for an hour (the juice must be cooked down and the peaches brown)

Serve hot or warm with real whipped cream.

In July I read Anne Tyler's *Ladder of Years* and loved it. I love the way she writes, and I felt very warmly toward her heroine. I wonder how many of us go through life without telling others that they are needed, wanted, and loved? Her husband didn't know the color of her eyes!

Our travels did not slow down much in the summer. For pure pleasure we took as many of our gang who could go and several friends on a cruise to the Greek Islands in June.

In July, we went to Krakow, Poland, for the Polish-American

Children's Hospital fund-raising dinner. We were told it was the first such dinner held in Poland. We had visited the hospital several years before, and on our return, saw some of the same people we had met on our last visit. That evening, the dinner was held in the salt mines. This was as fascinating a place as I have ever seen. The mines have been worked continuously for seven hundred years. They go down 1,200 feet, and have 200 miles of underground walks on seven levels. The top four levels are open to the public. Over the years, some caverns on the first four levels have been carved by the miners. We visited three. One was a lovely little chapel with a beautiful Madonna and babe, along with a glorious grown-up Jesus. The next is tremendous and holds five hundred people. The wall carvings are absolutely magnificent. Both these chapels and the large cavern where we had dinner had huge chandeliers, also made of salt crystal. This is used for church services three times a year and sometimes for concerts. Our guide had worked in the mines for twenty-seven years. It is on par with the lost city of Petra in Jordan as one of the great man-made wonders. Why have we never ever heard of this most unusual sight?

We went on to Warsaw and had a nice visit with Lech Walesa and his beautiful wife Danuta at the Presidential Palace. Lech presented George with "The Great Cross of the Order of Merit." I wrote my friend Patsy Caulkins that the contrast between this lunch in the Presidential Palace and that lunch in their tiny breakfast room in Gdansk a few years ago—when Lech was head of the opposition—was like night and day.

We then went to the British Open Golf Tournament at the Royal and Ancient Golf Course in St. Andrews, Scotland. For every golfer, this is Mecca. We stayed at Waldon House, with a view from our bedroom of the eighteenth green. We had a small balcony outside our room, and I twice climbed out a tiny window onto the balcony. Getting back into the room was almost impossible, and I had several friends who told me that they saw a less than perfect view of my body on television as I scrambled—really fell—through the window to get back in.

We met up with many friends, including Prince Andrew, an avid golfer and a very nice young man. We played on the Elie Golf Course while we were there, and I humiliated myself again.

We had to leave before the end of the tournament to go to London in order to have dinner with our dear friends, John and Norma Major, at No. 10 Downing Street. When we arrived, we immediately asked John who had won the British Open. John is a huge cricket fan and had absolutely no interest or idea who had won. To avid golfers, that seemed inconceivable. We had such a lovely time laughing and relaxing with them. Norma Major made the living quarters at No. 10 warm, attractive, and cozy.

From London we went to Potsdam, Germany, where we stayed at the Schlosshotel Cecilienhof, a beautiful palace built or finished after World War I in the British Tudor style. It had just been renovated and we were the first to stay in our lovely suite. It was one of the few remaining buildings left near Berlin after World War II, which is why it was chosen for the Potsdam Conference between Churchill, Truman, and Stalin. It was here that it was decided that Germany should not be divided, but have three sectors guarded by Great Britain, the United States, and the Soviet Union until they could get things regulated. Well, we all know what happened. The Soviets took over their sector, built the Wall, and like it or not, we had East and West Germany. We saw the round table where the agreement was signed and ate the exact same meal as the three of them. There was a poignant moment when we realized that Clement Attlee, not Churchill, had signed the Potsdam agreement. While Churchill was at the conference, the British people had voted him out of office.

It was here that I first heard my George referred to over and over again as the father of German reunification. After hearing Lech Walesa give him credit for the peaceful turnaround in Poland, one does get even more respect for this great husband of mine. So many people are living in freedom thanks in part to George Bush.

We went to a briefing at a former Soviet military facility called Bornstedter Feld. This very run-down base covers many acres next to a lake. The Soviet occupiers had brought their families, but were naturally isolated from their captives. They had left six months earlier taking everything that they could with them, including, in some cases, the floorboards. George remembers Gorbachev telling him that many soldiers were going home to no jobs and no housing and that it was going to be a dreadful problem for Russia.

My main impressions after this marvelous, very interesting visit were that although the Wall was down, it was as though there was an invisible wall left. Everything on the west side was clean and neat. Everything on the east was unkempt and uncared for, windows broken, etc. Evidently maintenance was low on the Communist list of priorities. From talking to folks on both sides of the invisible wall that remained, I got the feeling that it was going to take years to change the mindset of people who had little or no work ethic after 45 years of living under Communist rule.

 ﾟ On September 3, George and I took an unbelievable trip to Vietnam—unbelievable because I never expected to set foot in what had been North Vietnam. We first went to Hanoi and then on to Saigon, now called Ho Chi Minh City.

We drove through narrow streets clogged with many bikes, both motorized and regular. They come at you from all sides and it is very much like mainland China of 20 years ago, the big difference being that the streets were wider in China. . . . Everything looks very run down to me. I was told that the Vietnamese are entrepreneurs, each and every one of them. The architecture is unique when it is other than covered shacks and lean-tos. The buildings are thin (one room wide); tall (3 stories) and seem to have windows on two sides only. It's as though they are waiting for a house to be built next door and they just haven't come yet. They are colorful and have very decorated porches and balconies. . . . As we got closer and closer to town there were more and more people and the roads were lined with lean-tos and shacks which turned out to be "Mom and Pop" stores and homes either behind the open stores or upstairs. The narrow roads were filled with bikes pulling every conceivable thing behind them; even well-dressed ladies with hats, gloves up to their elbows, and often with umbrellas, pedaling or riding; many bikes with large bucket seats in front and passengers in the bucket. These look very strange as the passenger cannot see the driver. As in China, there are boxes, whole families, and every household thing you could imagine on the back of the bike. Cars are barely able to move through this jumble of humanity because of the narrow-

ness of the streets and the size of the crowds. We were a motorcade with sirens and there was no pulling over or getting out of
the way—no place to go.

We had lunch with the foreign minister and his wife, and also met
with President Le Duc Anh and the party secretary, Do Muoi.

George gave a great speech to a group of maybe two-hundred,
largely Vietnamese. I especially liked the question-and-answer period.
He was asked some tough questions: "Why did it take your country so
long to come to our aid? Look what you did for Germany and Japan
after World War II"; "Bob McNamara said in his recent book that the
United States was wrong to get involved in the Vietnam War. Do you
agree with him?" George answered them truthfully and well. I remember when Bob's book came out, I saw Tom Johnson—then head of
CNN but once a cabinet secretary under Lyndon Johnson—at a Mayo
Clinic meeting, and I asked him if Secretary McNamara was against
the war as he suggested in his book. Tom said that he certainly never
heard any opposition to the war coming from McNamara's lips! Of
course, in retrospect, we were all against the war. Some felt we should
not have fought at all; some—like George—regretted the way our
military were constrained by the politicians.

We visited a hospital for severely handicapped children named for
Olaf Palme, the assassinated prime minister of Sweden whom we had
visited a year or so before his death in 1986. This was a very moving
visit, but the hospital was pathetically primitive. It reminded us again
that we are the most fortunate country in the world.

We also went to "The Ranch," the nickname for the MIA/POW
Headquarters. We were told by a young captain that the Vietnamese
have allowed them accessibility to any site the American military
wants to examine. It was really amazing to hear the lengths they went
to to find missing Americans. They have gone through diaries and
journals of American veterans and worked with veteran organizations.
The Vietnamese are asking their vets to do the same. It is not easy to
find people who remember what happened twenty-five years ago.

Then it was on to Ho Chi Minh City, or Saigon, which most people still call it. What a difference! The streets were wide and there was
less of the squalor we saw in Hanoi.

*Listening to a briefing about the ongoing search for missing
American soldiers, during a trip to Vietnam in September 1995.
We visited this field site near Da Nang.*
FAMILY SCRAPBOOK

We went by helicopter to a field site in Da Nang where they were looking for a POW/MIA. The site was on a river that had grown around twelve feet wider in twenty-five years. A witness who had been there when they buried the American showed where he was by throwing a rock into the edge of the river. They had buried the man in the ground, but it was now under water. The recovery workers had built a bamboo dam—two rows of bamboo poles with woven bamboo screens which they were filling with thousands of sandbags—to isolate the spot they were looking for. The plan was, when the dam was finished, to pump out the water and dig. They hoped to find teeth, bones, dog tags, etc. The MIA they were looking for was reported by his buddies to have been talking to some young children looking for a "woman." The children obviously led him into a trap. How does the U.S. military tell that to a mother waiting anxiously for news of her child? I hope they do not!

This was a most emotional trip as George had invited several Secret Service agents who had served in Vietnam to accompany us. Standing in those rice fields brought back many memories of their friends, snipers, and all the horrors of war.

We went from Vietnam to Beijing and went almost immediately

upon arrival to have dinner with President Jiang Zemin at Diaoyutai State Guesthouse.

We couldn't get over the changes just since our last visit. The roads were jammed with cars and still lots of bikes, but they did have bike lanes so you were not in constant fear of running over somebody. The cabs and buses were everywhere. The men were in stylish western suits with ties, and I saw one lady in a long black skirt and a chic blouse. The waitresses were graceful, slim, and in long traditional dresses with slits up the sides showing pretty, stocking-covered legs. Twenty years ago we would have seen them all in ill-fitting Mao suits! We were warmly greeted by the president and several old friends. Our dinner was very relaxed, and the men questioned each other about all the happenings in the world, especially in the United States and the People's Republic of China.

The big happening in China at the moment was The Women's Conference, sponsored by the United Nations and being held right outside Beijing. This was a very serious, important conference, attended by several good friends—including Tom Kean, the former governor of New Jersey, and Julia Taft, the wife of the future governor of Ohio. They were very enthusiastic about the conference as they are interested in the education of women and girls—a tremendous need around the world. If you educate the woman, she will see that the children are educated. They, like me, feel that with education, so many of our problems would be solved.

However, most of the news about the conference revolved around Hillary Clinton's involvement and her criticism of the Chinese concerning the accommodations and their lack of civil rights. The president of China suggested that she go home and take care of some of our problems, pointing out something about lack of civil rights in Los Angeles. Also, the weather did not help as it rained and the site was muddy and difficult.

When we were in Vietnam, George had been asked about Hillary, and he said that he had a rule never to criticize the president or his wife. He went on to say—as a joke—that he did feel sorry for the Chinese with Bella Abzug running around Beijing. Bella had served in Congress with George, and he always liked her. Her answer was marvelous: "Poor George—what would you expect? He was in China speaking to a fertilizer group." We were actually there to attend the 44th Conference on Grain Production, as the guests of IMC Global, Inc.

On Sunday, we went to a "new" church; new in the sense that it wasn't the tiny, second-story chapel that we had attended when we lived in China in 1974. We were startled not only by the size of the congregation in the church but also by the tremendous, seated overflow in the courtyard. The congregation was Chinese, with a smattering of westerners. We could spot many from the Women's Conference, not because—as an article I read suggested—they had unshaven legs and armpits, but because they wore badges. We were greeted by several old Chinese friends and given the English-translation Bibles that we had used all those years ago. A small, elderly woman gave the sermon and went on and on and on for over thirty minutes, all in Chinese. Our friend, the tiny old minister who sat next to me, kept looking at his watch. Finally I gestured with my hands that I thought it was long. He smiled and stretched his hands farther and then gestured that she was going around in circles.

As we could not understand a word, George and I and our hosts, Wendell and Nancy Bueche (Wendell was chairman and CEO of IMC Global), read the lesson of the day from Timothy. It was a fascinating choice for the week of The Women's Conference. Paul had written to Timothy about how people should act towards each other, and his description of how women should act is probably the most chauvinistic passage in the Bible. If the women's lib group had understood Chinese, they would have gone right up the wall—Chinese Wall, if you will! It is not my favorite passage either: "Let a woman learn in silence with all submissiveness. I permit no woman to teach or have authority over men. She is to keep silent." George especially liked: "Women should adorn themselves modestly and sensibly in seemly apparel, not with braided hair or gold or PEARLS or costly attire."

I had to wonder if this was planned and was a secret joke the Chinese were having among themselves!

We went on to Japan, where we met with some old friends and also did some speaking. We had a visit with former president Jimmy Carter who was in Japan for a funeral, and with Jim and Elaine Wolfensohn who were on their way to China. Jim had just accepted the big job of heading up The World Bank, at an enormous personal financial cost to himself and his family.

After speaking in Tokyo we went to Sapporo, Nagoya, Kyoto, Osaka, and Fukuoka. I wrote in a letter to my good friend Andy Stewart:

> We loved Sapporo in the northernmost island of Hokkaido where we climbed mountains (GB) and rode a bike for miles along a river bank (me). The agents were prepared and had on sports attire. The poor Japanese security had on black suits and dress shoes. We toured Kyoto which is a lovely city filled with castles and temples. In one Buddhist Temple we were sipping green tea, sort of squatting on the floor after having had a glorious tour by a Buddhist monk with a bright interpreter, when out of the blue the monk, who had not spoken a word of English until that moment, said: "How's your doggie?" He then told us through the interpreter that he had visited the United States, and when walking by the White House had seen me walking my dog, and that I had waved to him. So a MILLIE'S BOOK is winging its way around the world to this monk.

Then it was back home to Maine.

〜 Among many things I did that fall was to visit the Reiche Elementary School in Portland, where I had been invited to come and read to the children during the lunch hour.

This event was truly amazing. This school is designated for children of mostly political refugees; I had not realized that Portland was a refugee center. At that time, the school had children from forty different countries. When I walked in, three children from Bosnia were being registered. Three or four students from Somalia had arrived the day before. For the first day, they have someone who speaks their language show them their desks, lockers, and the routine, and from that day on, they are on their own. All classes are taught in English, and the teachers told me that in two to three months they all speak English. Think how frightened those children are as they are in a new country, learning a new language, and among strangers. The lucky ones meet children who have arrived earlier from their home country and who speak their native tongue. It does make one wonder if all the schools that think we must ease children into school by teaching in their native language are wasting time and money when this seems like a very effective way to learn. I understand that some schools in our country teach in Spanish. It is important to speak several languages, but if you don't speak English in the United States, you are saying that you will never be a first-class citizen—never experience the American Dream. I was really impressed with a school that registers children all year long and manages to cope with so many languages and social problems.

     ∽ Earlier that summer I had been urged to visit with folks from the Maine Medical Center. They very kindly wanted to name a children's hospital after me. I told them that I really could not accept that honor as I was already overcommitted with projects. They assured me that I would not have to do anything, but I, of course, knew better. Finally, after a lot of urging, I agreed to at least hear them out and they came to Walker's Point. I really cannot remember exactly who "they" were other than one rather informally dressed lady named Elizabeth Noyce and a man named Owen Wells. We had iced tea, and I explained my worries. They assured me that I honestly would have to do nothing but lend my name. I was told that IF I would lend my name, Mrs. Noyce would give $3 million to kick the campaign off. How could I say no? I didn't. Let me say here and now eight years later that I was never asked to do anything for the hospital. They raised the money by themselves. By choice I visit the hospital and read to the children once a summer, have spoken once at a volunteer luncheon, and have done a few videos for them.

On September 28, George and I drove up to Portland for the announcement of The Barbara Bush Children's Hospital, which is part of Maine Medical Center. This was much more emotional than I expected. Imagine having a hospital named after me! They are really stretching my life. Long after I am gone this hospital will be there with my name.

George and I went to visit the children, and they brought back such memories of Robin—little babies with bald heads, although Robin never lost that sweet head of soft blond curls, but they had that "look." I read "Amazing Grace" to the children and they were so dear. Then they asked George and me questions.

George and I went on to become good friends of Elizabeth Noyce and also of Owen Wells and his wife Annie. Elizabeth was a great philanthropist in Maine, and although she died several years ago, her generosity is still felt across the state through her Libra Foundation, which Owen runs.

    ⤳ In early September, we flew back to Texas for the opening of the Nimitz Museum in Fredericksburg, the birthplace of Chester Nimitz, who was commander in chief of the Pacific Fleet during World War II. The museum included one whole wing dedicated to George's war experiences. We stayed with our great friends Mildred and Baine Kerr at Kerrplunk, their vacation house on the Guadalupe River. The next day we went to the museum, and there were George W. and Laura looking marvelous. I said: "George, you look so dressed up. Dad doesn't even have on a tie." George answered: "The difference is Dad doesn't have a job. I do." I believe it was here that George told the crowd that his dad didn't give him advice, but his mother always was telling him what to do. A good ole boy in the back yelled out: "And you'd better listen to her, Sonny!"

We ended with a parade through this great Texas Hill Country town. There were thirty thousand people along the route, and the town looked like the Fourth of July with flags and bunting.

    ⤳ I read John Berendt's *Midnight in the Garden of Good and Evil,* a true story about a killing in Savannah, Georgia. It is bizarre and beautifully written. I loved it. It occurs to me that I have not mentioned yet that I read every John Grisham book, every David Baldacci book, and every Mary Higgins Clark book as they come out. They are all so prolific and I can hardly wait for their next books.

    ⤳ Finally, on the 28th of September, the O. J. Simpson case went to the jury. This trial had dominated the news for what seemed like forever. I am not going to talk about the verdict, but just put in a comment I made in my diary:

> I was amazed that the TV stations only showed the Palestinian/Israeli Peace Treaty signing at the White House during a recess in the Simpson court case. During the recess they would cut to the White House and at the end of the recess they cut back to the trial in spite of the fact that real news was being made at the White House. Where is our perspective?
>
> The other big news of the day was that Pete Wilson withdrew from the presidential race because he was having trouble raising money and was having staff problems. I felt sorry for Pete and Gayle, but even more for our dear friends, Craig Fuller* and others, who left great jobs to help him. In spite of what one is told, politics is a thankless job for those loyal friends who often sacrifice so much for a candidate. George says, and he is right, that we can never adequately thank all those people who worked so hard for us—never!

∾ George's sister Nan Ellis gave me *The Stone Diaries* by Carol Shields and I really enjoyed it. Such fun to find books that one loves.

> And so September finally ends. What a month.
> A wing of the Nimitz Museum . . . was named for George.
> We traveled to three Far East Countries.
> I was sued for $4 million dollars for something I had said in my memoir.†
> A hospital was named for me.
> Life threatened.‡

---

*Craig had been George's chief of staff during his second term as vice president.

†I will not get in trouble again by repeating what I said but it involved a CIA agent. I did not have to pay the $4 million but it was a costly nuisance suit. I will hope not to have to go through that again!

‡I don't remember this now but it must have been a threat against George and not a nice fat old lady!

Talking about the Cold War they helped end are, from left:
Brian Mulroney, François Mitterrand, George Bush,
Mikhail Gorbachev, and Margaret Thatcher. October 1995.
SUSAN BIDDLE

Out of the blue [came] a gift of $100,000 to the Barbara
Bush Foundation for Family Literacy.*

┳ In early October, I flew to Colorado Springs and the fabulous Broadmoor Hotel to meet up with George, who had been on a
western states speaking tour. The first afternoon George played golf
with some good players and nice, kind Brent Scowcroft played with
me. I was pretty—no, very—bad, but Brent and I laughed our way
around the golf course. I think on one hole we hit seven golf balls in a
tiny pond. We were all there to attend the forum, "A World Transformed: Our Reflections on Ending the Cold War." The forum was the
first event hosted by The George Bush Presidential Library Foundation
and co-hosted by Brent's The Forum for International Policy.

The event started off with a dinner where one of our favorites, the
very funny juggler Michael Davis, did part of his act. George had met
him coming off the golf course and invited him to come entertain the

---

*Generously donated by a company based in Houston, called TransTexas Gas.

former world leaders who had gathered for the forum. He had performed for us when the G-7 Group* had met in Houston in 1990 and so many of the leaders were the same. Amy Grant also sang and was superb.

The next morning, the panel assembled and the discussion, skillfully led by Jim Lehrer of PBS, went from 9 a.m. until noon. The panel members were Brian Mulroney (Canada), Mikhail Gorbachev (the Soviet Union), François Mitterrand (France), Margaret Thatcher (United Kingdom), and George Bush. They had lively discussions about the reunification of Germany.

Baroness Thatcher, who was a great prime minister, was pretty outspoken, which is yet another reason why she is such a popular speaker around the world. At one time she disagreed with the other four and said something like: "I am certainly right on this, but then I am always right." Margaret was very opposed to the reunification of Germany, feeling that it would become a German Europe. George, Brian, and François disagreed. Of course Mikhail was opposed, but knew it was inevitable. It was fascinating to find that when the Wall came down, East Germany was not the jewel in the Soviet crown that we all thought it would be, but was rotting and run down. Brian summed it all up by saying that there were three attitudes: the European—FEAR; the Soviet—did not want to see Germany in NATO; and the United States and Canada—for reunification, but maybe because of the distance between them and Germany.

This was François' last visit out of his country, and it touched George more than anything. He obviously was not well. He and George had become great allies and, I think I can say, friends. He told George he would come and he did, but at some cost to himself. We liked him enormously. François died in January 1996 on the day we arrived in Beijing. George really wanted to attend his funeral, but had commitments that he couldn't break.

Brian Mulroney and his wife Mila are perhaps two of our dearest friends and we love their four children. We have become closer and

---

*G-7 stands for "Group of 7," the seven major industrial powers in the world. The heads of state from these countries met once a year: United States, Japan, Germany, France, Italy, Great Britain, and Canada. They have since added an eighth country, Russia.

closer to Mikhail Gorbachev, and during the summer of 2001, we had Mikhail, his lovely daughter Irina, and two granddaughters spend some time at both George's Library and at our home in Maine. Mikhail has a wonderful sense of humor, and I'd like to share two jokes he told us during those visits:

"Reagan tells Gorbachev that in our country we are free. Why, he said, in our country people can stand outside the White House and yell, 'Down with Reagan' and nothing happens to them. Gorby tells Reagan that's nothing. In their country, people can stand outside the Kremlin and yell, 'Down with Reagan' and nothing happens to them either!" How he laughed and loved that joke, which he promptly followed with:

"A Russian wanting bread waited in a queue for so long that he announced that he was leaving and was going to kill Gorbachev. After quite a while, he showed up again. When asked if he had killed Gorbachev, he replied, 'No, the wait in that line was much longer than here.'" Again Gorbachev laughed and laughed.

The meeting in Colorado ended with *Time* magazine's Hugh Sidey as the lunch speaker. He has covered every president since Eisenhower, and told informative and amusing stories about them all. We feel he is a great writer and friend. This was truly a perfect day and a half and lots of fun.

꩜ We left Maine around the middle of October. I drove to Boston and climbed on a tiny commuter prop plane to Washington. I joked about having seats 6A and 6B and the pilot said: "Oh, that's the safest place to sit if the propeller falls off." We thought that he was being funny, but he said: "Oh, no. A prop fell off a plane just like this one last month," AND WE CLIMBED ON.

On the plane we saw a copy of *USA Today*, which had a full page ad announcing that I was being presented The Freedom Forum Award of $100,000 on that very day. The ad was a surprise and so very nice. Many people on this tiny plane asked for autographs. A lot of close friends were at the event. Our old friend Alan Shepard, the astronaut, introduced me. We had known the Shepards, Louise and Alan, for years, first in Houston, and then Alan served as a public delegate at the United Nations when George was the UN ambassador. Both have since died. They were very special people. And the $100,000 for my literacy foundation was also very special!

 ⤳ I read *Beach Music* by Pat Conway and really loved it, all 621 pages. I honestly laughed out loud at times. This author is the most sensual writer, meaning that I can smell the tidal waters in South Carolina, taste the food he talks about, and see the scenes he describes. I had put off reading it because it got bad reviews. Isn't it true that one person's taste might be different from another's? Our bookcases contain a number of books that friends have recommended and neither of us enjoyed, books we started and did not finish. For years I struggled through books that I didn't like very much. For every good book I read, I am ashamed to say I read some awful ones. Finally, I have matured, and if I don't like it after 100 pages, I put it away. There are so many books I want to read. Our bookshelves mainly are filled with books that we have loved.

 ⤳ The fall was spent doing interviews for my book, which was coming out in paperback, and doing a variety of events for pay and for charity. I especially remember a visit to Laguna Niguel, California, where George was speaking at a Ford Motor Company convention. They had kindly arranged for us both to play golf. The men took off, and the most attractive young women were in my group. It seems to me that although we always send ahead the message that I am not good but fast, convention planners think I am being modest. So, every time I walk out on the first tee, there are three good young golfers swinging their drivers and stretching. For the first couple of holes they think I am just warming up. After they realize that I really am bad, we can all relax and have fun.

Among the charity events I attended was a dinner for a big Youth Internet program that serves five different programs which help kids in New York City; The Episcopal Women in Houston; a Dallas umbrella charity that supports two shelters, one for the homeless and the other for abused women and children; and the Montgomery Women's Club in Cleveland, which gives scholarships to students who might otherwise not be able to go to college. They also support the arts.

I wish I could list all the wonderful events we attended, but there are just too many. By the end of the year, the staff counted that George had raised almost $10 million for charity, either directly or indirectly, at thirty fund-raisers, and I had raised more than $5.5 million at fifty-one charitable events. I am not bragging, just trying to say we were doing our best to be Points of Light and to give back just a tiny bit of what we had been given.

∽ Colin Powell was the talk of the political world. Will he and should he run for president was the universal question. It was very interesting that the ten announced Republican candidates were still not attracting any enthusiasm.

∽ A lot of foreign visitors came to Houston that fall. We had a visit from President Berisha of Albania, with cocktails at our house and lunch at The Bayou Club. Sali and Liri Berisha are doctors, he a heart doctor and she a pediatrician. We have had several visits, two in Albania and this one in Houston, with this charming couple. The president seemed very confident and enthusiastic about Albania, which had been isolated from the rest of the world for fifty years.

We had President and Mrs. Jerry Rawlings of Ghana for coffee. They are extremely engaging. George asked the president about Africa and Ghana. He was interesting but frankly very hard to understand.

President Juan Carlos Wasmosy of Paraguay came for cocktails at our home and eight of us had dinner at The Taste of Texas Restaurant. Our grandson George P., who then was an undergraduate at Rice, joined us.

Later in the fall, President dos Santos of Angola came to Houston, and Lynne and Dick Cheney came down from Dallas for the dinner at our house.

∽ I was reading Rosamunde Pilcher's *Coming Home* and loving it. Easy read.

✑ Our friend of many years, Israeli prime minister Yitzhak Rabin, was assassinated in November at a peace rally. He was killed by a radical Jew, which added to the shock. President Clinton graciously invited George to go to Israel with him for the funeral, which he did along with Jerry Ford and Jimmy Carter. My heart broke for Leah Rabin and her family.

While George was at the funeral, I went to the CARE World Leadership dinner at Ken and Linda Lay's home (later in November we went to the big national CARE Dinner where George spoke), and also substituted for George at The Living Legend Luncheon in Dallas, a fund-raiser for M. D. Anderson Hospital. They raised $300,000—mainly because everyone thought George was the speaker! He did speak there several years later, and as I write this in 2002, Lance Armstrong—who has just won the Grand Prix for the fourth time—will be the speaker for this year. He is the miracle cancer patient and is dedicated to helping others fight this disease.

That same day I also went out to dedicate the President George Bush Highway near Dallas. It was really an honor for George, and I was so sorry he wasn't there. State senator Florence Shapiro, who sponsored the bill, spoke. The former mayor of Plano, Texas, she is a bright, peppy, feisty lady. Four mayors were at the dedication and one hundred people, even though the weather was really threatening. As we uncovered the highway sign, it poured rain. After I said thank you, I did suggest that when the first pothole appeared, they call the other George Bush—their governor!

✑ During a trip to Washington that fall, George and I went to the Smithsonian National Portrait Gallery where they unveiled his portrait by artist Ron Sherr. This perhaps is my favorite portrait of George, although Ron just finished painting a joint portrait of George and George W., which hangs in George's Library. It would be tough to choose between the two.

There are many paintings of George scattered in different clubs, museums, schools, and so on. One day we were led into a room and told that there was a big surprise awaiting us. Was there ever! There was a life-size portrait of a total stranger. We were told that the portrait was by a "very famous artist." Before I could ask who we were looking at, we were told that the artist had studied many pictures of George and how did we like it? We were speechless for a moment and then fumbled around saying nice things. Then we were told that the artist was here and this was the moment to get him to change anything we did not like. Ha! How about the whole thing? Both of us remembered the story about the woman who went to the funeral home to view her husband. The funeral director asked her how she thought he looked. She said that he looked well, but that she had asked them to bury him in his blue suit and he was in a gray suit. The director said: "I'm so sorry, madam. We'll take care of that right away." At which time he turned and yelled into another room: "Joe, change the heads on #5 and #7." That's just what we felt like saying. Some place that I shall not name is a portrait of George Bush that looks no more like him than the man in the moon!

✎ Kevin Costner and Don Johnson were in Houston that fall making the movie *Tin Cup* and we asked them for dinner one night. While waiting for Don, I asked Kevin to please do me a favor and walk down the street with me. I asked him to ring Mildred Kerr's door and tell her he was on a scavenger hunt and needed a green umbrella or something. Mildred answered the door and there stood this famous movie star. She was stunned and stammered. I stepped out of the shadows and she really laughed. When Don Johnson arrived an hour later, he did the same thing for me. The only problem was that Mildred had NO idea who Don Johnson was!

✎ In late November, George and I flew to Frankfurt, Germany, where he was to speak. We stayed in The Schlosshotel Kronberg. This house was built around 1880 for the Empress Frederick, the widow of Frederick III, king of Prussia and the German emperor, and the mother of Wilhelm II, known to the world as Kaiser Wilhelm. The empress was the firstborn daughter of Queen Victoria of England. Had there not been a male heir born, she would have inherited the British throne. As it was, she and Frederick expected to inherit the throne of Prussia and Germany, but his father lived to be ninety-one. Frederick finally inherited, came down with cancer, reigned for ninety-nine days, and died. The empress wrote her mother, Queen Victoria: "I disappear with him."

The empress died in this house. It is enormous and filled with portraits, treasures, and books, many of them in English. The parks and gardens reflect those in England. The ceilings downstairs are 24 feet high, I believe, and are maybe 18 feet on the second floor. Our suite was large and spacious with an entry hall, a large sitting room, an equally large bedroom, and a bath. The woodwork is lovely, the furniture old and fine. Ceilings are carved wood, floors are covered with beautiful oriental rugs, etc. This hotel suite was certainly worthy of an empress.

On this same trip we flew on to Amsterdam where we saw our longtime friend Rudd Lubbers, the former prime minister of the Netherlands. Her Majesty Queen Beatrix invited us for lunch, so after George's speech we raced to The Hague, where George changed into golf clothes. We had a light lunch and George and Prince Claus went to play golf. Her Majesty lent me some rubber boots, and she and I walked in her gardens with their two little dogs. Over the years Her Majesty and the prince have been very kind to us. We have found them to be interesting and interested in the world and many causes. She and George have had some very fascinating discussions on many different subjects.

This time the discussion was about Rudd Lubbers, who had been nominated to head NATO. The Dutch government put him up for the job when it looked like he had universal approval. French president Jacques Chirac had spoken to George about it at the Rabin funeral and later spoke to President Clinton about it through a car window. John Major had spoken to President Clinton, saying that they approved of Rudd. George had spoken to Secretary of State Warren Christopher about it on *Air Force One* on the way home from the funeral. Rudd went to the United States to be interviewed, which George felt was degrading. Two days later, with no word from Washington, the Dutch government put his name forward for NATO chief, assuming that silence meant approval. Wrong. Washington didn't approve, the humiliation factor was huge, and our friend Rudd was horribly embarrassed. Rudd is now serving as the High Commissioner for Refugees for the United Nations.

On our walk through the garden Her Majesty brought up the subject again. She said that she had mentioned her disappointment to administration officials when she was in Washington the previous week for the opening of the Johannes Vermeer show at the National Art Gallery. She was told the administration knew nothing about the matter. The queen felt someone was lying to somebody.

We attended a large dinner that night, and the next morning George left for Bombay, India, and lucky me, I flew home to Houston.

∽ All of that year I had some problems with my hips and knees. Neither traveled too well, and I took to swimming a mile a day which I had done at the White House. This is a very gentle exercise and hurts *no* body parts. I am slowing down. I used to swim a mile in forty minutes and now it takes me an hour. I am still swimming. Exercise is of great importance in our family. I try either to work out on a bike, on the Roman table (a torture table that strengthens the lower back muscles), lift weights, or swim a mile. Some days I do both and then have a little trouble staying awake beyond 8:30 p.m.

∽ After two days in India, George returned home. He is an amazing man and after a good night's sleep, he was at the office early the next morning. It is hard to believe, but we were at the annual Cancer League, Inc. awards ceremony at lunchtime that day. They raised $100,000, and we managed to get in and out before the lunch and fashion show. Just as George had announced when he was sixty-five years old that he no longer ate broccoli, I announced that I no longer went to fashion shows. I guess looking at me that does not surprise anyone!

At the eight o'clock service at St. Martin's Church that Sunday the sound system was off and the minister got up and said that he hoped we could hear him. He said that this had happened during another preacher's sermon and when the church engineer was asked what had happened, he said: "There's a nut loose by the mike!"

∽ In December, we gave a small dinner at our house for David Frost, the British reporter who does such interesting and fair interviews. Back in 1991, right after the Gulf War ended, David had asked George if he could come and debrief George, Brent Scowcroft, Marlin Fitzwater, and me about the war while the memories were still fresh. He taped the debriefings at Camp David. I sat in on one meeting with my diary open. My contribution was to say what other things of import were happening and who was visiting during those trying months. Brent, Marlin, and George recalled the planning, phone calls, dealings with Congress, the tensions, the press reporting that there would be a need of fifty thousand body bags, and so on. After two days of debriefings David gave George the reels. He never asked for a thing. He did a great service and the tapes are now part of the archives at The George Bush Library Center.

⌒ I attended several school Christmas programs, one at The Barbara Bush Elementary School and one at Kinkaid, where Neil's darling daughter Ashley sang. We went to Washington to speak and to see some of our family before Christmas. First we visited with Marvin and Margaret and children: Marshall, Walker, and Abigail Meyer. Abigail really isn't our grandchild, but she and Marshall have been inseparable since childhood. Abigail calls us Gampy and Ganny and we love her. The children looked marvelous and their parents relaxed and happy. Margaret was studying theater in New York City several days a week and looked radiant. She is still acting and manages to be in several plays a year and balance family life perfectly.

I went on to see daughter Doro and Bobby Koch and their children, Sam, Ellie, and Robert. The house was beautifully decorated for Christmas, and three-year-old Robert was really excited about Santa. Sam and Ellie were so sweet with Robert, who was the most loving, squeezable little fella—well, not so little.

I flew to San Diego to christen the world's largest container ship, the OOCL* *America*, for our old friends from Hong Kong, C. H. and Betty Tung. It was a beautiful day. The ship had five thousand personnel on board and held almost five thousand containers. If this much cargo were on a train, the train would be twenty miles long! The cere-

*OOCL stands for Orient Overseas Container Line.

mony was simple. We had known the Tungs for many years. C.H.'s father, C. Y. Tung of Hong Kong, had been so kind to us when we were living in the People's Republic of China. Imagine our surprise that C.H. became the chief executive of Hong Kong when, after a hundred years of British rule, Hong Kong reverted peacefully back to the People's Republic of China in 1997.

⮝ Christmas Eve, George and I went to the 9 p.m. service at St Martin's. Our minister Dennis Maynard told a funny story about a little boy who wanted a big red bike for Christmas, and so he wrote Santa a letter: "Dear Santa: I have been a good boy. I have done my chores and homework. I have obeyed my mom and dad. Please leave me a big red bike." Well, he got thinking about it and decided that wasn't enough, and so he wrote a letter to Jesus: "Dear Jesus, I really want a big red bike for Christmas. I have attended church, learned my lessons, obeyed the commandments." Then he got thinking that was not enough. He crept downstairs, went to the family crèche, very carefully lifted the mother Mary out of the scene, and crept back up the stairs. He wrapped the figure of Mary in Kleenex and tucked her away in the back of his closet. Then he continued his letter to Jesus. "And if you ever want to see your mother again . . ." Dennis gets your attention with marvelous stories and then gives fine sermons.

We also went by Neil and Sharon's, who had some close friends over with their children. Their house was lovely, filled with Christmas decorations, great food, and music. Some neighbors came by in a horse-drawn carriage and sang carols, and as we were leaving, Santa arrived. It was a sweet night.

Christmas Day, the Neil Bushes came to us for our tree and Christmas lunch. That night, we went to Lee and Joe Jamail's for their great annual Mexican buffet dinner. Joe is a famous trial lawyer, and both he and Lee are among the most generous givers in Texas. Many, many of our friends go to their annual dinner, a relaxed, informal come-and-go event for Christmas night.

The Tuesday after Christmas, our grandson Jebby arrived from Florida. I drove him out to watch his grandfather play tennis with Pete Sampras against the Houston Country Club pro David Dowlen and our friend Jack Blanton. As Pete was playing "polite tennis," George can now say that he is one of the few people who lost with Pete Sampras as his partner! During lunch Pete said that he loved golf, and so Jeb, George, Pete, and I played nine holes of golf. The golf wasn't very good, but it was fun. Pete and Jebby looked like brothers, and Pete was so sweet to Jeb. As we walked off the course, Jeb—who had started with a bang and faltered along the way—looked at his grandfather and said, "Next summer." He is a true Bush and very competitive.

We saw the New Year in at El Tule, our friend Nancy Negley's ranch in Falfurrias, Texas, surrounded by dear friends. So ended 1995.

*The Oak Ridge Boys and their wives visit us in Kennebunkport,
August 1996. From left: Duane and Norah Lee Allen,
Richard and Donna Sterban, George and Barbara Bush,
Brenda and William Golden, and Mary and Joe Bonsall.*
FAMILY SCRAPBOOK

In early January George and I went to the People's Republic of China again, this time with Martha and Mike Bowlin, who had replaced our friend Lod Cook as the chairman of ARCO. On this trip we stayed at the Palace Hotel on Goldfish Lane, Wangfujing, Beijing. Wangfujing used to be the street where we rode our bikes to buy stamps, and I remember when we first went to see the "new" department store named for the street around 1975. The Chinese stood ten deep with their mouths literally hanging down to their chins.

A year later the diplomatic community could talk of nothing else when Madame Chiang Ching, Chairman Mao's wife, designed some dresses that looked like something Eleanor Roosevelt would have worn. Wonderful as she was, Mrs. Roosevelt was not known for her great, stylish wardrobe. They were put in the department store window, and George and I rode our bikes down to see them. One must remember that in 1975 everyone dressed in Mao suits (at least that's what they wore in public). The street in front of the department store was jammed with folks peering over heads and under arms to see the dresses that were way too costly for them to buy. It was suggested that maybe they could copy them, but I never saw anything that resembled these dresses on people. Perhaps they had better taste than Madame Mao.

Today the street is largely changed although the department store is still there. Now here we were twenty-one years later, and I saw a CNN program discussing and showing the most gorgeous evening clothes with unbelievably stylish lines and made out of fabulous materials by Chinese designers. They have come a long, long way.

One night we had dinner with an old friend, Liu Huaqui, and his wife. He was in charge of all American affairs and had just been given another job, similar to our national security adviser. The conversation was on the same subjects we covered in September the year before: the U.S. elections; the relationship between Taiwan and the People's Republic of China; Boris Yeltsin; and the upcoming changeover in Hong Kong in 1997, when it would transfer hands from Great Britain to China. Amazing that when we lived there in 1974 we thought that 1997 was forever away.

On this trip we visited with several vice premiers and with President Jiang Zemin. I love sitting in on these meetings. The president and George exchanged all sorts of thoughts on many subjects. He is a very interesting man, has knowledge of the world, and seems to have a real sense of humor.

We went to Seoul, South Korea, after Beijing, and among other things, George had breakfast with President Kim. Have you ever noticed how many Koreans are named Kim? Lots.

We got a phone call at 5:30 a.m. on January 12 (it was still January 11 in the United States) telling us that Georgia Grace Koch had been born that morning. The baby was fine, and her mother was well. Gigi was named after her two grandfathers, George Koch and George

Bush, and Doro's great-aunt, Grace Walker. We talked to a happy Doro, who said that the baby was "perfect and tiny"—she weighed in at 8 pound 8 ounces! Obviously Doro produces BIG babies.

Before the birth, Bobby Koch had moved Doro and their son Robert to The Four Seasons Hotel, as Washington had a horrible blizzard and another big storm was on the way. The older children, Sam and Ellie, had gone to stay with friends. Bobby wanted to be sure that the baby was delivered at the hospital and not at home or in a car stranded in a snow bank.

We left Houston on January 8 and were back on the 12th. This is a typical George Bush trip! But I'd rather go than be left behind.

On January 18, I went out to San Diego to attend a luncheon for a hospital that my former aide, Casey Healey Killblane, was interested in and asked me to visit. Casey had worked for me in the White House and is still very dear to me. After the luncheon, my aide Quincy Hicks and I went to the Navy's submarine base to visit the USS *Houston*. It was fun to see "my" ship, as I had christened it fifteen years before in Newport News, Virginia. My great friend Andy Stewart had been my "Maid of Honor."* Admiral Rickover, known as the father of the "nuclear Navy," was there, along with Secretary of the Navy, John Lehman. George told me that the Navy had just made the admiral step down and John had accepted Rickover's resignation—although he hadn't submitted it! At this time Admiral Rickover was very old and very controversial. It was a little tense, but the spry, feisty admiral led the tour of this very compact submarine.

Through the years the commanders have sent me reports on the *Houston*. The present commander had written that it was being overhauled, and he'd love to have me come by if I was going to be in the area.

The ship has over a hundred crew members and it is tiny; it is largely comprised of engines and motors. I believe that they said there were two bathrooms for a hundred men. They sleep in three tiers of

---

*A Navy tradition that means nothing more than I was allowed to invite a friend to come with me.

Visiting the USS Houston *submarine in San Diego, January 1996. I felt a personal connection with the ship since I had christened it fifteen years earlier. Please note all the sailors are looking at my beautiful assistant Quincy Hicks.*
FAMILY SCRAPBOOK

bunks separated by about two feet. The officers have a slightly better deal. It was crowded, and we decided that it took a special type of person to serve on a sub, which can stay down sometimes for two months without surfacing. We crammed into a crew room, and they permitted me to present the "Sailor of the Year" award. I might say that my beautiful Quincy had all the sailors smiling and maybe even drooling. I told them that George Bush didn't miss Washington, but he sure missed the military. The Commander said he knew he shouldn't say this, but they all missed George.

January 27—Awakened this morning to see a CNN special on parents telling their children about SEX. It said that you should bring the subject up yourself and answer all the questions that your children ask. It reminded me of our experience with the present governor of Texas. George W. spent the night Jebby was born with Randy Roden, the son of one of my GYN doctors. Jake Roden was a dear friend, and he told me that he had thoroughly educated George on babies and sex that night. I was so surprised as George was only 7½ years old. I thought he was way too young. But our dear friends Jake and Gloria were much more liberal than we were—at least than I was—on that subject. I believe that GB thought it was fine. Well, several years later George and I took young Baine Kerr and George W. to the Texas-Oklahoma game in Dallas. To kill time before the game we walked the fairgrounds where the Texas State Fair was in full swing. We came across a scientific display and went in. There was a line going through the building, and as we progressed we found ourselves walking past pictures with a voice describing the birth of a baby. Suddenly, in a loud voice, George W. asked: "Where the heck does this birth canal come out anyway?" It was amazing. The room emptied, and there we were alone with our son. Even young Baine left. So much for Jake's great explanation. I wonder today with all the sexually explicit magazines, movies, and television if a 9- or 10-year-old would ask the same question? I doubt it.

This reminds me of another story, involving one of our great-nephews. He and his dad had a deal that when the child wanted to talk "off the record," he said something like, "Can we go into the closet, Dad?" That meant they could talk and whatever he said or confessed to, he wouldn't be scolded. So he asked his dad if they could go into the closet. Off they went to a quiet place and the child said, "Dad, what does 'dick' mean?" The father, choosing his words very carefully, went into what that slang word meant and that it was not a nice word. The child's face showed total amazement. "Dad," he said, "you are never going to believe this. There is a kid in my class named Dick!" Now that is funny, but there is a moral to this story which may well explain just why these children are so very nice. These are two gentle parents who listen to their children.

In February, we had a marvelous trip to England. While George did business, I visited Eton, where Sir Antony Acland was the provost. We knew the Aclands in Washington when he was the British ambassador. Antony and Jenny were two of the most popular people on Embassy Row and lots of fun.

The drive out to Eton was so interesting, and it occurred to me that I never see the countryside on our many trips to England or, for that matter, any foreign country. It was a forty-five-minute trip out, and as we got close, Windsor Castle appeared on the horizon. We went through several small towns and saw the famous entrance to Windsor, down which the queen makes her approach to the Royal Ascot race in a horse-drawn buggy. The town snuggles up to the castle. A little further on we crossed the Thames and soon we came to Eton's campus. This school is five hundred years old and very stately. There were boys on the campus wearing tails or morning coats. We had a lovely lunch with around fifteen of Jenny and Antony's friends, almost all of whom were friends of ours, too. I rarely remember meals, but this one was perfect. It started off with a nest of very small crisp fried onions on which sat tiny quail eggs. On the side was a hollowed-out lime filled with hollandaise sauce. This was followed by a fish course, a salad, and an apple dish for dessert. It was just right: pretty to the eye, delicious, and light. After lunch, Antony gave me a quick tour of the school and the beautiful chapel. Nearby we went into several rooms where the walls were covered with the names of past students. Antony showed me the great poet Shelley's; Antony's own name and that of his father; Foreign Minister Douglas Hurd's, and so many more all carved into the walls.

I read *The Horse Whisperer* by Nicholas Evans on this trip and enjoyed it very much.

> *February* 10—I could kill Jack Fitch—not really. But he brought George some Band-Aids that you put on your nose to keep one from snoring. He says that he wears them every night. Well, George never used them, but tucked them away and last night I had sinus [problems] and told George that I was afraid that I was going to keep him awake and would go into the guest room. He said, "Don't go into the guest room, try the Fitch snoring cure." I did, and George told me that I still snored AND, to add insult to injury, this morning when I pulled the darn thing off, I also pulled off the skin on my nose. Ugly!

ꙮ We did many local charitable events, all of which were pretty much the same. The one exception was the dinner we attended for The Museum of Printing History. Our schedule stated that the speaker was to talk for forty-five minutes, after the usual introductory talks. I was moaning before we even left home about the length of the evening as I was tired, having spoken at a luncheon that very day for The Children's Museum, which my friend Charlene Pate asked me to do.

The speaker was Paul Harvey. It was fascinating. For forty-five minutes Paul spoke and not one of the four hundred people in the room moved, shifted in their seats, looked bored, or was glad when it ended. He was spectacular. Maybe the best speaker I have ever heard. He was so funny AND—that voice! What a delivery. The next day I was walking with Baine and Mildred Kerr and was raving over the speech. They asked me what he said. I couldn't really tell them what his speech was about, just that he was spellbinding. I finally remembered that he was patriotic and pithy. (I love that word.) When pushed, the only thing I could remember that he said was, "If life were logical, all men would ride side saddle." How the Kerrs laughed.

Both George and I read James Patterson's *Hide & Seek* on a trip to visit Bayard Sharp in Boca Grande, Florida. It was really a scary book. He writes very much like Mary Higgins Clark in that his chapters are short and his novels are very suspenseful—except much scarier! James really surprised me by writing the most sensitive love story in 2001, *Suzanne's Diary for Nicholas.* I wept several times and loved that book. It was interesting that both John Grisham and David Baldacci also wrote very sensitive books in 2001—John's *A Painted House* and David's *Wish You Well.*

February ended with a trip that started in Seattle with my friend Andy Stewart. Andy was to go as my traveling aide, but then I realized that we both needed an aide if we were to get any place on time. So dear Quincy came along to take care of us both. We ended in Hawaii and visited our friend Esther Moore for several days before a speech I was to give there.

On the way out I read part of *Chicken Soup for the Soul,* a compilation of anecdotes. They are very sweet and thought-provoking. This book got me to thinking that while we are apt to be polite and kind to strangers and friends, do we sometimes forget our husbands and wives and take them for granted, not to mention our children? Do we remember to say "please" and "thank you"? Do we remember to say, "I love you"? We are grateful and we do love, but maybe we are just out of the habit of telling people. Shouldn't children hear and see more love and kindness at home?

I love the story of the wife who told her husband that she was leaving him after thirty-five years of marriage. The husband was shocked and asked, "Why?" The wife answered that in thirty-five years of marriage he had never once told her that he loved her. He said, "Now wait a minute. I told you the day that we were married that I loved you and that I would tell you if I ever changed my mind!"

That is not good enough. We must tell each other what we feel.

Before finishing this trip, Andy and I went to Seattle; Bakersfield, Caliornia; Phoenix; and Hawaii. In Phoenix, after my talk, we went to have dinner with Patsy and Jack Caulkins. They were housemates with us in New Haven all those years ago after World War II, and we have remained good friends. They live in a marvelous retirement community on a golf course outside of Phoenix and are very happy there. Jack shared something with me that sort of fit in with what I had been thinking about. He said that when he was very sick, all five of his sons and his brother George came to see him at the hospital. Corky, their eldest, came to the bed, took his hand, and said: "I love you, Dad." Jack said he was very touched, but Corky continued: "Now, you tell me the same thing." So Jack, who was not at all comfortable doing it, told me he did. After that, each boy came to his dad's bedside and said and did the same thing. When his brother George approached his bed and told him that he loved him, Jack said that he was overwhelmed with such a feeling of love and emotion that he wept. He asked me if my George was affectionate with his boys and I could truthfully answer, "Yes, they do hug." Jack said that he had a terrible time being a "hugger" with his boys before that, and he just wanted to be sure that George experienced the same happiness. He is a darling, gentle man.

This brings me back to: Are we telling our families "thank you" and "I love you, Dad" enough?

The day I left home I had a postcard from Ruth Graham, Billy's wife, saying in essence that she missed me and loved me. George had just told me that Ruth was very ill and not expected to live more than forty-eight hours. I was heartbroken and so touched by her card. I love Ruth Graham, and the card was so typically nice of her. Thank God that both Jack Caulkins and Ruth Graham are still alive today as I write this in 2002, but it is another example of not only loving, but showing your love.

This is turning out to be a "love" lesson, but it seems so important. I received a letter from a dear friend who has had Parkinson's disease for years. I started to say "suffered" from Parkinson's disease, but this friend is so generous and puts on such a great front that although it has been very tough, that word connotes so many things that she isn't. She gave her husband for his birthday an essay a month. Her first essay was on love:

These days when I go to parties and gatherings of all kinds, I've begun to feel the collective goodwill of my friends in supportive acknowledgement of my neurological predicament. It manifests itself as an extra pat on the back, an extra warm kiss on the cheek, an extra big hug, an over-generous compliment, and every so often a "hang in there" message of encouragement. All this makes me feel . . . well, loved.

When I got sick, my greatest fear was that my friends would pity me. Pity would have turned me into pitiful, pitiable, and I was not prepared to play that role. I'm still not. Fortunately, not one layer of friends-acquaintances has made me feel the least bit pitiful or pitiable. I am very aware that in order to incorporate me into their busy lives, they must slow down to match my erratic, unpredictable rhythms, but they do it so thoughtfully and naturally that I can't feel anything but gratitude. As for the family, both immediate and extended, they have been the constant sources of support from the start. These days, granddaughters take my arm at the slightest hint of a rough spot. Grandsons gently help me up after a fall. As it is with my friends, I am rarely aware of the family machinations involved in fitting the unpredictable me into their supercharged lives. To have such a lovely cushion of support is to understand the power of love.

I can't help harking back to a trip I took to an orphanage in Bucharest, Romania. Under the Ceauşescus, the government encouraged families to produce many children in order to create a pool of labor for the state. Many of them were sent to orphanages, with the understanding that the parents would retrieve them at some later date. As most of the parents were unable to feed what children they already had, these children, supposedly on loan and therefore not able to be adopted by anyone else, languished in orphanages till they reached the age when they could be useful to the state. At that point they became the slaves of the government, undertaking such efforts as the Ceauşescus felt necessary. Many—several thousand in fact—were put to work building the largest standing building in the world, The Palace of the People. Contrary to its name, the "palace" was solely planned as a monument to the Ceauşescus.

The children I was taken to visit were the youngest, those not yet walking. Some of them were tiny infants in cribs, perhaps a dozen or so, lined up in a long, dimly lit corridor. A woman whom I judged to be a nurse (although she fell far short of our image of the kindly, clean, and caring nurses of our experience), wearing a dingy, spotted apron and a martyred, sour, sour, bordering-on-anger expression on her face, trudged from crib to crib, bending over just far enough to place the nipple of the bottle in each tiny mouth. Not for one second during the entire process did a human hand make a contact with a baby. When I asked why the babies weren't held by a nurse while being fed, the doctor who accompanied me said that this was an unskilled nurse who knew no better. But I noticed he made no comment to the nurse. I also subsequently learned that the neglect was intentional, because the thinking was that once you picked up the baby, he might want to be picked up again, and that would be all together too time-consuming.

As I became more aware of my surroundings, I realized

how unnaturally quiet it was in that corridor, despite the presence of so many babies. I also noticed how dull-eyed and listless the babies were. They looked like little shriveled old men. Something I learned in my psychology class long ago came back to me, and I realized that I was witnessing for the first time, first hand, the tragic results of the withholding of love. Like an unwatered plant, a baby denied love and attention shrivels in its absence and could even die from lack of it, even if he is adequately fed. I wondered at the time how many of these cruelly neglected creatures would actually survive.

Like these babies, I feel that I too might have shriveled by now if I hadn't had the abundance of love to sustain me. Keep it up, oh my friends and family!

This all reminded me of a verse from a favorite hymn that I like for a blessing before a meal:

For the joy of human love
Brother, sister, parent, child
Friends on earth, and friends above
For all gentle thoughts and mild
Lord of all to thee we raise
This our hymn of grateful praise

❧ That spring it seemed George and I passed like ships in the night. George spent seventeen days traveling in the Middle East. I missed him, and also worried every minute he was there. Saddam Hussein was then still a real danger. Meanwhile, I traveled all over the United States. At one time we met up at Sunnylands, Lee and Walter Annenberg's beautiful home in Rancho Mirage, Caliornia, before going off in different directions again. Besides being surrounded by great beauty, we were with two very dear generous people. During George's last afternoon, we turned on TV and watched Greg Norman play the most amazing golf and end 6 up on the Saturday of the Masters Tournament. Sunday, the Annenbergs and I saw the saddest thing I had ever seen on a golf course. From the first hole it was obvious that Greg was "off his game." Having started 6 up, by the end of the tournament he was 4 down. It was heartbreaking, and he will go down in the record books as the man who lost with the biggest lead on the last day. It was so bad that the winner, Nick Faldo, hugged him when it was over.

In 2001, George invited Greg and Laura Norman to stop by for the night and a golf game. They were putting their daughter in Boston College and helicoptered up to Kennebunkport in the middle of the afternoon. They are the nicest people. The moment they arrived, George suggested that we run out and play nine holes. So before I could think twice, I agreed and then wondered if I had lost my mind. George snagged our nephew Hap Ellis, a good golfer, who was fishing off our rocks, to join us. On the way up in the car I asked Greg when he had last played with someone who shoots 105. He looked slightly startled, rolled his eyes, and said that the very first time he played golf he shot 105! We really had fun and got in our nine holes in less than an hour and a half. With lots of strokes and a GREAT partner, Hap and I won. I am thinking of having a T-shirt made up saying: "I played golf with Greg Norman and beat him!"

In April, during a trip to Los Angeles, we went by to see Ronald Reagan at his office. This was so very sad. He looked wonderful, and it was very clear that he had absolutely no idea who we were. It really made George very unhappy as he respected and loved Ron very much. He still was innately polite, and yet one got the feeling that he was faking. We didn't stay very long, and as we left, George told him that we just wanted to say hello, that we missed him, and loved him. He answered something like, "You must drop in anytime." He looked so confused, like he knew he should have remembered us or something. That was the last time I saw Ron. I won't remember the man we saw that day. I will remember that gentle, wise, decent, warm, funny man. We think of Nancy, knowing the pain she must feel. He is still alive as I write this six years later.

I must have been on lots of planes that spring for I read and enjoyed many books: *Guilty as Sin* by Tami Hoag; *In the Presence*

of the Enemy by Elizabeth George; and *The Persian Pickle Club,* a wonderful short novel by Sandra Dallas. I read a lot looking for books
that I think George would like. He reads so many briefing papers
and loves to relax by reading good books and mysteries. Lucky me,
as I love to read and can blame my spending so much time reading
on George.

    ❦ We worked our way up to Maine that spring. George
spoke or did events in Orlando, Florida; Manassas, Virginia; and
Washington, D.C. I flew to Baltimore and spoke at 8:15 a.m. to an
estimated twelve thousand people in the Baltimore Arena for a Peter
Lowe event, which are motivational seminars. As it was held in the
ice rink, it was not only very early, but very cold! These people
would sit through eight hours of speeches that day. You might well
wonder just how a person who makes the same New Year's resolution
every year and breaks it the very first week could possibly motivate
anyone to do anything? (I'm sure I don't have to tell you what that
resolution is.)

I went from there to King of Prussia, Pennsylvania, to a luncheon
at the Valley Forge Convention Center for the Baptist Children's Services. I had a nice visit with Lee Annenberg and my good friend Bertie
Bell, and they brought with them Marsha Rothman, whose husband is
the great neurosurgeon. Bertie's husband George was a childhood
friend of my George's, and we have known Bertie and loved her since
1948! One of the joys of traveling is seeing friends.

From there I drove to Valley Forge Military Academy and College and met up with George. At 3 p.m. George and I were awarded
the Bob Hope Five Star Award. We did a very long receiving line,
and then George spoke to the Corps in the loveliest chapel. It was
like an old English movie—*Goodbye Mr. Chips* maybe. So sweet. Then
it was back to the president's house, another receiving line with pictures, and a lovely dinner. How do I remember all this? Because I was
about to go to the Mayo Clinic for my first hip replacement and
standing for hours was agony. I bet every picture that spring looked
cross-eyed!

We flew to Maine that night, and it was so exciting to get to our summer home. There were Ariel, Paula, Don Rhodes, and Millie. What a joy to see all four of them who had driven up the week before. Three of the four had done the most marvelous job of opening Walker's Point, and the fourth was really glad to see us.

George had given me an adorable, bright blue Chevrolet convertible, and on my first day in Maine, I jumped in it, and although it was slightly cold, put the top down and drove to the hardware store downtown. I felt about thirty years old.

In 2001, he arranged for me to have a dark blue TransAm. Now that is a convertible! I still felt thirty with the top down as I glided down the street in this high-powered car. The car presented a problem with the grandchildren, who felt it was much more appropriate for them to drive than me. They were right, but I honestly could not see letting children drive a car whose speedometer reads up to 150 miles an hour. We then had seven grandchildren with licenses, and three more who would have learner's permits and licenses in another year. I resisted the pleading eyes. Marvin called the car the "Bat Mobile." Now how should I have taken that?

George went to Miami almost immediately after arriving in Maine for a fund-raising luncheon that Jeb's wife Columba was putting on for Ballet Folklorico. Colu has worked hard for years to help promote this program that not only brings the ballet to schoolchildren, but also brings the culture of Mexico to them. I teased George and told him that he was going for the "best in-law award," as he had done a dinner for Sharon Bush, a reception for Bobby Koch, and now a luncheon for Columba, all in a few weeks. I could turn that around and say that all our in-law children are "Points of Light" and work hard to make the world a better place. Margaret Bush, a cancer survivor, works for the cure and for the Gladney Home, where she and Marvin adopted their two children. We all know that Laura has been very active in reading, education, and the support of libraries.

From Miami, George flew to Pensacola, Florida, where he spoke at a naval aviation banquet. He told me the evening was a joy. I wrote in my diary:

George was introduced by the Chief of Naval Operations, Admiral Boorda, a decent man George knew and respected. A week later he had taken his life by walking outdoors and shooting himself in the head. *Newsweek* magazine was about to come out with a story that said that he was wearing a ribbon that he was not eligible to wear. The ribbon with a "V" on it showed that he had been in combat off the shores of Vietnam. The ship was not in actual combat, but all ships stationed there during certain dates were eligible for the "V" on their ribbons. A year ago *Newsweek* started looking into this story, and they were, as I said, about to break it. Admiral Boorda removed the "V" at that time although Admiral Zumwalt* and others said it was justified. George believes that since the Navy had been under such fire for many reasons,† this decent Admiral just didn't want to add to their problems. He left notes that said the same.

An ironic footnote to this tragic story: It came out later that officially Admiral Boorda was eligible to have the "V" on his ribbon.

     ◆ I also flew to Florida in May to speak to five hundred spouses at the American Association of Management General Agents Luncheon. They were a wonderful audience, responsive and generous.

That afternoon I went to Epcot Center at Disney World, where David Valdez, our official photographer during both the vice president and White House years, arranged a marvelous tour of the Festival of Flowers for me. A darling young cousin of George's, Lucy Carney, and Dave's wife Sarah joined us. It was a drizzly day, which kept the crowds down and as I was "wash and wear," I did not care if I got a little damp. We visited several pavilions and watched fireworks across the lagoon while we ate dinner. There is something so clean about the whole Disney organization. (I have also been to Euro Disney and Disneyland.) The grounds are fabulous. The employees have a dress code. There is

---

*Admiral Bud Zumwalt, who was retired at this time, had a very distinguished Navy career, including being the youngest four-star admiral in the history of the Navy and the youngest person ever to serve as chief of naval operations.

†Some of the controversies swirling around the Navy at that time (and all of which have been cleared) included improper procurement procedures for the F-18 fighter jet and a cheating scandal at the Naval Academy in Annapolis.

nothing smutty about the place. I felt good about the world after an afternoon and evening spent there.

The next day I spoke at a fund-raiser for The Salvation Army. I am especially fond of the Army, which is made up of the most unselfish people I know. The money they raised at this luncheon went to a shelter for women and children.

∾ Life was not all work. We were playing a lot of golf, and George had a great trip to Pine Valley to play golf with Dan Quayle; Tom Kelly, a friend of Dan's and ours from Indiana, and his dad Jim; Nick Brady; and three Walker Cup* players.

And the summer started in a typical fashion. George invited some friends from Dallas for lunch and then called me from the road to ask me if I thought it would be fun to take them by boat to Ogunquit to our favorite restaurant there, Barnacle Billy's. I said that I thought it would be fun, but what he was going to do about Lech Walesa, who was also arriving on that day? He said that Lech was coming on Memorial Day. I explained that Monday WAS Memorial Day. So the friends came after lunch, after Lech left, and we raced out to play golf.

Although he speaks little or no English, Lech was on a speaking tour of the United States. What a nice man. We had a great visit and were thrilled to show him a part of our life that we love. I gave him a tour of our house and Walker's Point, and seeing it through his eyes made me realize once again just how lucky George and I are. He asked a million questions, including how much everything cost. I finally came down to answering, "A lot."

Several weeks later, I went to nearby Portland to shop for bedspreads and a few things we needed to make our guesthouse a little more comfortable. I also went to a tremendous bookstore to stock up for reading for the Greek cruise we were about to take and for my upcoming hospital visit for the new hip. I wrote in my diary:

---

*The Walker Cup is a highly competitive bi-annual golf tournament between teams from the United States and the United Kingdom. This amateur competition is named for George's grandfather, George Herbert Walker, who helped start the event in 1921.

I now have 15 paper back books I want to read. Why does that make me feel so good? It's like having money in the bank or a fully-stocked pantry.

We then went on to Sam's Club, a great, mind-boggling store. My aide Quincy said that I should have taken President Walesa there. I would never have gotten him out!

Our summer, as usual, included many visitors, family and friends. George keeps us busy, and (he says this is not true) I know he is only happy when the beds on the Point are full. We can sleep thirty-four people and that is a lot of sheets and towels. To facilitate life I have put a note on the back of the bedroom doors:

BUSH CHILDREN AND GRANDCHILDREN

1. Please hang up damp towels and use twice if possible.
2. Try to make beds and keep room picked up . . . makes dusting and vacuuming easier.
3. Please collect your gear from around the house and keep it in your room.
4. If possible let the kitchen know your meal plans:

    —picnics
    —specific requests for you or your children.
    —missing a meal

5. Breakfast served from 8 to 9 a.m.—coffee beginning at 6:30 a.m. [It's really more like 5:30 a.m.!]
6. Please put dirty clothes outside your door every night.
7. Ask Paula if you can help her.
8. Above all—have a great time! This is our happiest time of the year!

I have at different times gone up to the dormitory on the top floor of the main house and waded through piles of wet towels and bathing suits, dirty socks, etc., to get to the unmade beds. I know they can read, but home is where the heart is and also where you can drop your things on the floor! I admit that the note was a little naive, but our houseguests (those who are unrelated, that is) often read the note and obey.

June 8—Today is my 71st birthday. I reminded George this morning that his Grandmother Walker (Ganny) at 70 or 71 could not come to our wedding as she had been thrown from a horse and broken her hip. I remember thinking: "That little old lady still rides a horse!" Now I am that little old lady!

∽ We left on our Greek cruise on June 12 with many friends and all our children and grandchildren who were able to come. As we left Walker's Point, we passed Jean Becker and Quincy Hicks, the staff we left behind, sitting in lawn chairs with beer cans in their hands. They had a big painted sign that said, TOUR OF WALKER'S POINT. GET YOUR TICKETS HERE. 25 CENTS.

We started this trip by going to Albania to visit our friends President and Mrs. Berisha at the presidential summer house. From the ship the beaches looked lovely, but the closer we got we realized that we were seeing fifty years of neglect under a dictatorship. The first impression from the harbor was of a rusty old hull about the size of a tug boat, half in and half out of the water. It was in a very prominent place, and all other boats that wanted to dock at the pier had to maneuver around it. As we drove to the neglected, run-down summer house, we passed the filthiest beaches. These people throw their garbage and bottles on the beach, and people were swimming in big surf off these rocky, dirty beaches. There was building going on, but there also was rubble everywhere. If real estate people are right—that the most important thing is "location, location, location"—this summer house had it, but that was all. The walks up and down the hill were cracked and stones were missing, the gardens were overgrown, the rooms unfurnished, and what was there was ugly.

That night, Sali and Liri Berisha came for dinner on the ship with their attractive son and their protocol chief. Liri told us that under the Communist dictator, Enver Hoxha, when three friends got together, "one was a spy." She also said that when three family members got together, "one was a spy." Sali talked about how isolated this country had been for fifty years under Hoxha, with the People's Republic of China as their only friend. Hoxha broke off that relationship when Nixon went to China, claiming that the Chinese were turning their back on Marx.

Our son Neil asked just how the country was doing, and the answer seemed very optimistic. Since the fall of Hoxha, the average annual income had gone from $200 to $800; inflation was down from 400 percent to 6 percent; unemployment was down from 20 percent to 8 percent. There frankly seemed to be some skepticism about all this optimism. Now we have been to the northern and southern part of Albania, and both are so run-down and poor.

      We had a lovely visit on the Greek Islands. I remember one day walking on the island of Erikoussa. My good friend Betsy Heminway and I walked to a lovely church and then through some winding streets to see farms and houses. The island was lush and filled with olive trees. George went on a long march with a more vigorous group and ran into a farmer who let him see olives being crushed and bottled. He gave the farmer his watch after the man gave him a bottle of virgin olive oil. The people with George said that it was a touching exchange between two men who didn't speak the same language.

This reminded me of the time when we were in Hungary and we arrived in a terrible thunderstorm. It was pouring rain. The president and his wife drove us to a square filled with people who had been waiting hours through the lightning and thunder to see and greet George, who was then president. Most of us got under umbrellas, but George refused. A Secret Serviceman insisted that George put on his stylish British Burberry raincoat. The president of Hungary gave a rather lengthy speech and introduced George. George stood up, tore up his speech, spoke from the heart, and then plunged into the crowd to shake hands. When he got to an older, absolutely sopping wet lady, he took off his raincoat and gave it to her. When he finally got back into the car sopping wet himself, I said, "George, how could you give away your raincoat?" He answered: "Bar, we have so much and she looked so wet and cold." He was shocked when I reminded him that the coat had not been his to give away; it was the agent's. He had forgotten. What a good, sweet, and generous man he is. He did replace the coat, but that agent must have been slightly surprised.

Why did the watch story remind me of that rainy day? George didn't have another watch with him.

Colin and Alma Powell were on this trip with us, and they were a joy. Alma is so serene, wise, and gentle, with a real twinkle, and Colin is so bright. I honestly felt that they loved getting away from all the speculation and urging for him to run for president. We all saw a side of Colin that I, for one, did not know. He learned the Greek dances and could dance with the best of the Greeks. I wrote in my diary:

June 20—When I got down to breakfast this morning I discovered that General Powell and the kids played Monopoly until 1 a.m. Pierce and Colin finally beat Jebby and Sam. Isn't that the dearest thing—playing monopoly with them at all. I wonder if these children realize that Colin Powell is probably the most popular man in the USA and was a great General. The children were tired today and why not?

After the trip I went right to Rochester, Minnesota, and had my hip replaced. I swore in the first chapter of this book I would spare you my aches, but I'm going to break my word by saying that I have now had two hip replacements and seven years later have forgotten that ever happened. Yea, Mayo Clinic and Dr. Bernie Morrey! I was playing golf in six weeks. I teased the doctor by saying that I thought he'd promised me that my game would improve. It didn't!

Jeb's youngest son Jebby played in chess tournaments all around the New England area that summer. He was twelve years old and often competed against thirty-five-year-old men and beat them. He came home from one tournament and claimed that he had won three out of five matches. It turned out he won one by default; and his grandfather explained that you can't count a default as a win. Jeb was a small twelve-year-old, and I would have loved to see the faces of the thirty-five-year-olds that he beat. I'm sure that they thought he would be a pushover! He got a little too confident, and one weekend Tom and Kathy Super (Kathy is George's scheduler) visited from Washington. Tom was kind enough to play with Jebby and whipped him pretty soundly several times.

It was also another summer of fishing for George and Jebby. How they love fishing, whether it is going after bonefish in southern waters, salmon in northern waters, or striped bass and bluefish right off the shores of Kennebunkport.

July 23—The days race by so quickly and are so happy that it is hard to keep up.

Our cousin Grace Holden was in the Wandby* with her husband and baby. The author Ric [Richard North] Patterson and his wife Laurie spent several days with us. George, Laura, and the girls; Doro, Robert, Ellie, Gigi and a baby-sitter all arrived on Sunday, and Sam and Bobby will follow soon. Jebby adores having the twins around and they are playing tennis and running around doing all sorts of things. I came in one night and found the twins, Jebby, Doro's Robert, and Neil's children all draped on the couches, watching television, and they reminded me of puppies. That night Marvin, Margaret, Marshall, and Walker arrived, and the children all raced over to say hello and then all jumped in the pool.

∽ George and I stole off to the Meadowlands in New Jersey to a Three Tenors concert. I hobbled a little, but hearing them was one of my goals after the hip operation. What a treat for us; I will never forget that night.

At the end of July we had a wonderful golfing visit from pro golfer Freddy Couples; CBS sports announcer Jim Nantz and his wife Lorrie; and our golf pro friend in Houston, Paul Marchand, and his wife Judi. The men all went out to play golf. It was an unusual "five-some"—Paul, Freddy, Jim, Ken Raynor—our dear friend and the golf pro at Cape Arundel Golf Course—and one of my Georges as George W. and George H.W. took turns. One day Lorrie, Judi, Anne Raynor, and I played. That was the day that Fred Couples broke the course record at Cape Arundel by one stroke with a 62. This club is over a

---

*One of the guest cottages at Walker's Point, named for a ship that had run aground in 1921 near where the cottage now sits.

*The day Freddy Couples broke the Cape Arundel Golf Course record
in Kennebunkport, July 1996. From left: Paul Marchand,
Jim Nantz, George Bush, and Freddy.*
FAMILY SCRAPBOOK

hundred years old, and many people have come close, but Freddy Couples succeeded on that day. Excitement ran high. By the way, the course record was once held by George's father, Prescott Bush, who shot a 64 there.

On the next night of that visit we had the nuttiest time. Some friends from Texas sent a marvelous barbeque dinner from Fort Worth, so Pop decided to gather a crowd. Then out of the blue the CEO of a large insurance company called. His board was meeting in the area and included two gentlemen from the People's Republic of China. He wondered if he could bring them by to call on George. NATURALLY George invited them all to the barbeque. So we had eight insurance people, two Chinese, the three golfers and wives, Ken and Anne Raynor, our cousins Debbie and Craig Stapleton, Doro, and George W. and Laura. (We also fed Marvin, Margaret, Marshall, and Walker as they had to leave early to return to Washington with friends who offered them a ride home on a private plane.) Then the younger set—Jenna, Barbara, Jebby, Sam, Ellie, and Robert—all ate in the kitchen before our dinner. Ariel and Paula did a great job. It is not easy to serve two groups, not to mention three, unless you run a restaurant.

When we have a group like this I usually take a pack of cards, cut them in half, and set the table with a red half, black half, red half, etc. I then ask the guests to choose a half—red for girls and black for boys—and ask them to find the other half of their card and sit there.

This night I cheated a little and set the Chinese next to my George. By chance, I had golfers Freddy Couples, Jim Nantz, and Ken Raynor and several others at my little table. One of the insurance ladies sat down and said, "I hope you are not going to talk about golf. It bores me!" As I recall, we bored her.

After dinner George showed a very funny tape that his office had put together of our bloopers. It is funny, but the poor Chinese could not understand a tape that made fun of a former president and his wife.

Then, to add insult to injury, Jebby and Sam filled a bathtub with balloons filled with water and lobbed them at the Secret Service guard house and guests as they departed. They were so pleased with their results that they went outside and threw the balloons at anything that moved. Overcome with success, they then went to another guard-house, opened the door, and bombarded the agent! The agents didn't squeal on the boys, but the Point was covered with broken balloons the next day and an unnamed younger grandchild told his mother, who passed it on to me.

I got really caught around that time for it was clear that someone had urinated in the sauna drain. I immediately blamed Sam and Jebby. For some reason Sam apologized and Jebby claimed innocence. Lo and behold, the same unnamed grandchild squealed on two of the grand-daughters and I had to apologize to the boys. I wrote in my diary: "I am way too old for this."

One day in particular when I was very annoyed by all the wet towels I found on the bathroom floor, and the constant opening and closing of the refrigerator door in the kitchen, all the half-drunk cans of sodas left sitting around, and all the barking dogs that didn't belong to us but to our children—I turned to George in exasperation and told him I was going to have to go out and scold them, just like I did forty years ago. Then he gave me some very important advice which I will now pass on to you: "Be nice to your kids. They'll choose your nursing home."

✐ August started with a party that George's Uncle Louis and Aunt Grace Walker had celebrating the 100th anniversary of their house, a cottage on Ocean Avenue. The house, called Inglesia, had been sold, and this was to be a farewell to a happy house and a happy birthday. The party rapidly outgrew the house and was at the River Club. It was a wonderful family and friends gathering with lots of funny stories by the children. Their son Jimmy told the story of his mother visiting him when he was stationed in Japan. She promptly fell in love with the art, landscapes, and anything Japanese. Shortly after they returned to this country, she and Lou passed a movie theater where Grace saw SATSUNMO on the marquee and insisted that Lou turn around, go back, and inquire when the Japanese movie was playing. Lou was humiliated when he was told that SATSUNMO was short for Saturday, Sunday, and Monday.

Grace had just turned eighty that year and is the most beloved of aunts. Lou, who was often an outrageous scamp, gave a little toast in which he said: "The past is history, the future is mystery, and the present is a gift. That's why it's called the present." I really like that.

Grace's namesake, Doro's Gigi, was christened at St. Ann's, the church where her great-grandmother had been married and many Walkers and Bushes had been christened, married, and buried.

✐ All this time George and Brent Scowcroft were STILL working on their book, *A World Transformed.* They were the most reluctant of writers. I had loved writing my memoirs in contrast to those two, who suffered. Of course, they had to be sure their facts were right, leave out nothing, and check with others. I could selectively choose what to put in or leave out, write the truth as I saw it, or "the world according to Barbara Bush." Their editor and publisher, Ash Green and Sonny Mehta from Knopf, our lawyer Terri Lacy, and Brent's right-hand person, Ginny Lampley, arrived for a day to urge them to get on with it!

✐ Around the first week of August I was playing golf again. I loved getting out in all that beauty and being with dear friends. Judy

Beman and I played, and her husband Deane joined us and helped me a lot. Judy and Deane, the former head of the PGA Tour, were a great new addition to the Kennebunkport scene and have become darling friends. I wrote in my diary that I shot a 105 that day. Just as I tried to spare you all the good meals I ate for sixty-six years in my first memoir, I am going to try to spare you all the bad golf I played in the last ten years. But as this was less than six weeks after my hip replacement, I felt I must mention it—for Dr. Morrey's sake.

Later that month, George and I—taking Sam and Jebby with us—went to the Republican Convention in San Diego via Vancouver, Canada, where we cruised for several days on the 120-foot *Nova Spirit*. We spotted a school of the graceful Orca whales, a black bear, American eagles, and lots of other wildlife. One day the men and the boys went by helicopter to fly-fish at Nimmo Bay Lodge in the mountain lakes. I read and relaxed, had lunch and then decided to take a short walk—ten minutes they told me—to see a famous carving on a rock that supposedly was put there by Captain Cook, who discovered Vancouver.

Well, we took a small boat to shore, climbed a rocky beach, and then up a steep slippery incline for about five more feet. Our guide said this was the hardest part. Ha. Nice Andy Almblad, a Secret Serviceman, was with me. We found ourselves in an Alice-in-Wonderland forest—huge trees with enormous twisted roots and sawed-off trunks. No sky was showing, and the uneven ground was covered with rocks and slippery pine needles. To our right, with a drop of eight to twelve feet, was a lovely babbling stream that I was told was full of trout. Unfortunately, the so-called path dropped often to the stream. I had my cane, and even with that, was slipping and sliding. The rock was nowhere in sight. About three quarters of the way there—after tripping, sliding, and climbing—we came across a spot where I was to slide down quite a hill, and I suddenly thought, "What in the world am I doing? How will I ever be able to get back up this hill? What if my hip goes out and I'm in these dark bumpy woods in Canada on a boat? They will need an army to hoist me out!" So I turned back. Later that day I talked George into going to see the stone because I wanted him to see what those dramatic woods looked like from the inside out. He loved the walk and took a picture for me. On the stone was a perfect circle with a triangle inside and a cross on the outside. They are sure that the carving was not made by the natives.

We fished, read books (I read Jeffrey Archer's *The Fourth Estate*), and watched movies. The boys charged around behind the boat on Sea-Doos, jumping the wake of our boat. We passed one virgin island after another. Several times an enormous cruise boat would slide in and out of the fog in the distance. The silence on these waters is amazing. We fished one day from small boats, saw beautiful waterfalls, and more than one rainbow—once a double rainbow. Our friends Mary and Jimmy Pattison had insisted we take this cruise on their boat, and although they were not with us, they planned these wonderful three days for us. They even sent their assistant, happy efficient Maureen Chant, with us to be sure that all went well. Every meal was a treat and we had a chance to really talk to our great boys.

While we were gone, Bob Dole chose Jack Kemp to be his running mate. When we arrived in San Diego, the Doles and the Kemps called on us at our hotel, which was very thoughtful and courteous. We, of course, would have called on them.

Jack Kemp told us that Trent Lott had called him and said, "Jack, I think you are going to get it. I really think you are going to get it. And you are going to be a pain in the neck." Since he told the story himself, I said: "Don't you dare." His lovely wife Joanne said, "Don't worry. I am going to stay with him and I'll watch him." Jack promised that he would be a team player: "Bob's going to be the quarterback and I'm going to block." He then winked at George and said, "I'm going to treat you, Bob, just like I treated the Bush administration." He was in George's cabinet as the secretary of HUD and often spoke about things that clearly weren't in his field and sometimes were not the policy of the administration. We like both Kemps very much, but we also know that Jack is tempted to speak his thoughts, not the president's. We never had a chance to know if he had changed since Bill Clinton won re-election in a landslide.

Jeb was leading the Florida delegation at the convention, and we went by and had a visit with him and Columba. I had visits with several of my White House staff. My former aide, Peggy Swift Kasza, was advancing the trip for us, and Anna Perez, my White House press secretary, was there as a member of Team 100, a top Republican donors' group. Anna was the very best of the best. She told me a marvelous story:

Her son Anthony, a great boy who was having growing pains, was picketing the convention. He called his mother to ask her if he could spend the night on a couch in her suite as he didn't have a bed. She turned him down. "No," she said. " You are picketing me."

Our much-loved son-in-law Bobby Koch was also at the convention.

George W. and New Jersey governor Christine Todd Whitman were the co-honorary chairs, and we got to the convention in time to hear George speak. In the midst of his talk he introduced Laura. She spoke about the Texas Literacy Initiative, and in the middle of her remarks, a film came on the screen showing George W. at a school with children. I was so proud of her. She is the least flappable person I know.

George W. introduced Jerry Ford and Betty, and then his dad and me. Both Jerry and George spoke, and then Nancy Reagan. There was a short film about Ron. Nancy spoke very movingly. There were a lot of tears. There was another short film and when the lights went on there was Colin Powell. He gave absolutely the best speech that could have been given. The crowd went wild.

After Colin's speech we went right to the airport and flew back to Maine with our boys and Bobby Koch, arriving at 5 a.m.

〜 Later that summer we had a visit from Ginny and Clarence Thomas and their son Jamal. It was a very relaxed and happy time. One night, during dinner at Mabel's, I asked Clarence how he came to live with his grandparents. Jebby was sitting next to me and heard every word that Clarence said:

"I just told the President that my dad abandoned us at an early age. My brother, sister, and I lived in a shanty. Do you know what a shanty is, Jeb?" Jebby sort of mumbled something, and Clarence continued: "A shanty is one room with no water or electricity. Well, my brother and cousin really get the credit for our going to our aunt first and then our grandparents. They inadvertently burned down the shanty. My mother had to move and she took my sister and went on welfare." Clarence was sent at age seven to live with his grandfather, who was illiterate. Although he was poor, he sent the boys to a private Catholic school for $25 a year. He never let the boys play any sports and kept them at their books, telling them that "education is the only thing that counts."

We all ate so much that the men decided to walk home. Ginny and I drove back and walked the dog down to the gate to wait for the men. At least a half mile across the bay we could hear Clarence's laugh as they rounded the corner. He has the most wonderful, joyous laugh and honestly it can be heard miles away.

Several years earlier, a very close friend had come to tell me that he and his wife wanted to fund a family literacy program in Maine, but they wanted to remain anonymous. He asked if The Barbara Bush Foundation for Family Literacy could administer the program. I talked to that miracle woman Benita Somerfield, the director of the foundation, and she agreed that we could do it. So on August 19, I drove up to Portland to give out sixteen more grants to The Maine State Literacy Initiative and to meet with some of the mothers in the program. I told them about Clarence Thomas. And I told them that because they were working so hard to read, and making sure their children could read and learn, they might end up with a Supreme Court justice or a president in their families.

Then we went into a large room where we awarded the grants. The Maine State Literacy Initiative works closely with government on all levels: federal, with such programs as Head Start; state, as this program is run out of the state education department; and local, in cooperation with volunteers working with the public schools, etc. We are hoping to attack illiteracy on two levels: shoring up the parents' literacy skills; and preventing illiteracy being handed down to the next generation by getting their children ready to enter school reading-ready. Sometimes we get discouraged, but on that day when I heard that one of these sixteen groups had eighteen children in the program, I got encouraged. Each of these eighteen has a parent that will insist they read, take an interest in their schooling, and be able to help them. In turn, they will have children and teach them the need to read and the love of reading. It sort of reminds me of what happens when you throw a pebble into a pond—the little circles of water will get wider and wider, and keep spreading outward. So will the ability to read and write keep spreading down through the generations.

That afternoon I relaxed by reading *Vanity Fair* magazine. Relaxed? I was wild. There was the most vicious article called "The Valley of the Doles," written by Gail Sheehy and mainly about Elizabeth Dole. I have known Elizabeth for years. This article was well written, very ugly, mean, and seemed to me filled with half-truths. Obviously the author was supporting Bill Clinton. This piece was further proof that the pen is the mightiest weapon of them all.

Doro left with three of her four children, leaving Sam with us for a few more days. I hate it when the children go, but they need to get back to school and their own lives. The good news is that Margaret and Marvin arrive with their Marshall and Walker for a week or so.

Jeb arrived for a quick visit to be with us and Jebby.* When he arrived he found about forty young people at the pool, boys and girls. He said, "Mom, what is this? I couldn't find anyone I knew and I wondered if you had rented out the Point." They were the Yale Whiffenpoofs and the women's rhythm groups† from the senior class at Yale. George had invited them to come out to the Point to swim, play tennis, etc. He gave them boat rides in the *Fidelity*, his high-powered boat.

In the evening we had a mixed bag of 80 friends come to hear these groups sing. We had wine and cheese on the deck overlooking the Atlantic Ocean and then singing by the pool. At exactly 7:30 an army of mosquitoes arrived and the party ended. We learned that from now on at this time of the year we should have an outdoor party from 5:30 to 7:30. The evening was great fun, mosquitoes and all.

We had a dinner the next night for twenty-four, and Ariel rose to the occasion once again by having a buffet of the chicken with stuffing

---

*Jebby was spending the summer with us.
†Officially called Whim 'n Rhythm.

casserole from Ruth Parker's cookbook, Paula's jalapeño jelly, carrots, fresh Maine corn, homemade biscuits, and since Jeb was here, baked peaches for dessert.

Ruth is Betsy Heminway's mother and a wonderful artist. In her cookbook, which she also illustrated, Ruth included a recipe from Linda Walsh, another Kennebunkport summer resident. Ariel and I refer to this dish as "The Linda Walsh." It's easy, can be prepared well ahead, and is great for buffets.

THE LINDA WALSH
SERVES 12

4–5 pounds breast of chicken, skinned and boned
1 can cream of chicken soup
1 can cream of mushroom soup
1 3-ounce container sour cream
1 package ready-mix chicken stuffing

Simmer chicken in water to cover until cooked. Reserve liquid, cool, and remove fat. Lay bite-size pieces of chicken in a flat baking dish or casserole. Mix soups and sour cream; spread over the chicken.

Make your stove top dressing as directed, but use two cups of the reserved liquid instead of water. Flavor the dressing generously with poultry seasoning and thyme. Spread over chicken and bake for 35 to 40 minutes in a 325-degree oven.

After dinner, the wonderful Father Vern Decoteau entertained. A few nights earlier, George and I were having dinner with friends at the Kennebunkport Inn when we noticed the man in shorts sitting on a stool at the piano. He had a glorious voice, and knew all the songs from the great Broadway plays. People gathered around the piano kept calling out songs and saying, "Sing it, Vern." Before we left, Betsy Heminway invited him over so we could tell him just how much we had enjoyed his singing. Since we were having a dinner later that week, George asked him if he ever sang for groups. He said that he really hadn't, but he would. Then he went on to say that he was on vacation with his mother and that he was a Catholic priest. I have been teased for years because I said to him, "You can't possibly be a priest; you're in shorts." Father Vern is not only a priest but a good one. His parish, St. Francis in Belchertown, Massachusetts is growing and many young people are joining his congregation. He has sung for us many times over the years, and he and his sweet mother, Ida, have become friends of ours.

❧ On the 29th we had a dinner for 29. Our friends, The Oak Ridge Boys and their wives, came to visit. We really enjoy their refreshing enthusiasm, wholesomeness, and patriotism. It was such fun as they sang to us all, and Bishop Jack Allin joined in with them on "Amazing Grace."

❧ We left September 3 for Asia via Chicago. We were to lose thirteen hours on that flight. We lost a lot more, as a man on the plane had a severe asthma attack and the plane had to make an unscheduled stop in Anchorage, Alaska. I found it interesting and took a little pride in the fact that the pilots got on the air to the Mayo Clinic in Minnesota, gave them the young man's medical record, and on their advice landed the plane. I found it inexcusable that this man had his asthma medicine in the checked-luggage compartment below and that he not only was in the smoking section, but lit up as soon as the plane took off. Imagine the inconvenience to people who missed their next connecting flight, not to mention the cost to the airline. They held the plane for us and the other Beijing passengers, but there were twenty others who missed their connections to other places.

We stayed at the China World Hotel, one of the very best. The traffic was so congested that when I tried to take Quincy to see the Summer Palace, it took a half hour to move half a block. We settled for a visit to the beautiful Palace Museum at the Forbidden City. They now have tapes in several languages giving a forty-five-minute walking tour. Actor Roger Moore narrates the English tape and does it very well, giving an amusing and true history of the Ming and Ching dynasties.

We did see an old lady with "lily" feet. They were outlawed in 1925, but some parents continued binding baby girls' feet as they were considered beautiful. So it is still possible to see ladies who are anywhere from sixty to a hundred years of age with those tiny, little tortured feet. Amazing.

∞ Quincy got a message that the president wanted to talk with George. At first she thought it meant our president, as Bill Clinton had just sent missiles for two nights in a row into Iraq to retaliate for Saddam's persecution of the Kurds. But it was President Jiang Zemin. Once again I was privileged to sit in on discussions by the two friends. As usual, they discussed current events—our elections and those happening around the world; Most Favored Nation (MFN) status; and Hong Kong.

We flew on to Hong Kong and spent several days there. What an amazing transformation: ten years earlier people there still spoke of the PRC in fearful, hated voices; then several years ago people—particularly

One of our many meetings with Jiang Zemin in China.
This one actually took place in March 2000.
FAMILY SCRAPBOOK

those in business—started speaking about the PRC with ease. Now it seems they are looking toward Beijing and not Taipei, although this is a generalization based on the people we saw. You got the feeling that all who were going to leave had already left. Vancouver, for example, is filled with Hong Kong Chinese who had British passports and used them to move to Canada.

I read two Anne Perry books on this trip, *Defend and Betray* and *The Sins of the Wolf.* These two are from her William Monk series. She is the most prolific writer and writes another series featuring Thomas and Charlotte Pitt. I am a fan of William Monk.

We had a long trip home during which a stewardess came and asked me if a couple could bring their adopted baby girl up to greet us. It turned out there were six American couples, all with adopted Chinese baby girls, on the plane. I went back, met them all, and had my picture taken holding each baby. They were precious, and the parents were thrilled to be taking them home. The Chinese are encouraging their people to have only one child, and so baby girls are not always greeted with joy. Traditionally, the Chinese want a boy. A few years later I received a letter from the happiest of parents with a beautiful picture of one of the babies. I loved that! As I write this in 2002, I just recently read that it has become a real problem for the Chinese, having so many more males than females in that age group.

September 9—Our darling Jack Steel* died on September 8. It was all right as all was failing in that tired body, but that doesn't make it any easier. He will be buried on Saturday. George and I will fly down for the funeral. I know I wrote about Jack before, but, oh, how we will miss him. Also Sheila Watson died this past week after a devastating bout with cancer. Admiral James Watson was a member of the Joint Chiefs and was George's Secretary of Energy. Sheila was also a marvelous person and beloved by all the Cabinet wives. When I close my eyes I can see Sheila's bright, smiling face. I guess it is our age, but we seem to be having a lot of old and dear friends die. [George's sis-

---

*Jack was one of our best friends in Houston and was one of George's earliest political supporters.

ter] Nancy Ellis once told me that she pictured Mom up there paving the way and gathering loved ones to greet us when our turn comes. Jack, Sheila, Loret [Ruppe] and my brother Jimmy will be in that group.

∽ We went to Houston for the funeral via Washington where we attended the opening of The Presidents Cup golf tournament. Laurie Firestone, our social secretary at the White House, and Penne Korth, George's ambassador to Mauritius, put on the tournament parties with that marvelous touch that only Laurie has. Another of our Washington dinners was honoring Sonny Montgomery, who was retiring from Congress. It was a tremendous dinner that raised some $100,000 for scholarships for the University of Mississippi. We were lucky and got permission to speak before dinner. And then—now I can tell—we went to the Peking Gourmet Restaurant for a relaxed, delicious meal with Jim McGrath, George's speechwriter, and our friend Lud Ashley.

It is hard to believe how much we worked into those few days. I had a small luncheon with Margaret, Doro, Winnie Palmer, Blanche Hawke—wife of Bob Hawke, former prime minister of Australia—and Holly Finchem, whose husband Tim is head of the PGA Tour.

We attended the opening ceremonies and then drove around for part of the first round with Arnie Palmer, the nonplaying captain of the American team. At one point Arnie said, "You can't imagine what agony this is." George said, "You mean watching them putt?" He answered, "No. Not playing myself." He then went on to say that when they had played together he realized just why he couldn't be a playing captain. He was such a great champion and is still very capable of having a brilliant round. What a nice man.

We left the golf tournament, changed our clothes, and flew to Norfolk, Virginia, to a huge fund-raising luncheon for Senator John Warner. John introduced our great friend Senator Al Simpson, who was to introduce George. He told the audience that Al was such a good friend, but that Al—who had been in the infantry—had tried to tell John—who had been in the Navy and the secretary of the Navy—what Admiral Farragut had said. John said the admiral said, "Damn the torpedoes. Full speed ahead." Al said he was wrong, that the admiral said, "Damn the torpedoes. Where is the head?" Al introduced George with humor, and it was a very successful fund-raiser.

We went on to the General Douglas MacArthur Memorial where George and John laid a wreath on the General's tomb. Jean MacArthur* was not there that day as she was not well, but both men did it for her. She truly was a lady beloved by us all.

One of my favorite stories about Jean took place years ago when she took us and Spike and Betsy Heminway to the "21" Club in New York for dinner. She obviously was a regular as she was led to "her table." She immediately ordered a drink that came in a martini glass, so we all ordered drinks as well. When she ordered a second martini, so did George and Spike, although they were amazed this tiny little lady did so. When she got her second drink, she whispered to me that it was only water with a lemon twist, but she always ordered it in a martini glass so her guests would feel comfortable having a drink.

That night we attended a military dinner where George received "The Order of the Carabao,"† and then we flew to Houston. This schedule is so typical of my George. He works in more into three days than anyone in the world! You cannot be bored and live with George Bush.

Neither George nor I felt we could speak at Jack's funeral. We knew we'd break down. Our son Neil stepped up to the plate and read letters from both my Georges that were very moving. Neil then spoke so lovingly and with humor of Jack. Our children cannot remember a time when Jack was not a big part of our lives. For thirty years he met our planes every time we came home to Houston. Jack volunteered in George's office for twenty-three years and represented him at civic and charitable events. He organized conventions, events, and parties. How we miss him.

---

*We became good friends with Jean when George was Ambassador to the United Nations and we lived in the Waldorf Towers, Jean's home as well.

†According to the document that came with the award, The Order of the Carabao was established in 1995 to recognize the contributions of a member of the military establishment, either civilian or uniform, who best exemplifies the highest traditions of service to our nation.

⌒ One of the fun things I did that fall was to go to a retrospective of forty years of Arnold Scaasi's couture at the New-York Historical Society, "Scaasi: The Joy of Dressing Up!" The money from that evening went to breast cancer research. The dresses were stunning, and the show was a joy to saunter through. Each room was more beautiful than the last. I know my friend Arnold Scaasi was thrilled, and I was thrilled for him.

On that same New York trip, George and I had lunch with Benazir Bhutto, the prime minister of Pakistan, who was in town attending the opening session of the United Nations. All that I can remember is that she mentioned she was in trouble at home. She was and eventually left office.

That fall George and I did many "Points of Light" events, campaigned all across the country for Republican candidates, and sang for our supper. (That does not mean either of us sang.)

At the end of October we took a short but fun business trip to Europe, with our first stop in Barcelona, Spain, where we attended a concert by Lady Sarah Brightman at the Palau de la Música Catalana. She started off with several opera arias and moved right into some songs from *Evita, Phantom of the Opera,* and *West Side Story.* It was a perfect evening. The building is exquisite and the program lasted an hour.

I discovered that I had forgotten my nightgown and raced into a big department store to buy a gown and a matching robe. Since I am no good at converting U.S. dollars into Spanish money, I picked one set among many that looked fine. When I paid for it, I realized that I spent more than I ever had before. When I confessed to George, he pointed out that I spend at least eight hours of the twenty-four in nightclothes and I should stop worrying.

Michael Dannenhauer, George's aide, and I decided to go see the fascinating Gaudí Cathedral. It really is a horrendously big sculpture with two huge towers, unfinished at that time. Just as we were approaching the gate to go in, we noticed what looked like a low-budget film crew setting up to take a picture. When we were about fifteen feet from the entrance, the doors of a van opened, a toilet was placed on the sidewalk, and a man stepped up, dropped his pants, and sat down. Quick as a wink our party of eight or so, counting our agents and Spanish security, took a 180-degree turn and marched away. I missed being in a pornographic film by a second.

While George gave a speech to a Johnson Wax Company group, I joined the spouses for lunch at a small, one-time royal palace and now a jewel of a museum. I was so pleased, for Johnson Wax gave $5,000 in my name to a Racine, Wisconsin, literacy program. Nothing could have pleased me more.

We flew on to London. I was to have lunch with Natalie Whittaker, and since this was the day that Her Majesty was to address the Parliament, Natalie suggested that we eat lunch at our hotel to avoid the traffic. The most amusing thing happened. George was lunching at the same hotel with Raymond Seitz, our former ambassador to Great Britain, who along with his wife Caroline had stayed in London. Ray was a superb career officer, and when George appointed him, he was sending a message to the State Department people by appointing one of their own to this most prestigious post. George had asked the young man who helped plan the trip on the London end to please invite Sir Peter Middleton to join them for lunch. Just before the lunch, George discovered that the wrong Sir Peter Middleton had been invited and accepted. Hard to believe that there are two Sir Peter Middletons and they both are in similar businesses. Natalie and I enjoyed watching George greet this absolute stranger to his table. Very quickly they were chatting away like the oldest of friends.

At a reception that night, Michael Dannenhauer was warned that "one short man" was not to be allowed to get near George as he was a known flasher—I guess a successful flasher, as he was invited to a reception that was filled with successful people from around the world. The next thing Michael knew, George handed him a small camera and asked him to take his picture with—you guessed it—the *Flasher*. I suspect Michael took a picture of their feet!

One side note about our many visits to London: George and I had become spoiled over the years by the fact we often were friends of the Ambassador to the Court of St. James, so we usually stayed at the American ambassador's beautiful official residence in London, Winfield House. One of our first visits was in 1976, when George was head of the CIA and Anne Armstrong was the ambassador in London. We were there the day she went for the first time to meet Margaret Thatcher, who was then head of the opposition party. I remember thinking how smart Anne looked in a beautiful suit. She was appalled and offended when all the British press talked about was what she wore. In fact, I believe the press said that both she and Margaret were "dowdy." No man would ever have to put up with that kind of criticism.

Anyway, the last time we visited London we were thrilled to once again stay at that beautiful house, this time as the guests of our great friends, Will and Sarah Farish.

⤳ We ended this trip with a quick visit to Belgium where George spoke. We had left Houston on October 20 and were home on the 25th.

On the 27th I flew to Chicago to speak to the Ophthalmology Association of America. Certainly, a far-fetched group for me to address. I suggested that they might be perplexed by my being asked to speak to them as certainly eyes were not my field of expertise, but were among my most favorite body parts. After all, eyes did not need to be dieted or exercised. Right they were to be perplexed, and right I was to say that eyes are my favorite body part, mainly because they allow me to read!

On Halloween, I left our house at 5 a.m. to fly to Tulsa, Oklahoma, to speak to Literacy Volunteers of America. I was introduced by Ruth Colvin, a grand lady who founded and has supported LVA for years, here and around the world. I then went to the Apache Manor Drop-in Learning Center. I was surprised that Tulsa has fenced-in, gated grounds at this housing project. It was explained that this was done to keep the drug dealers out. I was so impressed with this center that deals with all ages and helps with issues such as homework and parenting. I listened to the children read, and then—thanks to the fact they sent a plane for me—I was back in our house for lunch.

We campaigned those last days before the November election with the Doles and for some other candidates as well. I always swear that I am through campaigning and then have trouble saying "no."

⤳ On November 9 we flew to Dana Point, California, to take part in the second forum sponsored by the George Bush Presidential

Library Foundation and Brent Scowcroft's The Forum for International Policy. This one was called "The 21st Century: Dawn of an Asian Era?" However, we first went right to the Pecan Hill Golf Course, changed into golf clothes, and played. George played with four men, and poor Brent Scowcroft got stuck with me—AGAIN. But—and this is a BIG but—he also played with pro golfer Dave Stockton, Jr.'s, lovely bride of a year. Diane Stockton was a fine golfer besides being a glorious-looking young woman.

We had a quiet dinner with Jim and Kate Lehrer. Jim was going to keep the discussions going, as he had the year before at the "Ending the Cold War" forum. This year's panelists were invited to discuss the future of Asia, and because the earlier forum had been so lively, I was expecting to be disappointed. But from the very beginning, which was an informal luncheon on Sunday, it became apparent that this was going to be an equally interesting session.

Representing Russia was Dr. Andrei Kozyrev, a former foreign minister. He spoke English very well and was charming.

From South Korea came Shinyong Lho, and his wife, Mrs. Chung-sook Lho. We knew them many years ago when he was the foreign minister, then later as prime minister. We had seen them on our last visit to Korea. Incidentally, Mrs. Lho is a great beauty. They both speak English. We have become good friends with their daughter Helen and her husband, Roy Ryu, a very successful businessman both in South Korea and here.

Kiichi Miyazawa represented Japan. Kiichi is our old friend. He was educated in this country and speaks perfect English, as does his wife. She was not with him on this trip. Unfortunately, Kiichi was the prime minister that George very publicly threw up on when we were at a very formal dinner in Japan in 1992. George claimed when he wrote and invited Kiichi to come, he said in his letter: "Kiichi, this time the meal is on me!"

Shanghai mayor Xu Kuangdi came from China. He was bright and spoke a lot of English, but often answered in Chinese.

The very first question asked by Jim Lehrer was: "Are you optimistic about Asia's future?" Dr. Kozyrev's answer: "You know the definition of a pessimist and an optimist, don't you? A pessimist is a person who says, 'Things can't get any worse.' An optimist says, 'Oh yes, they can.'" On the whole, they were all optimistic. They gave us all a lot to think about, and they did it with humor. It was a fascinating day.

≫ On November 19, George flew to Venezuela, where he met up with Jeb's wife Columba. They had a marvelous trip through South America. George called and said Colu was a great traveler, always on time and stylish-looking. He said everyone really enjoyed her, and of course her Spanish was perfect. They had a fabulous trip to Caracas, Venezuela; São Paulo and Brasilia in Brazil; Buenos Aires, Argentina; and Lima, Peru.

While they were away, I went to Dallas for a lunch with the first lady of Texas to thank the Dallas supporters for all they do for "Celebration of Reading," our annual fund-raiser for The Barbara Bush Foundation for Family Literacy. It's a wonderful evening where bestselling authors very generously donate their time to participate in an evening of readings in Houston. Over the years we have steadily raised more and more money for the foundation, hitting over the $2 million mark in both 2001 and 2002, making Celebration the largest fundraiser for literacy in the country! The foundation has now given away more than $13 million to 400 programs in 44 states, and we have started separate programs in Texas, Maine, and Florida, and will soon in Maryland.

That same day, Laura and I also kicked off the M.D. Anderson Dallas Christmas Card sales, and from there we went to San Antonio to have a thank-you reception for our supporters there. Mary Higgins Clark and her daughter, Carol Higgins Clark, helped us that day by telling us about their mother-daughter team writing. They were amusing and good. The following week we had a similar Celebration reception at our house in Houston to thank the core members of our very hardworking committee who really make this event sing.

That same week I flew to Rocky Mount, North Carolina, to speak; wrapped Christmas presents; went to movies; and flew to Edmonton, Canada for another speech. On this trip—all fourteen hours—I read Scott Turow's *The Laws of Our Fathers*. This book was very different— a lot of ugly street talk, a lot of flashbacks to the protesters of the sixties, the Berkeley crowd, Black Panthers, etc. There were even some Jewish conflicts for the child of Holocaust survivors and a little romance. Once I got over the fact that it was not Scott's usual court-room drama, I really got into it and felt I understood more about the sixties and certainly Scott Turow.

Finally, George got home after a great trip. We went to spend Thanksgiving with our children in Austin. It was a happy day with Neil's family; Ben and Julie Crenshaw and their two daughters; Laura's very close friend Regan Gammon and her husband Billy; and, of course; the great Governor of Texas, his wife, and two beautiful daughters. We were seventeen in all. It was a marvelous family day.

On December 6, George took Marvin's wife Margaret on a two-day trip to the island of Nevis for a speech. He ended up cutting his trip short so he could meet me at Howard Baker and Nancy Kassebaum's wedding reception in Washington, D.C. I wrote in my diary:

This is one of the many nice things that have happened to us lately! They will be a perfect couple. Nancy retires from the Senate this January 3. In any case they both have good minds and will enjoy each other. George and I received an invitation to the reception. I wrote back that I would love to attend but that George had a commitment that he had to keep. Shortly there-after my phone rang and it was the bride-to-be herself. She invited me to the wedding and then said: "Don't you want to bring a child or maybe a friend, like Andy Stewart?" I had started to say ,"No, thank you," but when she suggested Andy, I knew that she would love being there and quickly said that I'd love to bring her. It was a really lovely wedding, filled with their families and friends at the St. Alban's Church. I honestly was so honored to be there with these two dear people. Not only had Howard been a great Senate leader, but he was also "our leader" on the Mayo Clinic Board.

Nancy Kassebaum's dad was Alf Landon, who was the Republican presidential candidate in 1936. I believe that Nancy took us to meet this dignified man in the 1980s. I know we met him, but am just not sure of the date. He was very old and charming and sharp as a tack. Nancy was the loveliest, tiny bride surrounded by darling, happy children and grandchildren, both hers and Howard's. George managed to make it to the wedding reception after all, and we were so glad to see so many friends and to share this happy day.

~~~ One day George and Jack Fitch drove up to Texas A&M via Brenham, Texas, where George addressed the Chamber of Commerce and toured the Bluebell Ice Cream plant with our new friends, Howard and Ed Kruse. George Bush is the biggest Bluebell fan in America. The Kruse brothers are big Texas A&M fans, so this is a nice friendship with a lot in common. We met them in a rather strange way, but typical of George. There was an article in the paper that was brought to George's attention. Evidently the brothers were asked who was the person they would most like to eat with. One brother answered, "Jesus Christ," and the other, "George Bush." So George invited the brothers and their wives to come have lunch with us, despite the fact that one had NOT necessarily wanted to eat with him. We immediately liked all four.

Bobbie Fitch and I drove up after lunch to Texas A&M and met the boys there. I wrote in my diary:

> We were overwhelmed by the Library/School/Museum which we could see from the road. I asked just what was that big building (looked like one as we approached, but is three) and was shocked to be told that it was the G.B. Library. It is sensational! It sits on 90 acres of fields, has a stream and now a small reflecting lake or pool on one side that is presently still filling with water. The buildings are very spacious and really lovely looking . . . so much grander and more attractive than I had imagined. We saw our apartment and it is certainly a very nice space and very comfortable. Everything was great and they expect it to be finished in time to open the George Bush School for Government and Public Service next fall. After the tour Bobbie and I were driven to see our burial site which eventually

will be reached by crossing a bridge over the stream, up a little rise where there are three large Post Oaks forming a semicircle. The site will be in the center and in the background, a field of wildflowers.

⌒ I joined the great Governor of Texas at a luncheon one day, where he told once again the story about speaking at the Nimitz Museum opening and some guy yelling out he better listen to his mother. It always gets a big laugh. He then went on to say: "Mom, Dad, Laura and me went . . ." then he introduced me as the woman who still tells him what to do. So I got up and said that I wouldn't have mentioned it, but—well—it is NOT "Mom, Dad, Laura and ME went . . . ." Later, a friend gave me a book called *Woe Is I*.*

That night we attended a gala for the Smithsonian Institute, which was sponsoring a touring exhibit. It was fascinating, and because this was Houston, they had included George's portrait and my Inaugural blue ball gown. They also had from Alfred Glassell, who is a philanthropic leader in Houston and a supporter of the arts, a big— well, huge—blue marlin. When the head of the Smithsonian made his remarks, he mentioned Ron Sherr's portrait of George and the "TREMENDOUS BLUE" . . . he paused, then said "marlin." I had a momentary heart stop as I thought he was going to say, "Barbara Bush ball gown."

The great Governor of Texas introduced his father by telling a story about calling his dad and offering to lend him money to buy some new evening clothes, knowing that he was without a job. He said that his dad turned him down. The Governor insisted, and his dad still turned him down, finally saying, "Look, George, READ MY LIPS. NO NEW TUXES!" Funny. He ended by saying, "Ladies and Gentlemen, the best father in the world, my dad."

George walked up to the stage and said something like, "Ladies and Gentlemen, how would you like to be married to the most popular woman in the world? Ladies and Gentlemen, my wife Barbara Bush." AND THEN HE WALKED BACK TO HIS SEAT AND SAT DOWN!

*By Patricia T. O'Conner.

I stumbled through something, who knows what, and got off that stage. I later heard that someone asked if we did that often. Ha! I'd kill him.

⮎ I spent one morning that fall with my new friends, Israel and Nancy Tapick, visiting his plant. He supplies hotels and restaurants with meat, poultry, cheeses, Styrofoam cups, napkins—in fact, almost anything you can name except fresh produce. It was a fun day for me, and on our travels through the area of Houston known as the Heights we came across the tiniest house where Jack Valenti grew up and an equally sorry-looking lot where Israel grew up. Jack worked for Lyndon Johnson at the White House and currently is head of the Motion Picture Association. What a wonderful country where two boys with brains can come from such humble beginnings and grow up to be so successful. Both had worked very, very hard. Israel told me that both of their fathers started out by driving carts with vegetables on the back and selling them door-to-door through the town. Amazing. I loved that day.

In mid-December, Ken Burns—known for his great documentaries—came to stay with us. George had read in the paper that Ken was coming to speak to the Houston Forum. I was surprised (shouldn't have been, I guess) that George invited him for the night AND even more surprised that Ken accepted. I bet he was also surprised when he saw the dollhouse we live in and love and our informal way of life, especially since the last time he stayed with us was at the White House.

He arrived while I was doing flowers for the table. He and I walked Millie and then sat and talked and talked. Since we had seen him last, his wife had left him to "find herself." He had thought that after his documentary *The Civil War* came out and for the first time money was no problem, they would have a perfect life. He was stunned when she took off. He told me about his two daughters, who spend much of their time with him. The parents have joint custody. His eldest daughter had gone to St. Paul's School in the fall. He was so sweet about his girls, and his former wife. He told me he cried when his daughter went to boarding school. I remember crying when Doro went to school and could sympathize with him. While talking to Ken

I was amazed by how young he looked and how open he was about his life.

His mother was ill from the time he was five and died when he was eleven. His father closed himself off from Ken and his brother, feeling the grief was his alone and not the boys'. In the last year or two Ken and his brother searched out the funeral home where his mother had been cremated, found it sold, and learned that all the people who had not been picked up were buried in a potter's field. The two brothers had a funeral service with a minister and put up a headstone for their mother. Their father had never picked up the urn with the ashes! All this I learned from the genius who made *Brooklyn Bridge, The Shakers, Baseball,* and *The Civil War.* He looks thirty-four years old with fairly long hair, a scruffy beard, and beguiling eyes.

For dinner we invited Don Wilson, former archivist of the United States and head of The George Bush Library Foundation; Françoise and Ed Djerejian, who is director of the Baker Institute at Rice University and a former ambassador to several Middle Eastern countries; and George's chief of staff, Jean Becker. We all found Ken interesting and charming.

The next day George left the house at the crack of dawn to have a cataract removed. It was a roaring success but meant that poor Ken was stuck with me again. Ken read the paper, had a bowl of cereal, and did errands with me. I didn't know what else to do with him, and he was so easy and cozy.

Finally it was time to go to the reception, lunch, and lecture. There were tons of people—maybe nine hundred when they usually have around five hundred. That small man got up and spoke for forty minutes in the most soothing voice and almost spoke in poetry. Somehow or other he wove the history of America into his speech through films he had made. He was sensational during the question and answer period. He is a remarkable young man, then forty-two years old. I really liked him, although I must be honest that I was very disappointed that he didn't support our son for President.

Will and Sarah Farish invited us to attend the opening of Andrew Lloyd Webber's *Whistle Down the Wind* in Washington, D.C. Will told us that Andrew says this is his best. Better than *The Phantom*? Better than *Evita*? We loved the play, and we thought the music was wonderful. We then dined with Andrew and his wife and David and Carina Frost after the show. A wonderful evening, and then we awakened to very bad reviews.

Doro came for Christmas with her little family, and I hated the day they left, but was so grateful that they spared us the time. I know in my heart that it is time for all the children to start their own traditions and have Christmas—in fact all holidays—at home.

So ended another great year.

A little hammock action in Kennebunkport, August 1997.
From left: Jebby Bush, Robert Koch, Gigi Koch, on top of
her brother Sam LeBlond, Ellie LeBlond, Marshall Bush.
BARBARA BUSH

D uring the first week of January, George was having a little
trouble with his leg. He had hurt it sometime during
December and refused to do anything about it, saying it was nothing.
We had gone down to the Negley Ranch for New Year's again (more on
that later) and had a relaxing time, but George's leg still bothered him
at night. When you hunt quail in South Texas, you walk miles on
uneven ground through the brush, so his walking certainly had exac-
erbated the pain. But then when you are seventy-three years old, one

expects to hurt a little after a day spent marching around through rough terrain.

Our doctor, Ben Orman, came by one night with Henry Wilde, an orthopedic surgeon. Henry looked at George's leg, and he and Ben suggested that George take it easy for a week or two. That lasted about three days, and then we were out on the golf course with Jimmy and Susan Baker. Although it hurt his leg, it was a great deal of fun to be with our friends. I mentioned to Ben Orman that George's leg still hurt and, contrary to "taking it easy," he was playing golf and planning another hunting weekend. Ben immediately set up an MRI and by that afternoon George was in a brace up to his knee. It was his Achilles tendon and, what's more, a third of it was split or torn. George was reluctant to go into the brace, but when Ben and Henry told him that it would take very little to tear the rest, the pain would be excruciating, and he would be in a body brace for six months, he let them put it on.

Jim Baker is a great friend and was a superb secretary of state. If he has a fault, it is that he takes criticism to heart. He mentioned to George again that day that several people had knocked him in books and newspapers. My George gets zapped daily, and it hurts me for him. Nobody mentions the many good things that George did: the Clean Air Act; the biggest Civil Rights Bill ever—The Americans with Disabilities Act, which improved the lives of 40 million Americans; The National Literacy Act of 1991, the first bill of its kind, which helped give the literacy cause some much-needed national focus; and the economy, which was growing at 5 percent when he turned it over to Bill Clinton. (The Clinton campaign, along with the media, had persuaded American voters in 1992 that the economy was terrible, by saying over and over, "It's the economy, stupid.")

But the greatest thing he did was to teach us how to keep the peace by staying close to our allies. So when Saddam Hussein invaded Kuwait, George was able to form a worldwide coalition, assemble an enormous force in Saudi Arabia, and—after trying every peaceful means—win a war against this aggressor and drive him out of Kuwait. This is never mentioned, and my brilliant George never complains. I know that I am considered defensive about my husband and children. It's a very fair criticism.

I pointed out Jim Baker's tiny fault. George Bush has one, too. He certainly was not great at "blowing his own horn," a lesson learned from his mother. "Don't be a braggadocio, George," he often quotes her as saying. "How did the TEAM do, George?" He gives credit to others and never ever felt that he, alone, did anything. And, of course, he didn't. He assembled a great team. That takes genius, and as I write in October of 2001, I am grateful that his son, our president, has done the same thing.

But back to 1997 and the house party at the Negley Ranch that began our year. Nancy Negley is such a joy: a mother, an artist, a free spirit, and an exceptional friend. Keith Wellin and Nancy were married at that time and George enjoyed hunting with Keith and the others. Johnny and Phoebe Welsh, Jack and Bobbie Fitch, Perry and Nancy Lee Bass, and Ann and Al Simpson made up the house party, all old friends of ours. Alan Simpson was just out of the U.S. Senate, after serving for eighteen years from Wyoming. Ann said that she was now going to be a "kept" woman. She sold real estate while Al was in the Senate to help put their children through school and college. Alan came into the private sector like a rodeo bucking bronco just out of the chute. He served on a few boards; became director of the Institute of Politics at the John F. Kennedy School of Government, a post he kept for several years; and toured to promote his book *Right in the Old Gazoo: A Lifetime of Scrapping with the Press.*

Al maintained that the media has forgotten that they are to print the five Ws: WHO, WHEN, WHERE, WHAT, and WHY. He said instead, reporters now slant their stories to fit their own beliefs. He showed numerous accounts of the media being untrue and unfair, and examples of both Democrats and Republicans who have been hounded by reporters. Al also wrote that the press expect others to live up to certain standards, and then they do not do the same. For instance, they won't reveal honorariums they have received from organizations, which might have influenced their writings, etc. Alan has a way about him that is beguiling. He refers to people as "my good friend," then gently points out their faults and knocks the whey out of them verbally—and then softens the blow again. His language is very colorful, slightly scatological, and amusing. It makes a good read. He and Ann were great additions to our New Year's group and keep us laughing all the time. Wonderful Johnny Welsh has since died and is sorely missed.

❧ We got back to Houston to find that someone was thinking about buying the lot next door to our house and putting up a three-story house that would run 5 feet from our fence. They had a perfect right to do this, but it would thrust us in the shade and take away any privacy that we had. Then there was a small problem of security. The lot on which we built our terrace house was around 64 feet across and 160 feet deep. When George was in office, the Democrats had held a picnic and/or a press conference there, saying that we would never move back to Houston and certainly not build on that tiny lot. We did, and we adore our house, neighbors, and way of life. So George bought the lot next door and before any money changed hands, we sold off a large part of it but kept 20 more feet for ourselves, making our lot now 84 feet wide and 160 deep. George treated me to a "current swimming pool"—a pool that is approximately 8 feet across and around 14 feet in length. You turn on a motor, set the time and the speed, and then swim against the current. It is the very best thing one can do to exercise the whole body, and in Houston you can swim outside all year long.

Eventually, because we were traveling so much, we asked Jack Fitch to supervise the project, and never has one friend done more to help a neighbor. He met with the electrician, the pool man, the plumber, the sprinkler system man, the landscaper, and on and on. He ran into more problems than one could dream up, mainly because that was the spring of the big rains. They would just get the hole dug, and the rains would start again. We had a small garden shed—"had," because it fell into the hole. We had large ligustrum bushes that we were trying to save, which also fell into the hole. We were a mess of mud. We couldn't move the fence until the last moment because of security and on and on. We had a deadline because, as I remember, the fiberglass pool was being delivered on a truck from Rhode Island and we had to get the concrete foundation in the ground. We delayed the shipment once, but finally, after two and a half months, the pool was in and going. Mike Anderson, a most talented and thoughtful landscaper, designed a garden and a terrace around the pool in that extra 20 × 160 feet. We planted a veritable jungle, and are now pretty private and happy as clams.

⤳ On January 20, 1997, we had lunch with Jean Becker; Pete Roussel, our friend and one of George's former staffers; Pete's partner in their public relations firm, Roxann Neumann; and Ann Brock, my White House scheduler. We talked about the openings for the George Bush School of Government and Public Service and the George Bush Library, which were eight and ten months away, respectively. Ann had come down to head up the planning for the Library opening, and Pete and Roxann and their staff were helping out as well. I couldn't believe the enormous planning that goes into the openings. I also thought to myself that day how little interest one has in someone else's inauguration!

Five days after Bill Clinton started his second term, we attended the Alfalfa Club's annual dinner in Washington. This was a first for me as this had been a men-only dinner for years. It changed after 1993 when Bill Clinton refused to attend if women weren't included. Members can bring guests, and George had invited me for several years. Feeling that it is okay to hold "men only" dinners, I had made a silent (probably stupid) protest and had turned him down. It's a generational thing, I think. But George W. was being taken in as a "sprout" in 1997, and his dad thought I really might like to go.

I enjoyed every moment. The only purpose of the dinner is to have fun. And fun it is. It is a great reunion with friends from all around the country. After many crowded receptions, the evening starts with the "President's Own" Marine Band playing marches by John Philip Sousa, the flag presentation with all branches of the armed services being represented and marching in with their stirring songs. A great singer, Master Gunnery Sergeant Michael Ryan, who had sung at George's inauguration, sang "The Star-Spangled Banner," and then finally, the very long but interesting dinner began. There were three main speakers: the president of the club, in this case Colin Powell; the incoming president, Jay Rockefeller: and the Alfalfa Club's nominee for President of the United States—in this case, Trent Lott. The latter is kept secret from the attendees. The nominee usually tells who their cabinet appointees will be and their platforms. The one rule is that IT MUST BE FUNNY. Both George and his dad, Senator Prescott Bush, were candidates, about fifteen years apart. Senator Bush gave his speech in syncopation to the beat of "The Music Man." I do remember he said one of his cabinet choices, his secretary of agriculture, would be "a man outstanding in his FIELD." George came home from the People's Republic of China in 1975 to give his speech, wearing a Mao jacket.

Eventually, Jeb was taken in as a "sprout," and Marvin became a member in 2002. One of my happiest years was the year all five of our sons (Doro's husband Bobby Koch being the fifth) were at the dinner and Governor George W. Bush of Texas was the nominee. George W.'s speech was really funny, and included a number of digs at his parents. Several years later, after George W. became president, there were many stories about the Adams and Bush families being the only father/son presidents. I wonder how many sets of grandfather, father, and son nominees of the Alfalfa Club there have been? I suspect only one.

But back to 1997. Jay Rockefeller taught us all something that night we probably knew, but just needed to be reminded of again. Jokes made about yourself are funny, but jokes about someone else, particularly if they hurt, are not only not funny, they are embarrassing. Jay, who followed a very funny Colin Powell, said, "Colin and I have something in common. He was born in Jamaica. My family owned it. He was brought up in the Bronx. My family preferred to live behind gates." That was funny. Then he went way over the line on Bill and Hillary Clinton. Bill had been criticized for taking money for his campaign from foreigners, and there was talk that Hillary might be indicted over Whitewater. (She wasn't.) Jay passed the president a briefcase full of money after telling him (and us) that he had just returned from Asia and was given the briefcase for him. And then he followed with something like, "Did any of you notice that the first lady has become really polite? She went around the room earlier tonight saying, 'Pardon me, pardon me.'" It was so bad that George W., George H.W., and I all went out of our way to speak to her. She was a good sport and smiled. I read someplace, "Good humor is like a rubber sword. It always makes a point, but never draws blood." The senator drew blood that night.

I might add that there were only about 25 women there that night, out of about 550 total attendees. But the number increases every year.

❧ Once more we were doing a great deal of traveling and speaking, with some emphasis on Florida since Jeb had decided to run for governor again.

One speech that I really remember was in Illinois. I flew to Chicago at the crack of dawn and joined George at a school in Elgin. *Money* magazine and several other companies had adopted Elgin, with the goal of making the whole city money-wise through the use of the school system and community meetings. The plan was to teach them how to invest and budget wisely. There were three thousand adults and two thousand students in the audience who had agreed to join in the program. I am wondering four years later if it made a difference.

In the spring I attended a dinner for the Star of Hope, Houston's extraordinary homeless shelter, where they serve endless people in so many different ways, always giving hope to desperate people. George had spoken to this huge dinner on a previous occasion. More than 1,100 people attended, and when I asked how much they charged for the dinner, the answer was "nothing." They pass the hat at each table and always come out way ahead. Houston is a generous city.

❧ In early February, Madeleine Albright, President Clinton's new secretary of state, came to our home in Houston for breakfast with two aides while she was in town for a speech at The Baker Institute. Her appointment caused great excitement as she was the first female secretary of state and because she was brought up a Catholic but had just discovered that her grandparents were Jewish. There was great speculation that she knew and just didn't care or was in denial. Frankly, I don't care. I always thought that Judaism was a religion and if her parents chose Catholicism, then they were Christians. She was born in Czechoslovakia, moved to England, and then migrated to the United States. Her father had been a diplomat. All four grandparents were killed in concentration camps.

Madeleine came bearing flowers and said and did all the right things. She was bright without being arrogant, and we were impressed. I could not believe it when several days after her visit I received a handwritten thank-you note from her, especially since I knew that she went on a whirlwind trip around the world when she left us. Whether or not we agreed with her policies, she is an amazing woman.

February 8—Talked to Doro Koch this morning and then four-year-old Robert. I asked Robert how he was. "Good," came the answer. "How's school?" "Good," again. "Are you doing any sports?" "Karate," came the whispered answer. "What else?" I asked. "Basketball," followed by "tennis" and "baseball," all in a whispered voice. Doro got back on the phone, and I asked, "What's with the whispering?" She told me that Robert whispers when he's lying, and he doesn't want them to hear. It did seem like a pretty busy schedule for a four year old!

We had lunch one day at Houston's Hermann Hospital,* and they announced that they were naming their cardiovascular center after George. It was done in a very touching, nice way and I was thrilled for him.

We went to a lovely dinner for the United Way at The Museum of Fine Arts. George had spoken the previous year and—without asking me—had told them that I would be glad to be their speaker this year. I spoke for a few minutes and then pulled on him what he did to me at the Smithsonian Gala, where he was the speaker but used his few minutes to introduce me and sat down.

. . . One big trip to Florida where there were five very divergent events: charitable, a YMCA Banquet; political events, fund-raisers for Jeb; civic, a visit to Liberty City Charter School with its founder, Jeb; social, lunched with dear friends Sally and Dick Novetzke; ending with a "Quest for Children" fund-raiser where Jeb introduced me. I am so proud of Jeb. He is so smart, inspiring and sincere. He is very handsome and so sweet and caring. I went to bed a very happy mother.

*Now known as Memorial Hermann Hospital.

My George sent out a notice saying that the new rubber boat he was buying for the younger members of the family needed a name. He offered an award. Several months went by and the names poured in—fifty-nine of them. Then in February this notice was sent out:

February 18, 1997

To: All the family
WE HAVE A WINNER
Yes, the Judge just reported in. After hours of deliberation during which he considered the speed of the boat, where and how the name might be applied to the boat, and other serious things, Judge Rhodes* narrowed the list down to two names: 1) Gull (submitted by Neil Bush family) and Maine Coaster. At exactly 3:48 Judge Rhodes announced the winner is:

MAINE COASTER

And the winning name submitter is:

MARGARET BUSH,
MOTHER OF WALKER AND MARSHALL, WIFE OF MARVIN.

Ok, Let's hear it for Margaret—to whom the prize of 25 U.S. Dollars is being mailed as I type. C'mon, no sulking. Let's hear it for her! That's better!
Attached is the full list of names as submitted to Judge Rhodes. You will note that the good Judge was totally unaware of the submitters' names. We did it the old fashioned way—FAIRLY.
All five families sent in entries. Everyone entered in. It was a heavenly contest. The boat, properly named now, will be ready for use by all of you by mid-May.
Oh, yes, a couple of families tried to bribe the Judge by

*That would be Don Rhodes.

sucking up to him, saying nice things about him, etc. He never saw those comments, though.

Thanks for what I can only term superb cooperation.

Devotedly,

Gampy

Some of the names might have reflected Don Rhodes's thoughts. I am not accusing the children or grandchildren of "sucking up" (an expression that I not only dislike, I hate), but all knew that Don loved George Bush, Texas, C. Fred and Ranger (the latter being two dogs of ours), and birds—not necessarily in that order. I rather suspect that someone was being funny and making fun of our present president when he or she submitted "killdeer," a protected Texas bird that the then-Governor of Texas accidentally shot one year while hunting.

This little rubber boat has turned out to be a great plus for our family. We see all ages using it, and it really gives us both great joy. One sunny day one of our grandsons and a houseguest were out in the *Maine Coaster* while we were eating lunch on the deck with Dan Jenkins, the great sports writer and author, and his wife June. George was saying how much he enjoyed seeing the boys in the boat, what great pleasure he got, etc. Suddenly, quite far away, the boat stopped.

George got out the binoculars that he keeps at the ready, hoping (I suspected) that he might have to go to the rescue. No such luck. The "grand" was relieving himself off the back of the boat, little knowing that his grandfather had him in full view.

The latest grandchild to be "checked out" on the boat was Marvin's Walker, who I watched "solo" on July 31, 2002. I wrote in my diary that day: Walker slept on the Lincoln Bed in the White House when he was several weeks old, and now he can go out in the *Maine Coaster* alone!

There are rules: You must wear a life preserver; you must tell your parents or grandparents that you are going and when you will be back; and you must share.

⌘ George loves fishing. He reminds me of the quote: "Give a man a fish and he'll eat for a day. Teach him to fish and he'll be on the

George and his Maine fishing buddy Bill Busch. August 1997.
FAMILY SCRAPBOOK

lake every weekend." I am amazed that he can spend hours talking flies with others of the same persuasion. There are millions of them out there, and they seem to be able to spot each other from across a crowded room. Bill Busch is a fishing buddy of George's in Maine. He and his wife have cottages down the coast from Walker's Point on the Saco River where George has spent many hours fishing for blues and stripers. George and Bill met quite a few years ago on the water, in their boats, exchanging hints on where the wily bluefish were hiding. Bill has become a close young friend to George, as only fishing buddies can. They call and report: "They're catching them at the mouth of the Moussam River," or, "They're off Boone Island!" There is no more welcome call than that! I used to fish with George, but those long stretches of just sitting seemed such a waste, so I would bring a book. His boat is not conducive to sitting and reading—no place to curl up. There is another reason, too. George likes to race along, pounding as you fly from wave to wave. He knows that I used to love that, but have long since not. So he thoughtfully slows down for me. I honestly don't like to ruin his pleasure. On a calm day I am thrilled to be out speeding across that glorious Maine water.

I got the sweetest letter from Bill right after my memoir came out in 1994. When he read the book—which was above and beyond the call of duty or friendship—he saw the story about the big jar of spaghetti sauce that George brought me from Sam's Club. Bill couldn't believe that his friend, the former President of the United States, would be fed canned spaghetti sauce. I have no excuse. I had not really cooked in twelve years, and we were enjoying quiet meals at home. All of this is leading up to the fact that Bill sent me a great family recipe for sauce to go over pasta.

BILL BUSCH'S "SICILIAN" RECIPE
SERVES 8

½-pound thin-sliced prosciutto di Palma (imported from Italy)
2 two-pound cans whole tomatoes (use imported Italian plums)
Olive oil
Fresh parsley chopped (about a handful)
1 large Spanish onion, chopped
Hot pepper flakes, to taste
½ teaspoon basil
Dash of oregano
Black pepper
3 cloves of garlic (more if you like)

Dice up the prosciutto and sauté it in 5 to 6 tablespoons of olive oil.
When shriveled up, add onion and garlic. Sauté with parsley,
pepper, and spices until garlic and onion are translucent. Crush
tomatoes and add. Raise temperature and cover until boiling. Then
reduce heat and simmer about 45 minutes.

Pour over bow tie or penne pasta. (I prefer angelhair.) Top with
Reggiano Parmigiano. (We use whatever parmesan we can find in
bulk and grate it as we use it.)

Bill wrote in his note: "It will be better than Wal-Mart's!" He was right, and we use it all the time. In fact, we had it one night that spring when we had a few friends drop by for drinks, and George invited them to stay on for supper. This sauce can be frozen and brought out for just such an occasion. A green salad, crisp French bread, and a piping hot pasta dish make a perfect meal and something even I can make.

I am writing this in the White House in December of 2001—
Laura having invited us to stay in the Queen's Bedroom while we were
visiting Washington—and I must share something that just happened
apropos of my cooking. The president had gone to Florida for, among
other things, a Town Hall meeting. His brother, the great Governor of
Florida, introduced him to six thousand Floridians and, as I later found
out, most of America watching on TV. A young girl during the question-and-answer period said something like, "Mr. President, my
mother says that it is important to eat together as a family. Did you eat
as a family when you were little?" And that bad son of mine said,
"Your mother is right. It's important to eat as a family. And we ate
together—unless my mother was cooking!" This brought down the
house. Jeb, sitting right behind George, was laughing and covering his
face. The president looked directly into the camera and said, "Just kid-
ding, Mom." When the laughter died down, he compounded the
felony by saying, "My mother was the fast-food queen of the world!" So
now the world knows the truth. I am not a great cook.

I was really surprised when my phone rang that afternoon and it
was George W. and Jeb laughing so hard that neither could really
speak. George said, "Mom, Jeb said I should call. We don't think you
should watch the evening news or, if you do, you better be prepared."
Finally, I persuaded Jeb to tell me what I should be ready for and
amidst much laughter, he told me. I have been asked quite a few times
if I had heard what the president said about my cooking and was it
true? I used it in my speeches for a while to lighten up my message as
I am always trying to find a story or a happening that is funny. This
was funny and was a joke on me.

Sometime later the president was sitting in his bedroom eating
pretzels and watching TV when he suddenly passed out. One explanation was that a piece of pretzel hit a nerve and momentarily cut off oxy-
gen. I chose to think that it was a heaven-sent message to George W.
that he should NOT make fun of his mother!

My George and I get huge pleasure out of the love, laughs, and
comfort our children get from each other. And we both feel very
spoiled by Neil's family, who meet us after church on Sunday at an
informal and favorite Mexican restaurant, Molina's. My excuse for not
cooking is that this way the children can bring friends and all diets are

catered to. Some are vegetarians and some are meat-eaters. Then we have that unnamed fine fella who honestly does not like anything green and tells the grandchildren that he thinks vegetables are bad for him and them. That is also where we catch up on the family news. Jeb's son, George P., was at Rice University during this time, and he often joined us and brought some of his friends.

    One night at the end of February I flew to New York City for the presentation of the Lifetime Achievement Award, from the Council of Fashion Designers of America, to my dear friend Arnold Scaasi. I might add, only for Arnold would I do this. This was the most amazing evening, held at the beautiful Lincoln Center. The reception was a mob scene of fascinating people. There were all sorts of dress designers—Mary McFadden for one; representatives from all the media; models; and I even met my first transvestite—in fact several. Finally, forty-five minutes late, the program started. The presenters were told to say what could be written on one 5×7 card only, as there were many awards to be given before the big one to Arnold. From the very first presenter they spoke forever. Among them was Lauren Hutton, the famous model of yore who still is a great beauty. She introduced an Italian jewelry designer. Sharon Stone presented the Humanitarian Award to Kenneth Cole, the shoe man. He certainly has done a lot for AIDS. She gave a very impassioned, long speech. She had on a lovely long, clinging satin dress, reminiscent of the actress Jean Harlow. She looked stunning and shared with us that her "underwear drawer was empty." She did not need to tell us—it was obvious! One rather unattractive woman in sloppy clothes presented an equally sloppy recipient an award. Someone behind me said in a shocked voice, "She's stoned."

Ralph Lauren was honored for his men's clothes. I had just seen something wonderful about his life and family, and it was great to meet this nice man. He was presented by Iman, that really extraordinarily stunning model from Somalia with classic features and a paper-thin body. Donna Karan was also honored. Her whole group had on that black, clinging knit dress that is so hard to wear with chunky shoes. Half the women in the audience had on that same black dress with different bodice treatments: thin straps, no straps, one shoulder, full sleeves, etc. I mentioned this to Arnold and he suggested that the dress "must pack well."

Finally, our moment came: a lovely film of the forty-year retrospective of Arnold's sensational clothes, narrated by a funny lady; and then I was on—looking like a large gray whale after those beauties. I was touched that this strange crowd of two thousand were so welcoming. When Arnold came out he was protested by two or three screaming women—well placed in the audience to get the most attention—for his use of fur on his clothes. I have never seen fur on his clothes and I don't know when he last used fur, but they were loud and rude. He coped very well and finally they were led out, and he gave a very nice, modest thank-you. All in all, it was a strange evening for me and, I suspect, a nightmare for the Secret Service. On the other hand, they may have enjoyed the ladies in the totally see-through dresses and Sharon Stone.

✍️ At the end of March, George and I flew to Scottsdale, Arizona, for our annual physicals at the Mayo Clinic and from there to the Air Force Base at Yuma, Arizona, where we met Hugh Sidey and Henry Wilde, the doctor who had treated George's torn Achilles tendon. George had been planning for months to jump with the Golden Knights, the Army's elite parachute team. As a Navy pilot, he had parachuted out of his burning plane in 1944 and felt that he really wanted closure on that jump. He had to get permission from General Denny Reimer, the Army's chief of staff, who told George: "The only thing that worries me now is that the next phone call I will get will be from Strom Thurmond!" Strom, then a senator from South Carolina, was ninety-four years old!*

George spent the afternoon practicing on the proper moves with Hugh observing while Henry and I took a rather disappointing ride down the Colorado River. We mostly saw trailers filled with "snowbirds" parked at the banks of this lazy river.

That night we dined with the servicemen and women, which was a highlight for us and a real feast. George spent a very restless night,

---

*I want to make clear that George and not the government paid all the expenses for his parachute jump.

going over his moves for the next day. He made a perfect jump and said it was "heaven." For someone like me who has acrophobia (fear of heights), it would have been more like hell.

⟋⟍ I had been planning for quite some time a trip with our daughter and four daughters-in-law to Egypt. The whole trip quickly got out of control—my control. And how lucky I was.

It began when George spent one night in Luxor earlier in the year and loved it so much he thought it might be fun for me. So I invited all the girls to go. At the last moment Doro had to cancel because Ellie's spring break plans had changed. The four others suggested we bring Ellie as they knew it would be more fun for all of us with Doro there. Ellie was a great addition. So we were one mother and grandmother, one daughter, four daughters-in-law, one eleven-year-old, and two aides—Andi Ball, Laura's chief of staff both in the Governor's Mansion and now at the White House, and my beautiful Quincy Hicks, who was in charge of tickets and keeping us all on schedule. (In 2001, Quincy went to the White House with Laura as her scheduler.)

Our trip was pretty much taken over by the Egyptians. President Mubarak's plane met us at the Cairo airport and whisked us to Aswãn, where we were taken immediately to a paddleboat, *The Liberty,* a five-star cruise boat that has won several awards for being the best on the Nile. I believe it. We were on the top sleeping deck, and all had nice rooms with separate bathrooms, although I believe I had the only tub. The food was delicious—big buffets with lots of eggplant dishes, lamb, rice, fish, and salads followed by yummy desserts. Perhaps the best thing the Mubaraks did was to arrange for the charming head of The Cairo Museum, Mohamed Saleh, to accompany us on the whole trip. He was marvelous.

Our first stop at the High Dam was obligatory, I believe. This dam was built in partnership with the Russians in the late 1960s. The Nile is more than 4,000 miles long and runs south to north. Its source is in Burundi, where it rains a great deal. Before the dam at Aswãn, the runoffs would flood the lands of Egypt for six months. So they would farm for half a year and flee the water the other half. Life in Egypt has changed, thanks to the dam. Now that the flooding has stopped, the

Egyptians can farm and have electricity all year long. The dam was the brainstorm of former Egyptian president Gamal Abdel Nasser and was carried out by president Anwar Sadat. For the girls, this was a rather boring stop. They sat and giggled and fought jet lag as the director of the dam, with a pointer in his hand, described at length the depth and width of the dam, the amount of water it stored, released, and on and on. When the girls noticed that the pointer really was a back-scratcher with painted red fingernails and a ring on a finger, they had real trouble controlling themselves. Thank heavens I didn't notice that as I was trying to stay awake and seem interested. When I could, I broke in and begged to see the dam. We were dying to get on to see the ruins and the antiquities.

We went from there to the Philae Temple, which was literally moved about 500 meters, stone by stone, from Philae Island to Agilika Island when the dam was being constructed. It is huge, and you can see the watermarks on the stone still from those years of the floods. It is amazing in that one wonders, although the granite comes from nearby, how did they get all those columns and pillars there on an island five, four, or three thousand years ago? There were Coptic crosses carved on the walls and columns where Christians took over temples and defaced many of the carvings. The ancient Egyptians learned to write in 1000 B.C., and we can read their diaries from the carvings on the wall. There were lots of steps involved in this tour, and I was delighted that my new hip gave me absolutely no trouble. Somewhere that day I looked up and saw Chuck and Gail Alling, dear friends from Kennebunkport. We could not believe our eyes.

We then went to the Unfinished Obelisk, in the pink granite quarries. It would have been over 120 feet high and weighed over 1,150 tons. You can see where they had carved out almost all the column and then the granite had cracked! From there we went to The Tombs of the Nobles and the famous Old Cataract Hotel, where we had tea and cookies. It was on this very porch that Agatha Christie sat and wrote *Murder on the Nile.* Then on to see and walk in the botanical gardens on an island. Much of this was done by riding on a large felucca, the ancient sailing vessels of the Nile. The two men who handled the felucca seemed very adept at it until it came to docking. They crashed into the dock, and that's how we knew we had landed.

We went down the Nile (up on the map), stopping at the temples Kom-Ombo and Edfu, ending the cruise in Luxor at the Karnak Temple and visiting the tombs of Tutankhamen and Nefertari. Going down the Nile was heaven, and the views were sensational: small villages on thin strips of green with crops, goats, camels, donkeys, people all in Arab dress, many lovely pottery jars, and many ibis and palm trees behind which we could see miles of desert with sandy mounds.

We ended this trip in Cairo, where we stayed for a full day. We lunched with Suzanne Mubarak and her daughter-in-law, Hedi, and met Mohamed Mubarak, Suzanne's three-month-old grandson. Suzanne is a gentle lady and a great beauty, and she and I had such a nice time remembering previous visits over the past twenty years. Before we flew home, we had a sunset visit to the Pyramids and the Sphinx with the usual pictures on camels with the monuments in the background, followed by dinner in the Souk. The whole trip was perfect and magnificent. George was certainly right: I loved it.

While we were gone George took Jebby, our fourteen-year-old grandson, to Italy. Jeb and his family are Catholics, and George wanted Jebby to meet the Pope. They had a nice visit, and we have a picture to prove it.

Visiting the Egyptian pyramids in March 1997. From left: Columba Bush, Laura Bush, Barbara Bush, Ellie LeBlond, Doro Koch, Sharon Bush, Margaret Bush.
FAMILY SCRAPBOOK

〰 In April, I flew to San Antonio, where I spoke to The National Association of Elementary School Principals. I got to watch a little of the Masters Tournament on the airport TV. I wrote in my diary:

> It was such a thrill. Tiger Woods wins the Masters with 18 under par—a 12-shot win—broke best 72 hole record in Masters' history and is only 21 years old. It was so sweet when his mom and dad rushed up to hug him. He broke into tears from the world's biggest smile. I believe all of America stands a little taller today.

〰 In mid-April, we attended the rededication of the Ford Museum in Grand Rapids, Michigan, along with Lady Bird Johnson, Caroline Kennedy Schlossberg, Jimmy and Rosalynn Carter, and many old friends from the Ford administration. It was great to see John and Michelle Engler, the really bright and effective governor of Michigan and his vivacious wife, who were such a vital part of my George's political career. Betty and Jerry led us through his fascinating museum; it was fun to see, especially since George's would open in November. The actual ceremony was held outside in the coldest, dampest weather and everyone cut their talks to a minimum. I was so touched that Lady Bird sat there freezing, but with a huge smile on her lovely face. She is such a remarkable woman.

That afternoon we popped into St. John's Northwestern Military Academy in Delafield, Wisconsin, for a dinner and then on to New York for the night. The next day we attended an academic conference on George's presidency at Hofstra University. This was so great for us, as many of the Bush administration people were taking part: Jim Baker and Hugh Sidey had spoken the night before we arrived; Susan Porter Rose, my White House chief of staff, was there serving on an afternoon panel about me as first lady; Mikhail Gorbachev and Dan Quayle were to speak the day after we left. Both George and I received honorary degrees, followed that evening by a huge banquet. Remarks were made by Dr. James M. Shuart, president of Hofstra University; Dr. William Levantrosser, the Hofstra professor who directed the conference; Andy Card, my George's secretary of transportation and the current president's chief of staff; H. E. Sheikh Saud Nassir Al-Sabah, minister of information of Kuwait and former ambassador to the United States during the Gulf War; followed by Brian Mulroney. George spoke to end the evening, and we flew home to Texas exhausted.

Chris Evert and her sister Clare Evert Shane arrived for lunch the next day, and along with George, they all played in the Chuck Norris "Kick Drugs Out of America" annual tennis tournament. Among the other players were our son Neil, who plays every year, and the world's nicest man, professional tennis player Vijay Amritaj.

At the end of April we attended the Volunteer Summit in Philadelphia. This was the brainstorm of the Points of Light Foundation. Although Colin Powell agreed to head the summit, George was (and still is) the active honorary chairman of the foundation. While working on the summit plans, George and Colin felt they must include the current administration. I wrote in my diary:

> The summit was attended by the President and First Lady and the Vice President and Tipper Gore. There is a feeling by the Points of Light people that the White House is trying to take over everything, and it is true. The President keeps saying that it is non-partisan and then talks about all the jobs he has created, etc. Former President and Mrs. Ford, Former President and Mrs. Carter, Nancy Reagan, many governors and wives, heads of large corporations, delegations from each state, many volunteer agencies are represented—the Red Cross, Communities in Schools, Literacy groups, Ronald McDonald Charities, etc., all were there. Our Laura Bush headed the Texas delegation . . . Colin and Alma Powell are not only here, but Colin is the chairman, in spite of the fact that there was great pressure by the White House for Al Gore to take over that job. I believe that Colin is the only person in America who could truly bring us all together to follow him.

George traveled a lot the rest of the year encouraging states and cities to get onboard with this great program.

Out of the Volunteer Summit grew America's Promise, the "alliance for youth" originally headed by Colin and now run by the former Democratic senator from Pennsylvania, Harris Wofford, a man truly dedicated to helping children. Thanks to many, America's Promise is still strong in the year 2003. Governors and mayors are joining the cause, realizing that so many of their problems could be solved if we fulfill the five promises made at the Philadelphia summit:

1. Ongoing relationships with caring adults—parents, mentors, tutors, or coaches (73 percent of teens report they do not have sufficient role models in their lives; and 71 percent report that their parents are not involved in their schooling).
2. Safe places with structured activities during nonschool hours (1.35 million children were homeless in 1999).
3. Healthy start and future. (There are many hungry children in our country.)
4. Marketable skills through effective education (64 percent of employers said that most high school graduates do not have the skills necessary to succeed in the workplace).
5. Opportunities to give back through community service. (If asked, 93 percent of young people volunteer, yet 49 percent of teens are not asked.)

Here are some disturbing facts I read in America's Promise literature:

- We have as many as 7 million latchkey children who return home to an empty house on any given day. In low-income working families, 22 percent of children lacked health insurance in 2000.
- Only one third of children and adolescents who need mental health services get them.
- Teenagers say that they spend 1,500 hours watching television and 33 hours in conversation with their parents over the course of a year.
- Nationwide, 37 percent of fourth-grade students and 28

percent of eighth-grade students score below the basic reading level.

- On school days, the hours from 3 to 6 p.m. are peak times for juvenile crime, crimes against children, teen sex, smoking, drinking, and using drugs.

Although Colin had to leave his post at America's Promise to become secretary of state, his wife Alma is still very active.

◁◦ After hearing rumors all year that this might happen, the Houston City Council voted unanimously to rename the city's biggest airport. On April 30 I wrote in my diary:

> This was a big day in our lives. We went out to the airport to a dinner in a hangar, then got on a Continental airplane with 200 city officials and friends and flew from Houston Intercontinental Airport around the city, landing 35 minutes later at the newly named George Bush Intercontinental Airport. The evening ended with glorious fireworks. What an honor for George and we are thrilled.

I still love it when the pilot announces, "We will land at GEORGE BUSH Intercontinental Airport in 20 minutes," or, "The weather at BUSH is . . ." Sometimes we fly from REAGAN to BUSH, and that's a thrill, also. Houston is our hometown, and although our city council is nonpartisan, I suspect they are mostly Democrats; for them to vote unanimously to name the airport after George was an even greater honor.

I think George truly thought at that time that nothing would mean more to him than putting his name on our hometown airport. However, two more wonderful "naming" surprises were in his future: when the CIA headquarters in Langley, Virginia, was renamed the George Bush Center for Intelligence in 1999; and when it was announced in 2002 that the Navy's next aircraft carrier would be called the USS *George H. W. Bush*. He was very touched and honored by all three.

❧ May always is a very busy month for us, what with graduations, conventions, and charities trying to raise money before summer sets in and people take off for trips. Plus, we move our whole gang—office and household—to Maine. May 1997 was no different. One day I met George in San Francisco where he had flown after being honored at Southern Utah University's centennial celebration, along with Michael DeBakey, one of Houston and America's great heart surgeons; C. Everett Koop, the former Surgeon General; and astronaut David Scott. We then flew to Maui, Hawaii, to speak to the Steel Distributors Convention, where we played golf with several different people who were attending.

Quincy had found two golfing jokes on the Internet that seemed appropriate for my talks, especially the one I gave to this group: "Do you know the difference between a bad golfer and a bad parachutist? A bad golfer goes WHACK . . . Darn! A bad parachutist goes Darn! . . . WHACK!" I can follow that with: "Aren't we glad that George is the former and not the latter?"

The other joke I really loved after the awful golf I'd played with those nice ladies: "I was so discouraged after my golf yesterday that I went upstairs to our room and told George that I was so bad, I was going out in the ocean and drown myself. He answered: 'Not going to happen. You couldn't keep your head down that long!'"

❧ On May 10, we had our annual fund-raising evening for The Barbara Bush Foundation for Family Literacy with authors Patricia Cornwell, Alan Simpson, Dominick Dunne, Jim Lehrer, Scott Turow, and Barbara Taylor Bradford. The evening started with the Governor and Laura Bush speaking for a few moments, followed by Miss America, Tara Dawn Holland, who had made literacy her cause. The night ended with George reading from his not-yet-published collection of letters, *All The Best.* Believe it or not, we were on schedule, starting at 7 p.m. and ending by 8:45 p.m., after which we fed 1,300 people and raised enough money to give the foundation $1 million!

The next day we were on a plane for China and Hong Kong. Two hours after arriving, we were at a welcoming banquet. The topics of discussion had really not changed from our last visit: Most Favored Nation (MFN) status and the divisions it creates in the U.S. Congress;

and the Hong Kong takeover by China that was to come in six weeks. As the day got closer, people were getting nervous, including the anti-China coalition between the left and the right in our Congress; one side was worried about human rights and the other was concerned with communism. We had a really nice visit with President Jiang Zemin in Zhongnanhai, the place where all the very top Chinese officials lived when we lived in China, including Chairman Mao. It is lovely, right on a lake and next to the Forbidden City.

We had lunch at Villa #5, Diaoyutai Guest House, with the vice premier and foreign minister Qian Qichen. This all brought back many memories of our days spent living there, and all subsequent visits. That night we had dinner with the ambassador, Jim Sasser, and his wife Mary, at our old residence. We were greeted at the front door by our Mr. Wang, who in 1974 had started in our residence as a young man; moved on to several other posts; and now was back with the U.S. Embassy, again as head houseman.

The ambassador had just returned from the United States, where he was lobbying the Congress for the Most Favored Nation treaty to be passed. George was too polite to mention that when Jim was a Democratic senator, he had opposed the bill every time George brought it up. (Finally, in 2001 when the People's Republic of China joined the World Trade Organization, this ended the need for the controversial MFN vote for China to be brought up every year. Yea for President George W. Bush.)

The residence looked lovely, thanks to the Friends of Art and Preservation of Embassies Committee that Lee Annenberg had initiated, and to Mary Sasser's warm touches and good taste. The meal was delicious and the evening great fun.

We flew to Hong Kong the next day and met with our friends C. H. and Betty Tung. He would become the chief executive of Hong Kong when it returned to Chinese rule. Some of C.H.'s new rulings were upsetting the outside world, such as the need for a permit to protest. The hue and cry in the U.S. papers and from the far right were loud, but nobody was mentioning that you must have a permit to protest in our country as well.

Chris Patton was the last governor of Hong Kong. I think it amused the Chinese that the British ruled Hong Kong for one hundred and fifty years and it wasn't until the last two years that they have tried to make it into a democracy by having free elections.

We had a large lunch and another huge meal at dinner before boarding a plane for home, making that a total of four big, nine- or ten-course meals in a row.

We left Houston on May 11 and arrived in Kennebunkport at the crack of dawn on the 15th. That is the long way to get to Maine, but by the time we arrived, Ariel had the house looking wonderful and ready for an onslaught of family and friends. That was the good news.

The bad news was that our precious Millie really was not well. She was just as sweet as ever, but would not eat. She was loving, slept through the nights—often at my side—awakening when we did, her little tail wagging to welcome the day. On Monday, knowing that I was leaving town after lunch, I took her to the doctor at 8 a.m. I felt so sorry for the young doctor, for after a thorough examination he suggested that I leave Millie for some tests. He called us after a few hours and told us that her X-rays showed a large hard mass, her blood count was awful, and she was in great pain, although she never whimpered or cried. George and I talked it over, had several phone calls with the doctor, and made the decision that we did not want her to suffer. So Millie was put to sleep. Her autopsy showed that she was riddled with cancer. I wrote in my diary that night:

> That angel of a dog is gone. It almost seems too hard to believe, but we have known for years that she had lupus and we were lucky to have her that long. What a dog! She never bit or barked. She was gentle, loyal, loving, and such a dear, dear dog. Oh, how we shall miss her. She truly is where she should be, with the other angels.

I had to go to Orlando, Florida, that afternoon to speak to the Pennsylvania Bankers Association. Quincy and I decided that we would not mention Millie because it might make people sad for me. When I awakened the next morning and turned on CNN, I was shocked to hear her death reported every fifteen minutes. So much for secrecy! George called me to explain that he had his office put out a press release because he noticed on my schedule that there would be a question period after my talk. He knew the first question would be: "How's Millie?" And I would have sobbed. How right he was!

The outpouring of letters, faxes, flowers, and telephone calls about Millie was unbelievable. People wrote things like, "I love her and will always remember her," or, "I am having a Mass said for her," this accompanied by a Mass card. At our First Congregational Church, they prayed for her on the Sunday after her death. One lady wrote that she "knew the pain we were suffering . . . you see my husband died last year." The Barbara Bush Foundation for Family Literacy got a $500 contribution in memory of Millie. It was amazing and truly sweet. People wrote letters about their dog's death, sent pictures of their dogs OR CATS, either living or dead. Millie would not have liked the latter one bit! Mildred Kerr, after whom Millie was named, had reporters call to interview her, and Jean Becker was interviewed by *People* magazine. Both ladies said that the interviewers said that they knew Millie had written a book and that she gave the proceeds to charity, but they wanted to know "the personal side of Millie. Do you know anything special that she had done lately?" Thank God for a sense of humor.

We were offered some beautiful puppies, but Will Farish—who had given us Millie all those years ago—told George that he would find the perfect precious little girl for us and that we should wait.

Several weeks later, we went to England and had the treat of going to Wimbledon for lunch and tennis. We saw many of our old friends, both British and Americans. I met Lord Astor, a young man who said that he really did like America as AFTER ALL, he had relatives there. As if I didn't know that! He went on to say that he had an aunt or a great-aunt there right now. I asked, and he said, "Brooke Astor." I told him that I knew and admired her. Then he told about the party where they had recently celebrated Brooke's ninety-sixth or ninety-seventh birthday. He said that a little old man with a cane got up and toasted Brooke, ending with, "Happy Birthday, Mummy." Lord Astor went on to say, "Imagine, that seventy-two-year-old man still had a mother." I could see that he suddenly realized that he was stepping on some very fragile ground. I did not tease him for he was being so polite by just talking to me, and I really didn't know if he had a sense of humor. I was dying to say, "We seventy-two-year-olds often still have mummies," but I did not. I might add that Brooke was then still taking two-mile walks and just had been in England for four days of shopping and visiting friends! Amazing woman.

It was on this trip that we picked up the perfect little girl dog that Will had found for us. The pup was two years old and we discovered that she had already delivered eight puppies. A Mr. Parnell, who trains Her Majesty's dogs, and his daughter brought her to Glympton, the home of Prince Bandar, our good friend and Saudi Arabia's ambassador to the United States. George and I stood outside in the drizzle and watched this sleek, trim dog work out. She was the absolutely best trained dog that we had ever seen. She responded to hand gestures for staying, sitting, going left, or going right, etc. She was trained to stay off the furniture and, of course, was house-broken. We were told that she was a great hunting dog. Her posture was and still is positively regal. We changed the pup's name from "Dart" to "Sadie," named for Sarah Farish. Sarah was never called "Sadie," but then Mildred Kerr was never called "Millie." Mr. Parnell suggested that I take Sadie for a walk on a lead while they drove off. I turned to look and it seemed to me that he had a tear in his eye.

We were lucky enough to get a ride home on a private plane, so could keep Sadie with us. We arrived in a horrible thunderstorm. When we went to bed that night, George suggested that Sadie might be lonely on her first night away from the kennel and lifted her up on our bed— something we swore we would never do again. Famous last words. To this day, Sadie starts with us, fast-moves to the chaise, and then comes back up around 5 a.m. when she hears us stirring. We have never had a bad dog, but this one is close to perfect. George adores her. When he's away and calls home, he teases me by saying: "How's my girl?" Before I get past, "I'm fine," he says, "Not you, I'm talking about Sadie!"

꩜ We got home from that trip to find a full house: Jeb and Colu, Doro's son Sam LeBlond; former staffer and friend Pete Roussel; George's brother Pres and his darling wife Beth; Sharon and Neil, their three children, and a friend of Lauren's and one for Pierce. Guests came and went all summer, and by the end, we had had 178 different people spend the night on the Point in 1997. That does not mean that I was responsible for feeding and caring for all those people, just most of them. Many of them were guests of our children. The Point was jumping. I wrote in my diary:

> One night George and I were in bed asleep when he awakened me, whispering, "Who's that on our couch?" He put on the light and there was Tres, the boy visiting Pierce. He said, "The other kids are watching the Rangers and I wanted to watch the Astros." It turned out he and Pierce had come together and both were watching the Astros, but Pierce had gone into the other room for a minute to check on the Rangers. George said, "Would you mind turning the set down a little?" and rolled over and went back to sleep. This is a mad house.

We had too many guests to mention, but one who was universally loved by family and friends was George's Uncle Jimmy Walker, who was ninety years old. Jim's wife Sarah had recently died, and he came up and stayed in the Wave, a tiny guesthouse on the Point. I loved seeing Jimmy and his younger brother, eighty-five-year-old Louis Walker, playing what looked like slow-motion golf. I know they found golf frustrating, especially for Jim, who was such a great golfer at one time, but I know they loved being together. Both men often met at the pool and just sat. They both confessed that they could no longer swim because they sank. Since Louis often came for a swim, that really scared me. And it does give one a lot to look forward to as I, too, love to swim.

I had one glorious golf match with my brother Scott, his wife Jan, and their son-in-law, Marty Brix. I'm sure that they never realized just how thrilled I was to have a 50 on the front nine and a 48 on the back nine, thus breaking 100 again after my new hip! Amazing how the little things in life thrill one!

Golf really was such fun that summer. George had a lot of good golf with many of our guests, but none more fun than with Paul Marchand and Jim Nantz, who came again with their wives, Judi and Lorrie, or with pro golfer Hale Irwin and his son Steve. Well, that's only partially true as the matches in the family are fun, and both Jeb and George W. visited and played very competitive golf and had lots of laughs. One great match was two foursomes: Deane Beman, former head of the PGA Tour, and Cape Arundel's golf pro Ken Raynor; Bobby Koch and pro golfer Jose Maria Olazabal; George and Hale Irvin; Hale's son Steve and Nick Cutler, who is married to one of my former aides, Kim Brady. Jose was not staying with us, but with other friends who live nearby. Actually, the Koch/Olazabal team won when the cards were matched. Jebby and Sam, fourteen- and thirteen-year-old cousins, played golf and, of course, thought they were VERY good. The truth was, they weren't bad.

I played a lot of golf that summer, including with my new friend Judy Beman and her many friends—the "Golden Girls"—all good golfers; and many of my dear friends—Betsy Heminway, Jane Weintraub, Dianne Moss, Anne Raynor, Sandy Boardman, Bertie Bell, Carol Walker, Bunny Burke, and Daphne Gawthrop, to name just a few. They all had one thing in common—they are better than I am. Actually they all had much in common—they tolerated me, and I am devoted to them all.

In addition to a great deal of golf, the CLINK-CLINK of horseshoes became the sound of The Point. Just before and even during lunch on the deck, and often late afternoon, there were very many competitive horseshoe matches.

A fun addition to our life that summer was the Portland Sea Dogs, the Triple-A farm team of the Florida Marlins.* Our friend Dan Burke, the retired CEO of Capital Cities/ABC, had bought the franchise—a dream of his—which helped revitalize downtown Portland. The team sold out the stadium, which upset Dan as he felt so badly when people came with their children to see a game and couldn't get in. So Dan built five hundred more bleacher seats for the nonseason ticket owners. He'll hate it that I wrote this, but it is true.

꒰꒱ We enjoyed a number of visits that summer from some of our author friends. Mary Higgins Clark and her new husband, John Conheeney, came for a night. We liked him so very much. Mary waited some thirty-eight years after her husband died to find John. She wrote me that "he was worth waiting for!" The next morning our nephew

---

*As of 2003, of the Boston Red Sox

Hap Ellis, big George, and George W. played golf with John and really enjoyed it.

Ric and Laurie Patterson came with their three children. In the fall I read Ric's *No Safe Place*. We both love his books and them, too.

Patricia Cornwell came for a few days. We became friends, like the other authors, after she read at one of the Celebration of Reading events. Patsy is the most generous person, has so many interests, and has become involved in literacy in her home state of Virginia. She has given the Barbara Bush Foundation, along with many other literacy programs, a great deal of money, plus her time.

Yes, our house was on overload. All guests sort of overlapped, so Walker's Point was really jumping. In addition, George's brother Bucky from St. Louis rented a house on nearby Parson's Beach with all his family. Our young cousins, Craig and Debbie Stapleton, have a lovely house closer to town, and Debbie's parents, Uncle Lou and Aunt Grace, had rented a house across from the Point. All of our family is close and are urged to use The Point—the tennis court, the pool, etc. That's the point of The Point—family. One day I wrote in my diary:

> Sometimes I think Ariel DeGuzman is a miracle man. He not only is a "good soldier" (Navy man), and a great chef, but nothing seems to bother him. We had the craziest lunch on Tuesday with the Pattersons (5), George and Laura's family (5),* and my friends, Dee and Vance Torbert (2).† Counting us, that makes 14. The Torberts were stopping by for lunch on their way down from visiting their daughter. As we were sitting on the deck getting ready for lunch, George told us that Kenny Ford (1), the doctor/fisherman,‡ was up here to film George fishing with Bill Busch (1), and he was joining us for lunch. Somehow or other that added Ken's wife (1), two children (2), another couple (2), and two photographers (2). That made 24 people sitting down to a lunch for 14. It was chaos. I don't think our children

---

*One of the twins must have had brought a guest.

†Dee, a member of the "Ladies of the Club," had recently remarried. Her first husband, Jim Collins, a congressman from the Dallas area, had died quite a few years earlier.

‡Ken, who was a neighbor and grew up with our boys, does a show on ESPN2 called *The Reel Guys*. He's also an orthopedic surgeon.

got fed at all. The chicken salad was stretched beyond belief. Poor Dee and Vance (who George called Lance) didn't know what hit them. Nor did I! Ariel DeGuzman is not only a miracle man, he might be a saint!

~~~ I got a break from all the action when I flew out to speak to Schlotsky's annual convention. I was gone less than twenty-four hours, door-to-door, and spent less than four hours in Las Vegas. I am lucky because I can snooze easily on a plane. It was a large convention, and a very nice easy group. I mentioned at my table that I had met a great many people at the reception and had not met one person named Schlotsky. They all laughed and said there was none and never had been one. The two founders sat around seventeen years ago, had several martinis, and tried to think up the perfect name for a deli. Of course— *Schlotsky's!*

That reminded me of how George and his partner Hugh Liedtke named Zapata, the company that later became Pennzoil long after George left the business world. They, too, had a few martinis, and since the movie *Viva Zapata* was the rage at the time, they settled on that name.

~~~ The madness continued after I returned. Tim and Holly Finchem and Deane and Judy Beman came for lunch with two of Deane's daughters and Brian and Mila Mulroney; Andy Stewart—who is about my closest friend; the president of Smith College, Ruth Simmons; Louie and Marilyn Freeh, the FBI director and their five sons, all dropped in. Only a few spent the night.

The Oak Ridge Boys arrived on a Tuesday in their huge bus, meeting their wives who had flown up on a plane from Nashville. The Boys spend almost three-quarters of the year on the road and so were glad to be reunited with their wives. One night they were with us we had a dinner for thirty-six, and then afterwards, a few of the Secret Service agents, the household staff, and grandchildren came in to hear those sweet Oaks sing.

George went on several fishing trips that summer, one to the

Northwest Territories with our grandson Jebby and Peter Pocklington, a Canadian friend. Jebby got the award for the largest fish caught.
They normally "fish and release," but in this case the fish was stuffed.
The great news is that it was to hang on Jebby's wall, not mine!
Another time George went to the Ristigouche in Canada for a few days
with Dick Cheney, also a great lover of fishing. George truly feels that
the "time a man spends fishing should not be deducted from the time
he spends on earth."*

We also went out several times that summer to whale-watch with
our friends, Alicia and Stephen Spenlinhauer, who live just a few miles
from us on the coast. There is something so magnificent and exciting
about seeing those huge whales in their natural habitat. The Spenlinhauers very generously offer to take our houseguests out and show
them this phenomenon.

The Spenlinhauers have a glorious boat named *The Fine Print.*
Steve is the largest employer in southern Maine; he runs a printing
company—of course! The Spenlinhauers have adopted, and been
adopted, by us and our office. They are a marvelous addition to our
lives. So much for the people who say that you don't make new friends
after you grow up!

∽ I read and enjoyed *A Firing Offense* by David Ignatius. I had
bought it for George and he liked it so much that he suggested that I
read it. David's mother, Nan Ignatius, is an old friend of mine. I used
to play tennis with her in Washington, and she is a dear lady.

I read Elizabeth George's *Deception on His Mind.* She writes about
a British police officer in nineteenth-century London and normally
works in some British nobility, which makes it even more fun. I
learned in 2001 that Elizabeth is a truly charming woman when she
came with her mother to read for A Celebration of Reading. I introduced her as "a favorite of mine." When she stood up to read from the
first chapter of her latest book, she used some really risqué words.
George couldn't quite understand her and probably couldn't believe

---

*This is one of George's favorite quotes and comes from Izaak Walton's *The Compleat
Angler*, published in 1653.

his ears. I was surprised as I have read her every word and never before heard or read anything vulgar. Later I teased her by asking how she dare read those words with her lovely mother in the audience. She answered quick-as-a-wink: "No problem, she's very hard of hearing." The first chapter was the only one with one off-color word. I enjoyed the book a lot and can't wait for her next one.

I started *Captain Corelli's Mandolin,* a novel by Louis de Bernières. I started it and then put it aside. Maxine Weintraub, a wonderful book-reading friend across the bay from Walker's Point, lent it to me. She called Quincy and left a message saying, "Tell her to stick with it. It gets better, much better." She said that it was the best book that she read this summer. Then Ginny Lampley said that she loved it AND she also said that it was hard to get into. I put it aside again after 100 more pages. It is a book that I can put down! I later listened to it on tape on a long trip and enjoyed it, and then George brought the movie home and it was fun.

I read Deborah Crombie's *Dreaming of the Bones.* Lisa Drew sent me the uncorrected proofs. She writes like Elizabeth George, and I enjoyed it so much that I called the bookstore to see if they had any of her other books. Later that fall I read *A Share in Death.* It must be obvious that I read to relax. I do read the newspapers and stay in tune to the news, but sometimes it really is too much for me. (As I wrote this on January 11, 2002, I heard on the television that my precious Jeb, the governor of Florida, had a viable death threat. George, who was out of town, called one minute later and told me that the threat was real, but Jeb was not worried. I immediately wanted to read a novel.)

I also read Baine P. Kerr, Jr.'s, book *Harmful Intent* in manuscript form and enjoyed it a lot. Baine grew up with George W. and is a medical malpractice lawyer living with his family in Boulder, Colorado. He also is the son of Mildred and Baine Kerr, our neighbors and very good friends. I'm very proud of Baine, who wrote a second book, *Wrongful Death,* which came out in 2002.

I read David Baldacci's *The Winner.* He and his wife, Michelle, were so dear to send it to us in galley form. David also is a "Celebration" reader, and we have become good friends. They have been to the Point several times with their two nice, well-loved children—Spencer and Collin—and Michelle's parents, and they all came to spend the night in 2002. During that visit, David gave my literacy foundation an extraordinary gift. A book had just come out called *The Mighty Johns: A Novella by David Baldacci and Other Stories by Superstar Authors.* Based on an agreement David made with the publisher, the foundation received an immediate donation of $10,000 and also will get all of David's royalties from the book. I am so touched by David's generosity and friendship.

꩜ Princess Diana was killed in a car accident in Paris on August 30. This caused an amazing shock wave around the world. I wrote in my diary shortly after she died that "she has already attained sainthood." She was a lovely-looking young woman and really endeared herself to the world by caring for the ill and children. She also loved her boys. The times I spent with the princess were very pleasant, and she was marvelous with the AIDS patients that we visited in hospitals in London and in Washington. Her funeral was a pageant.

We were all saddened by our own loss—our precious Uncle Jimmy Walker died. His children and stepchildren planned the funeral, and all came to Maine to tuck Jimmy away by his wife, mother, father, two brothers, one sister-in-law, and one sister at a graveyard in Kennebunk. It was a loving, quiet, and very gentle service with a family luncheon.

꩜ In September, we flew to Texas to officially open The George Bush School of Government and Public Service. I wrote in my diary:

> Things are really rolling along. First we visited the museum which is beginning to be put together. They are working around the clock and they swear that it will be finished on November 5. There are people working to get the exhibits in place, the terraces finished, and the landscaping in. We walked over and looked at our apartment. It will be wonderful when it is finished. Mark Hampton was with us and gets credit for making rather sterile rooms (no fireplace or bookshelves) into a warm, cozy, comfortable apartment.
>
> Then we went on to the school for a tour, a reception for

major donors, and in to a large lunch. George and Laura were there looking marvelous. George W. introduced his father twice and did a great job. It is hard for his father—he gets teary— especially as George W. gets teary, too.

We went back to Maine, where things were relatively quiet during the rest of September. The only worry we had was the number of people who kept telling us that they were coming to the opening of George's Presidential Library/Museum on November 5. George shuddered when he heard people say that, for fear that we wouldn't see them. It was amazing. We told one and all that we didn't think we would even lay eyes on them, but they didn't seem to care.

I received two awards that summer: Tara Holland presented me with a literacy award from the Miss America Foundation; and I received the Harold W. McGraw Jr. Prize in Education, along with three other much more worthy people. I mention this because along with these awards came two checks, each for $25,000, for The Barbara Bush Foundation for Family Literacy. I didn't deserve them, but I certainly accepted the money for literacy.

After the McGraw dinner in New York, I got on a plane and flew all night to Madrid, Spain; then took a small plane to Malaga where Uta Patiño, our friend Jimmy Ortiz-Patiño's wife, met me; and then we drove to Sotogrande and their home.

Meanwhile, several days before, George had flown to Boston, San Francisco, and Hong Kong. His trip to Spain, where I met him, had taken him twenty-seven hours. He was sleeping when I arrived. We were in a large guesthouse with our cousins Craig and Debbie Stapleton and Jim McGrath, George's speechwriter. Because my George knew Jim loved golf, he had asked Jim to advance the trip. We were all there to attend the Ryder Cup, which is the United States against Europe in golf; unlike The Presidents Cup, which is the United States against the world, except for Europe. We lost by one point to a great European team.

Jimmy had worked for six years or so making sure that the course, Valderrama Golf Club, was in perfect shape, and it was. Sad to say, it was a very rainy week, and Jimmy was up every night and out on the course with an army of volunteers raking and pumping water out of the traps.

Also staying in the main house were His Royal Highness Prince Bernhard of the Netherlands, father of Queen Beatrix; and Prince Andrew, Duke of York. Both men are avid golfers, both very amusing and nice. Prince Bernhard was eighty-seven and said anything he felt like saying. He was having some bad tummy troubles and felt free to share them with us. When he got to feeling better, he was a charmer.

The Duke of York is a fine golfer, and he and George had a round. The Duke won $6 from George. George gave him a ten-dollar bill and never got his four back in change. The duke loved that $10 and brought it out over and over again. Once I got up my nerve to remind him that he owed George $4, but of course dukes don't carry money, and it is much more fun to wave a ten-dollar bill anyway.

It was on this trip that Jeb sent us an e-mail and Jean Becker faxed it to us:

> The bad news is that I was campaigning in Palm Beach and Daytona Beach when it happened.
>
> The news, which gives me enormous pride, relates to the 29–14 first game victory of The Gulliver Raiders today. Running back Jeb Bush scored four touchdowns and had one two-point conversion, which gave him 26 points in the victory.
>
> Is there anything better in life than the success of a son or a daughter?
>
> Excuse me for bragging on a son I love more than life, but it feels pretty nice.

Now our son knows just the same feeling of joy that his dad and I feel about him, his brothers, and sister all the time.

∽ We went on to Monte Carlo, where George spoke and I renewed my friendship with Prince Rainier during a dinner. I had last seen him in 1990 at the opening of the Metropolitan Opera Season in New York. At that time, he and his handsome son, Prince Albert, were the honored guests and I was married to the President of the United States, so I was seated next to His Highness, who was charming and very nice. He had just arrived from his tiny little principality and was absolutely exhausted. When the opera started, he immediately fell asleep, and—to be honest—he snored a little and his head came my way. People around us in the center box poked me and said, "Wake him up." I didn't, but the prince came to every time an aria ended and said the appropriate thing: "charming," or "lovely voice."

Back to 1997. I had a momentary panic that I had put this little story in my memoir, because he said, "Oh, yes, I remember Mrs. Bush. We attended the Metropolitan Opera together." My heart sank. I must have put it in my book. Well, as luck would have it, our host on my right had a much more interesting dinner partner—or important to him—as he rarely spoke to me, and the nice prince had a raging young beauty on his left. But in a few minutes the prince said, "Mrs. Bush, I'm afraid you are stuck with me because the lady on my left speaks not a word of anything I do. I have tried French, Spanish, etc., and have yet to discover what language she speaks." We discussed almost everything, including golf clubs. (We both play with Callaways, but he had an 11 wood. I didn't then but do now.) We discussed Princess Grace's cousin, John Lehman, former secretary of the Navy in the Reagan administration. He told me about a hunting trip he had been on with our new friend, Prince Bernhard, where the prince brought with him a case of wine, which he proceeded to drink all day while shooting. Besides making Rainier nervous, he was never offered any wine! He asked me about Boris Yeltsin, and I told him the story about stepping on Yeltsin's foot during a state dinner. I knew the name of his dog and he knew the name of ours.

The evening went on and on. Finally, I leaned over to him and said, "Sir, I don't know the protocol, but I do believe that none of us can leave before you leave." He was so kind and asked me sincerely, "Do you really think that I could leave now?" I assured him that he could; that in fact he could do anything his heart desired. He answered, "My heart desired that I leave an hour ago." We got up and the long evening ended. He charmed me! I rushed home to look in my book and I never wrote about the opera night. I do not worry about it now as that nice man will never read this book and if he does, I hope he'll laugh!

The next day we flew to Zurich, Switzerland, where we were met at the airport by our friend Louis Marx and his daughter Pearson, and

his friends and business associates, Charles and Veronika Elsener, Jr.—
our hosts for this visit. Then as a surprise there were our precious son
Neil and his wife Sharon. We drove an hour and a half to Ibach, a tiny
little town with the most amazing postcard-type scenes. This darling
part of the world is on Lake Url. One expected people to break into
yodels from the hilltops.

We were there to help celebrate the 100 anniversary of the Victorinox factory, the Elsener family business that produces, among other
things, the Swiss Army knife. We had a marvelous lunch with the
family. Thirteen children of all ages ran around the lovely restaurant,
and we felt honored to be among such a happy family with at least
three generations attending. We spent a day and a half with these
extraordinarily modest and enormously generous people, who live very
humbly and happy to be surrounded by beauty and loyal friends. They
are proud because they have never "let anyone go"—even in bad times.
Although Switzerland is neutral, we were told that they were prepared
to sabotage their plant before they would let the Germans have it during World War II.

We did tour the factory, and both George and I put together a
knife. They have pocket knives of all sizes that are sold around the
world, from Tiffany's to Woolworth's. I would venture to say that
almost, if not every, person living in the Western world has owned or
held a Victorinox product in their hand.

They had the sweetest family party that night with the Swiss Pirate
Drum Corps. They banged away. Then we had some wonderful singing
by the same group. In between courses the children danced; Gospel
singers sang; and a relative played bottles accompanied by a pianist. It
was such fun. We were all given presents, and out of the blue the family
gave a most generous contribution to my literacy foundation.

The next morning we took a boat trip on Lake Url. The scenes do
look like every picture one has ever seen of Switzerland. We were in the
German-speaking part of the country. The green hills go sky high,
with rocks on the top. The country was founded on this lake seven
hundred years ago. We ate on board the boat, and before we left, we
toured the majestic Einsiedin Monastery, where we heard the loveliest
organ concert. This church is rococo style, filled with cupids, angels,
and frills, all in pinks and pastel colors with white walls.

From Switzerland we flew to Stuttgart, Germany, for a dinner hosted by Erwin Teufel, president of the Bundesrat, and his wife. Neither of the Teufels spoke a word of English, nor did we speak German, and yet we found them charming. She is a sweet, smiling lady who puts you at ease immediately.

We also sat with the son of General Irwin Rommel, known as the "Desert Fox" and considered a great German military tactician during World War II. Rommel was caught in a plot against Hitler and was given a choice of being shot or taking a suicide pill; he chose the pill. The son told George that he is a friend of the son of our World War II great, General George C. Patton. An interesting irony.

The next morning we had a brief visit with Chancellor Helmut Kohl and his wife Hannelore. She looked wonderful, trim and very stylish and beautiful. Helmut is running again after sixteen years in office. I wrote in my diary:

> There are many who feel this is a real mistake and certainly against the trend. The new age seems to be going Bill Clinton's way—charismatic and TV-aware. . . .
>
> The Germans give George credit for seeing a window of opportunity for the peaceful coming down of the Wall and seizing it. It was George who talked the other occupying countries—the Russians, French, and English—into reunification.* The Russians and the English were very reluctant, and Margaret Thatcher still worries about reunification. Speaking of Margaret Thatcher, George tells me that recently she said that George made a mistake by not going after Saddam Hussein personally.† I am shocked. She, better than most, knew the mission—getting the aggressor out of Kuwait; the worries about possibly getting involved in another Vietnam; and keeping the coalition together. Margaret seems to be isolating herself from all her old friends with the exception of Ronald Reagan.

---

*George was in Germany to commemorate German Unity Day.

†She was referring to Desert Storm. She believed George made a mistake ending the war when he did and not sending troops into Baghdad to get Hussein. To this day George is confident he made the right decision.

Just before George was to speak, I had to leave for the airport as I had long since agreed to give a talk in San Francisco. All in all, with a short stop in Atlanta, the trip was almost sixteen hours. I spoke in Stockton, California, and flew home all that night to Boston and then on to Maine. I had agreed to give this talk before the Europe trip had been planned, and I just hate to miss out. Jimmy Durante, a comedian of yore, used to sing a song that describes me to a tee: "Do you ever have the feeling that you wanna go . . . Do you ever have the feeling that you wanna stay?" Or something like that. I love being with George.

We flew home to Houston around October 11, working our way home. October was spent buying for our new apartment at the Library and getting things in place there. Brilliant Mark Hampton came and hung pictures and drapes and put all the furniture in its comfortable place. Mark had a touch that was magic. He died very shortly afterwards and how glad I am that George and I had known and loved him. He left a lovely wife and two wonderful daughters and a more beautiful world behind.

Every visit to College Station was exciting, and people were hustling around putting in terraces, planting, and getting exhibits in place. I was not convinced that it would be ready for the opening.

Meanwhile, we were speaking to groups all across the country and really seeing our Houston friends too little. One very special program was in Kansas City, where Margie Hall Pence, the daughter of two dear friends, Don and Adele Hall, was the chairman of a fund-raising dinner for The Learning Center. I visited the most amazing place at the center, called Earthworks, a museum/classroom/experimental lab where kids learn about their environment, the world, and its inhabitants. I was amazed as I never knew or heard that there were underground caves that have constant temperatures—no heating or cooling needed and no moisture problems—that are used for storage or, as in this case, for a museum along the Missouri River. How little most of us know about our great country.

We did several motivational talks for Peter Lowe, who organized these events around the country. I was speaking about the importance of family and the importance of reading to, listening to, and taking time to be with your children. George generally talked about the world and getting involved in community activities. Once, while waiting our turn in "the greenroom," we heard the marvelous health and fitness man, Jack Groppel, say, "Go into your bathroom, take off your clothes, look in the mirror, and jump up and down. If you jiggle, you are too heavy and don't pass the jiggle test." We thought that was so funny. Henry Kissinger was there that day also and said he was shocked that he was told he should speak twenty-five minutes only. He said a German could not say "hello" in twenty-five minutes. He gave a great speech and was right on time. Later, after we left, both Christopher Reeve and John Major spoke.

Several weeks later I heard such moaning and groaning coming from George's bathroom and a loud "DARN IT!" "What's the matter?" I called. He called back that he had taken and NOT passed the jiggle test.

∽ A regret—not my only regret, but one regret—is that I did not keep all the pictures I have gotten from the Barbara Bush look-alikes. I get at least four letters a month and have for years from ladies who have been told they look exactly like me. I am so common-looking that when I spoke to the Junior League in Toledo, Ohio, in October, they had TWO BPB look-alikes greet me. They can be 5 feet 2 inches tall to 6 feet 2 inches tall. They can weigh 120 to 220 pounds. They can be fifty-five to eighty-five years of age. They all have one thing in common—WHITE HAIR. I have finally learned to say, "I wish I did look as pretty as you do." And in most cases it is true!

As you can imagine, the mail often brings all sorts of funny surprises. One year, shortly after giving the commencement address at Texas A&M, I received a letter from a lady who thought I might be amused by something that happened after my talk. She had taken her granddaughter with her to the graduation, and when she returned the little girl to her mother, the child ran into the house yelling: "Mom, you will never guess what I did. I heard the mother of the President of the United States—I heard George Washington's mother!" I might have been more amused IF I didn't sort of really look like George Washington!

Another letter that truly thrilled me and amused my family came from a dear little girl who said something like: "Dear Mrs. Bush, Great news! I've named my heifer after you."

This nice child sent me fairly frequent updates on Barbara Bush the heifer. Barbara competed in the Houston Rodeo and Livestock Show (also known as Fatstock Show) one year, and came in eighth. I was sorry for my little friend, but was slightly relieved as I'm not sure I could have stood the headlines: BARBARA BUSH WINS THE FAT STOCK SHOW.

 Later in October, George and I joined Margaret, Marvin, Marshall, and Walker in Fort Worth for the Edna Gladney Center's 110th Anniversary Dinner. What a group. There were 276 "Gladney babies" at the party. The oldest was eighty years old! George, Laura, Jenna, and Barbara were also there to see our Margaret honored for the work she has done for the Center. Every time someone said something warm and fuzzy about the joy and love these adopted children brought to so many, Marvin would look at Marshall or vice versa with such love that Pop and I had trouble not weeping.

On October 28, Quincy and I flew with Janice and Bob McNair to Columbia, South Carolina. Bob McNair, one of Houston's most philanthropic and nicest citizens, had given a Science and Technology Building to Columbia College and named it after me. Janice had gone to Columbia College, where she and Bob met. I was flattered beyond words, but for the life of me I still think they should have called this lovely new building The Janice McNair Science and Technology Building. But these are two very modest people. I told my children, "Of course they should have named their building after me considering all I know about the subjects!"

 Our family and many friends started arriving in Houston on November 4 for the big Library opening. We went to Molina's for a family dinner that night with our children, grandchildren, aunts, uncles, brothers and sisters, nieces and nephews, and cousins by the dozen.

The next day, along with many friends and former staff, we all climbed on a special train donated by Union Pacific and rode to College Station. We heard later that we had friends whose rooms were thirty miles away. Every room within miles was taken. George and I were overwhelmed by the people who came not just from the United States but from around the world.

The very first thing we did on arrival was go to the horseshoe pit, where we met many members of the White House staff—some thirty-two or thirty-three of them who had come to the opening. George and Marvin took on the two gentlemen they used to compete with in the spring and fall tournaments when we were in the White House, Ron Jones and Bob Gallahan. They whupped my boys, but we were all so glad to see them and the others that even that did not matter.

That evening we went to the world's largest tent and had a barbecue with what seemed like thousands and met and greeted so many dear friends. Afterwards, there was truly an incredible show with Jim Nantz as the emcee; the Oak Ridge Boys; Michael Davis, the talented and very funny juggler; Van Cliburn, the great pianist; Loretta Lynn

Gathered for the dedication of the George Bush Presidential Library are, from left: Lady Bird Johnson, the Carters, the Bushes, the Clintons, the Fords, and Nancy Reagan. November 1997.
MICHAEL KELLETT

and her sister Crystal Gayle; and the A&M Choir and the whole famous A&M marching band. John Major spoke a few really kind words about George—all true—and the evening ended with fireworks.

November 6, 1997, was a very big day for George, as his Library/Museum finally opened. I got up at 5:30 a.m. and took Sadie out for a long walk. The day was absolutely lovely—sunny and bright, with a little chill in the air. Perfect. I was shocked to see that there were many people lining up to go through the metal detectors. (The crowd was eventually estimated at 25,000.) The place was teeming with people at that early hour, and we were really glad to get back to our apartment.

At 9:30 a.m., Sadie and I went over to the Library to catch up with George and meet all the governors and wives along with the other VIPs for coffee. After they started their tour, Sadie returned to the apartment, and we greeted a special group of VIPs: the former heads of state who came—the Kaifus from Japan, the Majors from Great Britain, the Mulroneys from Canada, Rudd Lubbers from the Netherlands, Sir John and Lady Swan from Bermuda, and Lech Walesa from Poland; all the presidents and first ladies—the Fords, Carters, Lady Bird Johnson, Nancy Reagan; three members of presidential families: Caroline Kennedy Schlossberg, and David and Julie Nixon Eisenhower; George's able and very nice vice president, Dan Quayle, and Marilyn. George and the Governor of Texas went out to the airport to meet the Clintons.

The six first ladies marched side by side up the ramp and out to the stage, and the four presidents followed, to a roar of the crowd. It was so moving. Jeb, who was then the president of the Library Foundation, was the emcee. He looked spectacular. He introduced the magnificent Billy Graham for the invocation, and then the Governor of Texas to welcome people to our state and speak about his dad. I later heard that some people thought George W. got too close to the line when he spoke about his dad's decency and honesty. That really bothered me, because I remember when I was campaigning for George and would talk about his decency and honesty, reporters would say: "Do you mean you don't think his opponent is decent or honest?" I would answer, "Who's talking about [his opponent]? I'm talking about George Bush." Well, we were here to talk about George Bush, and you can't mention George Bush unless you talk about decency and honor.

Then Nancy Reagan gave a very generous speech about George. She looked lovely in red, and tiny—about the nicest thing I can say about anyone! She was so nice and spoke for her "Ronnie." If George W. got close to the line, then Jerry Ford got closer as he raved over George's service to his country and all the other leadership qualities. He was glowing. He and Betty are dear, fine people. Jimmy Carter surprised so many people by giving a charming and very amusing talk. Bill Clinton gave a flattering and a very kind speech. All the presidents were received with cheers and standing ovations. I think the Democrats were surprised and thrilled! George then spoke and worked everyone into his words with skill and affection. He thanked Bill Clinton for his generous words and for making a "happy retirement possible."

The Clintons came to the apartment for a few minutes, but could not stay for lunch as he had a full plate: a fast track vote was coming up; Saddam Hussein was acting up and would not allow Americans to be on the UN weapons inspection team; and all those worrisome problems that a president has to face. They greeted our other guests and flew back to Washington. We fed all the former "everythings," plus Lee and Walter Annenberg. They had been tremendous donors to the Library and were dear friends—not only to us, but also to Nancy Reagan and the Fords.

At the same time that we were having lunch on our apartment terrace for forty, George and Laura were hosting a lunch for two thousand people in the great tent. For months afterward we heard from people who said they had loved being there. I know that both George and I wanted to see all those who came from all across the country, and yet, you can't be in two places at one time. We were so sorry we never saw them. Even our children left before we had a chance to say good-bye or to thank them for coming, as the grandchildren had school the next day.

As for thanking people, there are so many: Ann Brock, who headed up the planning; George's office, starting with the staff headed by Jean Becker, and those unbelievable volunteers; Don Wilson, executive director of the Library Foundation, and his crew; Pete Roussel and Roxann Neumann and their team; good friends Nancy Ames and

Danny Ward, who coordinated all the entertainment for the barbecue; and too many volunteers to mention. Together they literally planned every single thing from the family dinner, the train trip, the meals, the programs—just everything. Two thousand people were seated in color-coded sections and that worked very well, thanks to George's office. Jackson Hicks catered many meals, and the Texas A&M food service did the Governor's lunch.

The Texas A&M students were magnificent and steered all our guests in and out of crowded places and to their seats. Everyone commented on just how helpful and polite the students were.

That night, we met with some classmates of George's from Yale and then took Lech Walesa and his entourage out for dinner. Our other foreign friends had to leave for their homes or other commitments.

Friday morning, George and I went our separate ways. George cut the ribbon on A&M's International Center, which is housed at the Library, and I toured briefly The Barbara Bush Family Center at Texas A&M. It is a wonderful place that has a Project Head Start, an ESL Program (English as a Second Language), adult literacy classes; plus, of course, children's classes getting them reading-ready. The Barbara Bush Foundation had given them $50,000 start-up money.

George and I met back at the Library to attend Community Day opening ceremonies. We once again marched up the ramp and the crowd was large. We thanked the community for all they did to make the day before go so well. There was music and a few very short speeches.

At 10 a.m. I went out on the highway to help symbolically plant some crape myrtles that eventually will line the roadway from the Library to the airport, hundreds of them.

⤳ Some rather miscellaneous things happened the rest of November that amused me a little and made me a little sad.

We went to a dinner one night and I sat at the "I don't know" and "What did you say?" end of the table. Many of our friends can't hear well or are slowly fading in and out. In answer to the simplest question like, "Where is your brother living now?" the answer is, "I don't know," or, "What did you say?" That's sad.

George told me that one of the major networks asked him to tape a message about both Jerry Ford and Ronald Reagan so that when they died, the network would have it "in the can" and be ready to go. I knew that newspapers did this kind of thing. They have obits already written so they can get them out immediately. Well, George turned them down flat. After all, they were still with us! He then learned that Dan Quayle had gotten a letter requesting that he make a statement about George! Now I think that is sad and amusing in a sick kind of way. (I just learned in 2002 that Jean Becker, when she worked at *USA Today,* was asked to write my obituary before she left there in 1989 to come work for me at the White House! Thank heavens they haven't had to use it yet.)

And at the end of November I wrote in my diary:

My heart is broken this morning. 70 people, mostly tourists, were killed in Luxor, Egypt [by] extremists. Poor people. Poor Egypt. This will devastate tourism in Egypt and an already poor economy. Suzanne Mubarak must be sick. I hate it when a friend hurts.

George traveled in Canada and Europe and I traveled in this country. We met up Thanksgiving Day in Houston. Laura was in New York City with the girls, and so we had Neil and his family and George W. The sons and I played a quick round of golf in the morning before George got home from England. I love seeing my children together, teasing, laughing, and enjoying each other. It is as close to heaven as I may ever get.

In December I got a new hip, my second. Once again I planned it after I knew that George had scheduled a U.S./Japanese meeting at College Station and could not be in Rochester, Minnesota. I honestly feel that elective surgery, or any ordinary surgery, is a time for the patient to be alone so they can work to get well and snooze in between. This is if—and this is a big if—you are fully confident in the hospital and nursing care. I am both at the Mayo Clinic. If George came, I would worry all the time about whether he was being fed, wasn't bored, etc. To prove my point, on Wednesday at 6 p.m. I looked up and there was our precious Doro. She had planned on being there at 10 a.m., to surprise me when I awakened from the surgery. Her plane was eight hours late due to snow delays. Doro couldn't stand my being alone and left her family of five and flew to Minnesota. She stayed a little while and then went to the hotel. She was back in the morning for my first painful getting out of bed and walk. Then she had to leave at 2 p.m. to get home. She had come so far that I didn't want to miss a minute of her visit, so I struggled to stay awake. She said as she left, "Now I know why you didn't want anyone to come with you. You have been fighting to stay awake for four hours." Right she was, but I was so touched by her coming so far and being so thoughtful and loving.

Obviously the rest of the year for me was a happy, quiet one while George traveled a little and took very good care of me. I saw friends at home; walked and walked, as that is important with new hips; and I read and read, as that's important for the morale.

So now I am balanced—new hips on both sides. Dr. Bernie Morrey, the same marvelous surgeon at Mayo Clinic, took care of me, and again I played golf in six weeks. I honestly do not remember that I have two fake hips—until I try to get through an airport security checkpoint. I went by a hand-held machine the other day and asked the women to check. Both hips beeped!

The following seems very self-serving, but is so sweet and meant a lot to me. It was a good way to end a year.

George wrote this letter for a benefit auction for Literacy Partners in New York. He was asked to name his favorite author or authors:

Dear Reader,
This is a letter about two of the great authors I have known and loved.
The first, our dog Millie. I used to be President of the USA. Millie, young and fast, lived in the White House. She chased squirrels on the White House lawn. She ran like a dart through the lovely woods at Camp David and climbed,

surefootedly, on the rocks at Maine. She wrote a best selling book, ably assisted by my wife.

Then this summer she got cancer and died and we wept, for Millie had given us great joy and love and we missed her.

The second author is Barbara Pierce Bush, the one who helped Millie write. Barbara is my wife—has been for almost 53 years. She wrote a *Memoir*. She helps our country know the importance of reading. She is down to earth. She loves grandkids, gardens, and dogs.

She is a grand writer, but not scary like some authors. We laugh a lot together. We cry, too. We are two people, but we are one. I love her a lot.

Sincerely,
George Bush

With Barbara and Jenna in Venice, March 1998.

Once more we saw the New Year in with our dear friends at El Tule Ranch. We then took Ann and Alan Simpson to College Station to see the Library and spend the night in our apartment. We both love going there. George tells me that if something happened to me, that's where he would live. However, I love Houston—especially my friends there. George knows that, so a move to the Library is not imminent, and I secretly think that he feels so passionately about our great cancer hospital, M. D. Anderson—as I write in 2003 he is chairman of the Board of Visitors—that he would never leave Houston. He also would think twice about asking the office staff to move, not to mention the Secret Service families! We also count heavily on our little army of Houston volunteers, who have sustained George's office for years. So I am not going to worry.

On January 26, George hosted the first of many leadership forums at the Library.

One of the scheduled speakers was Gordon Bethune, CEO of Continental Airlines, which is based in Houston. He suggested we fly to College Station on the company's vintage DC-3 airplane. The ride brought back so many memories of those twelve-hour trips from Midland back east to visit our parents in the 1950s. We would bump across the country, and it was especially treacherous in the summer when we bounced over those air thermals. I got sicker than sick. This was a smooth ride, but it took us over an hour—and with the drive to the airport included—it would have been much faster if we had driven. But not as much fun.

The other speakers that day were Chuck Norris; Frank Bennack, Jr., CEO and president of The Hearst Corporation; our dear friend Bob Mosbacher, George's secretary of commerce and a successful businessman; and Laura Bush, first lady of Texas and very successful literacy advocate. At the last minute Gordon Bethune couldn't come because of pressing business matters, so George filled in for him.

All the speakers were asked to talk about five minutes on leadership, and then they took questions from the audience, made up of students, faculty, A&M graduates, and residents of Brazos County. This is the regular setup for these events, whether there is one speaker or five. At Texas A&M the person who asks the questions does so to learn something, not to embarrass the speaker.

This panel was interesting. Frank Bennack talked about many of the traits that one needed to lead. The one I remember that rang so true to me was ENERGY. To be a great leader, one has to lead with enthusiasm and energy.

We were so proud of Laura. Her passion for the importance of learning certainly was evident, and her charming, gentle self came through.

I was really surprised by Chuck Norris. He and his beautiful wife Gina are friends of ours, but I knew little or nothing about his early days. He grew up in Oklahoma in abject poverty. His mother was his sole means of support. He didn't go further than high school, went into the service and learned karate—as I remember—to defend himself as he was small. He talked about setting goals. He eventually became the world karate champion and, of course, an actor with his own TV program, *Walker, Texas Ranger.* He was very articulate. It is an amazing story, and it hasn't ended. Chuck has an annual tennis and golf tournament to help support his "Kick Drugs Out of America" program. Since 1992, more than thirty thousand Texas children, mostly middle school students, have taken part in these karate classes. This is an in-, after-, and summer school program. These children are performing better in the classroom, and many of them have gone on to college and are contributing citizens. Some are now back helping Chuck.

I love it when people who have overcome great hardships turn around to give a helping hand to others.

This was the year of tragic skiing accidents, as both Michael Kennedy and Sonny Bono died running into trees on the slopes. The very saddest thing was that both were fathers, and in both cases, their children were with them.

The other sad current events were the trials of Timothy McVeig and Terry Nichols for the Oklahoma bombings.

The thing that worries me is that some of the families of the victims are on television and seem so bloodthirsty. There was real joy by some when the first man got the death sentenc (which I felt he deserved), then despair when the second ma didn't. I guess if you haven't suffered their pain it is hard understand. I am not articulate enough to express my sorr over the reaction that some of these people are displaying.

This brings up another thought: Sometimes people su loved one has died in an accident. Maybe the word "acci become obsolete. Accident used to mean: "A: an event occ chance or from unknown causes. B: lack of intention or etc." I wonder if these grieving people think that money death all right? There are always exceptions—sometimes appropriate. Easy for me to wonder, but I do have frien lost children to accidental deaths. They have felt that getting involved in causes that will prevent the same accident from happening again will ease their pain and keep their child alive in a positive way.

For example, there's a program in Houston called "Bo's Place," which fills a real need. Bo Neuhaus, who died at age twelve of liver cancer, wrote a loving, comforting book with his mother, Lindy, in his last year of life. Later, Lindy started this program to help families cope with the death of a child or a sibling. I went to their annual luncheon in 1998 (and again in 2003), at which Susan Baker and her sister Klinka Lollar were receiving The Robin Bush Award. The speaker for the day was Louise and Denton Cooley's brilliant daughter, Dr. Susan Cooley. She illustrated with a story in a very moving way why "Bo's Place" is important and needed:

Years ago in Houston a man took his little boy by the hand, and, carrying a briefcase, walked into Poe Elementary School. He told the principal of the school that he wanted to enroll his son. The principal got the facts, age, where he lived, etc., and then said that he would go to another good school because he didn't live in the Poe district. The man said that he wanted the child to go to that exact elementary school, and if they didn't enroll the child, he had a bomb in his briefcase and would detonate it. The principal immediately agreed that the child could enroll on Monday and, as she talked, she led the man and child out of the school, which was filled with children. Just as they got outside the school, the bell rang for recess, the children raced over to embrace the very popular principal, and the bomb exploded. One little boy was killed, along with the man, his son, and the principal, and several more were injured.

Susan Cooley was a classmate and a good friend of the little boy who died. She came to her mother several weeks later and confessed that she had to tell her that she had killed the principal and her classmate. Her mother asked her how she possibly could think that. Susan said when the recess bell had rung she had not run outside, but gone to the bathroom. When she flushed the toilet, the most dreadful noise happened and all the windows blew out. Therefore she had killed her classmate and the principal. This sounds slightly crazy, but that's what the little girl thought. "Bo's Place" lets children talk, and teaches mothers and fathers how to talk and listen to their children. It is a place to talk, listen, and share.

Klinka Lollar also lost a child, and when she got her award, she ended her few words by saying that many years ago she told me that she never could thank all the people who had helped her and it worried her. She said I said, "Don't worry—just pass it on." I hope I really did give her that good advice.

Later that day I visited with the mother and father of the child who was killed all those years ago at the Poe Elementary School, who are now very close, dear friends. This little boy died after our Robin and just before we moved to Houston. Mutual friends had asked me to go talk to the couple because the wife was having such a hard time. We discussed the fact that I said then I couldn't possibly talk to people I barely knew about such a personal thing; now I felt badly that I had been such a coward. They laughed and she said, "But you did come, you know, and you really helped me. I was going out to the grave with flowers all the time and you told me that I shouldn't do that. You said that I should get on with my life and the life of my family, my husband, and two other boys." That sounded so cruel. I said that I didn't think that was very nice and she reiterated that I had really helped her. Her husband said with a smile, "That sounds just like you, Miss Frank."

So I got credit that day for two things I don't remember doing or saying. Do you suppose you only remember those things you want to remember? Or do you just plain forget at a certain age?

We went to see several movies—*As Good As It Gets*; *L.A. Confidential*; and our dear friend, movie producer Jerry Weintraub, sent us *Titanic*. We loved the first. George enjoyed the second and I hated it. It was all about "bad cops." I think "cops" are good, and I hate for children to see them denigrated. Having said that, many people really enjoyed it and Kim Basinger won an Academy Award for her role. As for *Titanic*, I wrote:

It is getting the biggest rave. George loved it. It was beautiful—lovely clothes, great scenes of the ship. But I felt that it was at least one hour too long. I can forgive the twisting of the story, leaving out the real heroes: the Strauses, John Jacob Astor,* or all the people who were locked down below. But there was one hour too long of water rushing up and down the halls.

One of the best we saw was called *To Live,* with English subtitles. It was set in China, before 1949 and after. It was beautiful, and both of us were enthralled.

George and I went to see the stage show *Gigi* at TUTS—Houston's Theater Under the Stars. It was marvelous. We had the added pleasure of sitting next to Leslie Caron, who had played Gigi in the movies forty years ago. She is an adorable, tiny-looking creature with all the Parisian charm in the world. She stayed to be with us for the first act and then flew home to Paris. What a treat. The newspaper panned the show. Wrong!

At the end of January we flew to Kona, Hawaii, where 1,200 Pepsi-Cola people were gathered to celebrate their 100th anniversary. It was absolutely the grandest event, with golf tournaments, speakers, and every place you looked, Pepsi cans hanging off trees, plants, and even chandeliers. They had many famous entertainers, but the only one I can remember is Mick Jagger. Margaret Thatcher flew from London, arrived just in time for dinner, gave a twenty-minute speech the next morning, and flew home before lunch. We visited for a few minutes before our early morning talks, and Margaret said that she found it very strange that these people seemed to like "previously prominent people," or was it " formerly famous fellows"? I never quite thought of her, or ourselves, in that way, but I guess she was right. She also told George that she wished she could have had just "four more years" and was surprised that George didn't feel the same way.

Just after we arrived in Kona, the sad scandal about the president broke. I am sorry to say that it dominated the conversation at the convention. I am sadder to say that it dominated the news for all of 1998. I wrote in my diary:

---

*I'm thinking of all the husbands who put their wives and children in the lifeboats and bravely sent them off. Ida Straus refused to leave without her husband Isidor and died with him.

We saw several movies on the plane going home—all Academy Award nominees. *Wag the Dog* was eerie as we could have been seeing a true-to-life movie. The President in the movie had been caught in an act with a very young girl just before an election. His staff manufactured a war with Albania to get the President re-elected. Here we are sitting with Iraq misbehaving again. I read that the people of Iraq are watching this scandal carefully because they are afraid that our president might take action to divert attention from his problems. That's ridiculous.

⤶ El Niño played havoc in our lives that year. I was flying out to Palm Springs, California, to visit the Annenbergs and meet George. Both Norma and John Major were going to be there one night, and I was going to a dinner for John while George spoke at another event. I got on a plane and flew to Dallas. Although our plane was late leaving BUSH Intercontinental Airport, we made the connecting flight. We had a very late takeoff, but still left in plenty of time for me to make the dinner. We circled the Palm Springs airport for quite a while and then had to fly on to Las Vegas and land. It was amazing, because everyone missed something and kept people waiting, but the whole plane seemed to accept their fate and there were no complaints. By this time we were all friends and chatting and laughing EXCEPT for the rather disheveled-looking man who slept next to me and made all sorts of revolting sounds—sort of like he was going to spit out some pretty bad stuff. He snoozed off and on and finally awakened when we landed and he heard the pilot say: "Welcome to Las Vegas." He sputtered and said, "Las Vegas? I wanted to go to Palm Springs." He looked stunned. I said, "I wish I had known that; you slept through the Palm Springs stop." Then he really looked shocked, and I had to tell him the truth. He turned out to be a really nice guy, and an exhausted rabbi at that, who was flying home from a trip to Israel.

When I finally arrived at the Annenbergs', Philippe de Montebello, the director of the Metropolitan Museum of Art in New York, was another houseguest at Sunnylands. Walter and Lee have left their glorious collection of Impressionist masterpieces to the Metropolitan. I wrote in my diary, " I guess [Philippe] has come to see his paintings.☺" At that time the paintings spent six months a year in New York City and six months in Palm Desert. Now, thanks to a new digital process, the original paintings stay at the Met, and hanging at Sunnylands are the most amazing reproductions. Lee had the frames hand-carved to duplicate the originals, and you cannot tell the difference.

We had some fascinating discussions about artworks that were sold or confiscated before and during World War II, between 1932 and 1945. In some cases, the families themselves sold the paintings for much-needed money, but no records were kept. Of course, many paintings were taken by the Germans and changed hands so many times after the war that ownership is hard to prove. In most cases, the buyers—whether private owners or museums—bought the paintings in good faith from legitimate dealers. It is a real problem. Until this is settled, Philippe says that there is no way that any museum would ever lend a painting again. As always, Lee and Walter had very interesting guests and were the most thoughtful host and hostess.

Walter had discovered that George loves fishing and stocked several of his ponds with largemouth bass and bluegill. So when George was not playing golf, resting, or eating, he was fishing and releasing. By now, these fish are a pretty good size. The minute the sun came up, George was out casting. I played golf, swam, and read. On this trip I read *The Tenth Justice,* by Brad Meltzer, which Frank Bennack had sent me; and James Patterson's *Cat & Mouse.* Both books were easy reads, and I especially loved them as I knew George would, too.

⟡ El Niño struck again, and AmeriCares sent a planeload of supplies, food, and medicines to Ecuador and Peru to help after devastating storms hit the west coasts of Central and South America. Quincy Hicks and Dr. Ben Orman volunteered to help and went on this exhausting trip. On Valentine's Day, Sadie and I went out to wave the plane off and do a few TV and newspaper interviews. I was given large hearts that I was to affix on huge container cases that were wrapped in see-through plastic. *"AmeriCares"* was written on the center of the heart. As the cameras rolled and the pictures snapped, I turned to affix the heart and noticed that I was looking at case after case of female sanitary pads. I wasn't exactly sure what their problem was, but bravely continued, later learning that sanitary napkins make perfect bandages in emergencies. After all, they are sterile and they absorb. It makes sense, but still was a surprise. This was a grueling trip for Ben and Quincy as they were in the air four times longer than on the ground.

We were both still doing a lot of speaking. While in Phoenix at a Mayo board meeting, I gave a talk at a fund-raising luncheon for "Childhelp USA," the most marvelous program for abused children. I have helped them a little in California, Tennessee, and Virginia, and now they were opening their flagship center in Phoenix. Amazingly, Phoenix has the highest number of child abuse cases in the country! This group raised $1.2 million at this luncheon.

A side note: In 2002, I was honored to receive the Sandra Day O'Connor Award from the Arizona Foundation for Women. This organization works to educate women on what to do about abuse, how to get help, and so on. Very often the children are also abused, and in many cases that is when the woman will seek help. Former ABC anchor Hugh Downs, whom we both like a lot, presented me with the award at a huge lunch. He and his wife of fifty-nine years have retired to Phoenix, and he is a co-founder of MAN, an organization made up of leading men in the community who are dedicating time and money to this cause. So I guess Arizona is really facing up to this enormous national problem.

꩜ We traveled coast-to-coast speaking the last half of February. George even flew to Tokyo on the 24th and returned on the 27th. My last diary entry for February:

This whole week has been a nightmare weather wise. California has had an unending barrage of wind and rain. They are having mudslides and beach erosions. Homes are slipping into the ocean or buried and crushed. Two policemen drove their car into a mud hole and drowned in mud. Tragic. Florida has had such a bad storm in the Kissimmee neighborhood. 40 people died. The other amazing thing is that a young child was snatched from her father's arms by a 200 mph wind. She was found ALIVE in a tree.

I think we all understood finally what El Niño is all about: A world turned upside down weather-wise.

~~ I read *Memoirs of a Geisha,* by Arthur Golden, which George and I both found fascinating. It amazes me that a young man wrote this book, but then the very sensitive *The Notebook* was also written by a young man, Nicholas Evans.

~~ We did some campaigning with Jeb, separately and together. Jeb is an inspired speaker and, in truth, is the best in the family—but don't tell the others I said this. If you don't tell them, they will never know as they told me before that they did not read my other book, but just looked up their own names in the index. Colu and I campaigned together one morning and then met up with Jeb at a large fund-raiser in Lakeland, Florida. I was introduced by a very nice and very bald man named "Baldy" Boyd. At my table they told me that I must call him "Baldy" since his own mother did. I just could not and so thanked "Mr. Boyd," explaining that I wouldn't dare call him "Baldy"; I was so afraid that he'd call me "Fatty." I loved the look on Jeb's face, not to mention the gasp and finally the laughter that followed. Will I never grow up?

~~ Jack Allin, the former presiding bishop of the Episcopal Church of the USA, our dear friend and summer minister, died in March. Jack was also the minister in Hobe Sound, Florida, to George's mother, Grace and Louis Walker, and other family and friends in the winter. We miss Jack's twinkle and smile. We miss his sense of humor. We miss his breaking into song in the middle of a service. We had a nice memorial service in Kennebunkport at St. Ann's the next summer for Jack. The current summer minister, M. L. Agnew, gave a lovely sermon and said two things that I hope I won't forget. He quoted Jack's wife Ann as saying, "It wouldn't be so bad if it hadn't been so good." He also said, "Whenever a member of our family goes away, we say: 'Remember me as loving you.'" I loved that.

Jack wanted George to win so badly in 1992, and he worried that the Bush campaign was doing everything badly. I remember he wrote me that he was distressed because he asked all his farmer friends about the "Weed and Seed" program that he had read about and not one of them had heard of it. Of course they hadn't! The Weed and Seed program was run by former Notre Dame basketball coach Digger Phelps. It was an attempt to solve gang problems. Its goal was to weed out the gang leaders and seed the others out of gangs and into productive lives. It was a great program that never got the press attention it deserved.

Campaigns are hard and difficult for those of us on the outside to understand. "Why don't you go door-to-door?" "Why don't you have neighborhood meetings?" "Get Jeb to call me. I can introduce him to some rich people." They want to help, but do not understand. Jeb has a big state to cover and although he needs money, rich doesn't count. VOTES COUNT.

And speaking of votes, Texas had their primary in March and the good news is: George W. got 97% of the vote. The bad news is that only 12% of the eligible voters voted. That seems so sad to me. The apathy in this country is awful. People are willing to criticize, but not willing to vote.

On March 12, I met Jenna and Barbara, George and Laura's daughters, at Bush Intercontinental Airport where they had flown from Austin. We flew to Rome, Italy, for the girls' spring break. Quincy came along as my "everything." She made all the plans, but her biggest job was to see that the girls were up, dressed, and packed when the schedule said they should be. I also decided that I would NEVER look into their room. Once or twice in the ten days, by mistake, I caught a glimpse and that taught me that my decision was certainly brilliant. They were two normal, wonderful sixteen-year-olds; just messy. Quincy had worked hard at getting hotel reservations, and we stayed at the three nicest hotels in Rome, Florence, and Venice. The Italian Embassy in Washington was very helpful; as it turned out, much more helpful than I realized at first. Ambassador Ferdinando Salleo and his charming wife had suggested that they knew a young man who would love to

show us around. I resisted, feeling that we didn't want to impose and
that we wanted to sort of poke around by ourselves.

We arrived in Rome and went right to the Hotel Hassler at the
top of The Spanish Steps. We had three rather small, perfect, very stylish rooms, with great views of the city. We bathed and went to the
Galleria Borghese and were met by Daria Borghese Salleo, the daughter-in-law of the Italian ambassador. Daria was an attractive brunette
about thirty years old and is a descendant of Cardinal Scipione Borghese, who built the villa and collected the works by Bernini, Caravag-
gio, Raphael, Rubens, and Titian, to name a few. Daria was
accompanied by Stefano Aluffi-Pentini (the young man the ambassador knew), who had helped Quincy plan our trip. And what a trip
they planned. Stefano leads museum and company tours around all of
Italy, and Daria is also a member of that firm. I NOW think that our
great trip guide was a gift from the Italian government, but he was so
kind and laid-back that he made it seem as though he was along
because he enjoyed showing us around.

We went from there to visit the Galleria Pallavicini Casino dell
Aurora, a privately owned collection and garden. There are three high-
ceilinged rooms filled with paintings and beautiful marble floors—the
multicolored marble brought to Rome during the Roman Empire
period from China, Africa, etc.

I wrote in my diary:

> I am amazed by the number of people who come up to me,
> both in The Borghese Museum and on the Spanish Steps . . .
> really all over Rome and say such nice things about our family.

We learned a good lesson that first night. The three girls and I
went to a fancy restaurant that had been highly recommended. We
waited too long for dinner, it cost too much, and sixteen-year-old girls
do not like fancy food! From then on, when possible, we ate in bistros
and street cafés. The food was delicious, fast, and cheaper.

We were so honored to have our old friend, Pio Cardinal Laghi,
show us around the Vatican. When George was vice president, the cardinal lived across the street from us, when he was serving as the Apos-
tolic Pro-Nuncio to the United States. I was touched that he took the

I wasn't quite sure what to think when *Outlaw Biker* magazine named me "First Lady of the Century" in 1995. At least they got the pearls right. (Back cover reprinted by permission of *Outlaw Biker*)

George W. becomes Governor of Texas, January 1997, as his father wipes away a tear. Barbara and Jenna are standing between their grandparents and parents. In the crowd behind us you can see Jeb and Neil. Right behind Laura Bush is one of George W.'s closest friends, Don Evans, now secretary of commerce. Way in the back, taking a photo, is cousin Debbie Stapleton and her husband, Craig. And behind Craig you can see another cousin, Elsie Walker Kilborne.
(*Star-Telegram* photo by Rodger Mallison)

We took Mikhail Gorbachev to one of our favorite lunch places in Maine,
Barnacle Billy's in Ogunquit, just down the coast from Kennebunkport. Here
we are posing with three waiters who happened to be from Russia. July 9, 2001.
(Family scrapbook)

Our Kennebunkport flagpole
keeps getting bigger. From the
top: the American flag, the
Presidential flag, the Maine flag,
the Florida flag at left, the Texas
flag at right. July 5, 2001.
In front of the flagpole, front to
back: Gigi Koch, Robert Koch,
Doro Koch.
(Barbara Bush)

The president and the governor play horseshoes, July 5, 2001.
(Barbara Bush)

The Monday lunch ladies, December 3, 2001. From left: Barbara Bush, Bobbie Fitch, Ann Peake, Helen Vietor, Phoebe Welch, Peggy Neuhas, Barbara Riddell.
(Family scrapbook)

We were thrilled when the NFL returned to Houston in 2002, with the arrival of the Houston Texans. This photo was taken as part of a billboard campaign to help the owner and good friend Bob McNair sell season tickets. (Courtesy of Pam Francis Photography)

With the students of Barbara Bush Elementary School in Mesa, Arizona, March 22, 2002.
(Family scrapbook)

Campaigning for the Governor of Florida in 2002.
(Office of the Governor Photo by Eric Tourney)

Reading to a group of preschoolers at Carver Elementary School in
Bryan, Texas, March 2003.
(Chandler Arden)

Misbehaving in Maine, Summer 2002.
(Family scrapbook)

Hamming it up with actors from
the production of *Kiss Me Kate*,
in Houston, March 25, 2003.
(Family scrapbook)

time to give us a tour of the Sistine and Paulina chapels. The renovations at the Sistine Chapel were almost finished, and although His Eminence had arranged for a guide to show us around, he took the tour with us. The little Paulina Chapel is where the Pope celebrates Mass; it's here that Michelangelo's last painting hangs. After our tour, His Eminence guided us by car to a back door of St. Peter's, where we could walk through some gardens. The view of the cathedral and the city was spectacular from this vantage point. The two Secret Servicemen with us were Catholics and couldn't get over the honor of having a real cardinal show us around. They confessed to me that they hope he will become the next Pope. We left the cardinal and walked through the beautiful St. Peter's Basilica; I especially wanted the girls to see Michelangelo's *Pietà*. I had not been to the Basilica since some awful demented person had damaged the sculpture; it was cordoned off and one could not see it as closely as one would like.

From there we went to the Trevi Fountain, where Quincy threw in two coins. They say one coin will bring you back; two will bring you love. It was jammed around the fountain, and we had to wait while she wedged her way in. I don't know if Quincy will return, but she certainly found love and was married in 2001 in Kennebunkport to the very nicest young man, J. T. Crawford. They now live in New Orleans, where J.T. is the head golf pro at the New Orleans Country Club.

We went to a luncheon with Stefano at Circola della Caccia in the Piazza Borghese with Daria and Carmen Salleo and her brother, Marcantonio Borghese. These were the most attractive people. I must also mention the lunch because it was delicious: a pasta with asparagus, a perfect fish, potatoes, artichoke hearts, and spinach. It was our first healthy meal, and the girls talked about it the whole trip.

I rushed off to the Villa Richardson to have tea and a visit with Lindy Boggs, our ambassador to the Vatican. She was eighty-two that day and looked young and adorable in a black velvet gown. I was thrilled to see her. Lindy had been a congressional wife, and after her husband Hale Boggs died, she was a very respected congresswoman. She is also a "gentlewoman." She is the mother of Cokie Roberts, then an ABC commentator.

I had told the girls before we left home that I really expected them to sightsee with me in the mornings, then in the afternoons they were free to do what they wanted WITH QUINCY TAGGING ALONG. (Poor Quincy!) As it turned out, the girls were marvelous and went with me everywhere—to gardens, galleries, and so on. From 5 to 8 p.m. I begged off and took a rest while the girls explored stores and side streets. We had lovely quiet dinners in places that were recommended by the Secret Service and we had lots of laughs. I adore these girls. They are always fun, but—as is true of all fourteen of our grandchildren— they are much more fun and interesting away from their parents.

Our last morning in Rome, I looked out my window and thought, "I am going to miss my view: red-tiled rooftops, domes in the far-off, tourists down below on the Spanish Steps, umbrella trees, and a wild-flower growing out of a roof right outside my window."

We took a morning train to Florence, which was clean and rela-tively silent except that every few minutes a phone would ring and a passenger would answer and start talking—well, shouting. This seems to be a universal problem. Why is it that people on planes, in trains, or even sitting on a park bench feel they have to yell on a cell phone?

Florence: what a city! WOW! I still feel that way.

We stayed in the sweetest place, Hotel Tornabuoni Beacci, recom-mended by Debbie Stapleton. We met up with Wendy, Debbie and Craig's twenty-two-year-old daughter, who was studying art history in Florence for a term from the University of Michigan. Wendy moved into the hotel for our stay. It is charming, in the center of the city and several blocks from the Ponte Vecchio, the fourteenth-century bridge, lined with jewelry stores that have been there since the sixteenth century. Florence is one of my—and everyone else's who has ever been there—favorite cities in the world. We were very lucky that George's brother Jon Bush had a great friend, Gordon Moran, living in Florence with his wife, so he and Stefano both showed us around, including the Uffizi Gallery, the walk through the corridor to the Pitti Palace over the Arno River, and through the gardens. We also visited the Accade-mia Gallery where, thanks to Gordon, we were led in a side door so that we immediately passed Michelangelo's four unfinished *Slaves;* a better word is *"prisoners,"* as they are prisoners in the marble. There, directly in front of us, was the *David,* that huge glorious figure of a man.

We had a fabulous lunch—Jon Bush's treat—at an outdoor restau-rant on the square near, the Church of Santa Maria Novella. And treat it was—pigeons, kids, dogs, tourists (many Japanese), and students eating, sleeping, and generally having a great time.

At Gordon's urging we took a forty-five-minute trip through the countryside to Siena, a darling little town. The Piazza del Campo is a big focal point, and as it was a warm Sunday afternoon, there were hundreds of people sitting with their families, walking, window-shopping, and visiting. Jenna, Barbara, Quincy, Stefano, and Secret Service agent John McClellan walked to the top of the Torre del Mangia, a 280½-foot tower, and waved to us while Gordon and I had a soft drink and talked. He told me about the Palio delle Contrade, the horse race contest among the fourteen neighborhoods, held on July 2 and August 16, which has been going on since the thirteenth century right here in the plaza. Gordon says that it is one of the most thrilling, colorful events and well worth coming back to see. It was hard to envision and certainly would be hot, but Gordon's enthusiasm made it very tempting.

There is a truly lovely cathedral in Siena that we walked to. It was started in the eleventh century and never quite finished because the Black Plague hit and the work stopped. The interior has black and white floors and pillars, and there are lovely frescos in a small library. I found it stunning.

On the way back to Florence, we drove into Monteriggione, a village that stands on a high hill and is girdled by a well-preserved thirteenth-century wall, reinforced by fourteen towers. The fortified site is described by Dante in his *Inferno*. Lest I be accused of plagiarism—even in my diary—much of this information came from a little guidebook, circa 1978, lent to me by neighbor and friend Bobbie Fitch. How Stefano teased me about this ancient little book, but since I can neither spell nor remember, it certainly helped me on the whole trip.

We took a 2½-hour train ride from glorious Florence to Venice and went by boat to the Hotel Gritti Palace, a perfectly beautiful first-class hotel. I could see the Grand Canal out my window, and the traffic was fascinating. The Venetians looked to the east toward Constantinople, and the Turkish influence is seen everywhere. After we ate lunch, Stefano walked us to the Marchesi Berlingieri Palace, where the most adorable, attractive couple met us. They had invited a few friends to tea, among whom were three funny, nice young men about the girls' ages. One was a redhead named Freddy who knew everything about the city's history; he had grown up there and was the most enthusiastic Venetian. It had been a republic for well over one thousand years. We walked from the palace to St. Mark's Square. It is enormous—290 yards—filled with people and pigeons. We went to the Doges' Palace—so different from the straight lines of the Roman and Florentine buildings and art. Everything is so Byzantine, so ornate, covered with gold leaf, etc. The rooms are grand and painted on every inch. We then went into the Doges' Chapel, also The Church of the Republic. The ceilings and archways are covered with gold-leaf mosaics and biblical scenes. It has a dome and statues of the twelve apostles, the two Marys, etc. Behind the altar there is a scene with some seven hundred precious jewels, gold leaf, and lovely enamel figures. The cathedral is filled with lanterns that hang down with red glass lights. It is the busiest church that I have ever seen.

We took many canal rides to the islands: Murano, where we visited a famous glass factory, Maazzega SRL; Torcello, a very important town in the ninth-century, where we went through the Cathedral of Santa Maria Assunta and saw the fine eleventh-century mosaics, and then walked next door to the octagonal Santa Fosca, a Veneto-Byzantine chapel; Burano, a fishing village known for its lace and painted houses. We walked over bridges, poked around, and had lunch there in a fabulous little restaurant. We ended the tour on the island opposite St. Mark's Square at The Institute and Church of San Giorgio Maggiore, begun in 1566 by Palladio. It is severe and rather refreshing after all the froufrou we had seen. We saw two paintings by Tintoretto, *The Harvest of Manna* and *The Last Supper*. The latter is remarkable for its perspective. It is not a frontal picture, but almost a side view. I loved the grandeur of this church, the Palladian arches, the simplicity. It was lovely.

By now, the girls—who had been saintlike—were really tired of all this, and I didn't blame them.

One night we went to the famous Harry's Bar for dinner. It was very nice and very expensive. Poor George. What a treat he had given us!

We flew to Paris and on to Houston. The flight took eleven hours and then the girls had to wait another two hours for their flight to

Ellie LeBlond and Marshall Bush in Rome, March 2001.
BARBARA BUSH

Austin. They were the best—great company, no complaining, and seemed to really have fun.

In 2001, granddaughters Ellie LeBlond and Marshall Bush and I took somewhat the same trip with Brooke Sheldon, my new "everything." We started in Paris and ended in Milan, with Rome, Florence, and Venice in between. The rules were the same and these two cousins were darling.

⮐ No sooner did we get home than it was time for us to get ready for "A Celebration of Reading." Our readers were all superb: mystery writers Tami Hoag and David Baldacci; spy author, the late Robert Ludlum; our old friend Christopher Buckley; James McBride; and historian Stephen Ambrose. Literally the day before Celebration, Stephen had to withdraw because of pneumonia, and Laura Bush suggested as a replacement Larry Wright, a friend and author from Austin, Texas. Although we missed Stephen, Larry was marvelous and truly brought down the house. George W. ended the evening by giving a shortened version of his very funny Alfalfa Club speech. It was a roaring success. Then all 1,400 of us went upstairs to supper that was on our tables when we arrived. How that genius Jackson Hicks—in my opinion, one of Houston's best caterers, who also has become a good friend—manages to have a perfect meal waiting is amazing. I am a great believer that charity dinners should not be long, drawn-out affairs. Having a delicious meal on the table is hard to do, but it is doable and allows people to get home at a reasonable hour. This event could not happen without many volunteers. They escort the guests, help everyone find their seats for the reading and the dinner, and fill the gift bags with books donated by publishers.

This Celebration may have been the best ever.* Christopher Buckley read from a book he wrote ages ago, *Wry Martinis*. His reading was about a trip to Paris, when Christopher was a speechwriter for then Vice President George Bush. We were staying at the very fancy Crillon Hotel. After Chris got out of his shower, he discovered that there were no towels or any other amenities in his bathroom. He called down and one tiny towel was delivered to his room. It turned out that the secretary of state had been there several weeks before and his entourage had swiped every ashtray, towel—in fact everything that wasn't tied down.

When Chris returned to the Houstonian Hotel that night, he found fifty towels in his bathroom. The Houstonian puts up all our authors as their contribution to literacy; obviously someone had called back to the hotel and decided to play a joke.†

All our readers were fabulous, but James McBride, author of *The Color of Water*, managed to be amusing, personal, and very moving. This was my favorite book in 1997; my sister Martha had sent it to me. His mother—"Mommy"—and his brother, Dr. Dennis McBride, came with him, and they were charming. Ruth McBride Jordan, his mother, is the most amazing woman, as is her story. At the end of his reading, James got very serious. He told the audience that his family of twelve sibling children had never been on welfare, had all graduated from colleges or nursing school, had been helped by two great fathers, the

---

*I say that every year, and mean it.
†The Houstonian is where George and I stayed when we came home to Houston during the vice-presidential and White House days. They have recently remodeled and it's more beautiful than ever, including a terrific spa and gym. The new owner, Gay Roane, has the best taste.

church, and grants from people like those in the audience. He said if it hadn't been for programs like ours, he might well have been waiting outside the door with a baseball bat ready to hit them over the head and rob them. I loved his courageous mother and have stayed in touch with Ruth. James very generously read for us again at the first ever Dallas Celebration of Reading in November 2002.

The day after Celebration we offer the authors and their guests a bus ride to College Station, a tour of the George Bush Library, lunch at our apartment, and a ride back to the airport. Continental Airlines gives airline tickets to our readers. As I have said several times, Houstonians are the most generous of people. Ariel had gone up earlier and had piping hot soup, chicken salad, and hot rolls on the tables when we arrived.

☙ That spring I flew to Amarillo, Texas, to help at a fund-raiser for a marvelous program, "Books for Babies." They greet new babies at the hospital with a book and talk to the new mother about the importance of reading to their children almost from birth. Many cities, and some states, have now adopted similar programs.

I wrote in my diary about the Amarillo event:

> From the airport we went right to the lunch and they did it perfectly: the food was on the table when we walked in; that speeded up the lunch and it was delicious. During lunch they showed a great video of their program on big screens. There were no waiters banging around. The Mayor spoke and I spoke . . . period. They did not need to tell us about the program or the sponsors as we had all seen the video. I flew home in time for a massage, early dinner, and bed.

I may seem obsessed by the meal being quick and the programs short—I am. And I am not just thinking of the guests!

☙ I had my hair done one day during this period and the nice man told me casually that his partner was an alcoholic and had AIDS.

In the same week an excited young man called to tell me that he was having a baby and getting married. Ten years ago, neither one of these things would have happened—well, they might have happened, but they would not have been so honest and told me. The really amazing thing was neither shocked me. I thought the former very sad and the latter very happy.

∽ On March 27 I flew to Orlando, Florida, passing George in the air, to speak to the Louisiana Bankers Association. Both George and I thought I was a funny choice. He swears that I am the woman who told her banker that she could not possibly be overdrawn as she still had twenty checks in her bankbook. It was a quick trip, and I flew back to Houston in time to drive to College Station and join George at a reception and dinner for former South Africa president F. W. de Klerk, who was the speaker for Texas A&M's Wiley Lecture Series. The next day, F.W., Brent Scowcroft, George, and I raced out to Pebble Creek Golf Course in College Station to play a round of golf. F.W. was the best. It was fast and fun. This course is a really nice one with lots of water and pretty holes.

The George Bush Library Advisory Council met on that same weekend. These are the dearest people, all of whom pay their own way down to College Station or to Kennebunkport (depending on where the meeting is held), and all of whom really have great suggestions. For instance, Julie Cooke—who used to work in my office—thought my section did not represent me very well. I confess I was thrilled to even have a place and thought it was pretty good. It is so much better now. Halfway through the museum you will come across a nice little area with an overstuffed couch and chair where you will often find an adult sitting with his or her arm around a child and reading a book from a bookshelf that we keep filled with children's books. Then there are some videos, photos, and other reminders of our White House days. I had suggested early on after the museum opened that we had to put more benches around this huge building. There is so much to see and people need to rest every now and then. To find a soft couch and overstuffed chair must be a joy. A place to collapse, rest, and read to a grandchild—who could ask for anything more?

Nearby is the beautiful dollhouse that Paula Rendon decorated while she was living in the White House with us. It has lovely petit point rugs that she made, pillows, etc. Paula insisted that it go to George's Library; I insisted that she give it to her grandchildren, until she pointed out that she has so many and she couldn't pick just one. Anyway, she wanted it to go to the Library. She takes great pleasure from the fact that not only children but adults spend a great deal of time studying her work of art.

      ⌒ The following are bits and pieces from a letter to Andy Stewart I wrote on April 25:

. . . I really had fun when I invited three ladies from Sea Island, Ga., to come to College Station, visit George's Library, and play golf the next day. These were three darling ladies that I had played golf with just after the White House days. Griffin Bell had arranged the match for me while he played with G.B. and two other men. One was Louise Suggs (age 79), LPGA early pioneer and champion; Caroline Carter (79) wrote with Margaret Mitchell on the Atlanta paper; and Fran Green (age 81). I met them at the G.B. Intercontinental Airport and drove them to College Station, fed them lunch, put them to bed for a nap, and then we had a private tour of the Library after visiting hours. Cocktails and dinner. The next day we played golf at Pebble Creek. Louise had an 80! And she had never seen the course before. Then we cleaned up and drove to Houston for a dinner at our house. These darling ladies charmed the Kerrs, Fitches and GB who had returned the night before from Europe. Mildred Kerr is a *Gone With the Wind*/Margaret Mitchell nut,* so she was beside herself.

We spent Easter with George and Laura and the girls at their little lake house near Athens, Texas. We had wonderful walks and the men spent hours fishing. The guesthouse left

---

*Sorry, Mildred, but that is what I wrote in the letter. Surely I meant "fan."

much to be desired . . . like there were two single beds . . . just not in the same room. Sadie adored running in the dogwood-filled woods although I worried about rattlesnakes and alligators. We did go to a tiny sunrise church service in the country. We froze, but the warmth of the other attendees was wonderful and so nice.

George P.'s days at Rice are numbered. He graduates in May. How we will miss him. One night this month we took George P. and seven of his friends to Morton's restaurant. My George challenged them to eat a 48-ounce Porterhouse steak. George P. and his friend "Packy" did! It was amazing because they also ate hot bread, potatoes, vegetables, and a huge dessert. Ah, youth.

We had tea with Kofi Annan and his lovely Swedish wife while he was here speaking at the Baker Institute at Rice University. He was charming, and she is not only a beauty, but warm and nice, too. . . . George loves all the diplomatic stuff and hates that we are [in] arrears in our U.N. dues.

. . . We both traveled back and forth across the country a great deal in April speaking, including a trip I took to Hartford, Conn., where I spoke at a lunch for The Children's Village; my sister Martha came in a wheelchair looking thinner, pale and really lovely. What is the matter with us? I was told that 52 out of 1,000 children in Connecticut are abused and there are 5 worse states. The lunch took forever and I felt free to tell the organization's president who sat on my right that next year they really should have the meal pre-set and that would speed up the whole process. George says that I am dreadful and should not say what I think all the time. This because at a great lunch in El Paso, Texas, several weeks ago I felt free to compliment the lady in charge on the fact that she had the most delicious lunch on the table, dessert and all, but after the speakers (a General, Governor and me) she stood and read off 140 names of people she wanted to thank. I just suggested that next year they put their names in the program and not make us all sit through all that name-calling! I tried to be tactful, but after attending what seems like thousands of charitable lunches I have learned that businessmen and women do not have time for two hour lunches.

That night my sister Martha had a small dinner party for me at Duncaster, a retirement home that she had settled into several years ago, and I spoke after dinner. I can say with total honesty that this was the nicest retirement community I had ever seen. It was perfect for my sister.

From there I drove to Springfield, Mass., and visited the site of the Dr. Seuss Memorial. I was the honorary chair of this memorial. What a man and what joy he brought to the children (and many adults) in this world. I use him sometimes in talks when I want an example of someone who never gave up. He sent the manuscript of his first book, *And to Think That I Saw It on Mulberry Street,* to 27 publishers, all of whom rejected it. The 28th accepted it and sold 4 million copies.

Governor Paul Celluci of Massachusetts* took me to visit a marvelous program called SPREAD THE WORD. Suburban schoolchildren collect books for inner city schoolchildren. They are asked to donate books in good condition that they no longer read and then each inner city child gets 5 books of their very own. It teaches the children to share and at the same time gives books to children who in many cases have never owned a book. Then we went and spoke at Salem College. I have been amazed by the number of small colleges across our country where one can get a first class education. This is one such fine school.

The congressional investigations [of President Clinton] are still going on in Washington. We heard from someone sitting on one of the non-partisan committees that the Democrats say one thing in the meetings and then go out and defend their guy in public. The Republicans say nothing, because they are afraid it will backfire on them.

*Now U.S. ambassador to Canada.

They are probably right. (I do wish they would defend their guy, too.)* I read where Sally Quinn said: "Nobody talks about 'it' in Washington, but 'it' is on everybody's mind. It's as though you went to a cocktail party where there was a tremendous elephant in the middle of the room and people act like it isn't there."

George has flown off to St. Louis for a Volunteer Summit meeting, a follow-up to last spring's meeting. He is doing these in many states. Neil's Lauren went with him to introduce him. She is lovely at 13 years of age. He said that she did a really fine job.

Poor Andy; I finally ended my letter with the wedding of Nancy Huang, my former aide. She married a fellow Harvard Business School graduate, Dan McCormick. I felt a little like her mother. Silly, but we all love her so. Her dad, Jimmy Huang, is an old friend who owns several very nice restaurants in Houston.

🙂 One other note about the congressional hearings: There was a great deal of pressure for the Secret Service to be called on to testify. It was during this time that George sent a SEALED letter to Special Prosecutor Ken Starr, saying he felt very strongly that the Secret Service should not be made to testify UNLESS they saw a law being broken. It was leaked. Too bad, as this was a strong conviction that George held and not meant to be used as a defense or any other thing.

🙂 I called my sister Martha to thank her for a book she had sent me that she really loved, *Intermission: A True Story,* by Anne Baxter, only to discover that she was recovering from pneumonia. As she had dreadful emphysema, this was scary. She truly had trouble breathing at the best of times. Anyway, she told me that she was reading this book in the beauty parlor when a lady asked her if she was enjoying it. Mart said that she really was, and asked the lady if she had been lucky

*I assume I meant Special Prosecutor Ken Starr, whom George and I respect a lot.

enough to know Anne Baxter. "No," came a rather abrupt answer. "I was curious as she just married my husband."

On May 3, Ariel and Sadie took off for Maine, and we went in different directions. George headed to Kitty Hawk, North Carolina, for a rededication of the Wright Brothers Memorial. The next day he went fishing in Beaufort, North Carolina, with Reggie Fountain of Fountain Power Boats. That's when George saw his new boat, *Fidelity 2*. George told me that the Library had begged him for *Fidelity 1*, and therefore he just HAD to give it to them. That sort of amused me. NO. 1 was twenty-five years old or more and had served us well, and if George wanted a new boat, he deserved one. I LIKED FIDELITY #1 better than #2, but since I don't ride in it that much, it makes no difference. They are both nice, and I can visit my old friend at the Library any time I want.

Meanwhile, I took in the Prudential Spirit of Community Initiative in Washington, D.C., a great program where they honor children thirteen to eighteen years old who volunteer and make a difference. We went upstairs to a reception/dinner; I never saw either, but saw lots of kids and their parents, all with cameras. Richard Dreyfus, the very talented actor, was there surrounded, and before I left I broke through his circle of children and reintroduced myself as we had met at a party Jerry and Jane Weintraub had given for us once at their home in Malibu. He was really nice and kissed me on both cheeks, and we had a little visit. I did not remind him that at the Weintraub party, when he came through the receiving line, he turned over his coat lapel and was wearing a pin that was uncomplimentary to George. George would have been pleased that I controlled myself—for once!

Quincy and I flew on to New York that night and did errands the next day. That night we attended "A Gala Evening of Readings," which I have attended for years and from where I got my idea for our own Celebration of Reading. Newspaper columnist Liz Smith, Arnold Scaasi, and Parker Ladd, a retired executive of the Association of American Publishers and a literacy activist, put this annual event on for Literacy Partners. It was one of their best, I thought. Their readers were Mary Higgins Clark, Frank McCourt, James McBride (who brought his darling mother and wife), Peter Gomes, and Gore Vidal. I have had the first three at our Celebration, and they were once again superb. Peter Gomes gave a sermonlike reading, and I thought that maybe this black-tie stylish group needed it—myself included. And as for Gore Vidal—the whole group, committee and audience, hung on his every word. "He usually doesn't do readings and came from Europe just for this evening," they said. No wonder he doesn't do readings. He read from the last pages of his *Lincoln* in a monotone that was hard to hear and understand. But New York loved him, and it was fascinating to watch.

From New York we went back to Washington, where I met George for a dinner for Iona House. Kitty Brady asked us to help with this dinner for this retirement home, and we were delighted to do it.

George and I went from there to Miami, where we had lunch with Jeb's good friends, Armando and Maggie Codina, and dinner with the University of Miami chancellor and his wife, Bosie and Tad Foote. We spent the night with Jeb and Colu, and the next morning we both got honorary degrees from the University of Miami. It was so hot that the graduation was at 8 a.m. As soon as it was over, we flew back to Houston, taking Jeb and Colu with us, and arrived in time to have dinner at the home of Malcolm Gillis, the president of Rice University; at eight o'clock the next morning, we were at George P.'s graduation. We had mixed feelings. We were proud that George P. made the honor roll. We were proud that he was graduating, but, oh, how we were going to miss our Sunday lunches with him. George P. was going back home to teach in Homestead, Florida, the next year.

Kurt Vonnegut delivered the graduation speech. It was short, amusing, well planned, and understandable. We both felt it was one of the best we had ever heard. He started out by saying: "Good morning, Adam. Good morning Eve. You have been in the Garden of Eden for four years, but unfortunately, you ate the apple of knowledge and you're out of here." He told the story about visiting his friend Joseph Heller, who wrote *Catch-22*. He said to him: "When you think about the fact that your book sold millions of copies and was translated into twenty-nine foreign languages, does it ever bother you that movie stars, basketball players, and TV commentators make more money in one month than your whole book made?" He said Heller thought a minute and said: "At least I know when I have enough." I'm sure he said other wonderful things, but that is what I remember. Also, I do remember thinking: "And we thought that it was hot in Miami!"

We went from the graduation to Houston's Volunteer Summit and then home, where I collapsed and George wolfed down a sandwich and a glass of milk and drove to Prairie View A&M's graduation, where he gave the speech.

After several more Houston dinners, the annual AmeriCares dinner in New York City, a Mayo Clinic meeting, and a graduation speech at Austin College, I finally got to join George in Maine on May 17. Sadie, Don, Paula, her daughter Teresa, and Ariel had the house opened and ready to go.

George was even busier. After the AmeriCares dinner, he gave commencement addresses for the University of Connecticut and Duke University, where the president is Nan Keohane; she was president of Wellesley when I spoke there in 1991. She is a really bright, nice lady and the first woman to be head of this huge establishment. George also spoke at the Disabilities Institute dinner in Chicago; got to play golf with our friend Bert Getz, CEO and director of Globe Corporation, at his marvelous Merit Club Course; and did an Eisenhower Exchange Fellowship dinner and meeting in Philadelphia. On May 23, he played golf with Bobby Koch, Lod Cook, and Jerry Weintraub at Pine Valley—I guess the golfer's Mecca. That night he gave the Lafayette College graduation speech and flew to Maine the next day. How often people worry about ex-presidents—what do they do? Are they busy enough? They ought to be asking George Bush what doesn't he do!

On May 28, we drove to Boston and George gave the ARCO Forum speech at Harvard. Al Simpson introduced him and was very funny. I think George was concerned about what kind of reception he would get at Harvard. No need to worry; it was fun and very pleasant. We also saw many friends and more family. In the fall of 2002, with fear and trepidation, I spoke in the same room for Harvard's John F. Kennedy School of Government and was also very well treated. I can't remember why I agreed to do this, but it turned out to be fun.

We took the train to New Haven for George's fiftieth reunion at Yale. It also was George W.'s twenty-fifth reunion, and although he didn't come, we saw many of his classmates and friends.

We stayed with Jane and Rick Levin, the president of Yale, whom

I had never met. I really am hesitant about staying with people I don't know. They turned out to be the nicest, easiest people, and both George and I immediately felt at home. So much so that I'm afraid we stayed with them again for Yale's three hundredth anniversary in 2001. When I arrived at The President's House, the Levins greeted me with their ten-year-old daughter, Becca. It was funny staying in that house on Hillhouse Avenue, right next door to the house we had lived in fifty years ago with eleven other families and thirteen children, where previously one woman and several maids had lived.

The next morning we walked on the campus, first looking into 37 Hillhouse Avenue, now cut up into offices; on to the old Yale Co-op, where I had worked part time, now a tremendous Barnes & Noble; and on to Woolsey Hall, where we saw lots of buddies, said hello to tons of people, had lunch, and unveiled a portrait of George by Ron Sherr that the class of 1948 had commissioned. Nice. We then drove to Greenwich, Connecticut, where we did a fund-raiser for Governor John Rowland for his re-election campaign. We flew back to Maine, arriving in time for dinner with Aunt Grace and Uncle Lou Walker, who had arrived earlier that day from Florida to stay in the Bungalow. They spent a week with us before moving into their rented house on Ocean Avenue.

We had planned to go out to dinner the next night with Dan and Bunny Burke when George called to say that Kevin Costner was coming for the night; so we changed the dinner to Walker's Point as we knew that people would never let Kevin eat in peace. We had a very fun evening, filled with laughter. Kevin brought a nice young actress, Susan Brightbill, who was acting in the movie they were making in Maine, *Message in a Bottle*. Susan played the dead wife. The next day they all fished after church, and in the afternoon we played golf. The heavens darkened and lightning appeared, and we girls disappeared and watched Freddy Couples win the Memorial Golf Tournament on television. The men finished and the storm blew over. (Besides being panicked by high places, lightning scares me if I am outside.) Kevin later sent us several videos of his movies, including *The Postman*. Although Kevin told us that this film had a deep meaning, we didn't see it that way. In fact, it was pretty bad. We like Kevin and most of his movies; just not this one!

    In early June we went to Singapore, where we stayed in the beautiful Ritz-Carlton Millenia, which they claim is the only six-star hotel in the world. It is grand. We lunched with Prime Minister Goh Chok Tong and his wife and several others. It was such an interesting lunch, and much of the conversation had to do with the financial crisis in the Asian countries, especially Indonesia.

The next day we flew from Singapore to Bangkok, Thailand, a place where I had never been. We were met by Thaksin Shinawatra, then a private citizen and now (in 2002) the prime minister; and Skip Boyce from the American Embassy, whom we had seen several years before on a trip to another Asian country. We stayed in a huge suite at The Oriental.

In the afternoon, George and I flew by helicopter to Klai Kunguol, the beach palace, and called on His Majesty King Bhumibol Adulyadej and Queen Sirikit with Thaksin Shinawatra. I do not know what I expected, but this compound was not it. There were very nice, small cottages, and although I know we were very close to the beach because we saw it from the helicopter—it was not to be seen from the cottages.

Some ladies-in-waiting showed us some of the really lovely handiwork that is being done through Her Majesty's foundation, which is teaching women to make products that will sell. Then we were led over to a very modest palace and presented to the king and queen. Somehow or other I was thinking of *The King and I,* and instead, there sat a perfectly normally dressed man and a beautifully dressed lady. George had an interesting but difficult conversation with His Majesty as the king is a "whisperer." I noticed that George was leaning forward. As the visit went on, he moved his chair closer. He then moved to the edge of his seat. It was almost impossible for him as the king's voice was difficult to hear and it seemed to get lower and lower. Meanwhile, Her Majesty and I had a very easy conversation in which she reminded me of a visit she made to the White House with two of their children. We had all stood on the Truman Balcony and waved George off to Africa that night.

I complimented Her Majesty on the truly lovely work being done by her foundation, and she immediately gave me an exquisite little evening bag, which to this day is my very favorite—a beautifully and delicately etched purse. I raved so much over it that Her Majesty then insisted on giving me the most amazing pin made from a green and blue beetle that is unique to Thailand. These beetles live for three months, die, and then their shells turn bright colors. This pin is gold, with diamonds and two beetles. I told her that I could not possibly accept the pin, but she would not take no for an answer. Then, as we were leaving, Her Majesty gave me three pieces of brocade. When Thaksin left, out of respect, he sort of slithered out on his side and did not turn his back on their majesties. So maybe *The King and I* mentality is not quite dead after all. George and I hosted a small tea for Her Majesty and the Crown Prince when they visited Houston in the fall of 2002.

We then flew to the Shinawatras' home. This is a huge city, and there clearly is no zoning. We drove from the airport through the smallest, shabbiest neighborhoods and down alleys to get to their stunning, enormous house. All along the way there were armed guards standing by the roads and alleyways. There was a huge dinner party gathering as we arrived, and I was led into a beauty parlor where a lady was all set to wet and blow-dry my hair! That is hospitality of the best kind as my hair certainly looked a sight after a hot and humid helicopter ride where the only air came from opening the windows and letting the wind have its way. This was a truly beautiful dinner.

We flew on to Hong Kong where we stayed once again in the same suite in the huge Island Shangri-La. Because of the economic crisis in Asia, the hotels were only 20 percent occupied. We went out to The Island Club, which is privately owned by the Tung family, and had a pre-dinner visit with our friends Betty and C. H. Tung, Hong Kong's chief executive, and their daughter Audrey, who had just had triplets—two boys and a girl. The other guests came and some twenty-four of us ate in the lovely Pagoda Room where we had eaten with C.Y. Tung, C.H.'s father, in the 1970s. I had to laugh as our friend David Rubenstein* announced the next day that it was the worst meal he had ever had! He hadn't eaten a bite, but went to bed eating potato chips. We on the other hand love Chinese food and thought it was one of the best meals we'd ever had. David is not into adventurous eating, but he is one of my favorite people anyway.

We flew on to Beijing and once again were overwhelmed by the changes. The traffic was horrendous, and the pollution was worse than

---

*David is one of the founding partners of The Carlyle Group, a private investment firm, which was our host on this trip.

ever. I celebrated my seventy-third birthday in Beijing and got three of the grandest cakes and was serenaded twice—once accompanied by an Erhu (sort of pronounced "R-Ho"), an ancient Chinese instrument that has two strings.

About this time I started mentioning in my diary that everywhere we went—overseas or at home—people talked about our son George running for president. My George said that this was natural; that any governor of the second largest state in the country would be considered as a presidential candidate. George W. was running for re-election at this time—NOT for president. This was even brought up in the People's Republic of China. I wrote in my diary:

> The expectations are so high and he will be the target for all others who are running. I read something he said the other day that made me so proud. All across the country the Republican Party was ripping itself apart, bashing gays, etc. George W. stepped in and told the party "to stop it." He said, "All individuals need and deserve to be given respect and dignity." He is so right.

We got home and had a very quiet celebration on June 12 with Neil's family for George's seventy-fourth birthday.

We both spoke the morning of the 17th, and then George flew that afternoon to Russia—yes, to Russia. He flew on a Wednesday and returned on Friday afternoon. During that period he spoke for Goldman Sachs, did a taping at the Kremlin and Red Square for David Frost, and met with Boris Yeltsin. He is a strong man.

∽ While George was gone, Kevin Costner called and said that he and his children would love to come for Saturday night. He did come and brought Susan Brightbill again and his darling children, Annie, Joe, and Lilly. Then, after dinner, Susan's Aunt Sue appeared, and we tucked her into the last available place we had. After church the Costner group fished, boated, and had fun. There was a very poignant moment at lunch when Lilly sang a song to her dad as her Father's Day present. The song was "Think of Me," from *The Phantom of the Opera*. Her voice was sweet and pure. These children spend alternate weeks with their mother and father when he is home. When Kevin is on a set, as he was then, they spend some time with him, but it is hard. He seems to adore the children and they him. He speaks very well of their mother, and that is nice. Kevin was very gracious to our grandchildren and their guests and posed for photos with everyone.

    〜 We did keep our household busy and occasionally wondered if someone had just wandered in off the street and joined us. One night we had invited Neil's family, including all their guests. They are wonderful about having friends of their children visit. We expected eight children and seven adults. George looked down the table and saw this totally strange young man sitting in our midst and asked me who he was. I didn't know. It turned out that he was Elizabeth Luck's brother, Steve. Elizabeth was visiting Lauren, and they just threw him in. Ariel counted heads and just set another place at the table and stretched one leg of lamb for nine children and seven adults. He is marvelous. It turned out the whole Luck family was in Maine to pick up Lauren and Elizabeth and take them with Steve and another brother to look at colleges. Elizabeth's grandmother was from Midland, and we knew her grandparents, Joe and Liz Walters. How small the world is!

Jebby, who was now fourteen, came for the summer and worked for our friend Jim Dionne, who owned the Northeast Angler, an Orvis store. He worked 9 a.m. to 3 p.m., Tuesday through Saturday, which still allowed him to boat, fish, swim, and play with the other kids. It certainly was déjà vu all over again, as George was paying his salary, which he had done for Neil when he worked for our friend Booth Chick at his marina one summer. Neither boy knew that's how they got their jobs; both boys came to me and complained about the fact that others were earning more and did I think they should ask for a raise? You know the answer.

Dave Valdez, George's White House photographer, arrived to do a book signing at the Brick Store Museum in nearby Kennebunk where they were having a Walker's Point exhibit. Dave had put together a beautiful pictorial history of George's years in office. He took the famous picture of us, the dogs, and the grandchildren all in bed. He had heard that we had coffee in the very early morning and read the papers, and that the little ones often came in as they awakened. So he popped in and snapped this picture at 6 a.m. It appeared in many different magazines, newspapers, and even books. You could say it doesn't show our best side—hair sticking up, etc.—but the truth is we love it.

About this time Gian-Carlo Peressutti, George's aide, asked me how long I wanted Prince Bandar to stay. I hadn't known he was coming, but was thrilled. I said he could stay as long as he wanted. He did arrive with a very nice couple, Bob and Jan Lilac. We invited Stephen and Alicia Spenlinhauer over for dinner, and since Neil had a crowd at his house, we invited them for cocktails. The next day Bandar announced that he was making lunch. I told him that it would hurt Ariel's feelings, but he insisted and cooked all morning. We all went about our business, and never have I heard such laughter coming from one kitchen. Bandar had everyone chopping and giggling—in fact, guffawing. I might add that he also was smoking a cigar and that caused a lot of excitement. "Does Mom know he is smoking a cigar IN THE HOUSE?" How could I not! To this day I do not let The President of the United States—past or present—do that. But Bandar was a guest.

Prince Bandar cooks up a storm in our Kennebunkport kitchen,
with Ariel DeGuzman, July 1998.
FAMILY SCRAPBOOK

Then, when the big moment came, we all marched into the dining room to the biggest meal I had ever seen. I really can't remember what it was we ate, but he made so much that Neil, at my invitation, came over that night and got pans of food, which he reheated and fed his ten guests. There was still food left over. Bandar stayed only twenty-four hours but made friends for life.

George traveled to New Orleans for another "America's Promise" event, and went right from there to Milan, Rome, Berlin, and ended in Birmingham, England, and was back in four days.

❧ George Bush fills each day, and Ariel manages to keep up with him. As an example, one morning he was out fishing with Peter Pocklington, a dear Canadian fishing friend who was coming for lunch. He also had Dr. Andy von Eschenbach from M. D. Anderson coming to brief him on some cancer-related subject, and had invited Andy and his wife Madelyn for lunch. Spike Heminway had set a tee-off time for George, Jeb, and Peter at 1:30 p.m., which meant all this had to take place on time. Ariel suggested clam chowder for lunch, which sounded great, BUT Peter can eat no dairy products, which we learned at lunchtime; so Ariel whipped up a salad for Peter in no time at all. George fished, was briefed, was fed, and was on the first tee at 1:30 p.m.

When giving talks, I love to tell the audience that life with George Bush reminds me of the girl who was getting married. She told the minister that she was so nervous she wondered if she would make it down the aisle. The minister told her he always told brides three things that helped: "First, look down at your feet and see the aisle. Then look straight ahead at the altar; and finally, let your eyes go to the right and there you will see your beloved. Just remember these three things and you will be all right." People attending the wedding were surprised to hear the bride as she walked down the aisle saying over and over again, "Aisle . . . altar . . . him; aisle . . . altar . . . . him; aisle . . . altar . . . him."*

*I stole this story from the Reverend Dennis Maynard, our former associate rector at St. Martin's Church.

Well, the truth is, I wouldn't alter one thing about George Bush. He really makes my life sing.

~ One recipe that saves us over and over again during the crazy summer days comes from Millie Dent, one of my childhood friends who moved south and married a childhood friend of George's, Fred Dent. Fred was President Nixon's secretary of commerce. This is a very favorite Bush dish. Even the grandchildren eat it—the real test! Every friend who has a vegetable garden grows zucchini and can't get rid of it! Now you'll know how. We freeze in containers, marked for 6 or 12, etc., and pull them out for those often unexpected guests.

Zucchini Soup by Millie Dent
Serves 6

1 pound clean unpeeled zucchini
2 tablespoons shallots (I often use onions or leeks)
1 clove garlic, minced
1¾ cup chicken broth
½ teaspoon salt
1 teaspoon curry powder
½ cup coffee cream

Chop unpeeled zucchini, shallots, and garlic. Cook in heavy skillet for 10 to 20 minutes. STIR TO KEEP FROM BURNING. Put all ingredients in blender and blend. Add cream. Serve hot with croutons or cold with chives.

(When it's for the freezer, I freeze without cream and add the cream later.)

~ Some place in here I had the most interesting conversation with a CEO of a big corporation about their company policy on health benefits for gay couples. Don't ask how we got on that subject! He

told me that at first he said, "Absolutely NOT." Then he got thinking about it and decided that if they met certain commitments, the
company would permit spousal privileges. There were six things they
demanded, including longtime commitment to each other; shared
bank accounts; and mutual ownership of property. He said there were
relatively few requests. I asked about unmarried heterosexuals. Didn't
that cause complaints? He said it didn't because if they were com-
mitted, they would marry. The gays couldn't marry in most states and
heterosexuals could. End of story—simple and fair. No wonder this
man was the head of a huge company!

༄ In July, during a trip to Boston, we decided to visit the
Kennedy Library, which neither of us had seen.

> We were trying to have a small visit to the Kennedy Library.
> It is a spectacular building with mile-high spaces looking over
> the Boston Harbor. We were met by the press and a bearded Max
> Kennedy (Bobby and Ethel's son named after General Maxwell
> Taylor) and his attractive wife and an 8-day-old baby. He did tell
> G.B. that he had been thrown out of Andover. He must have
> cleaned up his act, for he now teaches literature at Boston Col-
> lege and his wife does the same at Harvard, I think. George
> really had wanted to have a quiet visit and we popped in because
> Caroline Kennedy had urged him to do so. Max and his wife
> were very nice and the library was really interesting to see. Lots
> of pictures of Rose and Joe; good films; and best of all, benches
> and chairs to sit in to view some of the films. It seemed to me
> that Jackie was not mentioned as much as Bobby. There was one
> diary that Jackie kept on a trip abroad with her sister Lee that I
> admired enormously. She had illustrated it in the most charming
> fashion. She was truly a most talented interesting person.

༄ In the middle of July we went on the Greek Islands cruise
again with many family and more friends. We had a glorious two
weeks of swimming, water-skiing, hiking, and sauntering through

little villages and on beautiful beaches. While we cruised, there were backgammon tournaments, liar's dice games, bridge, always an ongoing jigsaw puzzle, and lots of reading. We all did our own thing and it was perfect. Since we were all ages—maybe five to seventy-six years old—we had the most unbelievably wonderful buffets to appeal to all tastes. The younger children passed up the caviar, smoked salmon, salad bars, eggplant dishes, goat cheeses—in fact, all healthy foods— and dove right into the French fries and pasta. There were many beautiful—and fattening—desserts, one better than the next, for us all to choose from. Most of the guests and our family went into town after dinner; George and I usually stayed on the ship and read, falling asleep early. Most shopping was done at night, for the world sleeps in Greek towns in the afternoon. As I am not a shopper, I didn't miss a thing. Sometimes during the day there were bus trips to ancient ruins or cultural sites, or to "good shopping towns." I only went if there was something of real interest, like a fort, church, statues, and/or paintings. We usually anchored off deserted beaches and tiny villages. The children played on the beach, and George went on five-mile marches—with a stout little band of followers—over huge hills and

Jeb's gang on the Greek cruise in July 1998. From left: George P., Noelle, and Jebby.
FAMILY SCRAPBOOK

around beaches. I tried to swim back to the boat, but July is a rough month to be on the Aegean Sea—lots of wind and sometimes rolling seas. It bothered some, but I have found those Sea Band seasick bracelets work for me, and I slept like a baby.

For George and me, these almost annual Greek trips have been the best. Our grandchildren live in Texas, Florida, Virginia, and Maryland, so they get to renew their friendships with their cousins, aunts, uncles, and great-aunts and uncles. We see each other during the year, but this time of laughter and joy is wonderful. We have been spoiled.

When we got home on August 1, George W. and Laura were there to greet their girls—who had gone with us—and spend ten days on Walker's Point.

> *August 3*—Condoleezza Rice is at the House. She is here for The George Bush School of Government and Public Service Advisory Board meeting and is staying with us. Condi is so attractive and very bright. She and George W. had long talks about the school and about foreign policy. We are so impressed with this bright young woman. George W. even said that he thought she might make a fine National Security Advisor.

One day George W. said, "Mom, I'm not turning anyone in, but you ought to know before you got home from Greece, I was up in the dormitory looking for my old leather jacket, and in the back of the closet I found the very worst porno pictures, really filthy. I am telling you because they were downloaded from the Internet off your computer." At that time we had several teen-age grandsons and guests staying with us, and I thought that I might just generally talk to them all about this at the appropriate time. This I did, and then put it out of my mind.

Several weeks later, I was working in bed at 6 a.m., answering mail, paying bills, and doing my homework. George was at my side, and several children and grandchildren were having coffee, reading papers, talking about the news or what had happened the night before. I opened the following letter and was stunned:

FEDERAL TRADE COMMISSION
OFFICE OF INSPECTOR GENERAL

Juliana Lopez
Chief Inspector

July 30, 1998

Dear Ms. Bush,

Our office is in charge of eliminating pornographic material from the internet. In doing a routine check, it appears you have recently been engaged in downloading pornographic material. We recognize that citizens of the United States have every right to avail themselves of any information on the internet, but when there is a continuous pattern of abuse, our office is authorized by Statute 12497 of the Federal Code to investigate. We respectfully request that you report to our regional office in Portland, Maine, for a hearing on August 17, 1998 at 8:30 a.m. If this is not convenient, please contact our regional inspector Maria Kent-Sloan at 207/-------. We can assure you that Ms. Kent-Sloan is an experienced prosecutor and will treat this inquiry with great discretion. Congress mandated that this material be held on a close basis.

Should you have any questions regarding this matter, please contact my assistant James Ramsey. He can be reached at 202/-------.

Sincerely,
Juliana Lopez [hand-signed]

Ms. B. Bush
Post Office Box 492
Kennebunkport, Maine 04046

FEDERAL TRADE COMMISSION 1800 CONSTITUTION AVENUE, NW
WASHINGTON, D.C. 200376

I must have gasped when I read this and was sputtering, "What is this? I am NOT going to Portland." All the room put down their papers and looked at me as I continued to read and say, "great discretion—I bet. I'm not going to any hearing. Can you imagine the press!" Finally, I gave the letter to George, and he read it to the room. Then I noticed there were lots of smiles, and it came to me that my husband had composed this letter! I fell hook, line, and sinker—again.

August 9—Up early as usual and the gang gathered in our room. George W. first, then Doro and Marvin. They were full of the surprise birthday party for Doro that Debbie [Stapleton] had the night before. (Her birthday is on August 18, so of course she was surprised.) They said that Jimmy Ortiz-Patiño [who was visiting] was great. He donned a birthday hat and blew a horn along with the rest of them. Jimmy joined us again at 6 a.m. Between Jimmy and Brad Freeman,* our bedroom in the morning is fun and certainly different. Gigi and Robert or both wander in, and there were more laughs and funny stories.

George and I love this time in early morning when our bedroom becomes the family gathering place. George tells everyone the story of how during one of those mornings, after George W. became president, he came in from a run, sat down on the couch in our bedroom, and put his feet up on the table. I immediately ordered him to remove them. George of course remembers saying, "Bar, he is THE President of the United States. He says I answered: "I don't care who he is . . . get your feet off the table!" True.

⌒ The bombing of two U.S. Embassies in Africa took place in the middle of August, haphazardly killing literally hundreds of civilians and twelve Americans. While I was at the August meeting of the Mayo Clinic, President Clinton rightly retaliated by bombing known terrorist camps in the Sudan and Afghanistan. I was shocked that sev-

---

*A great friend of George W. and Laura's who shows up when they do. We are always glad.

eral people immediately mentioned—again—*Wag the Dog.* I guess the embassy bombings were a precursor to the terrorist attacks on the World Trade Center and the Pentagon on September 11, 2001.

∽ One of the things I loved that summer and fall was to help Brent Scowcroft pick a tiny place where he and his daughter, Karen, could tuck in when they came to Maine. Brent gave me a check and said, "Okay, you talked me into this. Now furnish it." As it was a tiny condo on the river, it was a challenge and lots of fun. He probably rues the day that he asked me. Since I immediately decided that the tiny living room/dining room/kitchen area had three doors where one would do, I called in the builder. We took out two doors; painted the whole apartment; took down the curtains; and put up blinds that hid under a valance when they wanted to look at the river and let down for privacy at night. I bought and ordered furniture, some of which they liked and some they didn't. In the end they had a jewel of a hideaway. Karen is an attorney and works and lives in New York City; Brent's office is in Washington, D.C., and many weekends in the summer they meet in Maine. Their presence there has added immensely to our lives and those of our friends in Kennebunkport.

We had a terrific house party over Labor Day weekend. John and Norma Major came from England with John's aide, Arabella Warburton; Brian and Mila Mulroney came from Canada with their sons Ben and Nick; and for part of the time, we had Isabel and Leopoldo Rodes Castane, who was vice chairman of Banco Urquijo in Barcelona, Spain. They were friends George had met on a trip and were easy and charming. Sadly, Isabel has since died of cancer.

Most of us went out whale-watching with Steve and Alicia Spenlinhauer on their beautiful boat. We cruised out about twenty-five miles and crossed our fingers. When you get lucky, these huge beasts are through bottom feeding and are up on top rolling, snorting, making that umbrellalike spray over their backs, and most exciting, diving with a tail that bangs the water after a dramatic jump. We also often see porpoises on our way out. Unfortunately, on this day we saw very few whales and the wind kicked up and we raced back to shore.

On some days, you don't see whales at all:

On Tuesday the eighth George and I set out in the late afternoon to go whale-watching. We no sooner left Walker's Point than it started to sprinkle and then stopped. We went out on a relatively calm day and looked and looked. Not a whale, porpoise, or shark in sight. On the way back the heavens opened and we flew for home. It was smooth and exhilarating. We had hot baths, fixed an easy early dinner, and went to bed. I think we watched a pretty bad old Clint Eastwood movie. While we were gone poor little Sadie was seen underneath a table on the deck during the storm. She was in the house when we returned as somebody had seen her. Sadie is so dear and is doing such funny—maybe a poor choice of words—things like chewing up my slippers or bringing my sneakers to me. She ate Arabella's postcards which was not so funny and then hid some beneath the dining room rug.

Back to the house party. One night, George took the whole group to a restaurant that we enjoyed a lot, the Pepper Mill Steakhouse. (I guess others didn't, for it was gone the next year.) We added Eric and Jane Molson and Karen and Brent Scowcroft to the dinner. John and Brian of course knew Brent well, and the Mulroneys knew the Molsons—he is the Molson of Molson's Beer—who also are from Canada. They are a new addition to Maine and are great fun. The piano player at the restaurant played wonderful old songs, and before long we all—especially Brian—were singing along.

    Both George and I spoke a great deal that fall for varied and many causes. I was in Fort Wayne, Indiana, for a wonderful program, The Study Connection. People give an hour a week to an at-risk child. It has made a difference, and they had nine hundred volunteers at that time. I then went on to Warren, Ohio, where I spoke at the Buick Opera House for the Upton Foundation, to help save the 1830 Harriet Taylor Upton* Home. As we drove up we saw on the marquee: BARBARA BUSH in huge letters; and right below, "Coming attraction: WRESTLER. I wouldn't have taken that too seriously except that not

*A well-known suffragist.

long ago, a newspaper ad for a Peter Lowe seminar had listed all the speakers with their occupations printed below their name: GENERAL COLIN POWELL, Former Chairman of Joint Chiefs of Staff, etc. Mine said: BARBARA BUSH, Heavyweight Champion!"

On October 5, I drove down to Boston, where I spoke to the wives at a convention for plastic and reconstructive surgeons. I took a lot of teasing from family and friends about that, so I put in my speech:

"This invitation not only shocked me, but has family and less charitable friends laughing. BARBARA BUSH speaking to a convention involving plastic surgeons? My speaking at this gathering is kind of like that wild basketball player, Dennis Rodman, speaking to a convention of hairdressers! We both could use a lot of help.

"All I can say is I'm glad I'm speaking to you—and not your spouses. If it were the other way around, they'd all be rushing the stage to get their hands on me."

∽ I believe that people need to laugh, and so try to sprinkle jokes in my talks that make a point, keep you awake, and get your attention. Many of my stories are true and really happened to me. One of my favorites was in El Dorado, Kansas, where in a speech at the Butler County Community College I told the audience: "What I'd really like to do today is share with you some of the things I think I've learned in seventy-six years of life. That includes fifty-seven years of married life, six children, fourteen grandchildren, five wars, three dress sizes, two governors, two parachute jumps, and now two presidents."

Unfortunately, the reporter from the *Wichita Eagle* didn't hear it quite right and reported that I had said "three breast sizes." I couldn't believe she or he would think I would say that. I wrote a letter to the editor and told them that although I was "indeed a bosom buddy to two Presidents," I had been misquoted. And I added this P.S.: "I just wanted to get this off my chest!" It was all over the news, and for months, every time I used the "three dress sizes" line in my speech, the audience would twitter.

However, one of the funniest misprints ever happened to one of my dear personal aides. She was in the middle of looking for a new job and had sent out her résumé to about ten potential employers. When describing her job with me, she thought she had written that she had helped coordinate and attended hundreds of public events with Barbara Bush. Unfortunately, due to a tiny typo, the word "public" became "pubic." Several friends had proofread her résumé and no one caught it. Fortunately, she did find a job and a good one. I have NOT used this story in my talks.

     ʙ I have gotten some of my favorite stories from church. I love this story that David Wigley, the minister at First Congregational Church, told our last Sunday in Maine. I am still trying to work it into a talk:

Two nurses ran out of gasoline. Fortunately, they were near a gas station. They found when they walked to the station there was no container for them to carry the gas back to the car. They were at a loss for a moment, until they remembered that there was a bedpan in the trunk of their car. They were filling the tank from the bedpan when a car drove by with two men who slowed down and watched the ladies in amazement, "Now that's faith," they said. The men were further awestruck when the ladies got in the car and drove off! David got our attention with that story.

    October 8—The house and office are put away for the winter, and the office staff has started the long drive back to Texas. George went to Louisiana with Lod Cook to speak at LSU and then on to College Station. I flew to Benedictine University in Lisle, Ill., to speak to a lecture series that they have in the spring and in the fall. They had Colin Powell this past spring and Mikhail Gorbachev is coming next spring! I am flattered to be in such fine company!

I flew out and back and returned to an empty Walker's Point. I slept alone in that big house. Even Sadie had gone. And it rained and rained. It is always hard to leave Maine, but once George goes, and Sadie goes, and it is raining hard, I am ready to go, too.

All in all that summer, we had 152 different overnight house-guests on Walker's Point, many of them ours and many our children's. Some stay more than one night and some come back several times, but I am saying that there were 152 different people. I am not complaining, but awestruck. This is the happiest time of the year for us.

 ⮌ On October 10, I flew to Chicago and had dinner with Honey and Sam Skinner. Sam was George's secretary of transportation and then later his White House chief of staff. George arrived late that night, and the next morning we were on our way to Kauai, Hawaii, where we stayed at the beautiful, tremendous Hyatt Regency Hotel. George and I spoke to the Precision Metal Forming Association Convention, the nicest and easiest group, and they did not expect me to have any ideas about their business—thank heavens.

From there we went on to Japan, where we had a lovely visit with old friends, and George spoke at an Eisenhower Exchange Fellowship reception and dinner. We ate breakfast with Tom Foley, our ambassador to Japan, an old friend, and the former Speaker of the House. He and Heather had settled in easily to this lovely embassy and were doing a great job for our country.

We had dinner that night at a geisha restaurant with The U.S.–Japan 21st Century Committee. This relatively small group is made up of leading Americans and Japanese. We knew many on both sides, including former Prime Minister Kiichi Miyazawa, former Senator Bill Brock, Ambassador Tom Foley, and Bob Zoellick, who worked for Jim Baker at the State Department when George was president and is now U.S. trade representative for the current President Bush. The table was on the ground, but the good news was that in deference to the Westerners in the crowd, there was a trough under the table where you could put your feet. It was still very uncomfortable for me, for if you leaned back you were almost lying on the floor. All during the meal I worried about how I would get out of that pit without embarrassing our team, our country, and my husband. When there was a diversion—George was signing autographs and having his picture taken—I crawled out. Not pretty, but I was up and out!

We flew to Shanghai on October 16, and I was overwhelmed.

George had told me that I would not believe this was the same city I had visited with our children in 1975. It looked like Hong Kong—lights, crowds, modern hotels, and on and on. We stayed in the Ritz-Carlton Portman Hotel, but did have dinner with Shanghai's dynamic Mayor Xu Kuangdi in the Peace Hotel, where we had stayed all those years before. I remember looking out the same window at the Bund—sort of a grand promenade—and seeing people doing tai chi and singing, etc. Now we looked out the same window and all you can see are enormous buildings and lots of color. There are many colored lights all through the city where there was little or no light before. We have since returned to Shanghai, and the number of lights seemed to have doubled again!

During the whole trip I worried so much about Jeb's campaign that George suggested that I go home for his last debate. I knew I couldn't help him, but to ease my mind, George insisted I leave after Shanghai and surprise Jeb and Colu. So on October 17 George went to Nanjing, the old southern capital, and then on to Beijing, while I flew forever to get home to Houston with one Secret Service agent, William Redmon. The Secret Service are so great about changing plans, although I know it can be a logistics nightmare for them. William was eager to get home to his bride and new baby, so I didn't feel too badly.

On the way over I had read Victoria Gotti's *The Senator's Daughter,* a mystery that was great airplane reading, and on the way home I read *The Rector's Wife,* by Joanna Trollope, a book Richard North Patterson had sent me. I loved it.

The day after I landed, I went to St. Petersburg, Florida, for Jeb's last debate. I wrote in my diary:

> Doro and I met at the airport. Nan Ellis* was there, having spent several weeks campaigning where the campaign needed her and staying with people she had never met before. Neil and his friend Tim [Bridgewater] arrived; Betty Sembler;† and former Governor Martinez and his wife Mary Jane were there, all to

---

*George's sister.

†Betty and Mel Sembler are longtime friends and supporters. Mel was my George's ambassador to Australia; he is now ambassador to Italy.

support Jeb. Unfortunately, so was the very popular and nice retiring Governor Lawton Chiles. We all gathered before the debate and saw Jeb and Colu, Jebby, and Noelle. (George P. had a teachers' meeting.)

The debate was agony for me. Buddy McKay* came out swinging and accused Jeb of "having no experience" and "shady business doings." He stayed behind the podium and brought his right hand up and down in a chopping position. Jeb on the other hand looked tall, healthy, calm, and very cool. He walked around the stage a little. He talked more about the issues and was in less of an attack mode. There was no question that Jeb was much more impressive and sincere.

On reading what I wrote in my diary, I believe that this is true, but I bet the reader will say, "That's a mother talking." And they are right. I am a very proud mother. I must be honest and tell you that the next day the papers said the debate was a draw. The wife of the former president wrote in her diary, "Baloney!"

As for Nan Ellis: At age seventy-three—a widow, mother of adults and grandmother of nine—she had called Jeb's headquarters, asked where they needed help, and moved to Florida for several weeks. She is amazing, loving, and intelligent—she whips through *The New York Times* crossword puzzle every Sunday—and reminds me of Katharine Hepburn. She has that air about her. Sometimes she stayed with people she didn't know; she answered phones, made calls, carried posters—whatever she could to help. Nan is loyal. This is a trait that the Bush family values highly. She tells the story of being SO mad at the *Boston Globe,* she called and canceled her subscription, only to be told, "Mrs. Ellis, you don't have a subscription. You canceled it last week!" George and I adore her and are thrilled that Nan has a small house near us in Cape Porpoise, Maine.

⌦ The next two weeks dragged on, and we were so worried. We did keep busy. We were both honored at the Literacy Volunteers of

*Jeb's opponent, who was lieutenant governor at the time.

America's convention in Houston—George for signing the National Literacy Act of 1991; and me for my work in the field. One of the things I remembered most about that event is that I saw my longtime speechwriter from vice-presidential and White House days, Susan Green. She was a dear, loyal friend and I was very sad when she died of cancer in 2002.

George spoke in Dallas, and I visited a Children's Center at Texas A&M. We had a visit from Choo and Lee Kuan Yew, the senior minister from Singapore. He gave a talk to the students at Texas A&M, and most of the questions were about the economic crisis in the Asian countries. I then flew to Dallas and Chicago to give speeches and arrived home at 9:30 p.m., just in time to greet George and Carla Hills. They had just gotten home from a dinner George hosted for "Harry" and Choo Lee in Houston, gathering a group from around the country including Carla, who had been George's U.S. trade representative.

I met George W. and Laura in San Antonio to dedicate the new Barbara Bush Middle School, and then I flew on to Cincinnati, Ohio, where I spoke and then took to the bed with the worst sinus attack. George participated in the annual charity George Bush/Cheeca Lodge Bonefish Tournament in Islamorada, Florida, and in the annual Chris Evert Pro-Celebrity Tennis Classic in Delray Beach, Florida. We both attended M. D. Anderson's "Loving Hearts Caring Hands" dinner, where we both received awards. I had to go to Kansas City to speak to The National Tech Prep Network, an engagement I had accepted months ago. I was still feeling lousy, and George offered to go for me. It was very tempting, but I knew he needed to be in his office as he had been on the road forever. He chartered a plane for me and that allowed me to fly out and back before dinner. On the Saturday before the election, George flew to San Antonio and back to accept the Theodore Roosevelt Distinguished Service Medal for us both.

Jeb's campaign was going on during all this, and I was glad that Bobby Koch and our cousin Debbie Stapleton went down to help. I do think campaigns make the family forget other very important things. I notice that the last day of the month I have this diary entry:

Margaret Bush's play, *I'm Not Rappaport,* opened to raves in Washington on Friday night. Doro went. Marvin is so proud.*

✑ We went to George W.'s last rally in Houston with Jean Becker and Nancy Brinker. Nancy, a good friend and founder of the Susan G. Komen Breast Cancer Foundation, had come to Houston for lunch and to talk to us about the National Dialogue on Cancer that George and I had just gotten involved with. All the statewide candidates were on the stage, along with beautiful Laura and Jenna. I don't remember where Barbara was, but I do know that neither of the girls like politics, and their parents don't ask them to campaign. Although the polls showed George way ahead, he and Laura campaigned as though he was in a dead heat.

On election day, George and I decided that IF the exit polls looked good for Jeb, we would go to Miami to be with him and Colu. George called me around 2 p.m. and said that we should go; so we took off and arrived around 6:30 p.m. to a room full of Jeb's supporters. I wrote in my diary:

> When Jeb walked into the room I honestly think he was surprised. We all teared up a little. All his family were there, Jeb, Colu, George P., Noelle and Jebby. Nan Ellis, who had worked so hard, had gone home to vote in Massachusetts where she lives. No wonder we all love her so much. Jean Becker stayed on the phone getting candidates for George so he could congratulate them. We stayed much later than we expected, but Buddy McKay didn't concede until 10:10 p.m. We finally went downstairs and there was a mob scene in the ballroom. It was so thrilling. We flew home late and very happy.

> *November 6*—I am now the mother of two elected Governors of the second and fourth largest states. George won with 69+% of the vote and Jeb with 55%. George's victory brought in the

*I should note that Margaret was in the play, she didn't write the play! The author is Herb Gardner.

whole GOP state slate for the very first time ever! Amazing. Jeb and his nice Lt Governor* ran as a team in Florida. George and Rick Perry ran separate campaigns in Texas.

Several very special things happened election night. First of all, we saw George W. give his acceptance speech to a huge crowd in Austin. The first thing he said was that he wanted to congratulate his "little" brother in Florida. This brought back memories of four years before when Jeb lost in the closest governor's race ever in Florida's history. I was told that George W. was on his way down in the elevator to give his acceptance speech when he was told that Jeb had just conceded. He stopped the elevator and went back up to pull himself together. Our boys love each other and Jeb's loss hurt George W.

Jeb, and all of us, were really touched when Grace and Louis Walker suddenly appeared from Hobe Sound, Florida, to help celebrate. At eighty-five years old, Louis was the oldest member of the family. They had hired a driver, gotten a room in the hotel, and then talked their way through security to get up to the suite. Lou got teary when he walked into the room.

Along with many volunteers, we were especially grateful to see longtime friends and former staffers, especially David Bates, Chase Untermeyer, and Lanny Griffith, who had been helping Jeb for some time quietly plan his transition. I wonder if most people know that many candidates start this process well before election day, so they have a team in place when and if they win. This, of course, is not necessarily true if the polls don't look close. These men took time from their own businesses and lives to do this, and they and their wives deserve great thanks.

⤳ In November I spoke in Sioux Falls, South Dakota; Atlanta, Georgia; Lima, Ohio; and Joplin, Missouri. I dedicated the Barbara Bush Middle School in Carrollton, outside Dallas; attended a reception at Dick and Lynne Cheney's home for A Celebration of Reading Dallas Committee; and attended a Mayo Clinic Board meeting in Rochester, Minnesota.

*Frank Brogan.

On November 8, George flew to Honduras with Dr. Ben Orman to see the enormous damage done by Hurricane Mitch. Ten thousand lives were lost. George said that all bridges, roads, etc., were gone, and mudslides had buried people alive. One third of the population were homeless. He met an AmeriCares plane there, and they handed out food. Two days later, George appeared on *Larry King Live* to talk about what he saw and to tell the American people what they could do to help. George told Larry that he would only come on the program if they would discuss the hurricane and NOT politics. Larry not only kept his word, but he showed the most devastating scenes in Honduras and gave out the AmeriCares number (800–486-HELP) several times, which was great. He also put the Red Cross number up on the screen, and we were told later that the response to both charitable organizations was huge.

At the end of the program, Larry told George he looked well. George said that he felt like a "spring colt" and that he was going to parachute again on his seventy-fifth birthday, which was the next June.

At the end of that week George and Brent Scowcroft attended the Texas Book Festival in Austin, which was founded by Laura Bush. This has been a very successful event that is still growing, and still headed by Laura, although she has moved to Washington. Texas authors are invited to come to the state Capitol to read from their works, lecture, and answer questions. Laura missed it in 2002, when she and George W. were in Prague for the NATO Summit, but she told me she was thrilled that this event has "taken on a life of its own."

In 1998, Brent and George read from their book, *A World Transformed,* which had finally been published that fall. They were protested by a handful of people in the audience, who shouted things like "bombing children and innocent people"; "sanctions are starving babies"; and some words I can't print. They were quickly removed, but George told me that Laura was upset, and it caused Jenna to worry about her dad being in politics. We later read in the Austin paper that one of the protestors was a University of Texas journalism professor, who was accompanied by his students. Frankly, I was appalled when I heard that a professor was teaching students to disrupt. What happened to Martin Luther King, Jr.'s teachings of peaceful protest? A teacher's job is not to teach political views, but to teach students how to explore and form their own opinions.

Later that year Jenna was entering the University of Texas as a freshman and thought she wanted to study journalism. She was assigned to that same professor. She withdrew from his class. She did not need that. It is tough enough to be in college while your father is running for president—you don't need a professor who is against your grandfather and father.

      About this time, George and I became involved with a new project that has come to mean a great deal to us. A small group of people—including Dr. Andy von Eschenbach, who was then a doctor at M. D. Anderson and is now head of the National Cancer Institute; John Seffrin, CEO of The American Cancer Society; and Dr. LaSalle Leffall, a professor of surgery at Howard University and now head of the President's Cancer Panel—asked us to become involved in a new group they were trying to form, eventually to be called The National Dialogue on Cancer. It's an umbrella organization, that for the first time brings to the same table the leading cancer experts and activists in the country; media stars like Sam Donaldson, Paula Zahn, and Larry King; government officials, such as Senator Dianne Feinstein, who is vice chairman, and former Governors Tom Ridge of Pennsylvania and Roy Barnes of Georgia; CEOs of pharmaceutical and insurance companies; and on and on.

This group has met twice a year since their first meeting at George's Library in the fall of 1998, with George and I attending every single meeting. We also have hosted many smaller meetings of the different working groups and committees. We have come to feel very close to the Dialogue participants, and although we often don't understand the topics they discuss—the science is sometimes a little over our heads!—we believe passionately in their mission: to prevent one million new cancer cases and 500,000 cancer deaths by 2010. However, we certainly understand the "prevention" part of stopping cancer, and the one figure that always amazes me is that if everyone in America stopped smoking today, we could cut the number of cancer deaths in half—not to mention the people who would not die of heart attacks, emphysema, etc. Cancer is still the disease most Americans fear most, and George and I are proud to play a tiny part in this great cause.

⤮ Also that month George and I hosted a reception at the house for the Celebration of Reading Houston Committee and attended the Three Amigos event. Jim Nantz and pro golfers Freddy Couples and Blaine McAllister attended the University of Houston together and played golf on the college team. They, along with friend and golf pro Paul Marchand, have remained good friends and put on this charity golf tournament and dinner every year—another example of people who have done well in life giving something back. I sat next to the honoree of the night, that great gentleman and pro golfer, Ken Venturi.

⤮ December started with George traveling in the Middle East; I met him in Melbourne, Australia, where we attended The Presidents Cup golf tournament. The United States was soundly beaten. I went with the players' spouses to The Healesville Sanctuary, filled with Australian animals in their native habitat. We saw kangaroos with joeys in their belly pouches, who ventured out for a minute or two before they hid; Koala bears in trees; wild dogs, or dingoes; snakes; platypuses; underwater rats; and glorious birds. There were flies, but not too many.

We lunched that day at Yarra Grange, in the wine region, at a truly glorious private country home. The house was small, lovely, charming, and filled with treasures. The lawn was large, and we ate on picnic tables under the spreading branches of big trees. It was an exotic meal of marvelous oysters, prawns, chicken cooked on outside grills, fruits with clotted cream, and trays of bread and cheeses. Unfortunately, all these little wives were dieting. We were to go to a sheep farm and see one shorn after lunch, but I decided to go back to the hotel as I had seen this on a previous visit. Some of the other wives went with me. It had been a wonderful day, but jet lag and heat were getting to us.

One night we went to a lovely dinner hosted by Jeanne and Richard Pratt, head of Pratt Industries in Australia. The dinner was at their 120-year-old Victorian house, Raheen, which was more comfortable than our stiff Victorian houses filled with all that red velvet. On the back of this glorious house they had attached a totally glass addition. It is unbelievable, with views like you have never seen. It works.

The dinner was great fun as the hostess said that we all—there were sixteen of us—would talk together; no private talking. She started. Then George on her right spoke and called on me to tell them my Boris Yeltsin story. We went around the table, and it was a warm and funny evening with people coming up with embarrassing moments, funny stories, or just plain nice ones.

We went to several other dinners and of course also watched golf matches. It was SO hot—107 degrees one day. The players were amazing as, of course, they walked. Even more amazing were the flies. Where you have heat and sheep, you also have flies. One day George walked the course with a very nice and happy Prime Minister and Mrs. Howard. I had such a bad sciatic nerve that I walked a very short distance and watched the rest from the stands. Then the weather really changed. It went from a dry 104 degrees to a wet and damp 60 degrees. The fans stayed to the end and were joyous over their first victory in three tries.

The Australians are so easy, attractive and warm. They remind me of Texans.

SUNDAY DECEMBER 20—Today is our Robin's birthday. It is hard to believe that she would be 49!!! Amazing how real she is in my mind. She is still almost 4 years old.

I went to the 9 a.m. children's church service, instead of our usual service, as Pierce was one of the two narrators. He was very good.

On December 21 I flew to Atlanta to speak to the Rotarians' Annual Daughters' Luncheon, which I did at the urging of our friend Louis Sullivan, president of the Morehouse School of Medicine and secretary of health and human services in George's administration. I only mention this as I was amazed at the number of people who came up to ask me to please urge George W. to run for president in 2000. He hadn't even been sworn in for his second term as governor. I will say that George had told me that he would begin to feel pressure if he got re-elected. I just did not expect it so soon.

Christmas lunch was a happy one, with Neil's family, Pete Roussel, and Don Rhodes. We had a real trauma as Elizabeth, Ariel's wife, had to be rushed to the hospital and operated on in the afternoon. Thank heavens she is well, but that was painful and scary for them. I went by the hospital in the afternoon and was amazed by just how deserted the hospital was on Christmas.

The day after Christmas we flew to Boca Grande, Florida, with our Texas families; Jack, Bobbie, and Bill Fitch; and Dennis and Mary Farish Johnson and their two children, Hunter and Sarah. Oops, I forgot Sadie, who is allowed to stay at Gasparilla Inn, where we were headed. There we met up with Doro, Marvin, Jeb, and their gangs.

Two wonderful fun things happened on this trip. My George had laid down a challenge to all the grandchildren: The first one of them to beat him in tennis would win $100. BUT, if they lost, they had to go down to the bottom of the list—which meant after Doro's two-year-old Gigi—before they could try again. George P. challenged him. I don't like to say this, but the grandfather is a great talker and resorted to a lot of chatter that day. George beat him twice in very tight matches, so George P. went to the bottom of the line. It was the first time George had played singles in forty or fifty years. He was dead tired—and should have been—as he fished all morning, raced in and beat George P., and then rushed out to play eighteen holes of golf after lunch.

Another note on the tennis challenge: In the summer of 2001, Lauren, who is a nice tennis player, challenged her grandfather. George had an eight-month-old hip replacement and was limping a little. He gave her a choice: Would she like to play one set, or two out of three? She unwisely chose one set. He really couldn't run, but he had all the shots. He won again and then beat Pierce. I'm afraid that by the time they beat him, $100 won't seem quite so big! Gigi is getting closer to that money!

Also on that Florida trip, Jebby challenged his Uncle George to a 3½-mile race. He at first wanted a short race, but George W. knew that Jeb was a sprinter, and they settled on the longer race. This was another highly publicized challenge and a crowd gathered to watch.

Jebby ran the first mile in seven minutes, the second in six minutes, and the last in five minutes. Although George ran a sensational race, to quote him, he was "still left in Jeb's wake."

We spent five really perfect days there with our family of twenty-six, and the Farish and Fitch families, playing tennis, golf, swimming, sunning, walking, riding bikes, and unfortunately eating too much in my case.

We ended the year the way we started it, at El Tule Ranch with friends. The Simpsons arrived from Wyoming two hours after we returned home on the 30th, and the next day we flew to Falfurrias, Texas. Once again George and I were asleep way before midnight, and once again we did not miss seeing the New Year arrive. It had been a great year for us. Our children were well and happy, and so were we.

Jeb's first inauguration as governor of Florida, January 1999.
Left to right: Mary and Frank Brogan, the newly elected lieutenant
governor; Senator Connie Mack; Jeb and Colu. All the women wore hats
to support Mary Brogan, who was undergoing chemotherapy at the time.
OFFICE OF THE GOVERNOR PHOTO TAKEN BY JAMES GAINES

January was very exciting for us as two of our sons were sworn in as governors of Texas and Florida. Suddenly, one out of every eight Americans was governed by one of our sons!

On January 4, we flew to Tallahassee with Alice and Keith Mosing, two friends from Houston. We had dinner with some of the family and awakened the next morning to a freezing day, around 23 or 24 degrees. The early morning prayer service was moved inside, mercifully, and it was lovely. The great Gospel singer and songwriter and our family friend, Michael W. Smith, sang.* Congressman Bill Nelson and his wife Grace both took part in the service, and Senator Connie Mack gave a very moving talk.

After the prayer service we went to see the Governor's office in the "new" Capitol† and to meet his staff. Then the whole family met in a holding room for a delicious brunch. It was so good that when it came time to go outside, George's Aunt Grace Walker was busy talking to the chef—Eric Favier from Chez Pierre in Tallahassee—and writing down a fabulous recipe for a seafood casserole. They had to urge her to please go to her seat with Uncle Lou; she was unmovable. Thank heavens she was so firm. It is a delicious dish that we have served many times in Maine. I heard later that Grace and Louis never got to the inauguration, but listened from a heated car since it was so cold.

THE RECIPE THAT ALMOST HELD UP JEB'S INAUGURATION

(This was interpreted by Ariel DeGuzman who, in all honesty, had to guess, for although Grace had listed all the ingredients, she neglected amounts! But many thanks go to Chef Favier.)

SERVES 8–10

In a medium saucepan, melt ⅓ cup butter over low heat.
Sauté ⅓ small onion, chopped, until translucent.
Stir in and blend:
>   *1 tablespoon flour*
>   *1 teaspoon salt*
>   *½ teaspoon paprika*
>   *dash of cayenne pepper*
>   *3 cubes chicken bouillon*
>   *Add 1½ cups cream (coffee cream—of course heavy cream*
> *would be richer) and stir constantly until smooth.*

---

*He sang at Jeb's second inauguration as well, in 2003.
†It actually was built in 1977, but is still referred to the "new Capitol" since the old one, now a museum, was built in 1845.

In another bowl beat 3 large egg yolks.

Add a little of the hot mixture (cream, bouillon, etc.) into beaten egg yolk, then transfer this into the remaining hot mixture. Stir until thickened.

Add 2 tablespoons dry sherry and stir.

Remove and set aside.

Clean 1½ pounds asparagus spears; remove tough parts, then cut in half. Steam asparagus until tender but firm.

Layer bottom of buttered 12-inch casserole with asparagus and top with ⅓ of the hot cream mixture.

Layer over cream mixture:

½ pound cooked crabmeat, picked over

½ pound cooked lobster tail, cut in chunks

½ pound cooked sea scallops

½ pound cleaned, cooked shrimp, peeled, deveined, split lengthwise.

Gradually pour remaining hot cream over seafood and spread evenly toward edge of dish.

Prepare according to package directions half a package of bread stuffing mix.

Spread stuffing over seafood/cream mixture.

Sprinkle generously with shredded parmesan cheese.

Bake in preheated 350-degree oven 20 to 25 minutes or until bubbly and browned.

(May be served with noodles or rice, or just as is. I prefer it "as is," but sometimes when we expect ten for dinner and sixteen show up, rice is a life-saver!)

✑ Back to the inauguration. I wrote my friends Andy Stewart and Phyllis Draper:

Jeb's inauguration was splendid. A freezing day, so cold that besides a wool suit, I had on a cashmere overcoat and cashmere wrap that you, Andy, had given me several years

ago for Christmas. On the phone you mentioned that you
noticed that I had on a blanket—nope, the stole you gave
me—and I was glad to have it! I guess I was the only one to
look on Internet and see the cold front coming. I warned
George and we were among the few who were prepared
although who can be prepared for 23 degrees in Florida?

Mary Brogan, the wife of the incoming lieutenant governor, was
in the middle of her third round of chemotherapy as she had three
tumors on her brain. She always appeared to be happy and cheerful.
Colu and all Mary's friends wore hats to show their love and friendship
for Mary, as she was bald as a cue ball and wore hats; no wig. That sign
of friendship touched me. I won't forget her. She had a really beautiful
face, and I never saw her without a big hat and a huge smile. She died
around six months later.* Frank Brogan has been a real friend to Jeb
and seems to be one of those amazing politicians who are team players,
putting their own personal views in "mothballs" until their moment
comes. I think there have been many like him—Walter Mondale and
George H. W. Bush come to mind.

We were so proud of our beautiful Florida family. George P.,
Noelle, and Jebby looked wonderful and very proud of their
Mom and Dad.

Connie Mack was the emcee and was generous, warm, and funny.
"At one time we thought it would be a cold day in hell before we
would have another Republican governor in Florida," he said. He went
on to say that Jeb almost proved that to be true.

A bundled-up and frail Billy Graham gave the invocation. That
was so sweet and very meaningful to our family, as Billy was a friend
of George's mother and father, had sworn in my George in January of
1989, our son George as governor of Texas in 1995, and now our Jeb
in 1999. Billy has quite a Bush family history and is loved and
admired by all of us.

---

*There is a happy footnote to this story: Frank married a lovely woman, Courtney
Strickland, in December 2002.

The Bible Jeb used was the one that I had held in 1989 when George became president. When George W. was sworn in as president on January 20, 2001, he used the same Bible, which we then gave to him. Jeb used it again in 2003, for his second inauguration, this time borrowing it from the president. On this day, Jeb had the Bible open at Psalm 91: "I will say of the Lord, 'He is my refuge and my fortress, my God; in him will I trust.'" I had opened the Bible at The Beatitudes, Matthew 5, having in mind especially: "Blessed are the peacemakers, for they shall be called the children of God." This little Bible was signed by many of the people who took part in these three inaugurations. I suspect it will be quite a keepsake and have a place in George W.'s Presidential Library.

We went immediately to the Governor's Mansion—a spacious, antique-filled house, with gracious public rooms, gardens, a pool, and a gym. The guestroom on the first floor is where I had stayed when Mary Jane and Bob Martinez lived in the house, and George and I have spent several nights since in that lovely room. Jeb and Colu had a huge open house; we went back to the plane and flew home, two very happy parents. If possible, I think we were even happier when we attended Jeb's second inauguration in 2003. It was a nearly perfect day, and our son gave such a passionate speech about the future of Florida, I almost moved there!

∽ In early January, I wrote in my diary:

> The House of Representatives impeached the President of the United States. The White House has blamed the Republicans, but the very worst is that Larry Flynt, publisher of *Hustler* magazine, has offered $1 million to anyone who will prove that they know something sexually embarrassing about a Republican Congressman or Senator.* This is very scary. What has happened to our country? Iraq is acting up. This is very scary. What has happened to our world?

---

*Incidentally, Larry Flynt did not have to pay a dime to anyone.

On January 25, I continued the same letter to Andy and Phyllis:

> George has just flown to Dallas where he speaks and
> then flies on to Austin where I will meet him. We will have
> a big family dinner tonight. (Bobby Koch, our son-in-law,
> later pointed out that there were people there that he had
> never met or heard of before. Like 65 relatives at the
> dinner!) Tomorrow the Governor of Texas will be sworn in
> for a second term. I don't envy George W. these next few
> years. No matter what he does, he will be under great
> pressure. Please pray for him! I am so glad that our boys are
> friends, Phyllis. I am so hoping that IF George does get in
> the race for president he will generate backers from the
> young. Sh Sh Sh . . . but so many of our 70-plus friends
> think we know everything. WE DON'T AND GEORGE
> AND I KNOW IT.*
>
> The prayer service in the morning was one of the best I
> have ever attended. The Rev. Kirbyjon Caldwell from
> Houston took part, and George and Laura's minister, Mark
> Craig from the Highland Park Methodist Church in
> Dallas, gave a fantastic sermon with lots of laughter and a
> great message. As I remember it was a sermon about Moses
> not wanting to do what God wanted, but was made to see
> that it was his duty. Somehow or other I felt that the
> minister was speaking directly to George W. I didn't think
> he was talking about his heavenly duty, but his duty to his
> country.
>
> . . . Laura Bush continues to be George's greatest asset.
> She had on a heavenly lavender suit with the tiniest fringe
> and covered by a truly beautifully fitted lavender coat. His
> speech was marvelous and, once again, we went home two
> very proud and happy parents.

Later in the month we had another Leadership Forum at George's
Library. The members of the panel were: Karen Hughes, George W.'s

---

*I was trying to say that it was time for a new generation to take over.

press secretary and one of his top advisers; Gordon Bethune, CEO of Continental Airlines; Judge Bill Webster, former director of both the FBI and the CIA; Roger Clemens, great baseball pitcher, father of four adorable boys, and a fellow Houstonian: and Drayton McLane, owner of the Houston Astros. Since Drayton bought the team, Drayton and his wife Elizabeth have become a big part of Houston and our lives. They are such decent, good people and are generous, positive, and energetic. Houston is a better city because of the McLanes.

These discussions, along with several individual lecture series—which are sponsored by either The George Bush School of Government and Public Service or The George Bush Library Foundation—give the A&M student body and the entire Brazos County community a great opportunity to meet and ask questions of business leaders, athletes, celebrities, and political and world leaders.

     I flew with George to Washington and attended a beautiful dinner in the magnificent United States Supreme Court Building given by our dear friends, John and Sandra Day O'Connor. After a delightful dinner in a glorious, high-ceiling room filled with flower-laden, candle-lit tables, some of the guests entertained with their own special talent: singing, playing a duet on the piano, a sweet violin, or some funny, silly thing. Ebersole Gaines, former ambassador to Bermuda, was persuaded to play spoons or forks, at which he is very talented. He made them dance on his knee and seem almost alive; he had us all in tears we were laughing so hard.

On Sunday, I met Andy Stewart and we went by Amtrak to New York City to see the Disney musical, *The Lion King*. This was supposed to be a big treat for Andy. Some treat! We arrived about an hour before the matinée started and had planned to pop into a restaurant close to the theater and have a nice lunch. There was only one place nearby that was open—McDonald's. We ran in and did have a quick Caesar salad. We raised a lot of eyebrows in this tiny little fast food place when they saw the Secret Service and two old well-dressed ladies, one of whom turned out to be the wife of the former President of the United States. Andy was a good sport.

We were in our seats at 1 p.m. for the play. As this was a matinée it was packed with wiggly, noisy children and I worried about that. But I didn't need to worry. Once the play started, the children settled down for a happy three hours. What a play! The costumes were magic—hard to describe, but so inventive. The dancers were sensational and the music was happy. George was right when he told me this play was "a must." I did take Andy to Osteria del Circo for dinner, a charming Italian restaurant that was highly recommended. It was delicious, and the people were so welcoming. We were lucky as it was one of the few places open on Sunday night. I hadn't realized many New York City restaurants are closed then. Thank heavens for Secret Service. They like to know plans ahead of time, and therefore keep us from showing up to find CLOSED on the door.

I had fittings the next morning at Arnold Scaasi's for dresses to wear to the Celebration of Reading in April and the big birthday party for George's seventy-fifth, benefiting M. D. Anderson, in June. Arnold and Parker Ladd then took me to Le Cirque. Imagine, I learned that day that with all the hundreds of restaurants in New York, I ate in the two that were run by the same management.

I went to freezing Maine and drove to bleak Walker's Point to check on some renovations we were doing and those at Brent Scowcroft's condominium. It was dark when I arrived, and I went immediately to Windows on the Water, one of the few restaurants that remain open in the winter, with Sandy and Barry Boardman and Stephen and Alicia Spenlinhauer, who live in Kennebunkport most of the year. We caught up on news, and the next morning I talked to the builders and was glad to hear everything was coming along on schedule.

I love Kennebunkport, I love the people, I love the ocean; I discovered on that trip that I love it more in the spring, summer, and fall!

I got back to Houston a few minutes before George, who had flown in from Paris where he and Brent had gone to promote their book, A World Transformed, which was coming out in French. They had a visit with the president of France, Jacques Chirac, whom we have known since he was mayor of Paris in the 1970s. In May 2002, at age sixty-nine, President Chirac was re-elected for a second term.

The next night we went to the Wortham Center to hear the beautiful Frederica von Stade sing in *A Little Night Music*. George was exhausted, but we love her and her glorious voice. George lasted until she sang a favorite song in the second act, "Send in the Clowns," and then we tiptoed out.

Mostly my days were spent at home that week trying to get rid of the most devastating pain in my left leg—a pinched sciatic nerve that had been sore for ages and was now going full tilt.

But something very exciting also happened. My aide, Kara Babers, had set me up on a great program where she worked on my schedule at the office and it came to my computer and vice versa. It then transferred itself to my little hand-held pocket computer. It also holds some nine hundred names, addresses, and all those numbers we need in today's world. For age seventy-seven, this is pretty high tech.

I spoke one morning at 7:15 to seven hundred men and women attending the Handy Hardware Annual Convention in Houston. They were so nice that I felt I could ask them a question during the Q&A period. I asked them to please hold up their hands if they had ever been polled. Not a hand went up. This is the second time I have asked a group to do this, and no hands went up either time. How can that be? All we hear on TV is "The American people say two to one," etc. We are fast becoming a country that is ruled by polls, but who are they polling?

George went to two royal funerals in 1999, the first in Jordan in January:

> This whole week King Hussein of Jordan had been hover-ing between life and death. What a valiant man. He died in the wee hours of the morning on Sunday, and suddenly George was packing and was on his way on Air Force One with Presidents Carter, Ford, and Clinton to the funeral. George said that during the trip President Clinton came back and briefed the former presidents and that he was very well informed. I read in the paper the funeral was attended by men only. Custom meant that Queen Noor was not at the final good-bye for the husband she so adored and we all admired.

Then later in the year:

> George flew with the President to the King of Morocco's funeral. He told me that Chelsea came back and said that she had heard that one of our granddaughters was considering Stanford. She said that she'd love to talk to her if she had any questions. We both thought that was really nice.

❧ I met George in Lake Geneva, Wisconsin, where we went to help celebrate Promotions Unlimited's* twenty-fifth anniversary. This convention was attended by 1,200 drugstore and grocery store owners; in many cases, "mom and pop" family-run stores. We had been in the exact same place with Ira and Lorraine Greenberg, the founders of the company, at another event—the Ben Franklin Family Reunion—just the month before, and so we felt very much at home. This time, instead of eating with the Greenbergs and a number of other people, we ate with just the Greenberg family. They are real charmers and the teasing that ran around the table reminded me of our group.

We had lots of photos before and after dinner with the guests—not all 1,200, but it felt like it! We both spoke and then answered questions. I took my poll again and we did find one person who had been called. One woman asked a tough question, I thought: "What is going to happen to all those folks who run small family stores now that there are so many mergers and buyouts?" George was hard put to come up with a satisfactory answer, but he gave a truthful one. There is no question that the big stores can buy in bulk and sell cheaper. On the other hand, he said, the smaller stores would be able to give better, more personal service than the bigger conglomerates.

This reminded me of a recent visit I had to a huge bookstore in our neighborhood. I went in to buy a book by Brad Meltzer that I knew George would enjoy. A surly young man waited on me without looking at me. After I had searched the huge store, I almost had to beg him to look the book up on the computer. He finally came to the conclusion

---

*Promotions Unlimited provides advertising and promotional programs for mostly small retail stores.

that the book was not in stock, and he would have to order it. He asked, "Last name?" I said, "Bush." "First name?" I answered, "Barbara." He asked for identification. I gave it to him. He then asked for a telephone number. We finished our business and I longed for my neighborhood bookstore, where the owner would not only have known me but known if they had the book, ordered it if it wasn't in stock, and suggested one I might like in the interim. They would have made me feel welcome, taken half the time, and not given the impression that they were doing me a large favor. Incidentally, as I walked out of the store I heard the young man at the next counter say, "You idiot! Don't you recognize the mother of the Governor of Texas!"

George had found it hard to come up with a satisfactory answer to the earlier question about big versus small because this is what makes America great—people coming up with new ideas, being inventive, "building a better mousetrap."

From there we went to New Orleans, and George spoke to the International Telecommunications Association. I was given the most adorable cell phone for just being there. George is addicted to his phone; car rides that used to be a time to catch up with each other now are a chance for him to catch up with the world. Keeping in touch with family and friends is very important to George. I love my phone—it even goes into my evening purse, but I only use it for calling home or a friend to say that I am caught in traffic, etc. I told George that people hardly ever call me on it. He suggested that I turn it on!

From New Orleans I flew to Orlando, Florida, where I was staying in Winnie and Arnold Palmer's lovely guesthouse. Arnold met me on my arrival with the news that Winnie was in the hospital, having had a serious operation. My thoughtful friend had planned my visit but didn't let me know, or permit her family to tell me, that she was in the hospital. Their daughter Amy came by to say hello before rushing off to be with her mother, and Arnie had to go play golf. I had lunch with Arnie's brother Jerry, Amy's husband, and a marvelous lady named Pat Boeckenftedt, who seems to keep Arnold's Bay Hill Club and Lodge and the Palmer family together. Winnie also had planned a massage and a hairdo for me before I went to give my talk to the Golf Course Superintendents Association Convention. These are the people who really make the difference between a great golf course and a so-so one. They have to deal with environmental issues and temperamental club members—the grass is too short, too long, the roughs are too rough, and so on. They were such an easy group. I did a photo-op and saw our darling friend Jimmy Ortiz-Patiño, owner of the Valderrama Golf Club in Spain. He is "Mr. Wonderful" to this group. He was mentioned over and over again in the most glowing terms. I was thrilled. Jimmy said that he must come back to Maine this summer. We talked about dates and decided that the week before the Ryder Cup would be good. I found it very flattering that Jimmy, who is used to such grandeur, wanted to come back to our noisy, hectic, but very happy Walker's Point.

George W's campaign is warming up . . . in fact is hot! All the other candidates are "shooting" at George W. who has NOT gotten in the race or even left the state of Texas.

February 15—I think I wrote in January that Gary Bauer, Steve Forbes, Dan Quayle, and Lamar Alexander all attacked George W. and at the same time, George H.W. I don't give a darn about the first two, but the latter two really hurt. They are friends.*

What is said in the heat of a campaign is often harsh and one regrets it. Criticism, which can be interpreted as personal, usually isn't. It must have been frustrating for the others to see George W. not campaign and yet have Republicans line up to come to Austin to meet with him. He had told the people of Texas that he would not leave the state until the legislature went home, and he didn't.

⮑ We did lots of traveling that February. George spent several days with our friends Evie and Gene Williams at Nilo Plantation in Georgia. I had a visit in Amelia Island, Florida, with my brother Scott, his wife Janice, their daughter Kim, and three of her children. I spent a morning with them at the beautiful rare animal and nature preserve,

---

*In 2003 they are still friends. George enthusiastically campaigned for Lamar, who was recently elected senator from Tennessee, and keeps in touch with Dan Quayle by e-mail.

*My brother Scott Pierce
and his wife Jan.*

White Oak Plantation; then attended a Mayo Clinic meeting in Jacksonville, Florida; and then went to Disney World and spoke to the Mechanical Contractors Association.

Meanwhile George spoke in Atlanta, returned to Orlando (where he had been the day before to raise money for a symphony orchestra), and got home several hours after I did.

The last weekend in February we spent at College Station. The former President of France, President Valéry Giscard d'Estaing, a charming man, came to speak and we had a small dinner for him. It was a really interesting lecture as he is an expert on the Eurodollar, which is on the horizon, has a great sense of humor, etc. Betsy and Spike [Heminway] came for two nights to attend the Library Advisory Committee meeting and to see the Library. George and Spike also toured the A&M campus. The Heminways loved both the Library and campus. I love them, as they are so positive about everything: "It's the best"; "What a great guestroom"; "The beds are so comfortable!"; "The Library really surpasses anything I've seen"; etc.

On rereading this in my diary, I realize that this is so true, and it is small wonder that these two have more friends than anyone I know. Our children and grandchildren feel close to them both and their daughter, Alex Heminway Anderson.

I wrote this letter to the "Ladies of the Club" in March:

Dearest Ladies,

This has been a relatively quiet month for me. I have spent more than my fair share of time at the acupuncturist's office, the physical therapist's office, wearing magnets, taking mild pain pills. Finally I had all kinds of tests including an MRI and myelogram while feeling great all the time, especially when seated or lying down.* I have tried everything but a witch doctor. We have about decided that this darn sciatic nerve is caused by a structural problem and there is a simple operation that can relieve the problem. George and the doctor feel that I should not put it off until summer, which I had planned to do. So I may have the operation now IF the tests I am having today say I should. I would hate to do this as George and I are on our way to Palm Springs next Saturday to spend Easter with Walter and Lee Annenberg and have dinner with Shirley and Ben Roberson. (Shirley is a recipient of this letter and has much worse back problems.) I am to give a speech in Palm Springs and then on to San Diego to do a charity lunch for Covenant House. THEN we are going to Phoenix for our annual physicals at the Mayo Clinic–Scottsdale. Precious George says he'll give the two speeches for me IF I'll have the back operation. The haste is only because if I don't have the operation I may permanently damage the nerves so badly that I might drag my foot. Nice. The doctors here think I have let this go on too long to chance it. I really will feel guilty if I have to back out of Palm Springs as Shirley said in her letter that she is putting off her back operation until

---

*My editor says this is contradictory, to say I was "feeling great" while on pain pills and having tests. The truth is—I lie, so people won't think I'm whining!

after my talk. BUT who wouldn't rather hear George Bush? I certainly would! I must get back on the golf course. I must get back to walking.

On Monday I had the myelogram and on Tuesday I spoke to the MAGIC CIRCLE luncheon.* The President of the Club, Caroline Pierce,† gave the most loving introduction. Almost all of George's office volunteers were there, and the ballroom was filled. I did my thing and they presented me with a special Callaway 7-wood. It seemed ironic as unbeknownst to them, I was facing a back operation the next morning!

George did spend Easter as planned in Palm Springs with Walter and Lee Annenberg, and Neil's family came to our house and brought the lunch with them.

George did give the two speeches for me, as promised . . . I had to laugh for I got some very nice thank you letters—people struggling to say that they really missed me and adored my substitute!

People are so dear and took Sadie for walks and some walked me. Bobbie Fitch and her son, Billy, walked both of us early on. Don [Rhodes] walked us both and took Sadie for long runs. I was flooded with flowers. Dr. Richard Harper told me to walk and so I walked, but a frisky dog pulling on a leash and jerking is painful.

. . . now having bored you and me to death with my health—which is really top notch. . . .

We see Neil and Sharon and their delightful children a lot, every Sunday, if they are in town and if we are in town. I saw Marvin twice—once in Houston on a business trip and last night when he and Walker (9 years old) joined me at "The Final Four" in St. Petersburg, Fla., where I spoke to a group of coaches' wives in the morning. Darling Jeb also joined us with his sons, Jebby and George P. Doro's husband Bobby

---

* I believe "Magic Circle" is one of largest and most active Republican women's groups in the country. In the 1970s, they met in our living room. I spoke to them when George was vice president, and First Lady Nancy Reagan filled a huge ballroom several years later.

†No relation but a volunteer in George's office.

Koch, his brother Danny, and his son came for a bite in my room at the hotel before the game and then again joined us in our box. You, Ladies, might well ask just why I would be invited to speak at THE BASKETBALL COACHES ANNUAL CONVENTION? Clearly they knew who was the real "jock" in the Bush family. There was a carrot in the invitation. They offered me tickets and great seats for the game. That's all I needed as my boys, especially Marvin, always try to go to the "Final Four." So I was in heaven; I had three sons and three grandsons with me that evening.

While working on that talk, it came to me just how much coaches' wives have in common with politicians' wives. There is NO job security, the wives are often alone as their husbands travel and the press criticize their husbands all the time, too.

I also spoke in Oklahoma for several literacy groups, attended a Parkinson's Disease dinner in Houston with George, and this week flew to Carbondale, Ill., to do a literacy event for former Senator Paul Simon at the University of Southern Illinois. Paul was a big literacy supporter when he was in the U.S. Senate, and although he did not usually support George, other than literacy, we were friends. I did have a nice visit with Jeanne and Paul. I always liked her. She was really nice the year he ran in the Democratic primary for president and we ran into each other.*

I love the groups who invite me to speak—groups I know absolutely NOTHING about. I spoke to the SynerMed† Convention early in the month and the NonPrescription Drug Manufacturing Convention.

We spent two glorious weekends at College Station. We love our apartment, the college kids, and Sadie loves the runs along the creek and in the fields. One weekend we opened a new exhibit in the temporary exhibit hall called "AN ANCHOR TO WINDWARD." It is fabulous and is all

---

*Jeanne has since died of a brain tumor.
†SynerMed Communications coordinates medical education programs.

about the history of The Kennebunks and the Walker/Bush Family. About 120 people flew, drove, etc., down from Maine for the opening, bringing a lobster/chowder/clam/corn bake with them; lobsters that were in the ocean that very morning and cooked in the large courtyard between the three buildings—Library/School/Conference Center. A group of students, the Texas A&M Wranglers, danced for us before the dinner. Although I know you were all there for the opening you must come back and see this great Library and School now that it is going strong. . . .

I hope you all saw *Life Is Beautiful.* I wish we could clone ROBERTO what's-his-name,* his enthusiasm, his joy and talent.

My darling friend Andy Stewart had a small heart attack while she was in Florida. She sounds fine and the doc (Tabb Moore) says that if she takes her medicine, she'll live forever. That's great.

Love,
Bar

April 10—This has been a dreadful week in Kosovo, with bombing by NATO troops.

꙱ I read *Tara Road,* by Maeve Binchy. How I loved it. Her writing is a joy!

On April 9, I met George—back from his long trip to California, giving his talks and mine—at the airport and we drove to College Station, where we learned the most amazing thing. Brent Scowcroft had endowed a chair at the Bush School, helped by a matching gift from A&M University. That really touched us both as we are so grateful for his help in so many other ways. Over the years several people have endowed chairs, and that has allowed the Bush School to get the very best professors.

---

*Roberto Benigni, star, writer, and director of this wonderful film.

Brent's gift reminded me of something that happened many years ago. When George was vice president, I was invited to attend and speak to a fund-raiser for St. Joseph's Hospital in Houston. At a press conference before the huge black-tie dinner, a young reporter spoke up and said something like, "Mrs. Bush, you have spoken so highly of this institution and the need for us to all give money. How much are you going to give?" I honestly was shocked. Hadn't I given enough by just agreeing to be there and speak? And besides that, George had paid for my trip, down and back. I'm afraid I quipped: "I'll give if you will," and smiled. As I was being announced into the ballroom, this young man slipped by the Secret Service and handed me a five-dollar bill. He taught me an important lesson. It's hard to ask others to give if you don't care enough to give yourself. So I worked him into my talk, turned over his $5, and sent a check the next day from the Bushes.

We think Brent had truly given enough and then he did this. What a friend. He now has taken on serving as president of the board of directors of the George Bush Presidential Library Foundation.

∽ *New York Times* columnist Maureen Dowd sent me a haunting little book, *Silk,* by Alessandro Baricco. George had written and congratulated her on her recent Pulitzer Prize and had mentioned my operation. At the same time he invited her to come to Kennebunkport. She said that she might come and bring a friend who loves golf. She also said that she might have to bash George W. George said that was okay, but that she "might have to watch the Silver Fox." I used to enjoy Maureen when she bashed "them"—not us. From my diary:

> She was on Hillary this week. Her criticism came on several fronts—[Hillary's] book on entertaining in the White House—a book about entertaining and recipes from a lady who "was not going to bake cookies and have teas" but get into issues like healthcare, etc. Also "What was she doing in Africa with Chelsea for ten days when her country was at war?"

I honestly did not agree with any of her criticisms in this article. Maureen is a brilliant writer, no doubt. I really do not read her any more as she sounds so bitter, so unhappy, so negative, so clever, and straining to be different. Sometimes I don't even get what she is talking about! I'm sure this won't bother her, but it makes me sad. I am afraid George still reads her and likes her, although he, too, gets furious when she snidely attacks the president.

⤶ On April 13, a group of ladies from the Town and Country Garden Club went to College Station and toured the Library. This is a tiny club and these were friends whom I rarely get to see. I noted in my diary that "every day I notice that my old friends are getting older— not me." Most of us met at St. Martin's Church parking lot, climbed on a rented bus and, after waiting for one member who had signed up for the trip, finally left without her. It turned out she had seen a bus, asked if this was the bus for the Bush Library, climbed in, and didn't realize that she was on the wrong bus with a sorority that also was going to the Library that day. I might have thought she would have noticed that she didn't know a soul. She was delivered to us and the sorority ladies said they enjoyed her company. We are getting older!

It's sort of like the woman who went to a new dentist. The doctor's name sounded just like a long-ago high school classmate, but the minute she saw the balding, gray-haired man, she knew this could not be the tall, handsome boy she had gone to school with. Just in case, she asked if he had graduated in 1952 from the local high school. When he said yes, she couldn't believe it and her face showed it. "You were in MY class," she said. The dentist looked at her closely and then asked, "I'm sorry, I don't remember you, ma'am. What class did you teach?"*

⤶ On April 17, we once again attended the Chuck Norris "Kick Drugs out of America" event, saw his kids do karate, and watched celebrity tennis. Chrissie Evert and her sister Clare came for the night, and we four went out to Rice Stadium to say hello to country star George Strait and his wife Norma. We had a good visit and then we four, Everts and Bushes, went to a restaurant nearby and had a

*Of course it is nothing like that, but I like that story!

long dinner, then back to Rice Stadium to hear George's concert. There were three things wrong with the night as far as I was concerned: The singers and George Strait were miles away; we watched them on big screens. (Thank heavens we had gone by to see him before the dinner.) The music was so loud that if they'd opened the windows in the restaurant a mile away, we could have heard him. And George didn't even sing until way after our bedtime! It was a huge success as the night was lovely, the stadium was packed, and we were with people we loved.

▷ Iris Dart sent me her new book, *When I Fall in Love.* It is a sweet story, which I read in two days. I think she wrote it to highlight the problems of the handicapped. I didn't enjoy it as much as I did *Beaches,* my favorite of hers and certainly a favorite movie. I also read *Charming Billy,* by Alice McDermott. She writes beautifully, but it depressed me a little—sort of a black Irish story. I guess the secret is out: I read to relax and forget the world's troubles; not to have more worries.

GB and I spoke in Cincinnati, Ohio, on [April] 22nd. I returned home late and George went on to a big dinner in NYC honoring Helmut Kohl and saw many of his friends, Lech Walesa from Poland, etc. He went on to Washington, Andover, fished in Killingworth, Connecticut, and spent the night with Jody and Johnny Bush. I would have loved going with him, but I think I am doing a little too much. My left leg still hurts a little.

I needed to exercise more, and eat and stand less.

▷ For my monthly letter to my family and "The Ladies of the Club," I often start them on my computer and add to it until the first of the month.

Here are a few excerpts from the one in April:

I'm flying to Orlando to speak to a Volunteer Hospital Group and then on to Washington for the big Republican fundraiser that is honoring GHWB. I honestly didn't want to do this, but the dinner is being put on by a close and very persuasive friend, Mel Sembler.

. . . It was an amazing evening as $14.2 million were raised—the largest of either party in a non-Presidential year.

It was a very affectionate, nice evening . . . a little tense in spots but only with old friends who are backing Lamar Alexander. We certainly understand and are sorry that it worries folks who are not backing George W. I wanted to put a sign on my back saying: "We'll all be together after the primaries—STOP WORRYING." I heard that Lamar and Elizabeth [Dole] were there, but we didn't run into each other. After all there were 1,200 people there.

. . . The highlight of the month was the renaming of the CIA Headquarters to The GEORGE BUSH INTELLIGENCE CENTER. This was a huge honor for G.B. as he was the Director for one year only. The affection we felt for George was strong. We really liked the new Director, George Tenet, and his beautiful wife Stephanie. It was a long day for me to stand on the cold hard cement floor and greet hundreds of dear friends—from Congress, both parties were represented; former Bush Cabinet members; GB's office staff and mine; Washington friends: and, of course, CIA friends. It was such fun. The best was that our Washington-area children were there to see their dad honored.

. . . [George] did have a physical at the Mayo Clinic in Scottsdale and came through with flying colors . . . with the exception that George was a little low on thyroid! I don't believe it. If he had any more energy, we'd have to chain him down! George said they tested him twice. I guess they did not believe it either.

On April 15 I flew to Dallas and was met by Charles Wyly* and we drove out to Grand Prairie to visit the Barbara Bush Elementary School that opened in 1997, around the time the George Bush School at College Station opened, which explains why I hadn't been there before. We had a tour

*Charles and his brother Sam are friends and successful businessmen from Dallas.

and then went to a really sweet program. What a wonderful school.

Charles and I then drove back to Dallas for the Salvation Army luncheon. Charles has taken on the civilian leadership of the Salvation Army for this part of Texas for the next two years, and has just finished raising ten or twelve million dollars for them. There were more than 1,200 people there. I saw Dee and Vance Torbert and Caroline Hunt at the inevitable pre-lunch reception made up of several hundred givers—not the whole luncheon crowd, thank heavens. I was glad that I went although it was only ten days after the operation. I did ache a little but had no real problems. I think the Army is one of the best charities in the country. They are selfless. I didn't feel I could back out two weeks before the event, and it was okay.

~~~ Celebration of Reading was on April 24. It was a glorious day. The yard looked lovely, but it was just too hot and humid to sit outside for the lunch we host every year for the authors. Jackson Hicks had set up an extra round table that spilled over into the living room and we had fourteen for lunch in our dollhouse—the five authors, some of their family members, Benita Somerfield, Lisa Drew, and George and me. It was amazing that the authors all seemed to enjoy each other immensely. I think having them for lunch really makes them feel more at ease. It was so much fun at that lunch with lots of laughing.

The readers this year were Stephen Ambrose, Dave Barry, Frank McCourt, Jan Karon, and Baine Kerr, Jr.

At 5 p.m. we met at the theater, and there were George and Laura, faithful as ever. We rehearsed, tested the sound, etc., and then went upstairs for the inevitable big donor reception. Over the years we have assigned a volunteer to each author and now have big posters for them to stand near so that people can find their favorites. (Unfortunately, authors look like all the rest of us.) The volunteer is there to rescue their charge from pesky fans IF necessary and to help them in any way they can.

We start at 7 p.m. on the nose, and our audience knows it. They are in their seats on time. This year George opened the program with a very amusing film clip about great happenings and people from the beginning of time. One quickly got the picture that his book, *A World Transformed,* was the main feature, as famous people had it tucked under their arm or in their hand, including Castro, the Pope, Saddam Hussein, and baseball great Mark McGwire. At the end, the credits said: "Produced and written by George Bush." It was very funny and we all loved it.

Laura Bush spoke about the First Lady's Texas Literacy Initiative, which is a new statewide program separate from the national one.

As we do every year, we had a student reader—Dewey Stovall, with his adorable adopted five-year-old granddaughter at his side. He was magnificent. He was so good and moving that several of our readers mentioned Dewey in their presentations.

As always, our readers were warm and funny. It seems that year after year, they get better and better—if that's possible.

We were through on time and all went upstairs for a delicious dinner that had been pre-set. Over the years Jackson has fed up to 1,700 people, scattered all over the Wortham Center, and finally we spilled over into a tent—the meal and the tent having been underwritten by very generous people.

We no longer send invitations, but just reminders. I think we are successful for several reasons:

- The former president co-hosts and is such a great sport.
- The governor/president and his unbelievable wife have been there every year with the exception of 2002 and 2003.
- We try to make it a family affair, and over the years, Doro, Jeb, Neil, Doro's Ellie, and Ashley—Neil's youngest child— have all taken part.
- People appreciate the fact that you can come from the office; no black tie.
- We start on time and you may stay or leave before dinner. To my knowledge, everyone stays.
- Most important is the fact that we have great readers, and it is a very entertaining program.

This is a year-long project. The invitations to the readers go out in the summer of the previous year, along with reminders to the committee and faithful supporters to put the date of the next Celebration on their calendar. The letters are all signed by me, but George is the co-host and I know that is one reason why people respond so generously. Also, because the cause is so right!

The credit for this evening goes to so many: Benita Somerfield, the head of my foundation; David Jones and Carrie Eickenroht of the Dini Partners, the fund-raisers and logistics coordinators; Danny Ward and Nancy Ames, the program producers; Jean Becker and Jim McGrath, the scriptwriters; our whole office and an army of volunteers; our Celebration committee; our loyal patrons; the publishers who give books that are put in donated book bags; and most of all, our readers.

We have had one real problem: getting 1,700 people in and out of town is difficult, especially in a city that has no really good rapid transit. The wait for cars in spite of valet parking has been awful, I'm told.

Several days later Shelby Hodge, a reporter with the *Houston Chronicle,* wrote that our evening showed that a fund-raiser could be fun and run like clockwork. I'm always so happy when it works out.

⤫ George started the month of May in Bahrain, and I met him in Cap d'Antibes, Côte d'Azur, France, for two fairy tale–like days. We stayed with friends, Nemir and Nada Kirdar, who live in the most beautiful cliff-hanging house, Villa Serenada. They are two of the kindest and nicest people we know.

Nada met me in Nice and we drove to the villa, picked up George, and then drove toward Cannes to the famous Restaurant Tétou, known for bouillabaisse and jams. The soup was delicious, containing lobster and seven kinds of fish. (I will confess that I am yearning for this soup right now.) Unfortunately, the dessert consisted of a large plate of sweet little bread puffs and eight different jams. They put the jams on our plates, and we ended by eating it with a spoon. Unbelievable, and the Sugar Buster Diet was over after a twelve-hour commitment— nine of which were spent sleeping.

I went back to the villa to a long nap, and then went down to a beautiful cocktail party around a lovely, natural-looking pool which you reached by going down a long flight of winding rock steps with darling places to sit along the way and view the blue waters off the

South of France. The trip down is worth it as the pool is glorious, with a pretty fountain, and the water flows over the edge and recycles back up. This is all hewn out of rock. There were wonderful lookout spots and picnic places, up and down the cliff. These have been camouflaged so as not to be seen from the water and offend boaters.

We then went up to dinner in a long, narrow tent that snuggled up to two French doors that led into the house. Not any old tent. It was peaked and gathered. The flowers on the four tables reached high into the air and were lovely. The dinner was superb and I enjoyed my dinner partners, especially Nicholas Soames, grandson of Winston Churchill. He talked about him a lot, and why not; Churchill was a great man. Nicholas had many interesting stories about his grandfather, whom he knew until he was seventeen when Churchill died. Nicholas was a heavyset man, in his fifties, I'd say. I'd sat next to his father many years ago at our embassy in London, when he unloaded on his former sister-in-law, Pamela Harriman, in the most explicit and rather graphic way. I seem to know the parents or grandparents of the people we meet more and more these days.

After dinner we went into the living room, where we heard four opera stars sing arias from several operas, interspersed with songs from musicals, *Les Misérables, Show Boat,* etc. It was a magical, unbelievable evening.

We slept late the next morning, and then toured the grounds, where we found all sorts of hidden treasures: a tennis court, an office for Nemir, lovely gardens, and a beautiful graceful statue in a hidden garden.

We left Villa Serenada at noon to take a 40-minute drive to Monte Carlo, where we had lunch with Prince Rainier and his son, Prince Albert. We had been told by the head of His Serene Highness's household, a Colonel Derge Lemblin (a Bill Blass look-alike), that we were to arrive at "5 minutes of 1—not 6 nor 4, but 5." We left in plenty of time, but a 40-minute drive took 1 hour and 20 minutes, with George Bush squirming all the time.

George feels that being late is rude and thoughtless. He's right. I should add that I don't mind waiting for someone else, but I sure hate to have someone wait for me! That is the good news about cell phones. You can call and tell your host if you are going to be late.

We felt we were visiting old friends. The family dining room had one floor-to-ceiling glass wall, and the walls had several informal sketches and portraits of the lovely Princess Grace and the children when they were younger. The view, through carefully trimmed ancient tree limbs, of tiny Monte Carlo and directly below and across the harbor, was mind-boggling. George and the young prince talked world politics and it was fascinating.

After lunch we raced down to the harbor and went to sea on the *Lady Moura,* a huge boat owned by our friend, Nasser Al Rashid. It was a lovely forty-five-minute ride back down to a dock opposite our temporary home.

That night George spoke, and the next morning we flew home. I couldn't believe that I had been gone only ninety-six hours.

       We got to Maine around May 13 and started a lovely, lively summer.

> Sadie is in heaven and chases chipmunks and other varmints by the hour. She met her first porcupine, fortunately a young one, at 5 one morning when I was out having a cup of coffee and enjoying a stroll and the sea. I was beside myself as her mouth was filled with quills. I held her and Special Officer Elmer Brown pulled the quills out with pliers from her tongue, cheek, and mouth. I learned that they do not shoot quills; she had to bite the beast. I can only hope that she learned the same thing.

       I went to Rochester, Minnesota, for the Mayo Clinic meeting, and George and I both attended our annual AmeriCares dinner in New York, after which we both spoke in Connecticut. I had a quick visit with my sister Martha, who was fast going downhill. Mart was dying of emphysema and was on oxygen. Her daughter Corrine was there and was dear to her mother. Mart listened to us talk, dozed, and suddenly entered in with marvelous stories from the past that either I couldn't remember or never did know.

~~~ At the end of the month I wrote the "Ladies of The Club":

George is in the Far East for a week going to Japan, Hong Kong, and Thailand. I will be interested to hear what he found. We are looked on as a "bully" in other parts of the world and now with the China crisis,* I suspect that we have lost a lot of our friends around that part of the world, also.

. . . George came back from his trip on June 2. I think he enjoyed it, but was depressed by the feeling that people have about the USA. He told me that C. H. Tung told him that 90% of the Chinese people think we bombed the Chinese Embassy in Belgrade on purpose. (I hope they are using our pollsters!)

I barely saw George as I left town to speak in Chicago the next morning, and from there flew to Washington, where I popped into Sibley Hospital to check on Andy Stewart, who had just had a quadruple bypass surgery. She looked great, but I wondered, "Is there NO justice?" This darling, tiny, athletic little person has a heart problem and Fatty Arbuckle (me) is still chugging along.

I had detoured to Washington to attend the Marriott Foundation Dinner as their speaker had canceled at the last moment and I was asked to fill in. Bill and Donna Marriott have been friends for a long time, and Bill was a strong member on the Mayo Clinic Foundation Board with me. I was more than glad to do this for them. Their foundation trains disabled/handicapped/special people for jobs that they can do. They work with high school children and guarantee them jobs. I had heard, and heard again that night, that trained disabled people are among the finest workers. Doesn't it make sense: the Marriott Hotels need qualified workers, and the young who had no hope of a job are mainstreamed, have pride in a job well done, and are PAID? Everyone wins.

Our dear friends from Greece, Vaggelis and Fouli Chronis and

---

*American bombs had accidentally hit the Chinese Embassy in Belgrade during the NATO campaign against Yugoslavia.

their children, Sotiris and Eva, came to Kennebunkport for lunch. Their daughter Eva had just graduated from Boston University. Vaggelis works for the Latsis family, who hosts our family on our annual Greek cruise. During lunch, Vaggelis told us that we would be going to Italy and not Greece this summer. He was embarrassed to tell us that we might not be welcome in Greece because of controversy over the bombing campaign in Yugoslavia. He didn't think there would be trouble, but feared there might be an ugly scene or two.

How right he was. Several days later, the morning news reported that Greece would not let our peacekeeping troops land. Greece is a member of NATO, and it was NATO that was conducting the bombing. But Vaggelis told us reluctantly that we, not NATO, were getting the blame; neither was Great Britain, although Prime Minister Tony Blair had taken a leadership role.

> Earlier this week it looked like all this horrid bombing had worked and Slobodan Milosevic* was going to make peace. This morning the news said that all peace talks are off. My gut feeling, and it is just a feeling, is that we have tried to help, but have hurt those we wanted to help, killed many civilians, and solidified people behind Slobodan Milosevic.
>
> . . . We have lost so many of our friends around the world. When I think how hard George worked over the years in so many jobs to shore up our relationships, now to see it all go down the drain. . . .

On June 10 we celebrated our joint birthdays, seventy-fourth and seventy-fifth. For 4 LONG days we are the same age; then for 348 days I am married to an older man again.

Bob Mosbacher had asked George if they could make his birthday a fund-raiser for M. D. Anderson. George decided that we could coordinate several things—his next parachute jump, a tour of the Library, AND a huge gala in Houston, all in a two-day period. So we flew from Maine down to College Station with Jack Fitch. George went immediately to practice for the parachute jump. We three had dinner that

---

*The president of Yugoslavia.

night with Pete Roussel and Hugh Sidey; Hugh had been with us at the first jump in Yuma, Arizona.

The next morning George practiced again, and "Operation Spring Colt" took place on June 9 at the Library:

> Jack and I walked over to the grounds in front of Library. There was quite a crowd: many heavy-hitters for the birthday celebration, the Houston office volunteers, Alicia and Stephen Spenlinhauer from Kennebunkport, lots of press, and many others. There were clouds in the sky and I wondered if the jump was on. (We had been told that they could not jump if it was a cloudy day.) Dr. John Mendelsohn,* Bob Mosbacher, Jack Guy,† and I walked out near the landing mark and waited. A young girl ran over to tell us that they were out of the plane. Suddenly we saw them floating down. The top man in the white parachute was G.B. His chute had a huge sign on it: "Making Cancer History; M. D. ANDERSON."
>
> They landed on the mark. What we didn't know was that George had trouble getting in the right position and started to tumble. Falling at 125 miles an hour, he spun out of control while at first two men and later just one tried to get him on his tummy and righted. They got him straightened out at the last moment, and he floated through the clouds as though he had not had a worry in the world and all had been fine. The two men with George landed well before him and were ashen and sweaty. George later said that he didn't have time to get frightened and found it exhilarating!

Later we did see the tape and it was really scary. No wonder the men were ashen!

General Hugh Shelton, then the chairman of the Joint Chiefs of Staff, came down from Washington and jumped after George. He is a huge, very impressive man.

Bob Mosbacher had a lovely reception that night at his home in

---

*President of M. D. Anderson Cancer Center.
†One of George's World War II squadron mates and good friend.

Houston where we learned that $10.2 million had been raised for The
George and Barbara Bush Endowment for Innovative Cancer Research.
Bob had hoped that this one event would raise $3 million toward the
FINAL goal of $10 million. Instead, they had it all in hand. We were
flabbergasted! Many of our dear friends from all over the country made
this possible.

The next day we went to M. D. Anderson for a lunch hosted by the
great Governor of Texas for his dad. It was very nice, and George W.
gave the sweetest introduction of his father. This was the same group
of big givers, plus Mila and Brian Mulroney and George and Laura—
a total of 250 people. Then came the big gala that evening:

> Neil and Sharon had come down [from Maine] earlier in the
> week. That afternoon Marvin and Margaret, Doro and Bobby
> arrived for the big extravaganza. They all raced off to exercise and
> came home to dress. Jeb and Colu flew in late that afternoon and
> went directly to the event. We met up at the Astro Arena where

*This was taken in June 1999, at our birthday party, which helped raise more
than $10 million for M.D. Anderson. Standing from left: Sharon Bush, Laura Bush,
Barbara Bush, Columba Bush, Margaret Bush, Bobby Koch. Sitting from left:
Neil Bush, George W. Bush, George Bush, Jeb Bush, Marvin Bush, Doro Koch.*
DAVID VALDEZ

we attended a reception for some 700. We went to have dinner in one hall and then the concert for 3,000 in another. Jim Nantz and Bruce Willis were the two emcees, and we were entertained by the Oak Ridge Boys; Vince Gill (live via video); Scott Hamilton who, believe it or not, roller skated, not ice skated; the Ballet Hispanico of New York City; Chris Evert and Arnold Schwarzenegger. They were followed by three wonderful golfers via video—Arnold Palmer, Jack Nicklaus, and Hale Irwin. Next came our two Governors, Jeb and George, who were very funny about their dad; followed by Gerald McRaney [TV's "Major Dad"]; and the Texas A&M Singing Cadets. On video again—the Three Tenors, Luciano Pavarotti, José Carreras, and Plácido Domingo; followed by a live appearance from "our" three tenors—Larry Gatlin, Michael W. Smith, and John Berry. They were funny and truly have lovely voices. We ended with Van Cliburn and Reba McEntire. With all that talent, it is no wonder the evening ran 1 hour over time . . . an unbelievable and thrilling evening.

One of our children later told me that he loved us, loved the evening, but that the family was costing him too much money: anniversaries, Library/Museum openings, inaugurations, weddings, and now birthdays parties. He was joking, but what a lucky family to have so much to celebrate!

The next day, George went by Bob Mosbacher's for an early morning breakfast for the now discredited President Hugo Chávez of Venezuela,* and then flew to Kerrville, Texas, for the opening of the George Bush Gallery in the Nimitz Museum. No children and no wife went with him as we had a big family wedding in Kennebunkport that weekend. I got home in time to go to the rehearsal dinner for Gracyn Robinson, daughter of George's first cousin, Susue Walker Robinson, and Peter Whitman, a very nice young man.

Marvin and Margaret with Marshall and Walker; and Doro and Bobby and their four arrived at Walker's Point on Saturday. All the adults including George went to the wedding, which was absolutely lovely, with glorious flowers and tons of family and friends.

---

*As I write this in March 2003 Venuzuela is horribly divided and very unsettled.

By Sunday, we were all packed for the Italian cruise. We went to our dear First Congregational Church at 9 a.m. and when we got home, there were George and Laura. They had come from a very successful announcement that he was a candidate for president. We saw his announcement on television, and he was really great.

We had a small army (all our family, cruise guests, etc.) on the deck for hamburgers and hot dogs. At 1:30 George W. had a press conference on the front lawn, with one hundred or more media of all types. Some were familiar faces—mostly among the "photo dogs," an affectionate name for the press photographers who we always felt were our friends.

We left George and Laura at the Point and met up with a group of friends in Boston and headed for Italy. We had two glorious weeks with new people arriving and leaving in the middle of the cruise. Robert Koch was the youngest, at six years old, and I suspect that George and I were right up there with the oldest. George, Laura, Jeb, Colu, and Neil did not make the trip as they all had to work.

The Italian cruise was very different from the more casual Greek ones. We missed those beautiful empty beaches.

Capri was a huge disappointment to me: "'Twas on the Isle of Capri that I found her"—a song that has run through my head from my childhood. I did not imagine a huge rock that went straight up with no beaches; and at the top, stores that are on Rodeo Drive in Los Angeles, Park Avenue in New York, or three or four blocks from our house in Houston. I did not imagine many really beautiful manicured gardens behind gates. I imagined a glorious island with white beaches, etc. I am not against all of the above; I just did not expect to find them there.

In Nettuno, we went to the Allies Landing Museum and then to see the cemetery at Anzio. They both were so moving. The folks seemed so glad to see George again, as we had visited there on a Memorial Day when George was in office. Our friend Tom Moseley had landed here with his parachute outfit during the war. George wanted the grandchildren to see and learn about the men and women who made such a sacrifice for their country. We stood in that mammoth cemetery and the tears were running down George's and our friend Lud Ashley's faces. Lud's brother died in the war. I couldn't look at anyone else because it was so moving. There were thousands of pure white marble crosses and Stars of David all lined up perfectly—not in order of rank or religion, state, or unit, but just as they were processed; their serial numbers on the back, and names, states, and dates on the front.

We had a little tour of Naples and then went in a bus to Pompeii.

We really had a fine trip, surrounded by family and friends. The thing that made our trip absolutely perfect were our Greek hosts: the Latsis family, Vaggelis and Fouli Chronis, and the thoughtful, kind staff on the *Alexander*.

The rest of the summer of 1999 was rather like every other summer—lots of our own children, lots of grandkids, lots of their guests, and many friends. In my diary I seem to have written more often than not: "He or she is messy"; "no one ever picks up a wet towel or bathing suit off the floor, uses their towel twice"; "I keep picking on 'the grands'; they are so sweet and I give up."

In a letter I wrote:

Our "grands" are driving George and me crazy by 1. Opening the deep freeze for ice creams and Klondike Bars and leaving it open. Yikes; 2. They drink soft drinks and don't finish them. Every time I empty an almost full can I could choke them!!!

And later I wrote in my diary: "Lots of people to love and lots of people to worry about."

All our children came. A team of George W.'s advisers appeared one week to brief him. I noted that *The Washington Post* had run seven articles on George W., and all seven had been fair. "He comes out as a nice guy who is decent and honest . . . not perfect, but a really good person."

Speaking of perfect . . . the sweetest thing happened in church last Sunday. One of our summer ministers at St. Ann's by the Sea, the headmaster of St. Paul's School, asked the congregation if anyone had a perfect family? He was talking about "the family of man," and to make a point, he asked that question. All but one of us sat on our hands which, I guess, is what he expected, probably hoped for. But one hand did go up and it was George Bush's. The minister sort of made a little fun of that and I heard a quiet George say: "To me they seem almost perfect." We all felt badly that we hadn't raised our hands, and I certainly felt a tear coming. George Bush is the sweetest man.

꩜ I flew back to Houston several times that summer to take care of some business, and on one of the trips I read *All the Best,* George's new book, in galley form. It is a book of letters and a few diary excerpts put together by Jean Becker. Jean wrote some two hundred people and asked them if (1) they had any letters from George; and (2) they were willing to share them. The response was overwhelming, and Jean had a difficult time choosing from so many. For instance, Gerry Bemiss, a childhood friend of George's from his summer days in Kennebunkport, sent in literally dozens of letters that George had written him from his days in the service, at Yale, and from West Texas and other places. George's mother had saved many of her children's letters, and our children had saved their letters. Then, in many of George's jobs, all correspondence was saved, so the Library, the CIA, etc., were huge sources. All of this is to say I sat on that plane going to Houston laughing, crying, and loving every moment. When the trip was almost over, a woman asked me what in the world I was reading as she really wanted to read it, too. I was a little embarrassed to tell her that I was reading a book by my husband, which meant that I already knew the story! But it brought back so many wonderful memories.

George did NO promotion for the book other than a few interviews. It is a great book, and although George says he won't write an autobiography, this comes very close. It is a true picture of a sensitive, thoughtful, caring man. I honestly think it is both interesting and fun.

꩜ Obviously politics were everywhere in our lives that summer.

One day last week I flew down to Orlando and spoke to the Florida Home Builders' Association. I worked hard on my talk as I did not want to be political. The introducer, after a short nice introduction, dramatically ended with, "Ladies and Gentlemen, the mother of the NEXT PRESIDENT OF THE UNITED STATES." 1,000 people came to their feet yelling and clapping. Honest, I'm not making this up. So much for avoiding politics!

. . . The feeling for GWB seems to be running high. Everywhere we go people seem to love him and yearn for family values.

∽ We had a marvelous trip to Belgium, where we saw Margaret Thatcher, former Belgian prime minister Wilfried Martens, and David Frost all gathered to help celebrate the seventy-fifth birthday of our friend Roger de Clerck and forty years of his Beaulieu Company, which specializes in carpets of every kind. Prime Minister Martens filled in at literally the last moment as Mikhail Gorbachev canceled on the day of the ceremony. That was the first hint we had of Raisa Gorbachev's illness. Three of the de Clercks' sons and two daughters came from South Africa, France, and the United States, respectively, where they are all in the family business. They came with twenty children who all speak three or four languages. It was such a loving and a happy time.

The next day I visited the Flax Museum, and we had lunch with the adult side of this marvelous family. I was delighted to see that all the children were sent to a hamburger place for lunch. Delighted, because I would have done the same thing.

∽ About this time I wrote in another letter to friends:

The feeding frenzy over George's not answering the Big "C" question is driving me crazy. I confess that I had to ask what "C" stood for and was shocked when Doro told me that it stood for cocaine. His dad and I react differently. I am sick of it, yell at the tube, and go into another room. I feel like

Groucho Marx who once brilliantly said: "I find TV very educational. Whenever anyone turns on the tube in my house, I go into another room and read a book." His dad watches every holier-than-thou commentator and political opponent. My gut feeling is that he should not answer the question; not because he has or has NOT used drugs, but because what he did 25 years ago is not relevant now. Incidentally, nobody has come forward to say he did use cocaine, and I have not asked him, nor has his father. His opponents in both parties are really loving it all.

Doro, our baby, is 40 today. I can't believe it. She left Saturday after 5 weeks and we miss her so.

Marvin and Margaret and their two arrived with darling Abigail Meyer, Marshall's very close friend, and I call her my 15th grandchild.

❧ Lou Walker called and said that he had a classmate from college coming in several weeks for his "last" visit, and he'd love to bring him by to say hello—or was it good-bye? We adore Lou and Grace, and so invited them to a small dinner with their guest, whom we had known over the years. I had several phone calls from Grace saying that she would stay home as there were too many guests. I said that of course she would come, and then she said that now three more were coming, one of whom was ninety-year-old Moon Hannon. "It's too much, Bar. I'll stay home." Finally it was agreed that we had plenty of room and we were really looking forward to the evening. A week before the dinner, Grace called and said that she hadn't known just how bad it was: Joe was in a wheelchair and had a male nurse. I said NOT to worry. Then she called back and said it was worse than that. Joe's housekeeper had told her that Joe's drinks should be watered down and he should have only three watered-down white wines. Believe it or not, she called again and said that it was even worse than that—Joe was incontinent. By now we had worked out a menu that could be gummed if need be.

Her last phone call was to tell me who should sit by Joe.

The big moment arrived, and Joe was pushed up our handicap

ramp into our living room. George greeted him and then said: "What will you have, Joe?" Quick as a flash Joe said: "Vodka, and make it strong!" He did look frail and was so sweet. He also had the vodka.

Our ninety-year-old was three years older than Lou and Joe but looked and acted fifteen years younger. He volunteered at a rehabilitation center at home. At one time during the dinner, which had now grown to fourteen, Joe got such sneezes—really loud, harsh, and hard to ignore. It went on for quite a while when finally, ninety-year-old Moon Hannan yelled down the table, "Blow your nose, Joe." Which Joe did and all was well. The minute dinner was over, we sent them all home.

Sunday we went to church at the 8 a.m. outdoor service, and no sooner were we in our seats than George saw a frenzy of bait jumping and sea gulls diving and fishing right off the rocks behind the altar. I half expected George to bolt because it was obvious that the blues were in. It was a real test of his faith—and he passed!

I flew to Michigan to speak at an event in Grand Rapids, where I met a priest who told me that he had just had a really nice visit with George W. An ecumenical group had flown down to Austin to meet with him as they wanted to know what he was really like. For some reason I found myself telling him that Jeb was a Catholic, George a Methodist, and we were Episcopalians. He pondered all that trivia for a moment and said that being an Episcopalian was all right as he considered us just "Lite" Catholics. I was certainly glad that I didn't tell him that I was really a Presbyterian and that George and I attended the First Congregational Church in the late spring and early fall in Kennebunkport.

⤢ In the September letter to my family, I wrote:

This has been a whale of a month. Along with a lot of friends and a few relatives, we have had a name-dropping month of visitors. Some because of George's new book that is coming out next week. Sam Donaldson, Jamie Gangel, Paula Zahn, and a Houston press person or two have all dropped by. They did not spend the night. Nor did Prince

Andrew who came for lunch and golf. (I was in Houston and so missed him.)

We started the month with the Oak Ridge Boys and their wives. They are so warm and independent* and come annually for a few nights. One night of the visit we usually have a large group over for cocktails and dinner and a sing. Thank heavens George took pity on the household this year and we took them out for dinner.

We had Chuck Norris and his beautiful bride Gina for one night. They were to leave early Sunday morning, but waited until after our early 8 o'clock church service. Very sweet.

Patricia Cornwell came for a day or two for the third year in a row. She is a great sport and adores racing around the ocean in the *Fidelity,* George's really fast boat. Patsy's new book, *Black Notice,* was No. 1 on the *New York Times* best-seller list and [her] *Point of Origin* was No. 1 on the paperback best-seller list. Amazing.

Sonny Montgomery, a former Democrat congressman from Mississippi and probably one of George's closest friends in the Congress, was here at the same time. Sonny served in the Congress for 30 years. Patsy flew Sonny home to Washington. That was really thoughtful and nice.

Mila and Brian Mulroney arrived on the 7th with Nicholas for the night. Their children are bright, attractive, and clearly very loved. Nick is their youngest and was on his way to school.

We had the two great Governors and wives (Texas and Florida). George and Laura went back and forth to New Hampshire several times.

We had Hurricane Floyd barreling up the coast and, thank heavens, he just dumped tons of water and wind on us. Unfortunately, we had scheduled a dinner for 36 for the Mayo Clinic and some guests couldn't fly in and some others

---

*This must have meant that I didn't have to entertain them as they play tennis, take walks, and so on on their own.

couldn't fly out. We ended with 24 people and had a lovely evening.

We had a large group for the Points of Light Foundation, 100 for cocktails at the Point and down to the River Club for yet again another clam/lobster bake. That night we learned that our house can't cope with 100 without a little more planning. The bottleneck was terrible getting in and out of the living room to the deck.

We had Julie and Ben Crenshaw for one night before the Ryder Cup matches; Ben is the captain of the American team this year.

This weekend we will have 110 for The National Cancer Dialogue—cocktails at the Point and dinner at a restaurant.

Michael W. Smith and Debbie will be with us this weekend for golf, and he will entertain at the dinner. The next day George and I will observe the cancer discussions. . . .

George stayed home in September—mostly; he fished some, boated a lot, did interviews for his book, and played golf . . . fast golf. He played golf with Jock McKernan.*

On September 8 I drove up to Portland with Kara [Babers] to visit The Barbara Bush Children's Hospital. We visited the neonatal floor and saw tiny babies, less than 2 pounds at birth, etc. The whole feeling is one of loving care in a sunny, bright atmosphere. Then we toured the part where the older children were, and I read a book to them. It brings back such memories of Robin; so adorable and so painful.

Politics have really become nutty in our country. Here we are 14 months before the election and fevers are running high. In June there were nine people in the Republican Primary and George W., who had just come out of the chute, had raised more money than all the others put together—$40 million. It is amusing as now the opponents

*Jock is the former governor of Maine and married to United States Senator Olympia Snowe.

in both parties are claiming "Big money, undue influence, etc." One can only give $1,000 to any one candidate, and they know it. They are just jealous. Almost 80,000 people have contributed to George's campaign, and the average gift has been $480.

By September one candidate on our side (old friend of ours) was saying that: "This election can't be bought by GWB for $36 million! I want a people's campaign. I want one million people to give me $36." By the end of this month George's campaign will have raised $50 million from well over 110,000 people. GEORGE'S IS A PEOPLE'S CAMPAIGN. UGH. I don't think I'm going to make it.

⌒ I'd like to go back to the Ryder Cup, which we did attend. It was held at The Country Club* in Brookline, Massachussetts, where our nephew Hap Ellis and his wife Robin not only live and play golf, but Robin had a big job for the tournament. For instance, all the beautiful antique furniture and rugs were moved out of the club and rented furniture was substituted. Rooms and large tents were set aside for eating, corporate sponsors, and so on. Robin did a superb job.

The crowds were enormous. For security reasons, we were allowed to be inside the ropes, and since the response to our group was disrupting, we walked ahead and settled in three spots where we could watch the green and the players tee off on the next hole. George W. and Jeb joined us, and the response was big to our two sons. But the response to my George was honestly overwhelming and very affectionate.

The play was sometimes slow, so the players often would come over and sit in the shade with us. At one time Payne Stewart came over, gave me a hug, and sat and talked politics with my three men. Payne was in the last match against Colin Montgomerie on the last day. He conceded to Monty as the match had already been won and the Ryder Cup was ours. He said that Monty had been heckled by the fans and didn't deserve any more abuse. This was a show of not only good

*Incorporated on November 7, 1882, this is the oldest country club in the United States.

sportsmanship, but also a sensitivity that is unusual. That lovely man was killed in a freak airplane accident several months later.

❧ In October, George returned to Texas via Pittsburgh, New York City, Hong Kong, and Tokyo. He read twice from his book, *All the Best,* at charity fund-raisers before he left—once at a luncheon for the Barbara Bush Children's Hospital in Portland, and another time in Greenwich, Connecticut, for AmeriCares.

I worked my way home with several domestic talks and arrived on October 13. On the way we did a lunch in one city—Long Beach, California—and then a dinner in another—Las Vegas. Kara Babers and I left early in the morning without any breakfast other than a cup of coffee. On the plane I lectured my really pretty aide about going on a diet. She had gained a few pounds after leaving college, so I begged her to join me on the Sugar Buster Diet, and we both agreed to eat NO carbohydrates, sugars, etc., for a week. Well, we arrived at the luncheon at 1 p.m. starved. There was a table set with more silverware than you could believe, a basket of yummy-looking rolls, and a small, delicious salad with three shrimp pre-set on the table. We both passed on the bread, of course, and ate sparingly of the salad. NOW THAT WAS REALLY STUPID. Suddenly the wait staff picked up all the silverware and plunked down the most glorious apple crisp with a large vanilla ice cream ball on top. We both stayed on the diet, but oh boy, we were two sad, hungry people. Fortunately the dinner had a lovely salad, chicken, and green vegetables! Hurrah!! (Kara did stay on the diet and lost 17 pounds.)

And so another summer ended.

❧ In my November letter to the "Ladies," I wrote:

Earlier in November George took me to Europe on the most fun and thrilling trip that I have almost ever been on. We started with the celebration of the 10th anniversary of the Fall of the Wall and slowly built up to quite an exciting trip.

. . . We started in Berlin staying at a hotel on the east side of the Brandenburg Gate, the renovated Adlon. All the hotels we stayed in were so much better than the last time we were in this part of the world and so was the food. From our window we could see 60,000 people standing in the rain all afternoon waiting for the big celebration. Three times that day we heard dear Slava Rostropovich play [his cello], the last being on an enormous stage set up by the gate. George, Helmut Kohl, and Mikhail Gorbachev also appeared to the wildest cheers. There were huge projection screens [on the stage] so we could see them from our hotel balcony. All three men are considered the big heroes of the reunification. Mikhail is around 1% in the polls in Russia and 100% in Germany. Ditto GHWB and Helmut, who now is the most popular politician in Germany, believe it or not!!!*

One of the nicest things we did on the whole trip was to have a small lunch with President and Mrs. Rau of Germany, Mikhail Gorbachev and his daughter Irina, and two interpreters who managed German to English, Russian to German, and maybe Russian to English; I've forgotten. At one time I asked Mikhail how he was doing. He said: "Don't ask, don't ask." Theirs was a real love affair, that's for sure.†
The conversation flowed freely as the interpreters were very good. President Rau started by telling several jokes and that got the luncheon off to a good start. He told about President Nixon during the Vietnam War telling Golda Meir that he must have General Moshe Dayan, a famous Israeli general, to help win the war and that he would give her two of our generals in return. She said: "It's a deal. I'll take General Motors and General Electric." He also said that Golda told Nixon that they had something in common: "We both have Jewish foreign ministers, only mine can speak better English.‡ That got Mikhail going and he told several jokes.

---

*Helmut had just lost his bid for re-election in September; Gerhard Schröder was the new chancellor.
†Raisa had died September 20 of leukemia.
‡She was talking about Henry Kissinger, who was one of Nixon's secretaries of state.

The one I remember was: Gorbachev went to Stalin, told
him that he was having trouble with the Politburo and asked
for advice. Stalin said: "That's easy. 2 Points: #1. Kill all the
members of the Politburo. Point 2. Paint the department
store across from the Kremlin pink." [Gorbachev replied:] "I
understand point #1., but I don't understand what point #2
will do to help me?" "Oh, well," said Stalin. "Forget point
#2!" There were other stories and memories that were very
funny. Conversations that started with, "You remember
George when . . ." It was very nice, relaxed, and fun.

We went on to London where we saw our dear friends
John and Norma Major, David Frost, and our daughter
Margaret, Marvin's wife, who was visiting her sister Jane
Hines. The Blairs, Tony and Cherie, invited us to tea at No.
10 Downing Street and were very gracious. It was
announced the next day that she was having a baby.

While in London we went to a dinner where my partner
on one side was Sir Charles Powell, at one time Margaret
Thatcher's right-hand man who now consults for many
groups. I only mention this because we had just seen his
younger brother, who is Tony Blair's right-hand man. The
man on my other side was rather portly and I thought very
old. He looked it, but turned out to be 71 or 72.
YOUNGER THAN WE ARE! I don't know his name
because he mumbled. When I finally got into his cadence, I
didn't have the nerve to ask his name again. He was very
entertaining and nice. John and Norma Major were at the
dinner, and John introduced George who spoke for 10
minutes and then answered questions.

We were in Stockholm literally for 3½ hours on the
loveliest sunny day. Alice Rubenstein and I skipped lunch
and wandered the streets looking at Swedish antiques for
Alice and David's home on Nantucket Island. I was
surprised to find that I really loved the Swedish antique
furniture. There is a simplicity and yet a classic beauty
about the old. Alice bought a truly lovely table and chairs
that are perfect in their Nantucket home.

Alice is great fun to travel with as she has researched the cities where we have traveled and knows exactly what to buy and where to look. We went on to Paris from Stockholm where Alice grew up and again wandered the streets in old Paris, poking in and out of fascinating shops. I am a lousy shopper and so got through the whole trip without buying one thing, but feeling guilty as though I had spent millions! (We are at the stage in our lives where we are giving away and not accumulating more.) While in Paris we got a message that the new King of Jordan* was in town and would love to say hello. We walked over to his hotel, just around the corner, and ran into the President of France, Jacques Chirac, coming down the staircase. So we got a nice hug from Jacques and had a very short visit and on up to say hello to the young King. He was charming and very polite. He asked about George W. and said that he had called him when he was in Washington. He said that he'd love to help him if he makes a trip to the Middle East. We were impressed by the dignity of this young man. He walked us down a huge flight of stairs and to our car, which seemed above and beyond the line of duty. He seemed like his father—a high compliment.

On to Munich and ate in the dearest restaurant with the nicest German people, our hosts. George was honored in Munich. Bavaria is such a very exciting part of Germany, different and cozier.

In Switzerland we spent 24 hours of pure rest with our dear friends, His Highness Prince Sadruddin Aga Kahn and Princess Catherine. We have been friends since the United Nations days and have stayed with them in Geneva many times. They are always the same and that was a great fun time in their glorious Château de Bellerive on Lake Geneva, taking walks in the drizzling rain, taking naps, watching an old movie, *One, Two, Three,* that was about Germany just before the Wall went up and a Coca-Cola Executive. Since

*King Abdullah II.

we attended a Coca-Cola dinner in Berlin, this was very appropriate and very funny.

We celebrated the 10th Anniversary of the Polish Independence in Warsaw. So really nice to see how far they have come in ten years. They are so kind about George and to us. They do give George a lot of credit for their independence.

On to Prague where we were joined or we joined Margaret Thatcher, Lech Walesa, Danielle Mitterrand and her really attractive photographer granddaughter, Mikhail Gorbachev and his daughter Irina, Helmut Kohl, and our host Vaclav Havel and his bride, Dagmar Havlová, lovely former actress. We had a small wonderful dinner together in that unbelievable [Prague] Castle. Thank heavens that Prague was saved by Hitler from being destroyed because he wanted to have it for himself one day!

One rather amusing thing happened at a huge forum where all were given The Order of the White Lion Medals by Vaclav Havel. Each recipient was then asked to give a small thank you. (Danielle spoke a few words for François* who had recently died.) When Margaret spoke she said something like "Ron Reagan and I brought about the collapse of communism in Europe." Amazing. Sitting on the stage with men who had spent years in prison and claiming that she and Ronald Reagan had accomplished that alone. In fairness, she probably wanted to bring Ronald Reagan into the mix and he certainly deserved to be mentioned. But there is no question that many people brought about the fall of communism and the Wall—many known and many unknown heroes, men and women. And there also is no question in my mind that both Ronald Reagan and Margaret were a real factor in bringing freedom to Europe, but they were two of many.

We did lots of things like sitting through many speeches for all ten days. For the first few my head bobbed

---

*François Mitterrand was the president of France when George was in office.

and I fought a semi-losing battle against jet lag. We visited embassies and thanked the folks for doing such a great job for their country, had pictures taken with the Marines and the young embassy children. We ate and ate and ate. George was made a citizen of Berlin, awarded an honorary degree at the 700-year-old Charles University in the Czech Republic and The Order of the White Lion in Prague and was awarded the Josef Strauss Prize in Munich. All of these things were done in the most glorious buildings, halls, etc., that one can imagine.

As you may know I have written this letter to you all, plus Andy Stewart, Phyllis Draper, my sister Martha, my older brother Jim's widow Margie Pierce and my younger brother Scott and his wife Jan. That's quite a group of people to cover with one blanket letter, I admit. I would have thrown our children in on these long tedious missals [*sic*], but I am assured in my mind that they wouldn't read them as they don't have the time and they know all they probably want to know. All of this is to say that after a long, long painful illness my sister Martha, an uncomplaining widow of many years, died this month at 79 years of age. Bless her heart. Her children enabled her to remain in her own home with loving caretakers, which is what she strongly wanted. She was surrounded by her six children and many in-laws although frankly it is hard to tell the in-laws from "partners" as some of the women have kept their maiden names.

⤳ Mart died while I was in Europe and so I left George to fly to Hartford, Connecticut, and attend the most loving, warm, and happy ceremony. Her children all stood and told marvelous stories, and some other relatives also spoke about their memories of her. All in all, since her death was truly a blessing, this was a great good-bye for us all.

Meanwhile, the day George arrived back in Houston, everyone had awakened to the bonfire tragedy at Texas A&M University where twelve students had died. He drove up that evening to attend the prayer service.

I can't tell you how this tragedy touched us all. We had planned to spend Thanksgiving at our apartment in College Station with Neil's and George W.'s families, plus Jebby. All the children wanted to see the bonfire, which is a revered tradition at A&M before their annual showdown with the University of Texas Longhorns. Instead, we attended the extraordinary candlelight silent vigil around the bonfire site with literally forty thousand kids holding lit candles and each other, all weeping. We then moved on to the most moving "Yell Practice," which they have before every game. No yelling this time, but such a feeling of family and love from students from both universities, Texas and Texas A&M, as many UT students had driven over from Austin to take part in the ceremony. That was perhaps the most touching of all.

The game was exciting on the Friday after Thanksgiving, and in spite of the tremendous rivalry, there was only good sportsmanship shown. During the half-time, the UT Band ended their program with "Amazing Grace," and marched off the field with the Texas flags lowered and two A&M flags raised high. The famous Texas A&M Band ended by asking for a moment of silence for their twelve fallen classmates and marched off the field of a stadium filled with 86,000 totally quiet people. Then there was "Taps"—and tears. There was a great feeling in the stadium that day. Thank heavens there are still schools where the kids are not ashamed to cry, love each other, and God.

I joined Jeb one day in Miami where he announced the Governor's Family Literacy Initiative for Florida, which began on a small scale (just three counties) as a joint venture between the South Florida Annenberg Challenge and The Barbara Bush Foundation for Family Literacy. It now funds programs statewide and includes many new partners. I am so proud of the job Jeb has done in boosting reading, schools, and education in his state. I was thrilled when he stole our "Celebration of Reading" idea, which he now hosts in Florida every year. Of course I stole the idea from New York's Literacy Partners!

It's amazing to me how the foundation has grown over the years. Now we not only give out national grants, but also have established statewide initiatives in Florida, Texas, Maine, and soon in Maryland, in partnership with local literacy organizations. Each state is different as they have different problems, so they customize the national grant and program criteria to meet their needs. The First Lady's Literacy Initiative for Texas—of which Laura Bush is honorary chairman—is very different from the one in Maine, which is very different from Florida's, which will be different from Maryland's.

I'm also very proud of Benita Somerfield, the foundation's director, who plays an important role in and ensures accountability to all these programs. She also advises many states and the great first lady of the United States.

∽ It is wonderful for a mother to see her children become passionate about the things she believes in, such as literacy and education. We are so proud of our son Neil, who is pouring all his energy into his company, Ignite! As Neil explains it, Ignite! is a "multimedia publisher of middle school curriculum." Neil feels strongly that all students can learn, but they can't all learn in the same way. He does not believe in the traditional, passive method of learning—at least not for everybody. He strongly urges teachers to use a wide variety of materials and teaching methods, including interactive activities. Part of Neil's motivation and inspiration comes from the problems he faced as a student with dyslexia. He's determined to help all students find their educational niche, in which they can learn anything. His ideas and company are too high tech for me to really understand, but I do know that I love his passion and his drive on the subject.

∽ In early December, Doro, her sister-in-law Tricia Koch, and Doro's Ellie came down to visit the Library for several days, which was so much fun. Right after they went home, I flew to the Mayo Clinic and had my feet operated on as I was having great problems. I went in a perfect "10" and came out a slightly less perfect "9." When asked, I guess you would say that "the little pig that stayed home" has now gone to heaven.

George e-mailed all the grandchildren and told them to act like they didn't notice my feet when they saw me swimming in Florida after Christmas. Then he debated whether they should refer to me as 4 or 9? Very funny! I e-mailed them that they would never have to see these ugly feet—in fact, couldn't see them—and that I preferred to be referred to as "9." My brother Scott wondered if I teetered? Was I lop-sided? Not to worry, as in 2001 the other "little pig that stayed home" went to heaven and joined his brother. I am painless! Just call me "8."

We had a quiet Christmas at home with Neil's family. I wrote to my family:

> Well, Christmas has come and gone again and Santa was very good to us. Why-oh-why do the grapefruits all come on the same day? Why-oh-why do supposed good friends send not only candy, but the best crunchy chocolate covered nuts and caramel kind of candy? Great, but guess who eats it? I guess we'll never know the answer.
>
> The day after Christmas George treated our whole family, 10 children and 14 "grands" to Florida for five days of golf, tennis, swimming, eating (unfortunately), and being together. It is fun to see our adult children together and to see the support they give each other, their own children, and their nephews and nieces. It was also great to see George and Laura relax before the year that is coming up for them.
>
> George P. (24) is here from New Hampshire where he is working in his uncle's campaign and is looking at law schools starting in the fall. Noelle (22) is here from her term in Australia, looks beautiful, but too thin. Lauren (16), Pierce (14), and Ashley (11), all riding bikes, playing tennis, and "hanging out" with their older cousins. Jebby (16) and Doro's Sam (15) are having a great time playing golf and fooling around with Jenna and Barbara (18). Ellie and Marshall (both 14) are at the pool stretched out sunning, swimming, and riding bikes. Walker playing pretty good golf at 11, Robert (7) fishing with "Gampy" and his precious mother, and Gigi, the youngest, at 4, swimming and playing.
>
> We may not be a perfect family, but certainly we are blessed.

RANKING COMMITTEE
JUNE 8, 2000

*In honor of my seventy-fifth birthday, George decided to reveal for
the first time the members of the top-secret family "ranking committee."
For years this committee had ranked family members on everything
from the jokes they told to their tennis and horseshoe game. George stole
the idea from our friend Jack Lupton, as you'll see in this chapter.*

ALEXANDER ROGERS

January 1—This is the first day of the new millennium. For
months we have heard nothing but scary things that might happen—terrorism, Y2K problems with the computers that run our
water systems, banks, trains, and airlines, etc. Today all seems
well. The world has not come to an end after all!*

*As I read this in 2003, terrorism does not seem as far-fetched as it did in 2000.

George started the New Year hunting with Jim Baker and took Sadie with him. He said that Sadie did remember a little from all those years ago when she was trained in England. What I remember from that hunting trip was that she returned covered with thousands of tiny, thin cactus stickers. We brushed her and brushed her and slowly they came out. I know they hurt. How do I know? I got one in my hand, AND I sat on one. Believe me—they hurt.

While George was hunting, I had lunch with my "Monday ladies"—a group of friends who have been meeting for years and invited me to join them when we left the White House. We have lunch the first Monday of every month. They are Ann Peake, Peggy Neuhaus, Barbara Riddell, Phoebe Welsh, Helen Vietor, Bobbie Fitch, and of course me. This is a treat and almost makes me feel normal, which I confess I don't always feel. I am not complaining, because my perks far outweigh any lack of privacy: no problem finding a parking place; surrounded by men and women who protect us with a quiet delicacy; no waiting in lines for airline tickets; and so on. Sometimes I will tell neighbors Mildred Kerr or Bobbie Fitch when the air conditioning has gone out or the dishwasher broke, "The nicest man came out in an hour." Their answer is almost always: "Of course—for YOU." Or I will say, "I don't find this or that person difficult." Their answer: "Of course—nice to YOU." And they are right.

Here is a good example: George and I have become very good friends with a wonderful couple here in Houston, Hushang and Shahla Ansary. Hushang was formerly ambassador from Iran to the United States, but has been an American citizen for years. He is a great supporter of education, literacy, M. D. Anderson, George's Library, and almost every other cause you can mention, including the United States. We saw them one day out at Shadow Hawk Golf Club, and Shahla and I discussed coming out one day to play together. Time went by and finally I called and invited her to play on the following Monday. I had called the club first to be sure that there wasn't a tournament and asked if the 9 a.m. tee time was available? "Oh, yes, Mrs. Bush," they answered, "That time is open, so come ahead."

Shahla and I drove out and teed off at 9 a.m., and it was marvelous. There was not a living human on the course, and we laughed and talked all the way around eighteen holes. We walked up to the club, sat on the terrace, and ordered lunch—a small salad. It took forever, but we had so much to share and talk about that I didn't think too much about it, especially since we began to see golfers on the course. I mentioned to the nice man who was serving us that I was amazed that on this lovely day there were so few people playing. That is when he told me that the club was closed on Mondays until noon and the kitchen was closed all day. That, he said apologetically, was why the lunch was so long in coming. They had gone next door to another club, bought the lunch, and brought it back. To make my point even stronger about being catered to or spoiled: Shahla and her husband both knew the club was closed on Mondays, called the club, and were told that in THIS case it was open.

          ∽ We again spent a weekend in Falfurrias, Texas, at the Negley Ranch with dear friends. We all sat in Nancy's bedroom and watched one of the Republican primary debates. This was the second night in a row for debates, the New Hampshire one being the night before. I did not watch New Hampshire, but did watch South Carolina.

I saw a cartoon around this time that expressed exactly how I felt. A man walked into a travel agency and said: "I don't care where the cruise goes as long as it doesn't get back before the election is over!" I hate to hear people lying about my son!

We were then and still are often asked this question: "Is it harder to run yourself [or in my case, "have your husband run"] or have your son run?" No matter how the question is asked, the answer is the same: "OUR SON!" I guess it is a normal instinct to want to protect your children from being hurt.

To this day George watches every single thing on television; I am not that strong. So, when it gets too bad, George puts on some marvelous Advent wireless earphones and turns the sound off so I can read in the same room. This may have saved our marriage! There is an added advantage to this for him—he can go from room to room and still hear all the awful things said about our sons.

Another solution to this problem for me is listening to a taped book. I turn it on while riding the exercise bike, walking the dog, and on trips. I love to do needlepoint as well, and it certainly makes long

trips in cars or planes a joy if you have a good book to listen to and
needlepoint to work on at the same time. All thoughts of campaigns
slip away. I have made seven backgammon boards over the last four or
five years, and a marvelous craftsman in Maine, Wade Junkins, has
made seven lovely tables for me. Four of them are at Walker's Point,
and I have given away the other three. Isn't it fortunate that we are a
backgammon-playing family!

Nan Ellis gave me Anthony Trollope's *Barchester Towers,* and I
spent hours listening to these tapes and have since listened to everything else of his I could find. I get these mainly courtesy of Mildred
Kerr, who is more than a great friend; she is an unending lending
library of take-your-mind-off-politics tapes and movies.

It probably won't surprise you when I say we did a great deal of
traveling and speaking in the winter of 2000. At the last moment,
before taking a long trip with George, I ran into the Jungman Public
Library close to our Houston house to pick out a tape or two and discovered that I didn't have my glasses. So I squinted and found a book-
on-tape by Amy Tan that I had not read. Then, out of the corner of my
eye, I saw *"Dutch."* I had wanted to read *Dutch: A Memoir of Ronald Reagan,* by Edmund Morris, but it is a huge book and to carry it around
the world seemed impossible. George had just read Morris's *Theodore
Rex,* and really enjoyed it. When I got home I discovered that it was a
little sad that we were not going to Holland as, now, thanks to my
blindness, I could learn to SPEAK Dutch!

꩜ All winter and spring there were debates. As George W.
was the front-runner, all the others aimed at him. The nicer he was, the
meaner they got. How I hate debates. I hated them for my George, and
now for George W., and for Jeb.

February 17—The McCain/Bush/Keyes* debate on *Larry
King* in South Carolina was such agony for me that I just could
not watch. George did and kept calling, "Bar, you must come

---

*By this time the only three Republican candidates left were Senator John McCain,
George W., and Alan Keyes.

and watch. He's doing a great job." I just couldn't. George then watched the post-debate roundup where the pundits then told him, and all the rest of America, who won and what they had just seen. So I stayed in my office working. While sitting at my desk the phone rang and without thinking I picked up the phone and it was George W., calling in to report to his dad as requested. Whoops! I lied: "You were great!" And quickly called George in the other room. I couldn't tell him that I hadn't watched. One of George W.'s team later called Jean Becker and said that John [McCain] had really unleashed on Alan Keyes during the break in the debate. He went on to say that everyone saw it and yet it was never mentioned by or in the press. I was really shocked to read that Senator McCain was not at two of the debates, but participated by satellite. I believe that he was in New Hampshire while the others were on the spot—probably smart, but not too fair.

There are enormous gaps in my diary during this time period that really are reflective of the agony of seeing a son run for president. I did note that by this time "38 Republican U.S. Senators and 175 Republican Congressmen and women have endorsed GWB."

I had one ally during this period—Marvin Bush. He, too, just could not watch.

We did some campaigning for George W.—mostly fund-raising—and also spoke at many charitable events and some for money. I read to many schoolchildren, visited hospitals, played some with friends, and spent time in College Station at the Library.

My diary says that in January of 2000 I was learning how to send letters over e-mail. Two years later, our computers went out for several days, and we all acted as though the world had come to an end! I don't quite know what this proves, but we are very spoiled. Seems really amazing that when George W. was born, we did NOT have television, and now we feel out of touch—almost lost—if our e-mail is down.

But this brings up another issue: I used to think that a huge problem was people who wrote all the time—in other words, wouldn't "stay writ to." Now I know there's even a bigger one. I love e-mail and even more, I love to hear from my family and friends. BUT, one should not give out their e-mail address loosely. It turns out there are folks who won't "stay e-eed to," either. I read in a column recently that there are rules that should be applied to e-mailers. Things like: "Don't send an e-mail to someone in the next office." Since I don't work in an office, that doesn't apply to me. My number one rule might be: DO NOT SEND ME THOSE THREATENING E-MAILS. You know—"If you don't pass this on to ten friends before sunset, a small child will die."

~ We were doing a lot of campaigning, including trips to Arizona, Iowa, and of course New Hampshire. It was unique as only New Hampshire can be, and the trips there certainly brought back many memories of 1980, 1988, and 1992. Former Governor Hugh Gregg had been my George's state chairman, and now his son, U.S. Senator Judd Gregg, was George W.'s. We saw many old friends; for instance, I was introduced on my first stop in Lebanon by Julia Fifield, a ninety-five-year-old, who had had a party for me—really George— in 1980. Loyal Amie and Edgar Mead were there with their daughter and grandchild. They had helped in 1980, and Amie served in George's White House.

Kathy Gregg traveled with me the whole two-day visit, along with New Hampshire congressman Charlie Bass and his wife, Lisa. We were met by Ohio congressman Rob Portman, another very loyal, dear friend. The senator and the two congressmen really were courageous as they all had fellow senators or congressmen running from their own states—Senator Bob Smith of New Hampshire and Representative John Kasich of Ohio. (Both these gentlemen dropped out early.) We appreciated the support of the governor of Arizona, Jane Hull, for the same reason, because of John McCain.

Maybe the best of all was that George P., our oldest grandson, was volunteering for the campaign and at this time was working in New Hampshire. He and I took an hour off from campaigning to go see thirteen-year-old Pierce, Neil's son, who was at boarding school there. It was a cold, slushy day and as we drove up to the top of a big hill, Pierce rushed out. He was expecting only me, but when he spotted "P.," he raced around the car and said with such enthusiasm to his teacher who was waiting to greet us: "It's George P., my cousin!" George jumped out of the car and they hugged. I cannot describe how happy it makes us to see how much our family members love each other.

In New London, there was dear Hilary Cleveland. Her husband Jimmy was with George in Congress and helped us in 1980; now Hilary, a widow, was with us again. The organizer, Ann Holmes, and Hilary had gathered a nice crowd at the Town Hall. I wrote in my diary that "this is turning out to be fun." We drove to Manchester, where I spoke at the Hillsborough County Lincoln Day Dinner. I sat at the table with my introducer and old friend from days of yore, Gerri Porter. They sent me to bed after that, and I slept in an enormous suite with very tall slanted windows that I could not see through as they were covered with snow.

The next day, I awakened to several TV interviews which I had already taped—one by Jack Ford and one by Jamie Gangel. Both were kind to me.

We drove to Rye, New Hampshire, and went to the waterfront home of Paul and Anna Grace Holloway. What a beautiful spot this is. George's Aunt Mary Walker spent her summers there as a child, and although I had heard of Rye, I had never been there before. It was a lovely, open house with a huge crowd. I spoke, took questions, and shook every hand in the place. We then did something that is rather traditional—we stopped in to have fish chowder at Gino's Restaurant on the harbor in Portsmouth. Old friend Evelyn Marconi, the proprietor, had packed the tiny place with friends, family, and supporters. It was jammed, and others in the entourage got some of that delicious chowder while I shook hands and posed for pictures. I often wonder if there are dresser drawers that are lined with pictures of us. Occasionally a mother will push a reluctant child next to me and say: "Johnny REALLY wants to have his picture taken with you." I bet if asked, Johnny would have absolutely NO idea who this large, white-headed lady was!

I read at McClelland School in Rochester, departed for Wakefield for a campaign event, and then a 2:30 p.m. event at the Town Hall in Sanbornville, where Dino Scala introduced me. At 3:30 p.m. we drove to Conway, where we had some private time before the 7 p.m. Carroll County "Night with First Lady Barbara Bush." This was a huge dinner, and I saw many more friends.

New Hampshire, along with Iowa, has an early primary. It is important that the candidates really cover these states, going from town to town, meeting, speaking, and touching as many people as possible. Surrogates can only rally the troops. I might add that this is all done at the coldest time of the year. Many of the candidates had practically lived in Iowa, and John McCain skipped Iowa and lived in New Hampshire. George W. covered the country.

After that exhausting trip I wrote in my diary: "My, what one does for their children." Then I thought just how silly that was—these same children did so much more for us! Besides that I was having fun!

George W. won Iowa and lost New Hampshire badly.

That winter we were having real problems with either an armadillo or a raccoon digging in our gardens. When we were gone and Sadie was not around, Ariel put out a Have-a-Heart cage; he finally caught a neighborhood cat! Sadie was very sad that he let it out and wanted to know: "Why do dogs have to be leashed while cats can run wild?" We did catch a huge armadillo later in the spring between the Fitch and Bush house; he or she honestly almost filled the cage. I still can't understand why we had to pay money to have someone pick up this destructive animal only to have it delivered to someone else's neighborhood?

I read Fannie Flagg's *Welcome to the World, Baby Girl!* and loved it. As I write this in 2000 I am reading an advance copy of her next book, *Standing in the Rainbow.* Fannie read for us at A Celebration of Reading in April 2000 and then read for us again at our first Dallas Celebration of Reading in November 2002. She sent me the new book and suggested that I pick a section for her to read. Honestly, from the first chapter, I found myself thinking: "This would be perfect," or, "No, this would be better." I am on page 254 and the book is 492 pages long. What fun to have the pleasure of 238 more pages to read.

There was a nice review of this book *in The New York Times Book Review* several weeks later. I guess they hated to be too positive for they did say that it was a "feel-good book," sort of implying that was bad.

So what's wrong with feeling good? If I want to feel bad, I can just read any one of the three major newspapers we get every morning.

I know things aren't going too well in the campaign as friends are calling to see how I am.

⟳ Toward the end of January I flew to Orlando to the National Center for Family Literacy's Ninth Annual Conference. I did this for Sharon Darling, head and founder of this group and truly one of family literacy's great movers and shakers. Sharon long ago realized that teaching an adult to read is not enough. We must also teach the child and the parent at the same time. We must teach the whole person. The child must go to school "reading-ready," healthy, and with parents who can help and encourage them—thus "family literacy." The parent must have the ability to fill out a résumé, learn a trade, get at least a high school diploma or GED. Most of the programs supported by The Barbara Bush Foundation for Family Literacy do just that.

We flew on to Clemson, South Carolina, for several receptions and a lecture. Late that night we circled because of a snowstorm and finally landed in Savannah, Georgia, and then drove to Beaufort, South Carolina, for a breakfast rally with campaign workers the next morning. These really loyal friends came out with snow on the ground. We worked a rope line, and then it was on to Charleston, where it had also snowed overnight. That certainly is unusual for Beaufort and Charleston.

I went by Ashley Hall where I graduated from high school. It was really lovely with so many new buildings, including a new swimming pool. I saw the grove where I used to be in school plays, and they had a blown-up picture of me in Shakespeare's *Much Ado About Nothing*. It had all changed so—from a day/boarding school to a much bigger campus and no boarders. They had gathered the whole school and a number of parents. But best of all they had gathered seven of my old classmates; when I say "old" I mean OLD, as we had graduated in 1943—fifty-seven years ago. That was fun. We had a quick and happy visit.

I then went into the school assembly, where I gave a talk and then questions and answers. Again, I was careful not to be political. The headmistress, Margaret McDonald, very kindly asked the last question, a tough one: "Mrs. Bush, would you please tell us about your son and his campaign?" That allowed me to tell about George W., his family, education, and character.

What I did not know at the time was that although school was canceled because of snow, they did not cancel my visit. Pretty nice.

I then went on to have lunch with Ann and Jim Edwards, former governor of South Carolina, secretary of energy in the Reagan administration, and president of South Carolina Medical School; Emily and Charlie Condon, who was the Attorney General; and Tom and Suzie Farsell, owner of the best restaurant I'd been to in a long time, Magnolias. The ambiance was just right and the food beautiful and delicious.

I also gave a speech at the College of Charleston; then flew to Myrtle Beach which, even though covered with snow, looked like a kids' heaven.

George went to Kuwait and Saudi Arabia to give speeches where he was treated like a king and then he came home "to Campbell Soup and me." (That was a note in my diary.)

We went to the Alfalfa Club dinner, and the great Governor of Florida was taken in as a member. The next night, UN Ambassador Richard Holbrooke and his very bright attractive wife Kati Marton gave a dinner for us at their residence and our old home at the Waldorf Towers in New York. The guest list was made up of friends in the media such as Barbara Walters, Helen Thomas, and Tom DeFrank, and some interesting ambassadors. In fact, all the guests were interesting. The dinner was fun, and they did the most flattering thing. Someone had read our books and clippings and taken small snippets of quotes about George's years at the United Nations—almost thirty years before—and slipped them to some guests. In between courses, Richard invited a guest or two to stand up and read whatever they were given. They were short and very funny. From the things they read it was clear—once again—that "the more things change the more they stay the same."

In January alone, we (one or the other of us or together) went to Arizona, Colorado, South Carolina, Maine, Kuwait, Saudi Arabia, Florida, New York and New Hampshire, and a day trip to Dallas.

⤳ On February 3, we had another interesting Leadership Forum at the Library. This time the panelists were: Charlie Cawley, CEO of MBNA; golfer Ben Crenshaw; Mary Matalin, TV commentator and political guru; and Chuck Krulak, the former commandant of the Marines. They spoke to a standing-room-only crowd.

Then on February 8–9 I headed to Virginia, back out on the campaign trail. I spent the night in Charlottesville and after an event there, went to Falls Church to a "Women for Bush" rally. Doro sat in the back with Gigi. She had just come from Delaware where the night before George had won the primary. She had given the acceptance speech on George W.'s behalf, in which she gave credit to many, especially our cousin Betsy Fields, who lives in Delaware and led the charge.

⤳ Around this time, while George was traveling, I saw several movies—I loved *The Winslow Boy;* caught up on my scrapbook, cleaned closets, packed and sorted out my life. I see that I noted in my diary that I DID NOT WATCH TV.

⤳ In March, we took a fascinating trip to The People's Republic of China. We went with our doctor and friend Ben Orman. George had just had a medical episode in Florida; it could not have been too bad as I can't remember what happened, but it scared me, and Ben came to keep an eye on him. (Ben recently reminded me that it had to do with George's heart being out of rhythm again.) Also along were Arnie Kanter, a friend and a China expert who works in Brent Scowcroft's firm; and our host, Charles Wang, the CEO of Computer Associates. Charles was an amazing fifty-three-year-old bundle of energy. As I mentioned before, energy seems to be a quality that is ever present in very successful people.

At one time during the short stay in a very polluted Beijing, Ben and I ran over to the Forbidden City, as he had never been to the Far East before. It is on 250 acres right in the middle of Beijing, and I loved showing it to Ben, although unfortunately we did not have time to really see it all—after all, it does have nine-thousand rooms. I am involved with Ronnie Chan—a good friend and a well-known, respected Hong Kong businessman—in a project to rebuild the very northwest section of the Forbidden City. Some say that it was here the "Last Emperor" lived, and that it was burned down so that nobody would know what the eunuchs had stolen. As the grandchildren say: "Whatever." I visited the site in May of 2002 and it is coming along. It is a huge project, and the work that is being done is absolutely mind-boggling—no nails, beautiful tilework, and so on.

We rushed back to the hotel and joined up with the others while they announced a $30 million gift from Computer Associates to train Chinese doctors to operate on children with cleft palates and for research. One baby out of every seven hundred to one thousand in China is born with this condition. Interestingly enough, Central America also has a very high incidence of this problem, while Africa's is small. Why? The program is called "The Smile Train," as the babies cannot smile, talk, or eat. I believe that "Smile Train" is active in twenty countries. Doctors volunteer to go to a country, operate, and return home. Certainly, training the local doctors is the better solution.

After the announcement, we went to visit the hospital where they will train the doctors and operate on the children. We saw babies ready to start the operations; those who have already had several; and those who are finished with the many painful procedures they have to go though in order to live normal, healthy lives. A group of the latter sang and then turned and smiled at us. I don't know when we've ever been so moved.

We had a good visit with President Jiang Zemin, at his invitation. It brought back many memories of other visits. We lined up on one side, and the Chinese on the other with note-takers galore on their side. After greeting the rest of us, Jiang Zemin said to George: "You start." And start he did; they exchanged their thoughts on the U.S. election and politics, Taiwan, Russian elections, the Falun Gong,* the trade problem, and "Smile Train." No one else spoke. It was fascinating.

A side note: George and I were thrilled to finally get to host President Jiang at George's Library in October 2002. The visit came during perhaps the worst rainstorm I had seen in ages, but it did not dampen the enthusiasm for the president—or the crowds. Well, let me

---

*A controversial religious group in China.

put that differently: The crowds were really damp, but the excitement was clear. The president gave his whole speech in English and that thrilled everyone.

Later we raced over to The Great Hall of the People, where we missed a large reception—thank heavens—and went right into a banquet for two thousand–one thousand of them surgeons. We left after some six courses and many speeches.

The next day, we flew to Tokyo and had lunch with Ambassador Tom Foley and his wife Heather. Then we flew on to a very polluted Seoul, South Korea, to the Grand Hyatt Hotel, one of the world's loveliest. Our suite was the most tasteful, filled with antiques, beautiful flowers, books in every room, fireplaces, and on and on. We took a Jacuzzi and had massages. We had left on Tuesday and got home on Saturday afternoon—almost too fast to have jet lag.

꒰꒱ Meanwhile, former Senator Bill Bradley was losing in a very ugly campaign with Vice President Gore in the Democrat primaries. Senator Bradley was such a gentleman and was gaining ground, but by the time all the lies and rumors about him were sorted out, it was all over but the shouting. At the time I was glad because I felt that Al would be easier to beat. Ha.

Incidentally, what is said in the heat of a campaign is often forgotten after the election. It must be hard for the voter to understand, but that's the truth. I have always thought that the Democrats are better at mending than Republicans. After a short period of time, Senator Bill Bradley backed Al Gore.

March 7—SUPER TUESDAY. I worked all day in Tennessee. I am glad to be busy.

In Memphis, I attended a fund-raising lunch for George W., given by Fred and Diane Smith. Fred is a fellow Mayo Clinic Board member and the founder and CEO of FedEx. Before the lunch, Fred laughed and said: "If you had told me back in my Yale days that George Bush would run for President of the United States and that I'd be supporting him, I'd have bet the moon against you." I asked Fred if he thought

George and his classmates would have foreseen that he would found and head an international company? He immediately said no, but I am tempted to disagree with him. Fred gave me a CD with the score from *My Dog Skip,* the movie based on the Willie Morris book. I told him that I had heard that this was a "must-see" movie for us. He confessed that he and Diane had never financially backed a movie before, but they got talked into this one. We later saw it and adored it.

There have been several low-budget movies that I really enjoyed in the last few years and so did the American public. Besides *My Dog Skip,* there was *Life Is Beautiful* and *My Big Fat Greek Wedding,* to name just a few. They were very funny, touching, and memorable; not violent and/or vulgar. Hollywood movies have a huge influence on Americans and they should, in my opinion, use this great power for the good and not the bad, the ugly, and the promiscuous.

꒜ I had my annual physical and it seemed like they found all bad things. But they kept saying, "For a woman your age, you are in great shape." The truth hurts. I am crumbling, but feel great, especially "for a woman my age."

꒜ On Tuesday March 14, at 7:15 a.m., George and I voted for our son for President for the first time, in the Texas Primary.

At 9:15 a.m. I was attending the Mayor's Literacy Leadership Awards Breakfast, hosted by the Houston Read Commission. Many really worthy people were honored for their work in the field, and then Eleanor McCollum presented me with the First American Bible Society Houston Read Commission Award. During the presentation of a beautiful crystal obelisk, she held it up and read from it the most glowing, rather long citation, and then handed it to me. I took it and realized that it was totally blank. I thought I must be going blind and turned it and turned it. I whispered to Eleanor that I couldn't see anything on it; she explained that it was to be engraved and that is what it WILL say. I have it sitting on my desk at College Station and it truly does NOT say much but her name and mine in big letters. But it reminds me of a lovely lady.

Eleanor was born Eleanor Searle in 1908 in Plymouth, Ohio. She was ninety-two years old at this time and had just made up the whole citation!

She studied opera as a child and became an opera singer of some renown, which she gave up to marry the social "Sonny" (Cornelius) Whitney. Many years after her marriage ended, Eleanor married Leonard "Mc" McCollum, a well-liked, retired CEO of Continental Oil Company and a widower. Eleanor remained in Houston after "Mr. Mc" died and truly became a leading citizen. She was a guiding force of many charities but especially Orbis International, which literally is a flying eye hospital.

How do I know that she came from Plymouth, Ohio? Several years ago Eleanor called and told me that she heard I was speaking in Ohio VERY close to her hometown and she would love to have me cut the ribbon on a museum she was opening in Plymouth. I explained that this was a really long, hard day and that I really didn't have any time. Eleanor was one of those people who did not take no for an answer, so I landed in a rainstorm, was met by Eleanor, and we drove quite a distance to Plymouth. It was very sweet as the town was really old and really small, and although it was raining, there was a small hard knot of folks, all waving flags in the rain. The mayor said a few words of welcome and we cut the ribbon. At that time the storefront museum had a few pieces of furniture, some old newspaper clippings, a little history, and many White House pictures of Eleanor and "Mr. Mc" with various presidents and wives, mostly President Reagan and George. This took no time at all to tour.

We then drove forever, leaving little or no time to rest, dress, etc. I was speaking to a large group who had subscribed to a lecture series. Eleanor introduced me. I couldn't believe my ears—I had seventeen grandchildren, eight children, was a genius, and on and on. About the only thing she got right was my name. And who cared? Not I.

In August 2002 Eleanor Searle Whitney McCollum died, surrounded by family and friends. What a remarkable lady.

    By the end of March, George was the Republican candidate for President of the United States. I wrote in my diary:

WHAT A VICTORY!!!! But now our children will have 8 more months of agony. Fortunately they don't feel the same way. They have one more day at home in Austin and then take off for another week of campaigning.

⤳ Kara Babers and I ended March by taking the most exciting trip with the Rubensteins—David and Alice and their three children, Alexa, Ellie, and Andrew; some good friends of theirs who have become friends of ours, Fouad and Nagwa Said, who were our hosts; their friends, Kailash and Indu Chandaria; our granddaughters, Lauren and Ashley Bush; and Dorie Mayne, a Denver friend of Lauren's. Besides being the very nicest people, the Saids take all the pain out of a trip by picking the hotels and camps, and so on.

We met in Paris, then flew to Nairobi and spent the night in the famous Norfolk Hotel, with tall ceilings and ceiling fans; pictures of celebrities such as actors John Wayne and William Holden, and the chimpanzee lady Jane Goodall; and a big-game wall filled with animal trophies.* There even was a picture of a very well dressed man in a morning coat riding a zebra. I especially enjoyed the many old pictures of second and third sons of European families at very formal black-tie dinners in this ninety-five-year-old hotel. They came to Kenya where they could live like kings and make a life since the firstborn was the heir to the estate back home.

The next morning we flew to the Mount Kenya Safari Club, which is at 7,000 feet. I fortunately had my high-altitude medicine with me, which I started in Paris and felt wonderful. We had a really brief but stylish and easy transition into Africa. My beautiful room straddled the equator. We were high enough to be very comfortable. A small group, including Bill Holden, originally owned this club, and one of its principal residents now is actress Stephanie Powers, who owns a house there. We did see the orphan park, which I believe is Stephanie's passion: rescuing babies abandoned at birth by whatever animal and for whatever reason. The beautiful Miss Powers happened to be in residence, and she generously called to say hello. I was sorry that we left

---

*Killing of game is now outlawed in Kenya.

before we could meet again. She did say that she still gets to Kenya three times a year still and then has to work to "bring home the bacon."

Early the next morning we flew to Masai Mara Reserve and stayed at Little Governor's Camp. Before the trip started, I told my girls that it showed my real love for them to "camp out" at my age. I really thought that a tent would be difficult; well, let's be honest—dreadful.

You have never seen such a fancy tent, which was on a permanent concrete base. There was a small porch outside with two chairs and a tiny table to hold my coffee, delivered the three mornings we were there at 5 a.m., the hour my eyes open. Inside the tent there was a double bed and a small tiled bath with a very simple shower. There was no electricity and we went to bed with a lamp—too dim to read by, but by holding up a flashlight I could read a little or keep a few notes on my little laptop computer until the battery ran out. So much for "suffering for the girls."

Our camp was on a small, marshy lake that had a resident hippo. He snorted and blew all one night, which made it even more fun. A family of elephants came wandering through the camp with babies one morning. It was quite a shock to see them ten feet away. There was also a family of warthogs who seemed to feel quite at home in the camp. Masai guards stood watch all night long, and when you weren't worried that they might be Mau Maus, these tall, handsome-looking warriors made one feel very secure. This is my imagination stirred up by Robert Ruark's book *Something of Value,* written in 1955 and read and never forgotten by me.*

We settled our luggage into our tents and immediately went out in funny old trucks. First, we had to cross a small river on a tiny boat that held only three or four people at a time. The nicest, brightest man named Stanley drove our truck. He made the trip for me as he knew all the animals and could spot them from miles away. We would drive, find some animals, stop, stand, look, and take pictures. We were lucky as it had rained several days before, so there was little or no dust and the weather was pleasant. We saw many animals "up close and personal." I did learn that lions need twenty hours of sleep every day and

---

*The 1955 description of the Masai: Fierce fighting tribes of Bantu origin who live in southern Kenya and Tanganyika (now Tanzania). Mau Maus are ruthless warriors.

A rather interesting river crossing during a Kenyan safari, March 2000.
FAMILY SCRAPBOOK

eat a huge amount of food caught by the lioness. I decided that the lion is NOT the king of the beasts. I believe the hideous hyena is. He has huge strength, and although they cannot outrun the gazelle, they can outlast them. They travel in packs and surround their prey and wait. We saw three lions abandon their kill as they were surrounded. I got a picture of a rather young lion so frightened by these ghastly, ugly animals that he or she climbed a tree.

One morning we were roused before sunrise and got into hot air balloons and skirted the tops of trees and tremendous plains for forty-five minutes with the sun rising over the hills that lead into Tanzania. The engine was in the middle and we sat four to a bench, seated back to back, with a firm divider in between; and eight on each side of the engine. So we were sixteen in all. We were told to stay in our seats. The balloon came down perfectly, and then, like slow motion, it tipped slowly over and some of us were lying on our backs looking at the sky. Climbing out was very funny. Secret Service agent Jimmy Rogers couldn't have been more surprised, nor could I. In about ten minutes the trucks picked us up and we were taken to a breakfast set up in the middle of nowhere. Roughing it in Kenya was not so rough.

The children, accompanied by David Rubenstein and Fouad Said, skipped one morning of the safari and went to a Masai village fairly close by. This is what I wrote about their trip:

> Lauren said that this was one of the most interesting things she had ever seen. There were around 25 huts made of cow dung in a circle, close together. At night they bring all the goats and cattle into the center of the circle and close the gate so the wild animals won't get to them. Our group paid to get in and the mayor led them around. He had five wives and 18 children. The men take care of the cattle, and the wives do the work. Only two of the wives live in the hut with him at one time. Maybe ten people to a hut that is about 12 feet by 12 feet. Of course no windows, just a low door. David said that the smell was awful with all that dung in the buildings and center yard. The wives are bartered for cows—you get the daughter and the father gets the cows. Cows are money to them. They eat them and drink their blood. They seem to live forever as they have *NO* stress. Sounds to me like a pretty stressful life for the ladies! Lauren told me that she did go in a hut and it was so sad. She said that the babies had flies all over them, even in their eyes and nobody brushed them off.

We went from Kenya to Egypt, starting at Luxor. We ate on the plane and charged the minute we landed to visit many of the places that I had seen several years before with our daughters and Ellie. I took it rather easy one early morning, staying in King Farouk's rooms in the Winter Palace Hotel overlooking the Nile, while the rest of the group visited the Valley of the Kings. My wonderful agent, Jimmy Rogers, and I walked down to a small mall. We were surrounded by Egyptian security, which was blocking traffic. Jimmy asked them to please give me a little room to breathe and to give me some air. They said they wished they could, but that I was the mother of the next President of the United States. It seems strange now, but at the time it still seemed really far-fetched to me, and I laughed. We went on to Cairo, where we stayed in what used to be a royal hunting lodge and now is the Mena House Oberoi Hotel and Casino. I again had Farouk's suite, this time overlooking the Giza Pyramids.

The next day was a huge day, starting in Memphis, the first capital of Egypt, where we saw a tremendous statue of Ramses II. We went to a papyrus paper museum and a rug factory. In our country we would have found the factory completely unacceptable, as the workers were eleven- and twelve-year-old girls. Obviously the plant man could tell that I was not only shocked but surprised by the age of the children, and he posed a question to me. He said they only worked four hours a day and went to school two days a week. Would I prefer that they did not work and therefore they would have no food? No shelter? And probably no schooling? Of course not.

The drive down and back along a canal was fascinating. We would pass a spectacular villa, and directly across the canal we would see a shantytown—dirt floors, palm-leaf thatched roofs, and lots of garbage, with children, chickens, dogs, and donkeys all milling around and some foraging in the piles of garbage.

We toured the Giza Pyramids with a guide, and the girls all took camel rides. We came back that night to see the light show after dark at the Sphinx; it was beautiful—and freezing. Then the Saids had planned a lovely birthday party for Alexa Rubenstein, who was fifteen.

As we were driving by the majestic Sphinx, one of the children said with longing in her heart, "Oh, look, a KFC and a Pizza Hut!"

On our last day we toured the Cairo Museum, shopped, and had dinner cruising up and down the Nile River.

What a glorious trip—really a once-in-a-lifetime adventure. A year later, much of this same group (without the children!) plus Alicia Spenlinhauer traveled together to Rio de Janeiro to attend Carnival. Needless to say, we had a wonderful time, and I'll never forget all those magnificent floats and yes, beautiful and nearly naked bodies, dancing down the street.

∾ George and I started the month of April in Chattanooga, Tennessee, helping to open the new ballpark for the Chattanooga Lookouts, the Double-A team for the Cincinnati Reds. The team is owned by Frank Burke, the son of our close friends Bunny and Dan Burke. Many of the family were there and that was really fun.

Even more fun was staying as guests of Alice and Jack Lupton at The Honors Course and playing golf. We had a really nice dinner the night before with a few of their friends in this attractively decorated club. Over the mantel in one room was a picture of the board of directors, all sitting around the board table with a portrait of the founder in the background. When you looked closely at this painting, you saw that EVERY face was Jack Lupton's, including the founder's. George loved this and tucked it away in the back of his mind for future use. The Luptons seem to know everyone that we know. Jack arranged a golf game for George and nice Alice played with me.

The following week, George went fishing in Venezuela with Doro, the second time they had made this marvelous trip. They love the family who hosts them, Gustavo and Patty Cisneros;* they love the fishing; and they love each other. Our family is so large that getting to be alone with George is almost impossible. He seems to make time for us all.

April was the same busy mix of travel and speeches. I spoke to two thousand senior citizens outside of Chicago, and I admit to a little—quite a little—shock when I realized that some of these "ancients" were a year or two older than George W.! How could two young people like George Bush and me have a son who will be a "senior citizen" in a year and two months? George gave speeches in Nassau and Puerto Rico.

One weekend we spent with Lee and Walter Annenberg at Sunnylands. As usual, she was most thoughtful hostess and invited friends and people she thought we'd enjoy. On this trip we ate or played golf with Marsha and Bobby French, who was an old friend from West Texas years; Jerry and Betty Ford; Dianne and Bill Moss, also a friend for many years with West Texas roots; Carol and Charlie Price, former U.S. ambassador in Belgium and England; Gerry and Robin Parsky from Rancho Santa Fe, California; Jerry and Jane Weintraub; Jim and Marilyn Fitzgerald, who are relatively new friends who had a one-night stay at Walker's Point in 2002; Ed and Patty Haggar, dear friends from Dallas of many years; Ben and Shirley Roberson, a member of the "Ladies of the Club"; and Jimmy Pattison, from Canada, who bought Frank Sinatra's desert house which he uses for guests. It looked rather like a motel in some ways. Jimmy and Mary have a home of their own where they

---

*Gustavo is CEO of Cisneros Group of Companies, a huge broadcasting and media company that owns, among other things, Univision.

stay. There were several other couples that I really didn't know, but all fascinating. Believe it or not, this all happened in a three-day visit!

Dear Walter died in the summer of 2002, leaving behind an incredible legacy of friendship and giving. His philanthropy made him perhaps the brightest Point of Light any of us ever knew.

⤳ One day in April, George W.—thinking we were just ninety minutes away in College Station—called and suggested that we drive up to the ranch for lunch. We were in Houston—three hours away—but as we were dying to see the children—whoops, "the old children"—and had not seen their newly purchased ranch, we decided to go. I had seen pictures, but no one prepared me for the beauty of this part of the world:

> We saw the tiny barn and fairly close by was the little house that George and Laura redid. It is a dream cottage as Laura had found old large windows and put them on the back. The views are sensational. We sat and talked and out the windows saw cattle grazing away in beautiful meadows. She has made it into a lovely wide-open cottage with a small living room with a fireplace and an open kitchen/dining room/sitting room and three tiny bedrooms.*
>
> Laura and George have total privacy as the ranch house is out of sight of any other building. The site where the main house is has the most beautiful trees. In front is a live oak with a 70-foot spread; there are cedar elms at the end of the living room; and the horizon is covered with motts (a new word I learned that day, meaning a canopy of trees) of pecans, live oaks, and cedar elms, all growing out of the most heavenly green meadows filled at this time with bluebonnets, Indian paintbrush, and some yellow flowers. I saw verbena and a beautiful white poppy. As this has been a year of drought in Texas, I can't wait to see it when we have a normal year. A seven-acre man-made lake has been

---

*Now that the main house is finished, this is where some of the White House staff or guests stay when George and Laura are at the ranch.

dredged about 100 yards or less from the end of the living room where he and Laura will be able to sit on a small porch and watch the birds and animals come to drink in the evening and where he can fly-fish to his heart's content.

A short walk from the house is a total change in the terrain: a small river or stream, beautiful trees, huge cliffs, at certain times waterfalls, and marvelous secret places to explore. He bought this ranch a year or so ago after looking for ages. I was surprised when I read that "it is ugly." As you can tell I am smitten with the place and we are so happy for them to have a place to relax.

꧄ John Major was scheduled to lecture at the Library and participate in A Celebration of Reading, but at the last moment he had back surgery and had to cancel. We missed him, but Ken Starr filled in at the Library and was fascinating. He kept us riveted for forty minutes. He never mentioned "the recent embarrassments." He spoke about the fact that the system works—needs adjusting every now and then, but it works. He is very much for going back to the Attorney General appointing the special prosecutor, rather than a panel of three judges, as has been the law since Watergate. That way the Attorney General would either "defend him/her or fire her/him."*

He was not bitter nor whining, although he was crucified by the press and the Clinton White House every single day for years. He told us that during a previous question-and-answer period, a lady said: "I think what you did was right, but can you tell me why in the world you put your garbage out with CNN filming you?" That paints a great picture of what he and his family went through for years, with the press camped out across the street from his house.

He talked about the mistakes he made—the biggest, he thinks, was to accept new investigations at the request of Attorney General Janet Reno. He explained that when a special prosecutor is appointed, it costs the government a lot of money. You have to find office space, staff for the office, fill it with files, and computers, and so on. When Janet Reno

---

*Ken has gotten his wish. The attorney general is now back to appointing the special prosecuter.

came to him and asked him to investigate the "Travel Scandal,"* pointing out that "they were all set up," Ken now thinks he should have said no. All in all, she asked him to take on at least twelve more cases.

He said with sort of a wistful smile, "If I had turned her down that first time, I would now be president of a college out on the West Coast." (Pepperdine University had invited him to become their president.) He also said that he is loving life now. He takes his child to school, takes out the garbage, and nobody cares. He also was writing a book—not about the "late unpleasantness" but about the Supreme Court. *First Among Equals: The Supreme Court in American Life* was published in October 2002.

As for A Celebration of Reading—our readers were all perfect. Besides Fannie Flagg, we had Tracy Kidder, Robin Cook, and Al Roker—now half the size of the man we saw that night! My two Georges filled in at the last moment for John Major. George W. read from a book that had just come out, making fun of his malapropisms; he was very funny. George read from *All the Best,* ending with a letter he wrote to the children about growing old. George W. became very emotional standing next to his dad.

George W. and Laura's girls graduated in May from the huge Austin High School and had applied to many colleges. The acceptances rolled in; I was amazed that they applied to so many. When I asked why, they answered that they didn't think they'd be accepted. Both were—by every university and college they applied to, and after great debate, they chose to go to different schools: Jenna to the University of Texas and Barbara to Yale, as they have very different personalities and interests. They are two bright girls, and we are very proud of them. I am often asked if the girls are close. They are really close; so close that I would hate to pay the telephone bills between Austin, Texas, and New Haven, Connecticut. They have learned early the value of friends and family.

As usual, we moved the whole crew up to Kennebunkport before

---

*Most of the career government workers in the White House travel office had been fired shortly after President Clinton took office. They were later cleared of any wrongdoing.

the end of the month and took another spectacular cruise to the Greek Isles. The "grands" were just getting used to the topless beaches and now nude beaches. I wrote in my diary:

> I am shocked, not by the nude bodies, but by the FAT old nude bodies. UGLY.

Several years earlier on one of the cruises a grandson was given an underwater camera, one of those throwaway kinds. We found him swimming along underwater, coming up opposite a spot where he judged a naked lady to be, taking a picture and saying, "Gotcha!" and popping under again. Besides not taking her picture underwater, he was way too far away to get anything on film. I'm sure he was very disappointed when he tried to get the pictures developed.

We got home June 2 and almost immediately had guests—Jim Nantz; his co-announcer on CBS and golf great Ken Venturi; Gospel singer Michael W. Smith (Michael flew out that night after dinner to get to another event); and Susan Biddle, a former White House photographer. They were all there for the Gary Pike Charity Golf Tournament, which George attends every year, as do Jim Nantz and Susan Biddle. Gary was a young boy who died of leukemia, and this tournament supports a house in Portland for families to stay in when their child is ill— just like a Ronald McDonald House. There is a Robin Bush Room and this touches us. They have "stretched" our Robin's life—her life goes on in so many ways—and this seems important to me.

⤳ Unbeknownst to me, this letter had gone out earlier in the year to our family and close friends:

May 4, 2000

Dear [Blank],

This is a **Save the date letter**—an advance peek at a great event which lies just over the horizon.

There will be a **surprise birthday party on June 10, 2000.**

The birthday girl is **BARBARA PIERCE BUSH.**

Barbara Pierce Bush, aka Silver Fox* or Former First Lady, will be 75. The actual date of the birth was June 8, 1925, but the party will be on **Saturday, June 10th.**

The place—**Kennebunkport, Maine.** A block of rooms has been reserved at the Nonantum Hotel. OK, it ain't the Ritz but it is nice. A list of other hotels is attached. All of our immediate family will hopefully attend, but a handful of Bar's close friends must come, too. That's you!

Program—Informal Supper at the informal River Club. After dinner some entertainment—skits, singers, clowns, men jumping out of cakes, jugglers. Speeches needling the Silver Fox—laughter, tears, joy, and wonder.

SURPRISE is the key word here. SH-SH-SH-SH!!! If you are a definite "Yes" or "No"—let me know now. If you are a "maybe" just circle the date for now.

All the best from her husband and Bar's kids who want this to be very special for her. Your coming will help make it so!

George Bush

This is easy—Please fill out this form checking the proper boxes. Mail to address shown below, Attention Gian-Carlo Peressutti.

RSVP from_____

Dear Mr. President_____

Dear George_____

Hey You_____

Yes, I will be there_____

No, I cannot make it, so there!_____

Sorry I cannot make it_____

I'm a "maybe"_____

I know who Barbara Bush is but I need more
    information before I can decide_____

*Eventually George called the event "SF2" for "Surprise for Silver Fox."

George must have had a lot of fun and, I'm told, several other missives went out. I guess that I should have been suspicious, but we had a lot going on in our lives.

On my actual birthday, Kara Babers and I first drove to Biddeford, which is about twenty minutes from Kennebunkport, to announce that year's Maine State Literacy Initiative awards. There we met up with Benita Somerfield, head of my foundation and adviser to the Maine initiative, and Mary Herman, first lady of Maine and a terrific literacy advocate. We then drove from Biddeford to Portland (twenty more minutes), where Kara, Benita, Jean Becker, and I had lunch and discussed next year's Celebration of Reading. We talked about authors to invite, etc.

From there we went to The Barbara Bush Children's Hospital for the announcement of the Libra Foundation's gift to family literacy, "Raising Readers." Owen Wells is the driving force behind this statewide program where they give babies books at birth and on each succeeding visit to the doctor. Eventually, the child will receive twelve appropriate hardback books. This is the easiest way to get books to babies, but it is also a way to spread the word to parents that reading to children is important; to tell mothers—if needed—where there are family literacy programs or where the mother can learn to read, continue her education, learn how to fill out résumés, and on and on. For this program to succeed, it must involve pediatricians, nurses, and many hospital personnel. They have accepted the responsibility in Maine. Connecticut and Maryland also are showing a bit of interest in a statewide program.

In 2002, I was sitting next to Connecticut's Governor John Rowland at a National Dialogue on Cancer meeting when the discussion turned to how we can get the word to women and men about the importance of mammograms, breast examinations, prostate cancer check, and so on, and where they are available. I mentioned to him that this could be done at the hospital when the mother has delivered her baby, and through emergency rooms. I told him what The Libra Foundation is doing in Maine. He got very excited about the literacy program and his staff is now consulting Benita. So the word spreads. It occurs to me that the two could be accomplished at the same time— literacy and cancer prevention through this same network. The state of

Wyoming has adopted the Libra Foundation's idea of the "Raising Readers" program.

 ⮑ In early June, Marvin called and told me all the children were giving me a surprise birthday party. The WHOLE gang was coming for the weekend of the 9th—twenty-four of them—and I must save the beds. He also said the surprise was that THEY would take me out for dinner.

June 9—I got a phone call from Alan Simpson today. He said something like, "I know you are too smart and have caught on." I said, "Al, I don't know what you are talking about." He went on, and I said, "Al, I guess I'm not that smart, but you should probably hang up and pretend we didn't have this conversation." He then said: "I just wanted to tell you why Ann and I won't be with you tomorrow night." "Al, I honestly don't know what you are talking about. All our children are here." At which time he said a four-letter word and hung up.

Al is a dear friend, and I was telling Dick Cheney how funny and apologetic Al was later. Dick said that really was funny as Al had given away a surprise anniversary party that his children had given for the Cheneys in Wyoming. I have come to the conclusion that busy men only remember the things that are important to them. That may be true of women, too, but I am closely associated with a fabulous man who can't remember trivia. Trivia in his case includes events that really don't interest him: divorces, births, names, etc. So thoughtful Al forgot the trivia—i.e., it was a surprise—and remembered the birthday, which was thoughtful.

As Ann and Al are two REALLY close friends, I thought that maybe George had just invited a few other friends, too.

Saturday June 10—Our house is filled with OUR children. They all are here to celebrate my 75th birthday. They arrived yesterday and today. I love seeing the grands all yell, hug, and laugh at each other. They play backgammon, exercise, loll around, and leave half-drunk cans of sodas all around the Point.

They leave wet bathing suits and towels on their beds, chairs and on the floor. They are marvelous. [HOW COULD I HAVE WRITTEN THAT?]

Marvin came to me this morning and said that I was not to leave the Point. When I asked why, he answered that George W. assigned him the role to tell me that I should not go off the Point and that is all he knew. So I didn't go off the Point. Everybody disappeared to golf and tennis and Betsy Heminway came over to visit with me for an hour or so. [I now realize she was my baby-sitter.]

Eventually we all got dressed and Susan Biddle took a family picture on the rocks. It turned out to be a good picture. Michael Dannenhauer took several for me with my little digital. They turned out to be good; just not as good as Susan's.

Then George said: "The children will bring you down to the restaurant" in the boat, and he jumped in the cars with all the "grands" and in-laws and before I could speak they were gone. With Neil at *Fidelity*'s helm I was driven in glory to the River Club with Marvin, George W., Jeb, and Doro laughing all the way. Way before we arrived we could see a crowd on the boathouse porch and 20 large posters held by friends and the "grands" saying HAPPY BIRTHDAY BAR!

George had gathered 176 family and friends. I was overwhelmed and touched. He remembered every former aide of mine, The Ladies of The Club, the East Wing staff—although Jean told me later that he was a little hesitant as he thought his staff should come and she reminded him that it was my birthday. He invited friends who now live in California; from our days at Yale; my family; his family and our family; from Colin and Alma Powell to Jim and Susan Baker to the two sets of Weintraubs—not related, but both dear friends of ours: Herb and Maxine, he a retired physician and she a writer, who built the loveliest house across from our Walker's Point driveway; and Jerry and Jane, he the famous producer (*Oh, God!, The Karate Kid,* and *Ocean's Eleven*) and she the fabulous retired singer, Jane Morgan. And last, but not least, he had our local friends who make our lives sing—from the builder and lobsterman to the masseuse—they all came. It was so exciting. The old boathouse was decorated with every painting of me ever done, some of them pretty horrible. We had a seated clam/lobster dinner. There was too much to see and too many to hug and kiss. Not only was I seeing some friends and family for the first time in ages, so were the guests seeing each other as many had spread across the country after we left the White House.

Suddenly George jumped up and hustled us all over to the casino, where there were more pictures in the entranceway. Then the show began.

Evidently George had been very firm about no long-winded toasts about how great or bad I'd been and had limited the number and time of the skits. Marvin was the funniest master of ceremonies, with a wig and great wit. The "grands" all were in skits, along with several children. Doro, Margaret, Ellie, Marshall, Ashley, Robert, and Gigi danced and sang the funniest, cutest song. Sam, Jebby, Pierce, and Walker astonished us with their lip-syncing and dancing to "She's a Lady." George P., Noelle, Jenna, Barbara, and Lauren were announced, all in children's clothes, and out came their "teacher," Brad Freeman,* in a white wig and my relatively new Scaasi dress that had us all on the floor laughing. I didn't laugh quite so hard when I realized that it looked better on him and I could not possibly wear it to the convention after this. The children sang the song "The Twelve Days of Kennebunkport."

Someplace in here Marvin introduced my very funny brother Scott Pierce and two of his sons, Derek and Kent. They had written a hilarious song, "The Barbara Pierce George Herbie Walker Bush Blues," the gist of which was that occasionally it would be nice to be JUST a Pierce.

George appeared as "Carnac the Magnificent," imitating Johnny Carson's psychic act. One by one my aides appeared and handed him a sheet with the answers on it, and then he had to come up with the questions. The girls were loaded down with baggage and toy stuffed dogs—starting with C. Fred and ending with Sadie—representing all the stuff they had to carry as they traveled with me. They were funny. Was I glad to see them? You bet.†

---

*George W.'s great friend from California.

†Here is a list of my aides, starting in order of their appearance in my life: Becky Smith Beach, Kim Brady Cutler, Elizabeth Wise-Doublet, Casey Healey Killblane, Peggy Swift Kasza, Nancy Huang, Quincy Hicks Crawford, Kara Babers Sanders, Brooke Sheldon, and Tricia Hardy. Neither Brooke nor Tricia was there that night since they came after this party.

*At the time of my 75th birthday, all of my aides from the beginning of
my time attended. Top row from left: Elizabeth Wise-Doublet,
Becky Smith Beach, Kim Brady Cutler, Casey Healey Killblane.
Bottom row from left: Nancy Huang, Quincy Hicks Crawford,
Kara Babers Sanders.*

Michael Davis, our juggler friend of old—first the G-7 meeting in
Houston, then the surprise appearance at the Library forum in Colorado, then the Library opening, and now my birthday party—came to
perform and was wonderful. He was followed by Davis Gaines, who has
the most glorious voice and, I might add, gentle personality. Davis was
the lead in *Phantom of the Opera* on Broadway for a while, and George
and I saw him in Houston at the opening of Theatre Under the Stars'
new Hobby Center for the Performing Arts in the spring of 2002.

The finale came as a huge decorated cardboard birthday cake was
rolled out. Gigi was supposed to jump out and wish me "Happy Birthday," but at four years of age, she had fallen asleep in her mother's arms.
So they stuffed Robert—a healthy seven-year-old—in the cake. It was
warm in there and Robert also fell asleep. There was a little confusion;
Marvin had to knock several times before a VERY sleepy Robert poked
his sweet, confused head out and whispered: "Happy Birthday,
Ganny!"

I will confess that I always hated birthdays. I'm not sure exactly
why, but it did not have to do with age. I agree with Dave Barry when

he said: "There comes a time when you should stop expecting other people to make a big deal about your birthday. That time is age eleven."

Well, this one certainly made me change my mind. I loved this party and it was a BIG DEAL!

In 2002, on my seventy-seventh birthday, I received the following e-mail from our friend Hugh Liedtke that gave me great pleasure and a real laugh: "Dear Bar, I see by the paper you made the cut again. Happy birthday. Hugh."

All the children went back home on Sunday except for Laura and George W., who stayed on for debate practice and issue discussions with his advisers.

✎ During this time period, while on airplanes or car rides, I listened to Michael Beschloss's tape, *Taking Charge: The Johnson White House Tapes, 1963–1964.* Funny how people think that Nixon was the only president who secretly taped telephone conversations. I guess you could say he was the LAST president to tape conversations. I discovered that Lyndon and George had something in common besides being a president and a Texan. Lyndon managed to pass off the caller by saying: "Bird would like to talk to you." How many times has George finished what he wanted to say and then passed the phone to me. One of the many things George does better than me is to call people the minute he hears of a sickness or death. I can find five hundred reasons why it is better to write. I am not as courageous as George or as thoughtful.

June 18—I am reading the most wonderful book, *Time to be In Earnest,* a fragment of autobiography by P. D. James. Mildred Kerr sent it to me and I am really fascinated. She has such a way with words. Our lives have been nothing alike and yet I find myself thinking: "Yes, she is dead right." This is the way to write an autobiography. She has written a diary for one year and yet she goes back over her life while talking about her schedule each day in the year between August 1997 to August 1998. I love this book. At one point she is bemoaning the time she

spends answering mail, signing autographs, reading manu-
scripts, writing prologues for other people's books, etc., all for
people she does not even care about or know. She says, "I lack the
courage to follow the example of Nancy Mitford who sent out
postcards simply stating: 'Nancy Mitford is unable to do what
you ask.'" Baroness James goes on to say that it would be "churl-
ish" not to answer those nice folks who care enough to write. I
agree, but, oh, it would be nice!

This may have been the very first time I thought about writing
another book. It started me thinking that it might be fun. Then David
Rubenstein suggested that maybe I might think about another book.
He probably was struggling for something to talk to me about, but he
and P. D. James get some credit—or blame!

In 2001, Baroness James accepted our invitation and read at A
Celebration of Reading. She was in her eighties at the time and
charmed us all. She is a real lady—besides being honored by Her
Majesty!

June 24—Okay, so the urge to write a book has gone. But it
was there and I still may do it.

Pop got home Thursday from Korea and Tokyo. That was a
very quick trip and he is sleeping now with that crazy Sadie by
his feet and I am writing by his side on my little laptop.

This may be Saturday, but this surely is the day that the Lord
has made. You cannot believe the air—clear and crisp. The sun is
bright and soon it will be a warm day. When I let Sadie out, the
birds in those tall, wind-torn ancient blue spruces at the front of
the house were literally talking to each other—speaking in
tweeps, chirps and cheeps, high and low, and in very different
songs. The sea is fairly level after several days of big crashing
waves and the sun is bouncing right back at us. WHAT A DAY.

The *Rosa Rugosa,* white and dark pink, are unbelievable this
year. I wonder if it is because Tom Wellman* gave them a bru-
tal trimming over the winter?

*Our landscape man.

I cut my first bowl of peonies yesterday morning and they're heaven. I planted these peonies 16 years or so ago. Gene Taylor, a congressman from Southern Missouri, sent them to me. Gene called them peONIES and said they came from the peONY capital of the world. They came with very clear instructions: Dig a deep hole, mulch, put in a little fertilizer, spread the roots just so, tamp down the earth, and water. They went on to say that if I followed the instructions, they would not bloom the first year, but would bloom every year thereafter for the next 100 years. At the time I thought I am planting for our children, grandchildren, and great-grandchildren and on and on down through the generations. I have used this true story many times in literacy speeches. When you teach someone to read, you may not see the results, but you may be sure that their children will read and their children's children down through the generations.

Pierce Bush came to stay with me one night. I had the very best time with him. We read a little from his summer reading, *Slaughterhouse Five,* I think. Not my cup of tea, but the boy is.

One afternoon he told me that he was going over to the house where they were staying to cut the lawn. I was working in my office on the second floor. I could see the sea was really roaring and a storm was coming. I stepped out onto a little porch off my office to look at the waves. A gust of wind blew the door closed and I suddenly realized that I was totally alone on our end of the Point, locked out in the elements. Since George was gone, I had told Ariel and Paula to go home. I waved, jumped, and yelled, banged on the door and finally decided that I would climb over the railing and go down the fire ladder. I got a leg over and then got hung up. Neither foot touched the ground. Frankly, it was painful. I started to break a window and decided that I would cut myself. I waved frantically. People waved back across the bay, a quarter of a mile away, but didn't come, of course. They thought I was just being friendly! If they'd known just how unfriendly I was feeling with the world at that moment they'd have run for cover. Finally I saw Pierce's dog, Angel, at the pool. Then Pierce emerged from the sauna and I yelled and yelled. He looked over and waved. I yelled again, and he saw I was waving him over. My hero. What a cute 14-year-old boy he is and what good company. He had come to the house, looked around for me, left me a note saying that he was going to take a sauna and a swim. Of course, he couldn't hear me yelling above the crashing waves.

. . . GEORGE W. HAS RAISED A RECORD $90 MILLION DOLLARS FROM 268,000 SUPPORTERS WHO SENT CONTRIBUTIONS AVERAGING $240.15. And it is just around the first of July!

This is a tough week for George W. as he has another prisoner due for execution. God bless him. This really is the law in Texas . . . I guess I agree with the death penalty, as long as there is no doubt about guilt and the condemned's state of mind at the time of the killing. So often we bend over backwards for the killer and forget the victim or victims.

This diary entry reminded me of a question we were asked a lot when George W. was governor and of course even more now: "How can your son cope with all the horrible problems that our world faces every single day?" I answer: "He has enormous faith." He does. I would like to share two excerpts from his book, *A Charge to Keep,* which was published in 2000, in which he explains better than I ever could how he feels about the death penalty and about his faith.

. . . The death penalty is a difficult issue for supporters as well as its opponents. I have a reverence for life; my faith teaches that life is a gift from our creator. In a perfect world, life is given from God and only taken by God. I hope some day our society will respect life, the full spectrum of life, from the unborn to the elderly. I hope someday unborn children will be protected by law and welcomed in life. I support the death penalty because I believe, if administered swiftly and justly, capital punishment is a deterrent against future violence and will save other innocent lives. Some advocates of life will challenge why I oppose abortion yet support the death penalty. To me it's the difference between innocence and guilt.

. . . I could not be governor if I did not believe in a divine plan that supersedes all human plans. Politics are a fickle business. Polls change. Today's friend is tomorrow's adversary. People lavish praise and attention—many times it is genuine; sometimes it is not. Yet, I build my life on a foundation that will not shift. My faith frees me. Frees me to put the problems of the moment in proper perspective. Frees me to make decisions that others may not like. Frees me to try to do the right thing, even though it might not poll well.

꿈 That summer, George had a very interesting oral history session organized by James McCall, author and historian, who had been hired by the Library for this project. A group of former staffers got together with George to discuss domestic policy achievements; they also got a little into Desert Storm. Hugh Sidey was invited to ask questions and to keep them going. The participants were Brent Scowcroft; David Bates, cabinet secretary; Marlin Fitzwater, the press secretary; Boyden Gray, White House counsel; Roger Porter, domestic policy adviser; Chase Untermeyer, head of presidential personnel; Phil Brady, staff secretary; Fred McClure, head of legislative affairs; Ron Kaufman, head of political affairs; Kathy Super, scheduler; and Dick Darman, director of OMB. They sat for several days of filming and talking. It was fun to see these old friends, and they were very generous to take time to come and to help George.

I got a very nice thank-you letter from Hugh Sidey: "One thing that emerged again strongly during the talks were that the President's achievements were real, but so often unheralded. He did things and really did not like to talk about them that much. That may have been the administration's greatest failing. It just may be an essential part of leadership today to blow the Presidential bugle, not so much as some, but at least so Presidential actions get noticed and discussed in public forums, even though the venues are distasteful."

It brought back memories of George's great mother again, who always said to him: "Don't be a braggadocio, George." "How did the TEAM do, George?"

In the four years that George was in office, he never had a Republican majority—House or Senate—and yet accomplished so much. I believe that George feels that history will report all the good things that happened during his administration. I hope so.

༄ In July, Jeb and Colu came for a few days. It is such a joy to have them. He is the most amazing man. He has given out his e-mail address and therefore gets hundreds of e-mails and personally answers them all. He sets up his computer and works late at night. Sometimes I get e-mails from him that he has sent at 2:30 a.m.

July—Now I am thinking again about [writing] another book although I am not sure what I have to say. I wish I had kept more things.

I read Jonathan Hull's *Losing Julia* at this time. I loved something he wrote and it made me think of George's eighty-eight-year-old uncle, Louis Walker. Mr. Hull is speaking in the voice of an eighty-one-year-old:

And me? I look like I'm 120, give or take. A small ember from a once-roaring fire. The older I get the more out of place I feel, like a weekend guest still loitering around the cottage because he has no place to go. How awkward to feel a burden. Better pack my things and move on. But please before I go, isn't there supposed to be some sort of resolution? A denouement before the final curtain? Redemption? Atonement? Extreme Unction, perhaps? I feel none. Just loose ends that snap and crackle like downed electrical lines.

Lou Walker was a firecracker in his early years, and was now eighty-eight, bent and deaf, and many of his friends were gone. He was very quiet and looked confused to me—almost like he knew there was supposed to be a resolution or something. Lou seemed so sad to me.

Amazingly enough, at church on the Sunday after I read that sweet but sad passage, Will Billows, the school chaplain at St. Alban's School in Washington, D.C., was filling in for two weeks for M. L. Agnew, our regular summer minister. Will said that I had spoken to him about a sermon we heard him sing in Washington several years ago, one that George and I both remembered. I told him just how much it meant and how much the children enjoyed it, and he announced he was going to sing the sermon again. It was not the sermon we remembered, but—and this is the amazing part—it was a very happy, funny song about growing old. After *Losing Julia's* sweet but "down" passage, this was a great "up" for me. I hoped our funny precious Lou was smiling in that shell of a body. He died in 2001; I suspect he did not "go gently."

∝ Jebby and Lauren spent the month of July in Spain on a school program learning Spanish. I later learned that they had a really great time and spoke very little Spanish. They are good friends and that makes this grandmother very happy. In 2002, Jebby, Lauren, and Sam LeBlond, all approximately the same age, entered college as freshmen—Jebby at the University of Texas; Neil's Lauren at Princeton; and Doro's son Sam at the University of South Carolina.

∝ During this whole period the newspapers were saying that the convention plans were way behind, and there was huge speculation about the vice-presidential candidates. The convention problems were solved when close friend and a very wise Andy Card agreed to take on the convention. He took a leave of absence from his job and never returned. Andy spoke at George's Library in the fall of 2002 after the midterm elections. We have known and loved Andy and Kathy Card since the late 1970s. We had never heard him speak before publicly, and I can say in all honesty, Andy is truly a fabulous speaker. He speaks with humor and warmth.

The vice-presidential choice was not quite as easy. George W. learned when his dad was vice president and, more importantly, when he was governor that you can—in fact you must—be able to draw on your number two for wisdom and strength. You must work together for the good of the state and the country. Although Bob Bullock was a dyed-in-the-wool Democrat, he put Texas first and Bob Bullock second. They were a great team.

George mentioned that there were many qualified people. Several people asked to have their names withdrawn—Elizabeth Dole and Colin Powell for starters. Dick Cheney headed the search team for George W. George told his dad that they were looking for a candidate that was qualified to be President, must be a woman or a man that he could trust and work with, and must be loyal. The more he looked, it came down to one man— Dick Cheney. For Dick, that was a problem. "I looked all around and found—myself." He certainly is qualified having been a congressman, a chief of staff, a Secretary of Defense, and a success in business. The more George W. met with Dick, the more he realized that he respected him and admired him and could work with him. Dick certainly added "gravitas" to the ticket. That seems to be a problem in other people's minds. So I think this is the choice. Now let's see if it can be kept a secret until George wants to announce his choice. Dick changed his registration from Texas back to Wyoming where he has a home. As George would say, "It would not take a rocket scientist to guess that Dick was the choice."

We awakened one morning to hear that Paul Coverdell, our very dear friend and the senator from Georgia, was in the hospital with a brain problem. His venus vein had clogged and filled his brain with blood. Paul had no symptoms other than a really severe headache for several weeks. He died rather quickly in the hospital. Paul and Nancy first visited us in 1980 in Kennebunkport. He was a gentle man who had accomplished many things. He was a peacemaker with a quiet, calm voice. Paul served in the Georgia state legislature and was George's state chairman when it was hard to find a Republican in Georgia. He served as the head of the Peace Corps in George's administration, and in 1992 was elected to the U.S. Senate, where he was a reliable point man. At the time of his death he was George W.'s Georgia state chairman.

I was so glad that Pop invited Paul and Nancy to my surprise birthday and that they came. Both Democrats and Republicans have told me that they miss him. We loved Paul and still love Nancy.

⤳ We had Ann McDaniel and Jon Meacham for lunch one day from *Newsweek*. They wanted to interview us about George W. as a child. Everyone seems so disappointed that he was a normal child and caused us NO trouble.

I get asked that question so many times or something like it: "Tell us, Mrs. Bush, some funny or bad things that George W. did as a child—was George W. a naughty boy?" I now hope I will be asked that very question these days. The answer was and still is: "George was a perfect child—I seem to remember it was his brothers and sister who caused all the trouble." I get a chuckle out of that and to be honest, NOW I don't remember one bad thing any of the children did.

⤳ In the middle of July, George and I did a campaign event for George W. in Indiana. Betsy Heminway joined us on the trip, which started with a huge fund-raiser at a private home. Dan Quayle and General Norm Schwarzkopf were also there. Dan is such a nice man and was so butchered by the press. It makes me sad. He told Betsy that he was not going to the convention. All the press would do is twist what he said. It was a joy to see both men again. Norm looked so trim and handsome. I read recently in an interview the general was asked if he didn't think there was room for forgiveness toward the people who have harbored and abetted the terrorists who perpetrated the 9/11 attacks on America. His answer was classic Schwarzkopf: "I believe forgiving them is God's function. Our job is simply to arrange the meeting."

We three flew to Libertyville, Illinois, to Stonehenge, the farm of Bert and Sandy Getz, arriving late at night. There were Bert and Sandy waiting on the doorstep to greet us. Betsy, in the lead car, got out first, and Sandy Getz, whom she did not know, gave her a big hug. So sweet and so typical of that gentle lady. The color and materials in this beautiful house are perfect. The house is filled with pictures of their darling family and friends—including, I'm glad to report, a few of us. We said we were not hungry and then sat down to a cold golden gazpacho soup. It was lovely and in the middle there was a scoop of frozen soup. This was pretty and very tasty.

When I came home and told Ariel about the soup, he managed to recreate it and maybe even made it better. Our guests just can't get over how delicious it is.

FROSTY GAZPACHO
SERVES 6

2 medium ripe and firm tomatoes
1 large cucumber — peeled
1 rib celery
1 small Vidalia onion
½ green bell pepper
½ red bell pepper
1½ cups tomato juice
1 tablespoon olive oil — light
2 teaspoons freshly squeezed lemon juice
Avocado slices
Sour cream
Sage leaves or sprigs — fried
1 teaspoon sugar or artificial sweetener
1 teaspoon Worcestershire sauce
½ teaspoon Tabasco sauce
2 teaspoons Italian parsley — chopped
2 tablespoons red wine vinegar
1 small garlic — finely minced
2 teaspoons fresh chopped cilantro
Salt to taste
¼ teaspoon freshly ground pepper
Basil — chopped
Cilantro — chopped
Lime wedges

Chop tomatoes, celery, cucumber, onions, and bell peppers into chunky bits (same size, if possible). Transfer vegetable mixture to a large bowl and combine with remaining ingredients. Refrigerate until cold. Transfer ⅓ of Gazpacho mixture into a separate bowl and freeze mixture 45 minutes before serving time or until mixture starts to crystallize. Chill remaining Gazpacho in refrigerator until ready to serve.

To serve: Fill 5 to 6 serving bowls with refrigerated Gazpacho. Scoop out frozen Gazpacho and top center of soup. Sprinkle around frozen mixture diced avocado, forming a ring. Dab top with sour cream. Top with fried sage leaves. Sprinkle with chopped cilantro and basil. Garnish with lime wedges. Serve immediately.

With the soup, Sandy gave us BLT sandwiches and cookies with milk. For people who were not hungry, we demolished the whole meal. It was perfect. The farmhouse has such lovely little nooks and crannies, filled with magazines, books, adorable knickknacks, etc. I really can't do the Getz family justice. They are the most thoughtful, kind people ever. They have three children—Lynn, George, and Bert—all married to darling people and all so hospitable and sweet. This family is filled with love.

Bert and I served on the Mayo Foundation Board together, and in 2002 he became chairman.

We were there for the U.S. Women's Open, put on by the LPGA with the largest purse ever—$500,000—for a women's tournament. Small compared to the men's purses, but certainly getting up there.

The next morning, we had breakfast with the family. Louise Suggs came by for a visit and we walked over together to watch the ladies golf on the course right next door, The Merit Club, built on Bert's family farm. Louise was an honored guest. She must have been amazed as she used to be paid peanuts, drove herself from tournament to tournament, and stayed with friends or slept in her car.

Everywhere George went, people asked him to sign hats, golf balls, programs—you name it, they wanted it signed. I had some requests and suddenly realized that some of the children had surely never heard of me. I asked one little boy who I was and he answered, "I don't know." Obviously he had seen others asking and he just got in line. Another boy thought a minute and came up with "a former great golfer?" Would that this were true! They got their autographs. Then several ladies asked me to sign their shirts, and I asked them if they

BARBARA BUSH

were for George W. They said yes, and so I spun them around and
signed:

GEORGE W. BUSH

Signed by his mom

BARBARA BUSH

And these nice ladies became billboards for GWB.

That night Sandy and Bert had a lovely party in a tent with enter-
tainer Mike Carney playing all through dinner. It was a truly busy,
happy visit.

George left us there, and Betsy and I took a political swing
through Nebraska and California for George W.

In Nebraska, one of our co-hosts was a young woman, Peggy
Sokol, who had written me the sweetest letter about her son, who had
died at age eighteen and a half in the last year or so. She was a lovely
young woman and seemed to be strong. She shared with me that she
had read my book and it had given her comfort. This happens often and
not only touches me, but makes me feel good. It is another way of making Robin's short life on earth important. She has become a symbol, or
maybe a saint is a better word. So much money has been given in her
name, so many people have been comforted by our child. I am not good
at explaining this, but many people talk to or write me. I hope we help.

My first aide ever, Becky Beach, met us there, along with Liz
Karnes, wife of former Senator David Karnes, who really organized this
very successful fund-raiser.

We flew to San Diego to the stunning home of Art and Veronica
Engel. The reception was outdoors and the view from this house overlooked the Naval Base, the Coronado Hotel, and the Pacific Ocean.
What a climate—no bugs, no screens, doors wide open, cool breezes,
and great views.

We had dinner with Robin and Gerry Parsky and her mother at
their beautiful horse farm in Rancho Santa Fe, and I campaigned up
the coast with Jerry the next day.

I spent a night with Dick and Margie Jenkins in their treehouse
in Santa Rosa. Of course it isn't a treehouse, but that's all you see from

their windows. Margie was in my class at Smith and Dick was a friend from Yale days, and we have stayed in touch with each other through the years. Dick and Margie had some friends in for cocktails, and then Patsy and Jack Caulkins—also from Yale days—who were staying close by to escape the Arizona heat and to see one of their sons, came to have cocktails, and we five went out for dinner.

The next morning, the Jenkinses went out to the airport with me to meet John Major and George. We had a chance for a nice but too short visit, and then John, George, George's scheduler Kathy Super, and John's assistant, Arabella Warburton, and I flew to Vancouver to set sail again on the *Nova Spirit.* We had several happy days of cruising, walking, reading, and napping. I can't remember which body part I had removed, mended, or taken care of, but I loved the rest after so much standing on the campaign trail at endless receptions. We saw glorious bald eagles; at one time we saw five of those magnificent birds perched on trees or logs, then soaring in and out. We were there for several wonderful days, and we all needed the rest.

    Finally, the first week of August, it was time to go to the Republican Convention in Philadelphia. From start to finish, it was wonderful. I don't know how Andy Card pulled it together in such a short time, but he did, and it was a really joyous and happy gathering with no real tension or arguments that I could see. I believe that it was the most entertaining, on-time, positive, and tension-free convention of either party. George and Laura were generous with their time, and we loved every moment. My George did some daytime travel, like golf at a nearby course, and was back for the evening events. I saw friends. Mostly I just loved every moment and admired all our family.

The theme the first night was "Education." Laura's speech was thoughtful, and she was backed up by the best team, a group of children from the unique Kipp Academy in Houston. Sharon Bush has been on the board from almost its beginning, and Laura came to a fund-raiser in Houston in 2002 for this amazing school.

Norm Schwarzkopf gave a rousing speech from the deck of a ship. He talked about the 40 percent cut in military spending—with four times as many troops—and the disgrace of having many of our mili-

*Surrounded by family and friends at the Republican Convention
in Philadelphia, August 2000.*
FAMILY SCRAPBOOK

tary families on food stamps, among other things. This was the first presidential endorsement that Norm had given.

The last speech of the evening was given by Colin Powell and was inspiring. He made us very proud and does to this day. He is honest to the core and a true public servant.

For the first two nights, George W. came into the convention hall via video. He was wending his way through the states the GOP had lost the last time around. Jennifer Dunn, congresswoman from Washington, introduced him the first night; it was late at night and he was surrounded by exhausted, bored-looking students. Not all plans work out. I hoped that people watched George W.'s face and not those sleepy, uninterested children.

The former presidents were honored Tuesday night. I sat next to Jerry Ford and Betty. They are such gentle, kind people and I feel Jerry is a true hero. He stepped into office at a tough time. When he pardoned President Nixon, he allowed our country to look forward and not spend years trying a former president. He also ensured a loss for himself in the next presidential election.

I honestly did not notice a thing wrong with Jerry that night at the convention other than he said he had a small cold. I did not notice a slur. Later that night he went to the hospital and scared us to death when we learned he had suffered a small stroke. We love the Fords and respect them enormously.

A beautiful and frail Nancy Reagan was there with Maureen, her husband Dennis, and their lovely adopted teenage daughter. Nancy flew in and out for the tribute to her husband. Maureen was a loyal daughter who tragically died of cancer in 2001.

After my George was introduced, I introduced our son—still on his way to Philadelphia. I had left my glasses at the restaurant where we had dinner and had no TelePrompTer. Fortunately, we had worked hard to keep it short. "Welcome. I hope I am the first to welcome you to Philadelphia—the city of MOTHERLY love. Ladies and gentlemen, I am proud to introduce you to a man that we love very much—the next President of the United States, GEORGE W. BUSH." George W. then introduced Condoleezza Rice, who gave a very moving, insightful speech. She was followed by both Doles, Bob and Elizabeth, and Senator John McCain. They all gave supportive and generous speeches.

On Wednesday, Bill and Donna Marriott offered to have a family dinner for us. It was a joy and I would have worried about the size, but then I remembered that they, too, have a loving, huge, immediate and extended family.

Many toasts were given—some funny and some moving. George's brother Jon gave a toast to Jeb, Neil, Marvin, and Doro. He said that he, Pres, Nancy, and Bucky bequeathed to them the joy of being a sibling to a president. He went on to say that if you did business in a foreign country, you become a lobbyist for that country; or if you have a car accident, you were headlines on the front page of every paper saying you are a drunk; etc. He was funny.

In retrospect, all our children already knew the hazards of being the son and daughter of a president. It is not easy. Maybe he should have made the toast to our grandchildren!

I was fortunate enough to sit between George W. and Jeb, thanks to Laura Bush. We were all so touched by Jeb, who said something like: "I have watched you, big brother, and about five months ago I noticed a change. You began looking and sounding presidential. Now when I see you, I see a president. I'm awed by you, I'm proud of you, and I love you." At which time George W., with tears in his eyes, stood up, leaned over me, and they hugged. I cried. I'm sure others did too, but I just couldn't see.

Wednesday was the Cheneys' night. Lynne's speech was really good, and Dick's was perfect. He was strong and quiet and I think surprised everyone with his great humor.

Our grandson Pierce Bush got a lot of "airtime." It almost seemed like every time we turned on the TV, Pierce was being interviewed. Although he was fourteen at the time, he sounded like a thirty-year-old, with an opinion on every subject. He was loving every moment. He is an amazing child, now a young man of seventeen.

I will let the article that appeared in the *Palm Beach Post* tell you about George P.'s appearance on Thursday night:

GEORGE P.'S DEBUT SPEECH WOWS 'EM
BY BRIAN E. CROWLEY, *Palm Beach Post*
POLITICAL EDITOR*

Philadelphia—In a rousing 13-minute speech mixing English and Spanish, George P. Bush brought tears to the eyes of his father and his grandfather as he gave his first nationally televised campaign speech to the delegates of the Republican Convention Thursday.

The 24-year old nephew of Texas Gov. George W. Bush spoke directly and earnestly about his mixed heritage, telling the cheering crowd that if his uncle is elected president he will look out for "those of us whose faces look different."

The son of Florida Gov. Jeb Bush and his Mexican mother, Columba Bush, took to the stage as if he had been born there. He waved to the crowd, pointing to people he recognized, throwing a kiss and pausing just long enough for the excitement to build before he spoke.

So strikingly handsome that he is being called the "Ricky Martin" of the Republican Party, Bush showed the crowd the political skills he has inherited as the first member of the fourth generation of Bushes to be involved in politics.

Calling his uncle someone who "has been determined to do what is right," he said the two of them "not only share the same name, we share the same dream. The dream for a leader who will bring people together to solve problems, not create them. Who will get the people's work done for the good of the people not for political careers.

"And a leader who really cares about those he was elected to serve, including those of us whose faces look different. You see, I'm American, but like many I come from a diverse background and I'm really proud of it. I respect leaders who respect my heritage."

Bush, who taught ninth graders for a year after graduating from college, said he and his uncle also share a passion for education. "He will give teachers and our schools and parents the support they need to help all children in our country get the best education they possibly can."

During his speech, both his father and grandfather—former President George Bush—had tears in their eyes. His grandfather and grandmother, Barbara Bush, appeared not only thrilled but awed by his performance.

When it was over, Barbara walked over to Columba and gave her a kiss.

"It's a new day. Now is the time to end the cynicism and the fussing and the fighting in Washington," Bush said as the cheers grew louder. "Now is the time to make sure the American dream touches every willing heart no matter the color of your skin or the accent of your speech. You can do that by electing my uncle. Now is the time to restore a sense of honor and decency to the White House. We can do that."

Then with a final flurry of Spanish, repeating what he said in English, Bush raised his fist in the air and the crowd jumped to its feet as he strolled off the stage.

George P. took a year off from school to help his uncle run for president, as his dad had done in 1979 and 1980 for George. By this time, however, George P. had been accepted at the University of Texas Law School and was thinking of leaving the campaign and going back to school in the fall. The campaign, of course, wanted him to stay, and having seen him in action in two states, I was secretly hoping he would, too. His dad was opposed, and I could certainly understand his feelings as it would have put off his entering law school for another whole year. Then George P. suddenly appeared in *People* as the fourth most eligible bachelor out of one hundred in the country. That article helped me change my mind. What constitutes being "eligible"? He had not finished his education. He had NO income. I guess being very handsome AND unmarried were the criteria. That is not enough in my eyes!

George P. made some marvelous political ads for the campaign, spoke at the convention, and worked some weekends in the fall for George W. The good news was that he did not pay attention to his press, did very well in Austin, and graduated in the spring of 2003.

At 10 p.m. that night George W. gave a really good talk. I am his mother and I am prejudiced so I will say NO more. We love him so much and I am not a fair judge.

Friday August 4—We awakened this morning to an 18 point lead—a bump from the convention.

Almost all the "grands" came back to Maine with us. Our teenagers are fun, and they are having all sorts of adventures together in Maine with their friends and cousins.

I learned a great lesson that year: Not only should the young have babies, but they should also run for office. I was tired.

⮑ In early September, I had a scheduled speech in Switzerland, and George suggested that since I had gone on exotic trips with all the other granddaughters, this might be a great time to take Noelle, Jeb's daughter, with me. Nosy* and I talked about it, and since I had always wanted to go to St. Petersburg, Russia, and since this was

*My nickname for Noelle.

near, it was decided that was where we would go. This was, of course, a joke as it certainly is NOT near Switzerland, but George not only went along with it but encouraged me. So Noelle and I, along with Brooke Sheldon—my brand-new "everything"—left September 4, Labor Day afternoon, and met Alice Rubenstein, my former and future traveling companion, and flew to Zurich, where we met Nagwa Said and her daughter Dina, a darling bright girl around Noelle's age. We then flew to St. Petersburg. We arrived and were taken to the Grand Hotel Europe. This is within walking distance of many of the sights one wants to see. We rested in our rooms, and at 5 p.m. we met with the most perfect guide, Polyakova Yevgeniya (we called her Eugenia), who took us to the "Spilt Blood" or Church of the Resurrection. This is the most rococo, decorated Victorian church I have ever seen. It has every tile design, fresco, turret one could ever imagine and I am just talking about the outside. The inside has famous glass mosaics. They are huge, and I thought they were lovely. There were many different marbles, lots of giltwork, and tremendous chandeliers. One can see this strange ornate church from all over the city.

As this is a city of many islands, the "Venice of the North," we went on a boat ride to see the city from the canals and the Neva River. There are 500 palaces built on 101 islands and 366 bridges. It was cold on the water, but each boat had many blankets which we wrapped around ourselves; it was a joy.

We ate a delicious dinner that night in the hotel and all went to bed, happy and tired.

> This was a great chance for me to take my mind off the campaign, I thought, but no. I awakened at 4 a.m., turned on BBC to see and hear that George W. was overheard whispering an aside to Dick Cheney, calling a reporter an ugly name—a very ugly name. The reporter was making a big thing about this. So I stayed awake worrying about our precious son. Then I had sort of fun making up answers if I was asked what I thought of George saying this man was an ——. I thought of several great and funny answers, but alas nobody asked me as I was hoping to say: "How can I answer that? I have never met the man in question."

We toured the city, went to St. Isaac's Cathedral, The Hermitage Museum that houses more than 3 million pieces of art, and the Russian Museum. I was interested that both museum directors went out of their way to tell me how much they hated communism. Of course artists—like the rest of us—would hate the lack of intellectual freedom. They showed their dislike by mentioning that Picasso and Matisse were both Communists and they did not like their work very much. I mentioned that both had painted for great capitalists like Nelson Rockefeller and Armand Hammer. (I remembered the Matisse ladies draped over two fireplaces that Nelson and Happy had in their New York City apartment, which we had seen and admired during our UN days.) We came across a painting given by Armand Hammer and the director said: "He was the worst Communist-lover of them all." I said that I had heard that he brought medicine to the Russian people when they really needed it. The man sort of pooh-poohed that. We did know Armand when he was very old, and he seemed a sweet old man. I remember eating at a dinner at the Russian Embassy with him after his wife died. He sat right opposite me and spoke not a word, but ate and ate as people who have had strokes often do. He was a hero to the Russian people, Soviets at that time.

This was a truly grand visit for me. During World War II, this city was under attack for nine hundred days and never surrendered. I admired the Russian spirit in rebuilding this city, almost from the ground up; their workmanship; and their vitality. I believe this may be the most interesting and beautiful of cities.

We flew to Geneva, drove to Interlaken, and all went to bed. The next day we sat in the sun at an outdoor restaurant and admired the hills with people floating down with colorful parachutes from the tops. I knew that if George Bush had been with me, he would have joined the parasailers! In the background we could see the snow-covered Alps. We all went to a reception and dinner; I spoke and then to bed. The next day we all said good-bye and flew as directly as possible to our homes.

When I got home to Maine, there was a marvelous group to greet me: the president of The Czech Republic, Vaclav Havel, his wife Dagmar, and her attractive twenty-three-year-old daughter Nina; five other Czechs; plus an interpreter. Also there was Brent Scowcroft,

Larry Eagleburger,* Nan Ellis, Jean Becker, and of course George and me. We all went out on the deck for lunch. Later, Jean told me that the interpreter was asked where she wanted to sit to interpret. We had been told that she would not eat. She said that she would eat and that she would sit between the two presidents. Usually interpreters sit behind the guest and eat either before or after the meal. In a loud voice her exact words were: "I have a stomach, too." So Jean quietly gave up her seat.

The discussions before lunch and during, when the interpreter didn't have her mouth full, covered many things: the European Market, NATO, the Eurodollar, etc. What a fascinating group to have greeted me on our arrival home. We last saw Vaclav and Dagmar at a dinner at the White House in 2002.

The night before, George had the Azerbaijan president Heydar Aliyev for dinner; George reported that Ariel had prepared a dinner "fit for a king."

✑ Mildred Kerr brought me Maeve Binchy's *Scarlet Feathers,* which was not in print in this country yet, only in England. She knew I love her books. I do and did love this one, too. I also read *Winter Solstice* by Rosamunde Pilcher and enjoyed it a lot.

✑ On September 16, George and I went to Caroline Mulroney's marriage to George's friend Tony Lapham's nephew, Andrew Lapham. It was held in the beautiful Catholic cathedral in Montreal, Saint-Léon, and was really an international wedding, with Mila and Brian's friends coming from everywhere. I have rarely seen a more beautiful wedding. The whole magnificent cathedral was filled with pure white huge hydrangeas, and since the inside of the building is very ornate, this was perfect. Caroline and her three brothers have visited us off and on for quite a few years. Andrew graduated from Princeton and Caroline from Harvard and got her law degree at New York

---

*Larry was number two at the State Department for most of George's presidency and finished as secretary of state.

University. She and Andrew now live and work in New York City. These two bright young people came with her parents in the fall of 2002 to spend a weekend with us. They left at 5 a.m. on a Monday to catch a plane to New York so they could be in their offices by 9. Sadie and I saw them off.

⟡ I campaigned for George W., but I am not too proud of the fact that I still could not watch the debates. I saw reruns and certainly saw and read the comments in the papers. After one debate, the papers and TV were full of the fact that Al Gore sighed, tore or shuffled paper, and even groaned while George W. was speaking.

> Generally speaking our folks feel good about the campaign and the debate. I don't know if it is true, but the next day the papers said that the Vice President had stretched the truth in several cases and was caught by the press. The strange part is that he doesn't need to exaggerate.

This brings up another point. It absolutely amazed me that Al Gore let his "handlers" try to change his image—brown suits, new hairdo, etc. I am convinced that the best candidate is positive and happy in his or her own skin.

Which, of course, reminds me that for several months after an election my George used this in his speeches: "People told me to just be myself. I took their advice and . . . lost."

In early October, Laura and George's daughter Barbara arrived from Yale with four other attractive freshmen girls. She seemed bubbly and very happy. They arrived exhausted, and we immediately took them to Mabel's for dinner. They were very interesting, from England, Portland, Oregon, New York City, Houston, and Austin, Texas. They spent a lot of time lolling around, going to late movies, sleeping, and some even studied. Then they all piled into a tiny car and drove back to New Haven. George and I loved that visit.

We had several more guests before the summer ended: Craig and Elaine Dobbin from Nova Scotia, and Michael and Debbie Smith from Nashville. They helped keep us distracted.

October 11—This is that glorious time of year when the monarch butterfly comes out of its cocoon and my gardens and fields are filled with them. They especially like the wild asters that have sprung up everywhere. We see the geese starting their trek south.

This was the day of the second debate at Winston-Salem, N.C., at Wake Forest University. Doro, Marvin, and Jeb all attended. (Neil was overseas.) George and I watched it alone. It was amazing. A whole new Al Gore appeared. Not the scoffing, rude, moaning, arrogant Al Gore of the first debate, but "Mr. Nice Guy." He seemed uncomfortable and fake. George was especially knowledgeable about foreign affairs, which folks felt he would not be. This, added to Dick Cheney's great showing in his debate against Senator Joe Lieberman, really helped. Colin Powell was in the audience and later in the "spin" room after the debate. There is a great comfort level in knowing that Colin and Dick are on our team.

At the end Jim Lehrer, the moderator, asked George if Americans should be concerned by Gore's stretching the truth. (He has been caught over and over again exaggerating, claiming that he had done things that he didn't do, or flat out saying he was some place where he hadn't been.) I held my breath as that was a really hard question, I thought. Of course a President must be trustworthy, but the way he answered was important. George thought a minute and gave a very polite and serious answer by saying: Yes, that the Congress and our foreign friends should know that the President of The United States is honest and tells the truth. He said that it was "a worrisome pattern."

The very next day the Middle East exploded. This had been festering for two weeks when a little Palestinian boy and his father were shot. The 12-year-old boy died and his father was wounded. Fortunately, or unfortunately, this was all on film. The boy and his father were caught in a cross fire and were huddled down. An Israeli soldier, in the heat of battle, had shot the unarmed father and killed the boy. There had been protests and skirmishes for several days, and the Palestinians captured and tortured two Israeli soldiers, threw them out the

window, and beat them to death—most on film also. At the
same time a small craft with two men aboard approached the
USS *Cole,* a ship that was refueling off South Yemen, rammed
into it killing at least 4 American sailors and 12 more are missing.* Bob Gates† told me that he is not sure that there is any
connection between the outbreak of hostilities in the Middle
East and this act of terrorism.

George told me that one of the Vice President's operatives
was on the air saying that Gore should be elected because of his
great knowledge in foreign affairs. I think that a better argu-
ment could be made for the wisdom of George W. and the
people he has surrounded himself with—Colin Powell, Dick
Cheney . . . seasoned advisors—people who are trusted worldwide.

. . . Our whole family is involved and we are all handling the
election in different ways. George suffers and listens to everything. He is on the road helping candidates. I listen to nothing
and am doing fund-raisers. Marvin is in a blackout like me. He
travels some with George W. at George's request because he can
relax with him. Neil attends fund-raisers and Jeb does also and
is working in Florida, a very difficult state for Republicans. Shy
Doro Koch is traveling the country for her brother and that wonderful Bobby Koch is raising money and seeing that all four children get to school, etc. plus a full time job.

Around this time there was a flap about George W. and the subliminal use of the word "rats" in one of his ads. George and I gave a talk
in Philadelphia, and I spent a minute explaining that I did not believe
that "subliminal ads" are effective and frankly couldn't see them anyway. All the time I was talking, on two big screens behind me, they
kept flashing: VOTE FOR OUR SON, VOTE FOR OUR SON,
VOTE FOR OUR SON. Thank heavens it brought five thousand
cheering, clapping people to their feet. I had permission from our hosts

---

*Unfortunately, the final casualty count was much higher: 17 dead, 39 wounded.

†Bob Gates is a former director of the CIA. In 2000, he was dean of the George Bush
School of Government and Public Service. In 2003, he's the new president of Texas A&M
University.

to do this, of course. I'd love to take credit for this, but Jean Becker, my speechwriter/editor and George's chief of staff, came up with it.

> *October 12*—This is my last day [in Maine]. GB left in the morning for a campaign trip for GWB. He will end the day in our bed in Houston, and I will meet him tomorrow afternoon at College Station where we will attend the opening of the Presidential Portraits traveling show that is touring some of the Presidential Libraries.* There has never been such a day as today. It literally sparkles, is warm and so beautiful and the leaves this year are so colorful—more vibrant than ever, I believe.
>
> Why is it that the day we leave is always so sunny, brisk and perfect so we don't want to leave? (Of course that isn't always true—it just seems that way.)
>
> . . . Paula and Ariel left on Tuesday driving to Houston, Jean and Brooke left on Friday . . . poor old Sadie thought she was going to be left as the people she loved left and the bags went out the door. She stuck to me like Velcro.

> *Tuesday, October 17*—Last debate in St. Louis.
>
> We watched in our Houston home's tiny library with Jean Becker and Peggy Kasza† who happened to be in town.
>
> George was very laid back and Al was sort of aggressive. Early on Al came rushing over to George and it almost looked as though Al was going to push him or hit him. I'm not sure what this was all about, but it certainly looked strange. We thought George was very good. Al has been three different people in all three debates. Jean Becker told me the next day that the swing towards George is great, that Al came across as "menacing." Who knows what will happen?

༒ On October 18, I flew to Grand Rapids, Michigan, to join Laura; Lynne Cheney; Condi Rice; Michelle Engler, wife of the gover-

---

*This was a wonderful show from the National Portrait Gallery in Washington, D.C.
†Peggy was my aide during the White House years.

nor; Candice Miller, the secretary of state; and Jane Abraham, wife of Senator Spence Abraham* on a "W is for Women" bus tour. We started at the Van Andel Museum, then on to Lansing, where we visited a children's hands-on museum; and to Brighton, a darling little suburb where 85 percent of the stores are owned by women. My great friends, Olga and Marvin Esch—Olga is a "Lady of the Club"—were there in that huge crowd and I was so touched that they were there for a quick hug only. It was then on to our last rally in a suburb of Detroit and out to the airport to meet George W.'s plane. We were dead tired—probably *I* was dead tired. We stayed for George W.'s press conference and then climbed on Laura's plane and flew to Philadelphia, where we visited the marvelous Fox Chase Cancer Center. The press event was held on The George Bell Terrace that Pop had helped dedicate in honor of his longtime childhood friend. I left Laura at this time and flew home to Houston.

The next week I spoke in Austin to The International Convention of Elbow and Shoulder Surgeons—thus maintaining my record of addressing people who are gathered to discuss subjects about which I know nothing, other than having two of each in this case. We met at the newly renovated Driscoll Hotel, where they have kept the color and the beauty of the Old West. I was met at the door by Louie Bigliani and Bernie Morrey and his wonderful wife Carla. Bernie was the chair of the group and our "hip" doctor at the Mayo Clinic; Louie is a great doctor whom we have known since he was young and summered in Kennebunkport and now is chairman of Orthopedic Surgery at the New York Orthopedic Hospital at Columbia-Presbyterian Medical Center in New York. We had a very nice visit, during which time I prepared Bernie for the fact that I believed that George would be a very difficult patient when Bernie gave him a new hip in December. George was already planning on hunting two weeks after the operation. As I write this, it occurs to me that "patient" is something that one must be after an operation. I also must admit that George did not prove to be a difficult patient at all. He behaved himself pretty well and didn't complain once.

I had a call from Patricia Cornwell urging me to look at her Web

* Now secretary of energy.

page. She had endorsed George W. big time. She also had pictures of us and a charming review of George's book, *All the Best.* What a nice friend she has been.

I met up with George in Illinois and we drove to Benedictine College. We visited with high school students and faculty; did a photo receiving line and lunch with around one hundred board members and big givers; gave our talks; and then went into a small reception where we "gripped and grinned" again.

It was here that the most touching thing happened. A lovely young woman, trim, beautiful skin and hair, very pretty, came up to me in the receiving line. She may have been thirty years old. There was a handsome man with her, but I honestly did not look at him as she softly said, "I am a Gladney* mother." I said that we had two Gladney babies which, of course she knew, and weren't they perfect—or something like that. She shook her head and with tears in her eyes said: "Oh no, I WAS a Gladney mother," meaning that she had a baby there and had given it up for adoption. By this time, we both had tears in our eyes—hers for her baby and mine for her and gratitude to her. I gave her a hug. The attractive man with her smiled and said, "It did have a happy ending," and they moved on. She married this nice man and I hope they now have their own babies. This made me think. As a child, this young girl went to the Gladney Home to have her baby because her religious training did not permit an abortion. It also made me think of the joy she brought to another little family. She just MUST have a happy ending.

October 26, Brooke Sheldon and I flew to Kansas City, Kansas, for a rally in a dark theater; I was introduced by the attractive wife of the governor, Linda Graves. On to St. Louis for an airport rally gotten up at the very last moment. We were met by Patty, Scott, and Lindsey Bush. Retired Senator Jack Danforth introduced me. We flew on to Chicago where I attended a "Women's Coffee" at 6 p.m. It was very well attended by the governors' wives—past and present. I was so glad to see Brenda Edgar again. I had worked with her husband Jim Edgar on literacy programs when George was vice president and Jim was the Illinois secretary of state. He later was a great literacy governor. Lura Lynn

---

*The Gladney Home in Fort Worth, Texas, is where two of our grandchildren came from and so many other beloved adopted babies.

Ryan, wife of the then governor and a dear friend, introduced me. I went right back to my hotel and fell asleep for ten hours or so after eating the cheese and crackers left in my room by the hotel management.

The next morning we flew to Wisconsin, where we were met by the governor of fourteen years, Tommy Thompson—now secretary of health and human services—and his wife Sue Ann. We drove immediately to a senior citizens' home where both the governor and I spoke. Then there was a Q&A session, and one man said that he just wondered why if Al Gore invented the Internet how come all Web pages started out "WWW." I thought that was very clever until I was told that it was all over the Internet. We went outside to another big rally, then went back to the airport and flew to Cleveland, Ohio. We took a tour of Strongesville Manor, a really sparkling new center; Hope Taft, the elegant wife of Governor Bob Taft, introduced me to a good crowd. We had Q&As and departed for the airport.

We were flown right to College Station and there were George Bush and Sadie. He had been campaigning in Pennsylvania and Maine.

On the 30th, George flew to West Virginia and I went to Florida, where I visited two retirement centers with Jeb—one in Fort Myers and one in Sarasota. Then we flew to Tallahassee, and there was Colu standing on the doorstep looking lovely; George had arrived and was resting on the bed. I was so touched to see that Colu had things in the guestroom that I had given her.

On Halloween, we met with Jeb's staff in the Capitol and then we took off again. George stayed in the north and Jeb and I went south to Clearwater and then on to Bartow, where we were in the Fall Harvest Parade with Jeb walking the whole way surrounded by volunteers carrying BUSH FOR PRESIDENT or BUSH/CHENEY signs and handing out bumper stickers. The streets were lined with children in Halloween costumes and many adults. This was America at its best, with all races living side by side. It was a sweet little town, with some of the loveliest old homes, surrounded by huge live oaks covered in Spanish moss, across the street from some rather small ones. It was hot, and I was put on the back of a convertible. I must have looked very funny— a huge, white-haired lady looking like she thought she was a homecoming queen.

When we left Jeb there, he was hot and tired and had about three events still ahead of him. Brooke and I flew to meet George in Orlando for a Harvest Festival in a big Baptist churchyard. It was so dark, but we worked our way through the crowd shaking hands. We made a really short visit and then flew home.

We were met at our house by Jean Becker and Andy Card. Andy is the greatest. He has been asked to be George's chief of staff IF HE WINS. This is a great first move. Dick Cheney has been asked to head the transition IF HE WINS. The press still does not have GWB winning.

"Miss Pessimistic" (me) really doesn't think he is going to win as we are at peace and because we have a strong economy.

Poor Andy spent the night on one of those hard guestroom beds.

November 1—We did a little taping at George's office for the *Dana Carvey Special** that will show this Sunday night. That night we went briefly to a reception for M. D. Anderson and left before the dinner.

November 2—George and I voted at 7:30 a.m.—an early vote hoping to encourage others to cast absentee votes.

Can anyone imagine how it feels to have a child run for President? Can anyone know what it feels like to vote for a son or a daughter for President of the United States? Awesome.

That night we went to a big M. D. Anderson dinner. The George and Barbara Bush Endowment for Innovative Cancer Research is now up to 16 million dollars.

That night, the media was full of a story that George W. was arrested for DWI (driving while intoxicated) in 1976 when he was

---

*It really was a *Saturday Night Live* special, but we agreed to do it because of our friendship with Dana. Dana did George a big favor after the 1992 election loss by coming to the White House to cheer the staff up. Everybody felt so discouraged and sad. After he lost the election George always got a laugh when he would say that Dana was one person who really missed him, as his "Saturday Night Lampoon" of George was a classic. The two of them became friends.

thirty years old. I had forgotten that this even happened. The story came from a Fox News reporter in Portland, Maine. George W. was with Pete Roussel—our friend and at that time, one of George's staffers—and tennis star John Newcombe. They had been to the House-on-the Hill, I think it was called, which is about half a mile from our house. They had been drinking and George was arrested on the way home for DRIVING TOO SLOWLY. I thought then and I think now that this was much ado about nothing twenty-four years later, my George could barely sleep worrying about this, and the next morning we awakened to CNN saying that the polls still showed George W. ahead, BUT that was taken before this "scandal broke."

Driving while drinking is wrong—it's awful. No question. But George has not had a drink in fourteen years, and he had long since told the world that at one time he drank too much. I suspect that he, too, had forgotten that incident. Frankly, I think that instead of the effect that some hoped for, this might have reminded people that George had the discipline to give up drinking and that he was strong.

∽ On November 3, George and I split again—he to the West and I to the East. I headed for Pittsburgh to a "WEAR YOUR PEARLS, GIRLS" brunch that our good friend and longtime supporter Elsie Hillman had arranged. I say "arranged" for she had a little heart problem and introduced me from her house via satellite. It was a huge overflow crowd and all seemed very optimistic. Brooke and I, joined by Pennsylvania National Committee Woman Christine Toretti, then flew to Bucks County for a Victory 2000 rally in the Christian Life Center with several thousand people; then on to the Reading airport for a marvelous Victory 2000 rally. I saw many volunteers from Texas, all of whom had paid their own way. As George says so often: "How can we ever thank all these people who have volunteered for the Bush family?"

We flew on that night to Cedar Rapids, Iowa, and were met by Becky Beach, who was executive director of George W.'s campaign in Iowa. She and her husband Charlie were very optimistic. The rally was wonderful. Congressman Jim Leach introduced me and it was déjà vu all over again. (A quote attributed to Yogi Berra. I wonder if he really said all those marvelous things?) Jim endorsed my George twenty years ago. Many of our old friends were there and lots of new faces. The crowd was huge and enthusiasm ran high. Sally Novetzke, another early supporter of George's and then his ambassador to Madagascar, was in the crowd and looked beautiful. Sally and her husband Dick are real friends.

Then back to Wisconsin with Governor Tommy Thompson and Sue Ann for some fast campaigning in two different sites. We spent the night and then flew to West Virginia to a huge outdoor rally. Carol and Guy Vander Jagt—she a "Lady of the Club" and Guy a former congressman—were in the group, having been campaigning in close-by Ohio for our son. They were optimistic and felt that he had a real chance. The folks there thought we are going to win by 8 to 10 percent. I was beginning to think someone was smoking some funny stuff!

In all three states—Pennsylvania, Iowa, and Wisconsin—the troops were all very optimistic. We lost all three. The Democrats just got out all their vote in minority areas. They did a better job. As it turned out, there may have been real voter fraud in Wisconsin as some students claimed that they voted two or three times. How could we have been so wrong? We did win West Virginia and elected a congresswoman, Shelley Moore Capito, daughter of a friend of ours. Shelley's opponent spent $6 million to her $1 million. I asked George how much he spent on his congressional campaign in 1976, and he couldn't quite remember. He thought between $100,000 and $200,000.

Brooke and I then flew on to Ohio with Congressman John Boehner who had been campaigning all over the country for George and congressional candidates. We went to John's district for a rally and were met again by Ohio First Lady Hope Taft. She introduced John, and John introduced me. I looked down and there was Nan Ellis, our precious sister, who had spent a week in Ohio doing whatever she was asked to do—making calls, anything. Sitting next to Nan was our longtime Columbus and Kennebunkport friend, Carol Sue Zacks. There was also a group of Texans including Nancy Lisenby from George's Houston office. We flew from Ohio (where we won!) to Michigan and our great friends, Governor John Engler and his Texas wife (and mother of his triplet daughters), Michelle. One event, which was outside, had a nice crowd and another group of Texas volunteers. John reported that we were one point ahead and that meant the vote could go either way. (We lost big. The Democrats did a great job of busing in their voters.)

Finally, some absolutely great news. My Houston nephew Jim and wife Dabney Pierce had a daughter that they named Barbara Pierce. The child has a middle name, which of course does not mean quite as much to me! I am thrilled.

This is the last day before the election. Our hopes are so up and then they plummet. It's like a seesaw. The polls show it too close to call, but our people feel confident. One minute I feel it will be a landslide and the next a squeaker. The press says it could be a popular vote win for George, an electoral college win for Gore and then Gore would be the next President.*

Election Day—We went to Austin via College Station, where George gave a talk to the students at the George Bush School of Government and Public Service. I rather suspect that he was a little distracted. We arrived at the Governor's Mansion to find George and Laura pretty calm. Jenna and Barbara were there, as was Laura's mother, Jenna Welch. We all got dressed and drove over to a family dinner. All our immediate family gathered, with the exception of Robert and Gigi, who were too young, and Noelle, who was in a hospital in Florida. All of my George's brothers and sisters were there with the exception of Nan, who had flown home from Ohio to vote in Massachusetts.

There were cousins and a FEW very close friends. There was a lot of excitement and a lot of noise when all of a sudden a hush came over the room because the networks announced that Florida had gone to the Vice President. Jeb was shocked and said that just could not be. The polls in Florida had not closed yet, as Florida has two time zones. The panhandle is in Central Standard Time and the polls were still open. Florida was a key state that our team needed and this was a blow. Jeb was devastated.

---

*I wonder if any press people would admit to that prediction now.

He had knocked himself out for his brother and the press had been gloating over the closeness of the race for weeks and how come Jeb couldn't win his state for George? Jeb came over to his brother and said that he had let him down and they hugged. Such an emotional moment and so sad! George W. told Laura that he'd like to watch it from home. We joined George W., Laura, Jenna Welch, and went back to the Mansion to watch the returns, and George W.'s top staff popped in and out. It was the closest race and as the night wore on it looked like we were going to lose. I must say that our children were great. My George suddenly looked old, tired, and so worried. I went into the Pease Bedroom where we were staying and started to read a book Laura gave me, *Sister,* about Sister Parish who Mark Hampton studied and worked with before he had his own decorating firm. From my room I could hear thousands of people shouting, cheering and singing, and when an especially loud cheer would go up, I'd rush into the small living room to see what had happened. George W. called for his brother Jeb to come over and he arrived with Jeb, Jr. Around 9 p.m. Florida was taken out of the Gore column and put back up for grabs. Then Tennessee and Arkansas, the Veep and the President's states, came to the Bush column. For four hours George and Jeb watched every precinct from Florida. Around 3 a.m. or so the networks gave the election to George and Dick Cheney. Gore called and conceded and we all hugged, kissed, and cried and were the happiest people alive.

For thirty glorious moments we were the parents of THE PRESIDENT-ELECT OF THE USA!

Barbara and Jenna's Inauguration shoes, January 20, 2001.
This is possibly the last time anyone has seen them.
BARBARA BUSH

We all know what happened next. Al Gore decided not to concede the election and all was thrown into chaos. I have often wondered just what would have happened if George W. had gone out and thanked his people who had stood in the cold rain for hours and sent them home, saying that he would speak to them and the country in the morning. We'll never know.

The next few weeks—thirty-five days—did NOT rush by. But as we never dreamed that the election would not be over on November 7— or at most, November 8—we had planned a full schedule.

We have never been prouder of our two older children. Jeb recused himself from the recount and vowed to have election reform in Florida. George W., with Laura at his side, went to the ranch and stayed quiet, knowing that the recount in Florida was in good hands—Jim Baker's and some forty or fifty lawyers who went to Florida to oversee the count, plus many other volunteers.

There were certainly irregularities in the election in 2000: polls held open well after the stated hours in Missouri; students bragging about voting twice or three times in Wisconsin; certainly the press calling Florida for Vice President Gore before the polls had closed; and for some strange reason, votes from our military could not be counted. This all came to be known well after the election. There were stories about the homeless being bused in and given three packs of cigarettes to vote. Polls were kept open until 12 a.m. in some cases while people were being bused in. The law reads that if you are in line when the polls close, you may vote; these folks were bused in afterwards. In fairness, there were claims of fraud on both sides.

(In 2002, in the Florida Democratic primary between Janet Reno and Bill McBride, there were ballot problems again in the same two counties—Palm Beach and Broward—and this was totally a Democrat-run affair.)

Hillary Clinton won big in New York. Her first statement was that she was going to work to change the Electoral College, "that it was outdated." Virginia senator Chuck Robb, a Democrat, was defeated by former governor George Allen. Montana senator Conrad Burns, a Republican, won re-election after a very tight race. The Republicans ended with a slim majority in the United States Senate, but we had no president.

⤸ Long before any of this happened, we had agreed to attend the 200th Anniversary of the White House dinner, scheduled just two days after the election. We never dreamed that our son would be in this position. For months I had worried about the agony of that evening if George W. lost the election. My George said we would go, win or lose—even "if we had pneumonia"—although it would be hard after a loss.

So, on November 9 we attended a huge White House dinner held in the East Room. Before we were led into the dinner, we went upstairs to join the head table group. It was amazing. We were greeted by a jubilant Hillary Clinton, the U.S. Senator-elect from New York, and her husband, the outgoing president. Our precious fellow Texan Lady Bird Johnson was there with her daughter and lame duck son-in-law, Chuck Robb. That must have been tough for Lady Bird, Chuck, and Lynda, but they were very good sports.

Betty and Jerry Ford and Jimmy and Rosalynn Carter, along with us, made up the group of "formers." Anne and Hugh Sidey—Hugh was head of the White House Historical Society—and Phyllis and Jamie Wyeth, the great artist, made up the upstairs party, completed by some top White House staff. Jamie had painted a picture to commemorate the 200th anniversary.

We were finally led downstairs for a group picture and then dramatically led into the East Room and seated at a long, raised dais. The room was packed with round tables and frankly lots of well-known Democrats and a few Republicans. We were given no guest list, and so I kept looking for Dottie Craig from Midland who raised the majority of the money for the White House Trust. (I called the next day and both Earle and Dottie had health problems, which is why they couldn't come.) I did see darling Lee Annenberg; she and Walter have given so much to the White House including the spectacular Benjamin Franklin portrait by David Martin; and dear Julie and Charlie Cawley who had paid for the Wyeth painting, *Dawn at the White House*. This was given to the White House on a long-term loan. As I understand it, the White House cannot accept a painting until the artist has been dead for at least twenty-five years,* so in the far distant future this will be part of the White House collection. This makes sense, for I can imagine the agony of receiving thousands of paintings from "wannabe" artists. What a logistical nightmare!

Bill Clinton started the evening with a toast to the former presidents and then recited the prayer that John Adams wrote to his wife Abigail, who was still in Massachusetts, on his first night in the White House. This prayer now is carved in marble over the hearth in the State Dining Room:

*An exception is made for the official portraits of presidents and first ladies.

I pray heaven to bestow the best of blessings on this house and all that shall hereafter inhabit it. May none but honest and wise men ever rule under this roof.

Hugh Sidey introduced all the presidents with humor and kindness. All the former presidents gave short and nice messages.

The Clintons invited all the formers to spend the night. The Fords and the Carters accepted; George was flying to Europe that night and I was just not ready to stay in the White House, so I flew home and was glad to be there.

I wrote in my diary the next day:

So there we were—a winner (Hil), a loser (Chuck), and Mr. And Mrs. In-Between (us). It was tense. Although I must add the Clintons were very gracious.

George left after the White House dinner for Spain, England, Florida, and finally returned to Houston on the 18th. During this trip, besides shooting with old friends from around the world (birds in Spain and England), he helped M.D. Anderson open a satellite hospital in Spain, and met with President Jose Aznar of Spain. Because I don't hunt, and because Christmas was hanging heavily on my mind as I had done nothing to get ready, I stayed home. Therefore I missed another dinner given by Their Majesties, King Juan Carlos and Queen Sophia of Spain.

George kept the telephone wires from Europe busy, asking: "Any news?"

On his way home, he stopped in Florida and did a press conference for the kickoff of "The First Tee," a wonderful nonprofit project sponsored by five major golf organizations. The goal is to create affordable and accessible golf facilities for all children, especially those who have not been exposed to the game. But truthfully, their mission is much bigger than that. They teach these kids responsibility, sportsmanship, leadership skills, how to set goals, and so on. It's a wonderful program of which George is honorary chairman.

Then, on November 18, George stopped in Starkville, Mississippi, for a "Salute to Veterans" event honoring our great friend, former congressman Sonny Montgomery. He finally arrived home that early afternoon.

Meanwhile my friends kept me busy.

> I got home from the Washington dinner at 3 a.m. and Sadie and I were walking at 7 a.m. I went to a movie with Mildred [Kerr] and saw *Meet the Parents* or something like that with Robert DeNiro. So-so, but it took my mind off my problems.*
>
> . . . Mildred and Baine took me to see *Remember the Titans* and out for dinner. It was a really good movie about a high school football team during the integration of schools and school busing. A truly sweet and important movie—we have too much racism—and kids will like this movie and get a not too subtle message from it. Denzel Washington was the star and was good.
>
> . . . I went to church with the Fitches. We sat with Catie Walne. I was touched and surprised when the minister prayed for "The anguish the Bush family is going through." Nice.
>
> . . . I have been reading Ric Patterson's latest book, *Protect and Defend*. I've had to stop reading it as it is about partial birth abortions, late term. The ads that Al Gore ran against GWB on that subject were too much for me.

I did finish *Sister* and loved it. First of all, Sister Parish—a famous interior decorator—helped and knew many people we knew. But best of all, I felt great about our hodge-podge of a house when I got through reading the book. She seemed to feel that a house should be comfortable, should be a home, and that family should be considered when planning a home. She liked collections and things that are meaningful to the inhabitants. So what I was thinking was clutter, is okay!

In my November letter to family and friends I wrote:

> While George was away, I jumped on a commercial plane and flew to Washington to see Margaret Bush in

---

*I must have been exhausted because I later saw this movie with George and loved it.

The Last Night of Ballyhoo.* She was wonderful, so talented.
This was really the first time that I have gotten to see her act
in the theater. I literally flew up in the late afternoon, said
hello to Walker and Margaret, rushed with Marshall to an
Italian restaurant for dinner with Doro, Ellie and Doro's
friend, Theo Hayes. We were in the theater by curtain time.
Margaret loves acting and is good—very good. I spent the
night in their new guest quarters and flew back the next
morning early. Sister Parish would love their home.
Margaret has made a dream house for Marvin and their two
beautiful children.

People were so nice to me and on one flight, when I
arrived at the airport, eight airline employees greeted me
at the bottom of the steps with signs, all supporting
George. [I should explain that many times I am driven
right to the plane.] Other times when I walk through the
airport, I hear people whisper as I go by, "We're praying
for your son."

Our phone has rung off the hook and the e-mails are
long. People are so kind.

November 13—Henry Kissinger called last night to tell me
that he and Nancy are outraged. I had to laugh because when
the phone rang, a voice asked for President Bush or Mrs. Bush.
I said: "Henry, is that you?" He said: "Yes, but how did you
know who it was?" How did I know? At one time Henry
Kissinger and his voice were probably known by more people
in the world than anyone other than, maybe, Chairman Mao.
The Chairman qualifies only because there were 1 billion people in the PRC and believe me, they all lived and died by his
word.

⌒ This was the most frustrating time for all Americans, but
worse for both the Gore and Bush families, I suspect.

*Written by Alfred Uhry.

We had a phone call from Doro. Doro, Sam, Ellie, and Robert had gone and stood across the street from Gore's V.P. House and yelled and picketed. Doro said there were 200 people, give or take a few. She was in disguise with a scarf and dark glasses. They had signs that said: LET OUR SERVICEMEN VOTE OR BRING THEM HOME! She said there were servicemen there or maybe retired servicemen and women. They had megaphones and they yelled chants, etc. Cars went by and honked and waved. She said it took care of a lot of her frustrations.

(Having lived in that house for eight years I know that the Gores probably couldn't hear a word or a shout.)

The rest of us could not yell and shout, but felt like it. George followed every word.

I attended a Mayo Clinic Board meeting:

People have been so kind about NOT speaking about the election. Some people have whispered to me that they hope he will win, but they must feel that I just don't want to think or talk about it AT ALL. They are right.

Incidentally, Dick Cheney was then a fairly new member of the Mayo board and of course would have to resign if George W. won.

November 17—I still cannot watch the news as the ugliness is overwhelming. I ache for our children and especially the country. There is all sorts of anger racing around stirred up by Jesse Jackson, Al Sharpton, Alan Dershowitz, etc. It will be hard for either man to restore civility after this battle.

Thank heavens Jim Baker went to Florida to watch over things. They were counting votes where there were no votes: "Well, they voted for all the Democrats, but just didn't vote for President, therefore they meant to vote for Gore." Or, several thousand people "voted for Pat Buchanan who meant to vote for Gore, therefore their vote should be counted for Gore." And on and on. Among the many lawyers on our team was John Kerr, son of our neighbors and friends, Mildred and Baine Kerr.

On November 20 I wrote:

> I woke up this morning with what seemed like brilliant thoughts at the time. I am not articulate enough to put them on paper, but will try. There have been several articles of late about both candidates and the influence their fathers had on them. When George put his arm around George W. in New Hampshire and called him "my boy," the press went wild with ridicule. There have been some pretty hurtful cartoons and stories about George and George W. I awakened thinking that it was so sad. My dad was my hero. George's dad was his hero. We looked up to our dads. Didn't the press have dads they loved and looked up to? Now we are on the other side and we look up to our children, all of them. They are our heroes and still, no matter how old they get, they will always be "our boys and our girl." Can't they [the press] understand this? All our children are sweet and thoughtful to us and adore their father and we adore them. Why do the press ridicule this? I will never know the answer to this unless it is because they don't respect and love their own fathers and mothers; or worse, their mothers and fathers don't love them. I knew I couldn't put into words what I mean.

I often do my most brilliant thinking in those few minutes before I really wake up. And it usually is gobbledygook. It seems so clear and then is gone with the wind. These worrisome days I had solution after solution, until I awakened.

⚭ We kept busy during the next few weeks. We had a small lunch for the planning committee of the National Dialogue on Cancer. I flew to Dallas for a reception Caroline Hunt put on to thank the Dallas Celebration of Reading committee for their help. Marlin Fitzwater came and read excerpts from his two novels: *Esther's Pillow,* which I read and enjoyed, and *Oyster Music,* which he's still writing.

On Thanksgiving Day we ate with Neil's family and then flew the next day to Austin and watched the University of Texas beat our Texas A&M football team. From there, George and I drove to Crawford to be with George W. and Laura at the ranch:

> We arrived in time for a dinner. George cooked small steaks and Laura had some wonderful squash dish, potatoes, and salad. Both George and Laura look marvelous and seem in very good spirits. The phone rang all the time with news of the Florida count. By this time there have been three counts, the original and two hand counts. George has been ahead in all three by the slimmest margin. The next morning we walked from the guest house to the almost finished main house about ½ mile away. On the way we passed a small gym. The whole visit was reassuring for this old mother. Our children seem relaxed and on top of it all. I wish I could say the same.

Speaking of feeling a "little" older, several of the "Ladies of the Club" had written that they and their husbands were thinking of moving into retirement communities. I wrote back:

> My darling sister-in-law, my brother Jim's widow Margie Pierce, told me that she is considering doing the same thing. So smart. These places are very attractive now and do take the burden from our children. I told Pop the other day that our children are beginning to treat us like we used to treat them. Recently Marvin called and said that George W. had told him that we had taken several long walks on a visit to the ranch last weekend and that was wonderful. I expected him to say: "Good girl, Mom."

Margie came to visit her children, Jimmy and Scott and their families, who live in Houston. I took Scott, Stephanie, and Margie to College Station to tour the Library and have lunch.

I had a small lunch for Dabney Pierce, my nephew Jimmy Pierce's wife, and the mother of my namesake, to introduce her to some members of the Houston Garden Club. Dabney is the most talented woman—

mother of four, has a small business, is a sensational hostess and mother. I have since heard she is also a real addition to the Garden Club.

November 21—STILL NO WORD FROM FLORIDA. George went to Islamorada, Florida, for his annual charity bonefish tournament. Evidently it was cold and windy and the bonefish were elusive. He ended that trip and the month in College Station at a George Bush Library conference.

I opened a Women's Home in Houston with Susan Baker on the morning of the 29th and flew with Brooke Sheldon to Cleveland late that afternoon and tucked into bed. The next day I spoke to the Cleveland Town Hall. Joe Gorman, CEO of TRW, introduced me. We had met in 1991 when Bob Mosbacher, then secretary of commerce, invited businessmen to accompany George on a trip to Japan to promote trade between the United States and Asia.

We started December with a luncheon speech in Kentucky, a dinner speech in Tennessee, and a late night arrival in Washington, D.C., for George. Jean Becker and I flew directly to Washington and had dinner with friends. The next morning, we spent around six hours at the National Dialogue on Cancer meeting. The discussions were led by ABC newsman and cancer survivor Sam Donaldson; Dr. William Roper, who had been one of George's top policy advisers at the White House and is now dean of the School of Public Health at the University of North Carolina; and Mickey LeMaistre, the former head of M.D. Anderson. There was a group of about eighty of us from all over the country. Dr. C. Everett Koop spoke about the three stages of cancer—detection, prevention, and treatment; and under prevention he mentioned the three greatest causes of cancer: smoking, obesity and alcoholism.

On Sunday, George played in the Chris Evert Charity Tennis Tournament. George said it was "show business" tennis, but George and Chrissie won their match against Regis Philbin and tennis star Jim Courier. George was in agony, but didn't want to let Chrissie down. He had some spectacular shots, which were duly recorded and shown on TV. He had been in pain for ages, but that old competitive spirit kept

A triumphant George Bush and Chris Evert at her
annual charity tennis tournament, December 3, 2000.
George had hip replacement surgery two days later.
FAMILY SCRAPBOOK

him going. He left from there for the Mayo Clinic and a hip replacement. One can only imagine what they thought at the Mayo Clinic
when they saw him on television, knowing that they were going to
operate the next day.

I spoke in Oklahoma on the day of the operation and got to
Rochester, Minnesota, to find that he was resting well, surrounded by
the most caring doctors and nurses and more flowers than can be imagined. Jean Becker told me he called her as soon as he came out of
surgery to see if there was any news on the recount; George fell asleep
while she was trying to give him an update.

I left after two days and flew to New York City to give a speech.
George got home on December 8 and was a really good patient, much
to my pleasure and surprise.

On December 13, thirty-five days after the election, we watched
the vice president's concession speech with our dear friends the Kerrs
and Fitches. It was finally over; our son George was the President-elect
of the United States.

∽ We had Christmas at home with the Neil Bush family and
the next day the whole family met again in Boca Grande, Florida, at

that wonderful Gasparilla Inn. It was then that we realized that it was impossible for the President or the President-elect to go to a place available to the public. You can't blame people, but it is hard to rest, play golf, and eat in a restaurant within sight of the world. And it is inconvenient for the regular residents and for the other guests.

That is why the last few years George W. and Laura have invited the whole family to Camp David for Christmas, and then some of us went to Boca Grande while they went to the ranch. For a change of pace, in 2002, George treated seventeen of us, ages six to seventy-eight, to three glorious days on a Disney cruise. We saw every child and grandchild that holiday.

One day in Florida during the 2000 trip, I was going to the beach restaurant to join the family for an informal buffet lunch. I was a little late, and as I rushed up the steps, a big man stopped me and suddenly pulled out one of those hand-held metal detectors and started to run it over me. A Secret Serviceman, who had been discreetly hanging back,

Christmas 2000, at Gasparilla Inn in Boca Grande, Florida.
We now had a president-elect in the family. From left:
Marvin Bush, George W. Bush, Barbara Bush, George Bush,
Doro Koch, Jeb Bush, Neil Bush.
FAMILY SCRAPBOOK

rushed up and said: "Stop. Don't you know who this is? This is Mrs. Bush, the mother of the President-elect." The poor security man looked stricken and apologized profusely. I assured him that he was just doing his job and then, as an afterthought, said that I hoped he wasn't doing this to the other people walking into this family restaurant. He looked relieved and said: "Oh, no, Ma'am. Just the people who look like reporters or dangerous." To this day I have wondered which category I fit in?!

∾ The days leading up to the inauguration were slightly frantic because we already had scheduled some engagements and because, frankly, I am a little—well maybe very—superstitious. I don't believe in counting the chickens until they hatch, so I just had not allowed myself to believe that George would win.

So there was a lot of last-minute planning to do. Of course where we would stay was easy—Blair House, where we had all stayed in January 1989 and would again. Our group was larger now as four more "grands" had been born: Ashley, Neil and Sharon's; Walker, Marvin and Margaret's; and Robert and Gigi, Doro and Bobby Koch's. Laura's bright, beautiful mother, Jenna Welch, rounded out the family; now we were twenty-seven in all. Clothes had to be planned, and Arnold Scaasi whipped up some outfits for me that were waiting at Blair House when we arrived, thank heavens. Not that anybody would have noticed, but I felt that I could not wear the same clothes that I had left in eight years before.

Blair House is the official guesthouse for the President of the United States. It is here that heads of state stay during state visits. At other times the secretary of state, the protocol chief, or the vice president and their spouses might use it to entertain foreign dignitaries at the request of the president or State Department. During the 1980s, Blair House was closed for a much-needed complete overhaul, including replacing the wiring and plumbing and refurbishing the antiques. The committee—headed by Mrs. Archibald (Lucky) Roosevelt, chief of protocol for President Reagan, and former ambassador Anne Armstrong—hired Mark Hampton and Mario Buatta to redecorate this beautiful house. The results are lovely, and when we were there in January 2001, Blair House was run like a five-star hotel by a charming Mrs. "V."—Benedicte Valentiner. She didn't seem to mind the children and made us all feel at home.

On Inauguration Day, George and I awakened early, had coffee, and read newspapers in bed. All our children came by with coffee, starting with the president-elect, another early riser. We were tucked all over this rabbit warren, antique-filled building. Blair House is made up of maybe four or five town houses that were joined by breaking through their mutual walls but whose floors were not necessarily on the same level; hence the rabbit warren description. Girls were running up and down small staircases getting their dresses pressed and hair done, and parents were awakening children. Breakfast in the Garden Room from the 24-hour buffet was being urged on the children as it was to be a long day.

We went to St. John's Church* for a prayer service, a repeat of 1989. Although George W. and Laura are Methodists, they had attended St. John's, an Episcopal church, while they lived in Washington briefly in 1987 and 1988, helping George with his presidential campaign. George W. said then that the Methodist minister's sermons were political, against his dad, so he and Laura attended St. John's. The service, attended by members of the Cheney and Bush families and a few very close friends, was sweet but short because the morning was tightly scheduled. The Reverend Luis Leon officiated.

After the service, we waited outside in our car for quite a while for George W. and Laura. We were to go directly to the Capitol, and they were to go first to the White House for coffee, then drive up to the Hill with the Clintons, which is traditional. Our motorcade could not leave until theirs did, so my George got impatient and sent a query through our agents to theirs: "What is holding it up?" The message came back that the Clintons were not quite ready to receive them. We did learn later from the news reports that Bill had worked late into the night, so he probably was tired. In any case, we spent close to thirty minutes sitting in the car with Barbara and Jenna. They were eleven when we left the White House and were now freshmen in college and nineteen years old. They had lovely outfits for the inauguration, including some very

---

*Every single president has attended at least one service at St. John's, starting with George Washington.

fancy and very stiletto high-heeled and pointed-toe boots and shoes. During this period, I think it was Andi Ball, Laura's chief of staff, who came up to our car and asked the girls if they were happy with their shoes or did they want another pair that Laura had thoughtfully tucked in the car for them. They seemed very happy as they were, and they did look so stylish.

Finally we arrived at the Capitol and were led up and down what seemed like miles of marble: stairs, long corridors, and all around, coming at last to a little holding room. All during the walk there were kind, cheering people. When we got to the room, those stylish shoes and boots came off with great sighs of relief. I later took a picture of them, and that was probably the last time they will ever be seen. The four of us remained isolated and eventually heard great cheering; we looked out the window and saw the motorcade. The long march reversed, and we were led up and down again to go out on the platform. It was a drizzly day, and we were given plastic capes to put on. I resisted briefly, but on it went; I could have worn the same coat after all.

Laura and Lynne Cheney with their girls looked lovely and very happy, even on that wet day.

When George W. actually walked down the steps with a distinguished congressional escort, it was breathtaking, and hard for his dad and me to stay composed. I know people say, or think, that we have been there, done that, and this should be old hat for us. Not true.

First Dick Cheney and then George W. took the oath at 12 p.m. on January 20, 2001.

Farewells were said to former President Bill Clinton and U.S. Senator Hillary Clinton. Then we went to a beautiful lunch in the Capitol Rotunda, followed by the parade in the drizzle. George W. stayed until the last band marched by in the dark. There was a lot of family teasing from our children about how twelve years before, we sat by the heaters while they froze. It was cold and I must confess that I didn't stay the whole time.

I walked back to the White House and was greeted by the marvelous staff. There had been a few changes in the eight years since we had left, and we all shared lots of hugs and laughter. All our rooms had been assigned and our clothes were in place. From the moment the president and the president-elect drive away from the White House around 11 a.m. to go to the Capitol, an army of staff and volunteers move out the old and move in the new, filling and unloading huge moving vans on the south side of the White House.

I had a cup of tea in the Queen's Bedroom and a hot bath; that warm household was a joy. A cold George H.W. Bush arrived, having stayed for the whole parade, and climbed into a hot bath. No sooner had he settled down when the phone rang; it was "The President" who wanted his dad to come to the Oval Office. George leapt up, put on his clothes, and raced over to the West Wing to greet his son. Andy Card described this scene to us two years later, as he had just walked into the Oval Office from another door. He said to see the father walk in to greet the new president was very emotional. I would say that this was typical of George W. He knew how much this would mean to his dad, and he wanted to share his first moments in this revered office with him. You can take a hot bath anytime, but just how often can you walk into the Oval Office and see your own son?

George and I decided to skip the balls and to watch our children and grandchildren leave for the evening. The second and third floors of the White House were filled with cousins and lifelong friends of Jenna and Barbara's, beautiful girls in lovely gowns, giggling and laughing. I went down and took some pictures of George and Laura and Jeb and Columba in their ball clothes.

⤍ This was to be it—ending the book as it began, with George W.'s inauguration and the glorious moment when he took the oath of office and became the forty-third President of the United States. In a real world, that would have worked; but after September 11, 2001, this was not a real world.

*This photo was taken right after the President finished his remarks
at a prayer service at the National Cathedral, three days after 9-11.*
WHITE HOUSE PHOTO BY ERIC DRAPER

We flew to Washington on September 10, 2001, to attend several meetings and a dinner, spending the night at the White House. This house is completely secure and saves us having to stay in a hotel. We sometimes used to stay at nearby Jackson Place, a town house reserved for the use of former presidents when they visit Washington. But the White House is much more comfortable. Besides that, we know the very generous inhabitants.

The president was in Florida, but we had a nice visit with Laura. On September 11, George and I kissed her good-bye early as we were flying to Houston via St. Paul, Minnesota, where we both were to speak. Then we would go on to Texas for the kickoff of Houston's new professional football team, the Texans. Laura was to leave the White House an hour after we did for the Capitol, where she was going to testify before Congress about educational funding.

We had settled down comfortably on the plane, drinking coffee, reading the papers, and working on the computer when the co-pilot came back and reported that a commercial plane had flown into one of the World Trade Center buildings. While we were absorbing this— wondering how it could be—the pilot came back and said that we had to land at the nearest airport as the second World Trade building had been hit. All planes were being grounded. Now we knew this was not an accident but a terrorist attack.

We landed at the airport in Milwaukee, Wisconsin, and were driven outside the city to a motel. Like everybody else, we spent the day glued to the television. We watched in horror again and again and again the replay of the attack on the Twin Towers and the Pentagon, and heard rumors of a plane downed in Pennsylvania. We feared for our children and grandchildren. We were no different from most Americans with one huge exception—we had Secret Service, and so knew that George W. and Laura and the girls were safe. We talked to several of our children. Bobby Koch was in California on business, and Doro was alone with four worried children. We talked to Jeb, and he and his family were immediately secured by the Florida state police. We could not reach the others. Of course phone lines were jammed with frantic parents and children and spouses checking on each other and seeking comfort.

We later learned that Marvin had been in New York on a subway under Wall Street, on his way to a meeting. The train came to a stop and they had no idea what had happened. Eventually they were evacuated, single-file, onto a platform and then out of the subway. They were told either to walk across the Brooklyn Bridge or walk uptown; but get out of there. Marvin said smoke and debris were everywhere. He walked 70 blocks back to his hotel, stopping in front of an electronics store to watch TV footage of what had happened. Marvin told us the people of New York were very supportive, offering water and encouragement along the way. Needless to say, we were pretty shook up when we learned how close Marvin was to the disaster, and grateful he was safe.

I also learned later that my nephew Jim Pierce narrowly escaped injury or possible death. He was scheduled to attend a meeting on the 102nd floor of the South Tower, which was the second building hit. However, the night before, the meeting was moved to an adjacent building because the group had outgrown the conference room. Jim later learned that twelve people were in the room where he was supposed to be; eleven died.

Many Americans told similar stories of narrow escapes. Unfortunately, the nearly three thousand people who died that day were not as lucky. America—and the world—had been attacked.

After about five hours in our hotel room, we left and searched for walking shoes in a totally empty, closed-down mall. We finally found some in an almost empty sports store.

We took a long walk on a public golf course across the highway from our motel where people were playing golf. They were shocked to see George, and were so nice. I walked a hole or two, but couldn't manage much more due to a recent back operation. So I sat on a bench as George charged around the course talking to people. It all seemed so normal. I wondered if they knew exactly what had happened that morning.

I think now that I didn't really understand the ramifications of the attack. I know George realized that day that the world had totally turned around and upside down. I know he knew of the huge problems that faced our son, the President of the United States. It took me much longer to realize that September 11, 2001 was the day the whole world changed; certainly for the United States of America.

As we drove back to the motel, we saw an Outback restaurant and realized that we had not eaten all day. So we immediately went in. We have eaten in Outbacks before and know that they have good food and the service is fast. It was there that the nicest thing happened. It was a really hot day, and people wandered in dressed in informal clothes—well, that is a master of understatement. There were men in shirts with no sleeves, their arms covered with tattoos; others with body piercing on every known place that we could see. There were also well-dressed families. A preacher and his wife told us, "We hate to bother you, but please tell your son we're praying for him." As we sat in a booth, one by one, men and some women came over to talk to George: "I'm a truck driver. Tell your son we're with him." "I was in 'Nam and I'll go again." This is a great country.

The next morning we got permission to fly back to Kennebunkport, where the Secret Service were set up with full protection. Flying from a totally closed-down airport, through a totally empty sky, to a totally closed-down airport was eerie. But it was nice to be home.

The days after 9/11 were confusing for us all. How could people accept our hospitality for years, be educated at our universities, and live among us while planning to kill us?

Both George and I were deeply disturbed by the prejudice that emerged during this time period. So was the president, and he went out of his way to try to remind all Americans that racism and prejudice of any kind, at any time, is wrong. Since 9/11, I've been trying to make the point in my talks that it's more important than ever to remind ourselves that tolerance is one of the most important of human qualities. We need to learn to appreciate and celebrate the differences in people, rather than fear or resent them. I agree with the teacher who said we could all learn from crayons: Some are sharp, some are pretty, some are dull, some have weird names, and all are different colors . . . but they all have to learn to live in the same box.

~ All of us wondered what could we do to help our country? Of course there were so many instant heroes. I read a review of Michael Perry's *Population: 485*, a book about firemen. The author asks: "How come a person is a hero if they save somebody and not if they don't?" As I recall, the example was that if a fireman risks his life by charging into a burning building, breaks down a door, and saves a child, he is a hero. If a fireman does all the above and finds an empty room, is he not a hero also? How many heroes were there after that horrible day—in big and little ways?

We couldn't all be heroes, but there were other ways to help. The president encouraged everyone to become active in community service, and created the USA Freedom Corps to help everyone find their niche. He said: "If people want to fight terror, do something kind for a neighbor . . . love somebody, mentor a child. Stand up to evil with acts of goodness and kindness."

The president also encouraged all Americans to "get back to business as usual." Shortly after 9/11, I told George W. that I didn't know whether I should go to Chicago and give a talk that I had agreed to give to a convention. He said: "Mom, one of the best things Americans can do is to try to get back to a normal life." I repeated this to Jean Becker, and she later told me that the office got a call from the convention planners asking if I was coming. They were very surprised when she told them I would be there. When I got to Chicago, the hotels were almost empty, most conventions had been canceled, and the group I was speaking to told me that they were considering canceling theirs until Jean told them I would be there. By canceling flights and reservations, we were permitting the terrorists to win.

Even at this time, I thought a little humor might soften the blow. I said in my talk:

"I asked George W. what I could do to help and he said: 'Mom, if you really want to help, go out and BUY! BUY! BUY!' When I told his father that I was yearning to help and show my patriotism by doing what my president had asked, he wasn't quite so enthusiastic and said: 'If you really want to be patriotic we'll go out in the front yard, hold hands, and sing "God Bless America."'" It was funny, and they did laugh, thank heavens.

    The Friday after 9/11, George and I flew down to Washington and joined much of official Washington and the Fords, Carters, and Clintons at the National Cathedral for a prayer service. Laura and George came in and joined us in the front pew, along with President Clinton, Hillary, and Chelsea. It was a truly glorious ecumenical service with all the great religions represented. I found it very comforting. We had no visit with our children, but flew home as soon as it was over.

George W. immediately left for New York City, and never have I been so proud. It is one thing to give a talk that you have a little time to work on; but it's quite another thing to speak from the heart. When he put his arm around that firefighter—that was magic. Later he and Laura spent hours talking to and comforting families of the lost.

It's really hard to express how George and I felt watching our president during this time. The day before he was to throw out the first pitch at the World Series in Yankee Stadium, many speculated that he would be booed, and some even talked about how dangerous it was. Sitting quietly alone, watching our son stride confidently to the mound in front of thousands of cheering Americans, we were enormously proud. His father was even prouder when his son threw a perfect strike.

The next morning, while having coffee and reading the papers, I heard mumbles coming from 41 . . . "alleged strike" . . . mumble, mumble . . . "they can't even bear to say something nice". . . . This continued and I finally discovered the problem: *The New York Times* ran a front-page picture with a caption that said something like: "President throws an 'alleged' strike to home plate."

≈ I am writing this on Christmas Eve 2002 at Camp David, right after a church service of carols, Bible lessons, and communion with the families of the military. Most of our family are here visiting George W. and Laura for Christmas; we'll be with Jeb and Columba and their children in Florida tomorrow. Although we have the same problems that any large family would have, we are blessed to be surrounded by love and caring. If ever again a minister asks those of us who have perfect families to please raise their hands, mine will go up in a minute. I might add "almost"; then again, I might not.

The mission of the Barbara Bush Foundation for Family Literacy is:

To establish literacy as a value in every family in America, by helping every family in the nation understand that the home is the child's first school, that the parent is the child's first teacher, and that reading is the child's first subject; and to break the intergenerational cycle of illiteracy, by supporting the development of family literacy programs where parents and children can learn and read together.

The Barbara Bush Foundation for Family Literacy
1201 15th Street, NW
Suite 420
Washington, DC 20005
www.barbarabushfoundation.com

Appendix A

There are several groups of people I would like for you to know about, because they make such a difference in my life.

The first is the very hard-working staff in the Office of George Bush: Jean Becker, Tom Frechette, Tricia Hardy (my assistant), Melinda Lamoreaux, Nancy Lisenby, Jim McGrath, Laura Pears, Linda Poepsel, Don Rhodes, and Mary Sage. I also should mention Kathy Super, who works out of her home in Virginia and does all of George's scheduling and some of mine. Also, though technically he doesn't work for us, I have to mention Max Fritzel of Insource Technology, who never loses his patience when explaining what we've done wrong on our computers and blackberries.

Next are our wonderful volunteers, some of whom have worked for us for years. Without them, we would never get any mail opened or out: Carolyn Anglum, Marjorie Arsht, Betty Baker, Melza Barr, Ellie Bering, Barbara Comee, Nancy Crouch, Annyce Duffin, Nancy Eubank, Ida Fahey, Mary Louise Knowlton, Alicia Lee, Willie McCullough, Emily Moore, Barbara Patton, Caroline Pierce, Marianne Sawyer, Lorelei Sullivan, and Margaret Voelkel.

I also would like to recognize the people who served on the board of directors of The Barbara Bush Foundation for Family Literacy. They have worked hard over the years to give the foundation guidance and to make sure the grant money goes to the right literacy programs, to help the right people:

Dr. Joan Abrahamson
President
Jefferson Institute

Reverend Dr. Anderson Clark
Chairman & CEO
Thermal Systems International

Sharon Darling
President
The National Center for Family Literacy

Lisa Drew
Vice President & Publisher
Lisa Drew Books/Scribner

Dr. John E. Harr
Author/Historian

Harold W. McGraw Jr.
Chairman Emeritus
The McGraw-Hill Companies

Sydney Olson
Former Assistant Secretary for Human Development Services
U.S. Department of Health and Human Services

Susan Porter Rose
Former Chief of Staff to Barbara Bush

Benita Somerfield
Executive Director
The Barbara Bush Foundation for Family Literacy

Margot Woodwell
Former Executive Producer
Community Outreach WQED—Pittsburgh

Appendix B

I have to include this for my father, who I think was slightly disappointed when I dropped out of Smith College in 1944 to marry a Navy flier. I hope he thinks these honorary degrees I have received over the years slightly make up for it:

Arcadia University, Glenside, Pennsylvania—Doctor of Laws, 1972
Austin College, Sherman, Texas—Doctor of Humane Letters, 1998
Baylor University, Waco, Texas—Doctor of Humane Letters, 2002
Bennett College, Greensboro, North Carolina—Doctor of Humane
    Letters, 1989
Boston University, Boston, Massachusetts—Doctor of Humane
    Letters, 1989
Cardinal Stritch College, Milwaukee, Wisconsin—Doctor of Laws,
    1981
Centenary College, Shreveport, Louisiana—Doctor of Laws, 2000
Central State University, Wilberforce, Ohio—Doctor of Humane
    Letters, 1992
Hofstra University, Hempstead, New York—Doctor of Humane
    Letters, 1997
Hood College, Frederick, Maryland—Doctor of Humanities, 1983
Howard University, Washington, D.C.—Doctor of Humanities,
    1987
Judson College, Marion, Alabama—Doctor of Humane Letters,
    1988
Louisiana State University, Baton Rouge, Louisiana—Doctor of
    Humane Letters, 1992

Marquette University, Milwaukee, Wisconsin—Doctor of Laws,
1992

Morehouse School of Medicine, Atlanta, Georgia—Doctor of
Humane Letters, 1989

Mount Vernon College, Washington, D.C.—Doctor of Humane
Letters, 1981

Northeastern University, Boston, Massachusetts—Doctor of Public
Service, 1991

Pepperdine University, Malibu, California—Doctor of Laws, 1992

Smith College, Northampton, Massachusetts—Doctor of Humane
Letters, 1989

South Carolina State College, Orangeburg, South Carolina—Doctor
of Humane Letters, 1991

University of Miami, Miami, Florida—Doctor of Humanities, 1998

University of Michigan, Ann Arbor, Michigan—Doctor of Laws with
President, 1991

University of New England, Biddeford and Portland,
Maine—Doctor of Humane Letters, 2003

University of Pennsylvania, Philadelphia, Pennsylvania—Doctor of
Laws, 1990

University of South Carolina, Columbia, South Carolina—Doctor of
Education, 1990

University of St. Louis, St. Louis, Missouri—Doctor of Letters, 1990

Wake Forest University, Winston-Salem, North Carolina—Doctor of
Humanities, 2001

Washington College, Chesterdown, Maryland—Doctor of Public
Service, 1999

Index